Politics of Friendship

PHRONESIS

A series from Verso edited by
Ernesto Laclau and Chantal Mouffe

There is today wide agreement that the left-wing project is in crisis. New antagonisms have emerged – not only in advanced capitalist societies but also in the Eastern bloc and in the Third World – that require the reformulation of the socialist ideal in terms of an extension and deepening of democracy. However, serious disagreements exist as to the theoretical strategy needed to carry out such a task. There are those for whom the current critique of rationalism and universalism puts into jeopardy the very basis of the democratic project. Others argue that the critique of essentialism – a point of convergence of the most important trends in contemporary theory: post-structuralism, philosophy of language after the later Wittgenstein, post-Heideggerian hermeneutics – is the necessary condition for understanding the widening of the field of social struggles characteristic of the present stage of democratic politics. *Phronesis* clearly locates itself among the latter. Our objective is to establish a dialogue between these theoretical developments and left-wing politics. We believe that an anti-essentialist theoretical stand is the sine qua non of a new vision for the Left conceived in terms of a radical and plural democracy.

Politics of Friendship

Jacques Derrida

Translated by George Collins

VERSO
London · New York

This book is supported by the French Ministry for Foreign
Affairs as part of the Burgess Programme, headed for the French
Embassy in London by the Institut Français du Royaume Uni

institut français

First published by Verso 1997
This edition © Verso 1997
Translation © George Collins 1997
First published as *Politiques de l'amitié*
© Editions Galilée 1994

Verso
UK: 6 Meard Street, London W1V 3HR
USA: 180 Varick Street, New York NY 10014—4606

Verso is the imprint of New Left Books

ISBN 1–85984–913–X
ISBN 1–85984–033–7 (pbk)

British Library Cataloguing in Publication Data
A catalogue record for this book is available from the British
Library

Library of Congress Cataloging-in-Publication Data
A catalog record for this book is available from the Library of
Congress

Typeset by CentraCet, Saffron Walden
Printed by Biddles Ltd, Guildford and King's Lynn

Contents

Quocirca et absentes adsunt . . . et, quod difficilius dictu est, mortui vivunt. . . .

(Cicero, *Laelius de Amicitia*)

Foreword

This essay resembles a lengthy preface. It would rather be the foreword to a book I would one day wish to write.

In its present form, opened by a vocative ('O my friends'), its form is thus that of an address – hazardous, without the least assurance, at the time of what was only the first session of a seminar conducted with this title, 'Politics of Friendship', in 1988–89. The trajectory of an introduction of this sort is here quite long, certainly, but it is strictly respected throughout its argumentation, stage by stage, in its scansion, in its logical schema as well as in most of its references. Hence the explanation, if not the justification, of the inchoate form of the project: preliminary rather than problematic.

I count on preparing for future publication a series of seminar studies within which this one actually finds its place, well beyond this single opening session, which thus presupposes its premises and its horizon. Those that immediately preceded it, then, if it is anything but useless to recall the logical development at this point, were centred on: *Nationality and Philosophical Nationalism* (1. *Nation, Nationality, Nationalism* [1983–84]; 2. *Nomos, Logos, Topos* [1984–85]; 3. *The Theological-Political* [1985–86]; 4. *Kant, the Jew, the German* [1986–87]); and *Eating the Other (Rhetorics of Cannibalism)* [1987–88]. Subsequent seminars concerned *Questions of Responsibility* through the experience of the *secret* and of *witnessing* [1989–93].

Be it artifice or abstraction, if I here detach one of these numerous sessions, and only the first for the moment, it is because, for apparently contingent reasons, this session gave birth to several conferences.[1] In addition, this session has already been published abroad, in slightly different, generally abridged versions.[2]

In the course of the academic year 1988–89, each session opened with these words from Montaigne, quoting a remark attributed to Aristotle: 'O my friends, there is no friend'. Week after week, its voices, tones, modes and strategies were tried on, to see if its interpretation could then be sparked, or if the scenography could be set in motion around itself. This work, taking its time, replays, *represents*, only the first session. This representation thus repeats less a first act than a sort of preview. It is no doubt anything but a primal scene, although the figure of the friend, so regularly coming back on stage with the features of the *brother* – who is critically at stake in this analysis – seems spontaneously to belong to a *familial, fraternalist* and thus *androcentric* configuration of politics.

Why would the friend be *like* a brother? Let us dream of a friendship which goes beyond this proximity of the congeneric double, beyond parenthood, the most as well as the least natural of parenthoods, when it leaves its signature, from the outset, on the name as on a double mirror of such a couple. Let us ask ourselves what would then be the politics of such a 'beyond the principle of fraternity'.

Would this still deserve the name 'politics'?

The question is no doubt valid for all 'political regimes', but it is undoubtedly more crucial with respect to what is called democracy – if, at least, one still understands by this term the name of a regime which, as is well known, will always have been problematic.

The concept of politics rarely announces itself without some sort of adherence of the State to the family, without what we will call a *schematic* of filiation: stock, genus or species, sex (*Geschlecht*), blood, birth, nature, nation – autochthonal or not, tellurian or not. This is once again the abyssal question of the *phúsis*, the question of being, the question of what appears in birth, in opening up, in nurturing or growing, in producing by being produced. Is that not life? That is how life is thought to reach recognition.

If no dialectic of the State ever breaks with what it supercedes [*relève*] and from which it arises [*ce dont elle relève*] (the *life* of the family and civil society), if politics never reduces within itself this adherence to familial generation, if any republican motto almost always associates fraternity with equality and freedom, as for democracy, it is rarely determined in the absence of confraternity or brotherhood.

Literally or through a figure, but why this figure?

Democracy has seldom represented itself without the possibility of at least that which always resembles – if one is willing to nudge the accent of this word – the possibility of a *fraternization*. The fratriarchy may *include* cousins and sisters but, as we will see, including may also come to mean neutralizing. Including may dictate forgetting, for example, with 'the best of all intentions', that the sister will never provide a docile example for the concept of fraternity. This is why the concept must be rendered *docile*, and there we have the whole of political education. What happens when, in taking up the case of the sister, the woman is made a sister? And a sister a case of the brother? This could be one of our most insistent questions, even if, having done so too often elsewhere, we will here avoid convoking

Antigone, here again the long line of history's Antigones, docile or not, to this history of brothers that has been told to us for thousands of years.

As we know, what still links democratization, perhaps more today than ever before, to fraternization cannot always necessarily be reduced to patriarchy in which the brothers begin by dreaming of its demise. Patriarchy never stops beginning with this dream. This demise continues endlessly to haunt its principle.

At the centre of the principle, always, the One does violence to itself, and guards itself against the other.

In principle, then, we should also think – even though we did not mention it in the course of the sessions, even if we were not thinking *it* – about *the* political crime.

We are not referring necessarily to those crimes called political crimes, those assassinations with political motivation which litter History with so many corpses. Rather – a second hypothesis – a thinking of *that* crime in which, allowing for the difference of a repression, the political being of politics, the concept of politics in its most powerful tradition is constituted (the 'real possibility' of the enemy being *killed*, in which – much time will be devoted to this – Carl Schmitt identifies politics as such, and which he would desperately wish to distinguish from crime as well as from murder). Unless – and here is a third hypothesis – we must think the crime *against* the possibility of politics, against man *qua* political animal, the crime of stopping to examine politics [*arraisonner la politique*], reducing it to something else and preventing it from being what it should be.

One may say: here are three crimes and three hypotheses that very inadequately usher in prolegomena to friendship. A foreword would thus accumulate provisionally all the figures of *grief*. This word may be understood in French as: damage, blame, prejudice, injustice or injury, but also accusation, resentment or complaint, the call for punishment or vengeance. In English the same word means primarily pain or mourning, but *grievance* also expresses the subject of the complaint, injustice, conflict, a wrong that must be righted, a violence to be repaired.

'O my friends, there is no friend': this is perhaps a complaint, and a grievance, the complaint of one who complains, to oneself, of oneself, or complains of the other, to others. But here, with whom will the complaint about the other be lodged, given that we are addressing friends to inform them that there are none? That they are not *present*, that they are not there, present and living, be it only to receive the complaint or to deem it admissible? Be it only to understand, in a totally different way, the very grammar of this sentence, a kind of orphaned quotation in its original idiom?

Unless they should come, those friends, in small numbers.

How many are there? How many of us will there be?

(Yes, in small numbers, as Aristotle would characteristically insist, friends must be few in number, otherwise they could not be the friends of this friend.

– In small numbers, but what is a small number? Where does it begin and end? At one? At one plus one? One plus one man? One plus one woman? Or none whatsoever? Do you mean to say that it begins with all men and all women, with anyone? And does democracy count?

– Democracy counts, it counts votes and subjects, but it does not count, should not count, ordinary singularities: there is no *numerus clausus* for *arrivants*.

– It is perhaps still necessary to calculate, but differently, differently with one and with the other.)

Lest they come, perhaps, one day, the friends, whatever their number, and the unique friend would be enough as well, to receive the sentence for which each remains singularly the improbable addressee. Theirs is the task of countersigning the sentence to give it its chance, always, each time its first and only chance. Consequently, each time is the last.

But it will have been necessary to endure the crime. Three crimes, as we were saying, which are mutually exclusive. For we might perhaps, in the case of this *grievance*, have only the choice *between these crimes* which, however, seem irreducible. Between these incriminations and recriminations, between these forms of *grief* in which accusation mingles with mourning to cry out from an infinite wound. As if nothing could happen or be thought elsewhere than between these *imputable* crimes, between sentiments of guilt, responsibilities, compassions, testaments and spectres: endless processions and trials.

The infinite abysses of imputability open on to mourning in the shadow of each and every event of death. These events always threaten to carry limits away to their bottomless bottom. On the edges of the juridical, the political, the techno-biological, they risk sweeping away such very fundamental but today so precarious distinctions, more problematic and fragile than ever. Are we sure we can distinguish between death (so-called natural death) and killing, *then* between murder *tout court* (any crime against life, be it purely 'animal' life', as one says, thinking one knows where the living begins and ends) and homicide, *then* between homicide and genocide (first of all in the person of each individual representing the genus, then beyond the individual: at what *number* does a genocide begin, genocide *per se* or its metonymy? And why should the *question of number* persist at the centre of all these reflections? What is a *génos*, and why would genocide concern only a species – a race, an ethnic group, a nation, a religious community – of 'the human race'?), *then* between homicide and – we are told this would be an altogether different matter – the crime against humanity, *then* between war, the crime of war – which, we are told, would be something else again – and the crime against humanity. All these distinctions are indispensable – *de jure* – but they are also less and less applicable, and that cannot, *de facto* and *de jure*, fail to affect the very notion of the victim or the enemy – in other words, the *grief*.

We will then ask *ourselves* what a decision is and *who* decides. And if a decision is – as we are told – active, free, conscious and wilful, sovereign. What would happen if we kept this word and this concept, but changed these last determinations? And we will ask ourselves *who* sets down the law here. And *who* founds the law as a right to life. We will ask ourselves *who* grants or imposes the right to all these distinctions, to all these preventions and all the sanctions that they give rise to. Is it a living being? A living being purely and simply living, presently living? A living present? Which one? God? Man? Which man? For whom and to whom? *Whose* friend or enemy?

'O my friends, there is no friend.' Opening with an apostrophe, this essay could simply let a call be heard, certainly, providing the appellation of the call be drawn out, to call it in turn, well before any destination is set down in its possibility, in the direction of familiar sentences, sentences bound by two locutions: to appeal and to take one's mark [*faire appel, prendre appel*].

The decision 'to appeal' would involve a procedure of re-examination. There is a grievance concerning the judgement handed down, concerning its givens, and the most accredited concepts of politics and the standard interpretation of friendship, as to *fraternization*: with a view to *protesting* or *contesting* – that is to say, to appealing – before another testimonial agency, from fact to law and from law to justice.

As for the impetus in 'taking one's mark', this gathers up a stooping body, first folded in on itself in preparatory reflection: before the leap, without a horizon, beyond any form of trial.

Notes

1. In particular before the American Philosophical Association in Washington, in 1988, and for a colloquium of the Jan Hus Association at the French Institute in Prague, in 1990.

2. In the form of an article (in English: 'Politics of Friendship', in *The Journal of Philosophy*, vol. LXXXV, no.11, November 1988, New York; a longer version of this article appeared in *American Imago, Studies in Psychoanalysis and Culture*, vol. 50, Fall 1993, Johns Hopkins University Press, Baltimore, special issue on *Love*, Thomas Keenan, Special Editor, trans. G. Motzkin, M. Syrotinski and Thomas Keenan; in Italian, in *Aut Aut*, March–April 1991, 242, trans. M. Ferraris, Milan); and in Czech in book form (*Politiky Přátelství*, trans. K. Thein, Philosophia, Prague 1994).

1

Oligarchies:
Naming, Enumerating, Counting

'O my friends, there is no friend.'

I am addressing you, am I not?

How many of us are there?

– Does that count?

– Addressing you in this way, I have perhaps not said anything yet. Nothing that is *said* in this saying. Perhaps nothing sayable.

Perhaps it will have to be admitted, perhaps I have not yet even addressed myself. At least, not to you.

How many of us are there?

– How can you count?

– On each side of a comma, after the pause, 'O my friends, there is no friend' – these are the two disjoined members of the same unique sentence. An almost impossible declaration. In two times [*deux temps*]. Unjoinable, the two times seem disjoined by the very meaning of what appears to be at once both affirmed and denied: 'my friends, no friend'. In two times but at the same time, in the *contretemps* of the same sentence. If there is 'no friend', then how could I call you my friends, my friends? By what right? How could you take me seriously? If I call you my friends, my friends, if I call you, my friends, how dare I add, to you, that there is no friend?

Incompatible as they may appear, and condemned to the oblivion of contradiction, here, in a sort of desperately dialectical desire, the two times already form two theses – two *moments*, perhaps – they concatenate, they appear *together*, they are summoned to appear, in the present: they present themselves as in a single stroke, in a single breath, in the same present, in the present itself. At the same time, and before who knows who, before who knows whose law. The *contretemps* looks favourably on the encounter, it responds without delay but without renunciation: no promised encounter without the possibility of a *contretemps*. As soon as there is more than one.

1

But how many of us are there?

And first of all – you already sense it – in pronouncing 'O my friends, there is no friend', I have yet to say anything *in my name*. I have been satisfied with quoting. The spokesman of another, I have reported his words, which belong in the first place (a question of tone, syntax, of a gesture in speech, and so on) to a slightly archaic language, itself unsettled by the memory of borrowed or translated speech. Having signed nothing, I have assumed nothing on my own account.

'O my friends, there is no friend' – the words not only form a quotation that I am now reading in its old French spelling. They have a different ring: already, such a very long time ago, they bore the quotation of another reader hailing from my homeland, Montaigne: 'that saying which', he says, 'Aristotle often repeated'. It is found in the *Essays*,[1] in the chapter 'On Friendship'.

This, then, is a cited quotation. But the quotation of a saying attributed, only attributed, by a sort of rumour or public opinion. 'O my friends, there is no friend' is, then, a declaration *referred* to Aristotle. There will be no end to the work of glossing its attribution and its very grammar, the translation of these four words, three or four in Greek, since the only substantive in the sentence is repeated. Like a renowned filiation, an origin thus nicknamed seems, in truth, to lose itself in the infinite anonymity of the mists of time. It is not, however, one of those proverbs, one of those 'sayings' with no assignable author, whose aphoristic mode is seldom in the form of the apostrophe.

Quotation of friendship. A quotation coming from a chapter entitled 'On Friendship', after a title that repeats, already, an entire tradition of titles. Before naming Aristotle, Montaigne had massively quoted Cicero, his *De Amicitia* as much as the *Tusculanes*. Occasionally he had drawn the Ciceronian treatise within the genius of his paraphrase, precisely around this 'O my friends'. The 'sovereign and master-friendship' had then to be distinguished from 'friendships common and customary, in relation to which you must employ that saying which Aristotle often repeated'.

We have in memory our *Laelius de Amicitia*: we already hear the Ciceronian echo. Let us specify, in anticipation, just that the Ciceronian distinction between the two friendships ('true and perfect' or 'vulgar and mediocre') works only with an *arithmetical* twist. How many friends? How many of us are there? Determining a nomination and a quotation (*pauci nominantur*: those who are named or whose name is quoted are few and far between when true or perfect friendship is named), the distinction expresses rarity or the small in number. We shall never forget that. Are friends rare? Must they remain rare? How many are there? What account must be taken of rarity? And what about selection or election, affinity or proximity; what about parenthood or *familiarity* (*oikeiótēs*, as Plato's *Lysis* already put it), what about one's *being-at-home* or *being-close-to-oneself* in regard to that which links friendship to all laws and all logics of universalization, to ethics and to law or right, to the values of equality and equity, to all the political models of the *res publica* for which this distinction remains the axiom, and especially in regard to democracy? The fact that Cicero adds democracy as an afterthought changes nothing in the force or the violence of this *oligophilial* [*oligophilique*] note:

> And I am not now speaking of the friendships of ordinary folk, or of ordinary people (*de vulgari aut de mediocri*) – although even these are a source of pleasure and profit – but of true and perfect friendship (*sed de vera et perfecta loquor*), the kind that was possessed by those few men who have gained names for themselves as friends (*qualis eorum, qui pauci nominantur, fuit*).[2]

An important nuance: the small in number does not characterize the friends themselves. It counts *those we are speaking of*, those whose legendary friendship tradition *cites*, the name and the renown, the name according to the renown. Public and political signs attest to these great and rare friendships. They take on the value of exemplary heritage.

Why *exemplary*? Why exemplary in a very strict sense? Rarity accords with the phenomenon, it vibrates with light, brilliance and glory. If one names and cites the best friends, those who have illustrated 'true and perfect' friendship', it is because this friendship comes to *illuminate*. It illustrates itself, makes happy or successful things shine, gives them visibility, renders them more resplendent (*secundas res splendidiores facit amicitia*). It gives rise to a project, the anticipation, the perspective, the pro-vidence of a hope that illuminates in advance the future (*praelucet*), thereby transporting the name's renown beyond death. A narcissistic projection of the ideal image, of its own ideal image (*exemplar*), already inscribes the legend. It engraves the renown in a ray of light, and prints the citation of the friend in a convertibility of life and death, of presence and absence, and promises it to the testamental *revenance* [ghostly apparition of the *revenant*, the 'ghost', its haunting return on the scene (Translator's note)] of more [no more] life, of a *surviving* that will remain, here, one of our themes. Friendship provides numerous advantages, notes Cicero, but none is comparable to this unequalled hope, to this ecstasy towards a future which will go beyond death. Because of death, and because of this unique passage beyond life, friendship thus offers us a hope that has nothing in common, besides the name, with any other.

Why is the future thus pre-illumined, beyond life, by the hope that friendship projects and inspires in this way? What is absolute hope, if it stems from friendship? However underdeveloped it may be, the Ciceronian answer leans sharply to one side — let us say *the same* side — rather than to the other — let us say *the other*. Such a response thus sets up the given state of our discussion. In two, three or four words, is the friend the same or the other? Cicero prefers the same, and believes he is able to do so; he thinks that to prefer is also just that: if friendship projects its hope beyond life — an absolute hope, an incommensurable hope — this is because the friend is, as the translation has it, 'our own ideal image'. We envisage the friend as such. And this is how he envisages us: with a friendly look. Cicero uses the word *exemplar*, which means portrait but also, as the *exemplum*, the duplicate, the reproduction, the copy as well as the original, the type, the model. The two meanings (the single original and the multipliable copy) cohabit here; they are — or seem to be — the same, and that is the whole story, the very condition of survival. Now, according to Cicero, his *exemplar* is projected or recognized in the true friend, it is his ideal double, his other self, the same as self but improved. Since we watch him looking at us, thus watching ourselves, because we see him keeping our image in his eyes — in truth in ours — survival is then hoped for, illuminated in advance, if not assured, for this Narcissus who dreams of immortality. Beyond death, the absolute future thus receives its ecstatic light, it appears only from within this narcissism and according to this logic of the same.

(It will not suffice to claim exactly the contrary, as we will attempt to do, in order to provide a logical demonstration, in a decidable discourse; another way and another thought will be necessary for the task.)

This text by Cicero will also have been in turn, for a history (long and brief, past and to come), the glorious witness, the illustrious *exemplar*, of Ciceronian logic. This tradition is perhaps finished, even dying; it always will have been in its essence *finishing*, but its 'logic' ends up none the less, in the very consequence of the same, in a vertiginous convertibility of opposites: the absent becomes present, the dead living, the poor rich, the weak strong. And all that, acknowledges Cicero, is quite 'difficult to say', which means difficult to decide. Those who snigger at discourses on the undecidable believe they are very strong, as we know, but they should begin by attacking a certain Cicero as well. By reading him, then:

For the man who keeps his eye on a true friend, keeps it, so to speak, on a model of himself (*tamquam exemplar aliquod intuetur sui*). For this reason, friends are together when they are separated, they are rich when they are poor, strong when they are weak (*et imbecilli valent*), and − a thing even harder to explain − they live on after they have died (*mortui vivunt*), so great is the honour that follows them, so vivid the memory, so poignant the sorrow. That is why friends who have died are accounted happy (*ex quo illorum beata mors videtur*), and those who survive them are deemed worthy of praise (*vita laudabilis*).[3]

In this possibility of a *post mortem* discourse, a possibility that is a force as well, in this *virtue* of the funeral eulogy, everything seems, then, to have a part to play: epitaph or oration, citation of the dead person, the renown of the name after the death of what it names. A memory is engaged in advance, from the moment of what is called life, in this strange temporality opened by the anticipated citation of some funeral oration. I live in the present speaking of myself in the mouths of my friends, I already hear them speaking on the edge of my tomb. The Ciceronian variety of friendship would be the possibility of quoting myself in exemplary fashion, by signing the funeral oration in advance − the best of them, perhaps, but it is never certain that the friend will deliver it standing over my tomb when I am no longer among the living. Already, yet when I will no longer be. As though pretending to say to me, in my very own voice: rise again.

Who never dreams of such a scene? But who does not abhor this theatre? Who would not see therein the repetition of a disdainful and ridiculous staging, the putting to death of friendship itself?

This premeditation of friendship (*de amicitia, peri philías*) would also intend, then, to engage, in its very space, work on the citation, and on the citation of an apostrophe. Of an apostrophe always uttered close to the end, on the edge of life − that is to say, of death.

What transpires when an apostrophe is quoted? Does an apostrophe let itself be quoted, in its lively and singular movement, here and now, this impulse in which I turn towards the singularity of the other, towards you, the irreplaceable one who will be my witness or whom I single out? Can the transport of this unique address be not only repeated but quoted? Conversely, would the apostrophe ever take place, and the pledge it offers, without the possibility of a substitution?

We will read these themes of the apostrophic pledge and its quotation later on; they are no doubt inseparable from the theme of the name: from the name of the friend and, in the name, from the mortality of the friend, from the memories and from the testament which, using precisely the same appellation, these themes call up.

Familiarities. What is familiarity? What is familial proximity? What affinity of alliance or consanguinity (*Verwandschaft*) is concerned? To what elective familiarity could friendship be compared? In reading Montaigne, Montaigne reading Cicero, Montaigne bringing back a 'saying' 'often repeated', here we are already – another testament – back with Aristotle. Enigmatic and familiar, he survives and surveys from within ourselves (but how many of us are there?). He stands guard over the very form of our sentences on the subject of friendship. He forms our precomprehension at the very moment when we attempt, as we are about to do, to go back over it, even against it. Are we not obliged to respect at least, first of all, the authority of Aristotelian questions? The structure and the norm, the grammar of such questions? Is not Aristotle in fact the first of the maieutic tradition of *Lysis*, to be sure (*Lysis, è peri philías*), but beyond him, in giving it a directly theoretical, ontological and phenomenological form, to pose the question of friendship (*peri philías*), of knowing *what it is* (*tí estí*), *what* and *how* it is (*poíón tí*), and, above all, if it is said in one or in several senses (*monakhôs légatai è pleonakhôs*)?[4]

It is true that right in the middle of this series of questions, between the one on the being or the being-such of friendship and the one on the possible plurivocity of a saying of friendship, there is the question which is itself terribly equivocal: *kai tís o phílos.* This question asks *what* the friend is, but also asks *who* he is. This hesitation in the language between the *what* and the *who* does not seem to make Aristotle tremble, as if it were, fundamentally, one and the same interrogation, as if one enveloped the other, and as if the question 'who?' had to bend or bow in advance before the ontological question 'what?' or 'what is?'.

This implicit subjection of the *who* to the *what* will call for question on our part – in return or in appeal. The question will bring with it a protestation: in the name of the friend or in the name of the name. If this protestation takes on a political aspect, it will perhaps be less properly political than it would appear. It will signify, rather, the principle of a possible resistance to the reduction of the political, even the ethical, to the ontophenomenological. It will perhaps resist, in the name of another politics, such a reduction (a powerful reduction – powerful enough, in any case, to have perhaps constructed the dominant concept of the political). And it will accept the risk of diverting the *Lysis* tradition. It will attempt to move what is said to us in the dialogue elsewhere, from its first words, about the route and the name, the proper and the singular name, at that moment when this 'maieutic' dialogue on friendship (*è peri philías*) begins, at the crossing of who knows how many *passages, routes* or *aporias*, with love (*érōs*). It begins as well, let us not forget, by 'diverting' Socrates from a path leading him 'straight' (*euthu*) from the Academy to the Lyceum.

Yes, since when – whether we know it or not – have we ceased to be Aristotle's heirs? And how many of us? And turned, by him already, towards the heritage itself, towards the theme of some last will, towards the testamentary in itself? The *Eudemian Ethics*, for example, inscribes friendship, knowledge and death, but also survival, from the start, in a single, *selfsame* configuration. The same here is none other than the other. It has at least the figure of the other. The necessary *consequence* of this strange configuration is an opportunity for thought. Beyond all ulterior frontiers between love and friendship, but also between the passive and active voices, between the loving and the being-loved, what is at stake is 'lovence' [*aimance*].[5] You must know how *it can be more worthwhile* to love lovence. Aristotle recalls not only that it is more worthwhile *to love*, but that you had better love *in this way*, and *not in that way*; and that hence *it is more worthwhile to love* than *to be loved*. From then on, a singular *preference* destabilizes and renders dissymmetrical the equilibrium of all difference: an *it is more worthwhile* gives precedence to the act over potentiality. An activity carries it away, it prevails over passivity.

Ever-ready Aristotelian scholastics would tempt us confidently to take this a step further: this *it is more worthwhile* would acknowledge the pre-eminence of form over matter. And after a deduction of this sort, one would no longer be wary of a worrisome consequence. Rushing to the end, such a pre-eminence would then come, for once, with Aristotle, for a single time, not only to link lovence to dying, but to situate death on the side of act and on the side of form. For once, but irreversibly.

How does this come about? How would act, *this time*, bear itself over to death's side? How would it bear death? For it bears death in itself in this case; it contains death. Preference and reference. But it bears death in itself in bearing itself over to death. It transports itself in death by that which, in it, at the time of death, addresses its reference in a single stroke.

Let us then see death coming on the road of this argumentation. Is not death, moreover, in question – death in so far as one sees it coming, and even in so far as a knowledge knows what it knows in seeing it coming, only in seeing it coming?

Aristotle therefore declares: as for friendship, it is advisable to love rather than to be loved. Let us not forget the general horizon of this affirmation. Justice and politics are at stake. This passage from the *Eudemian Ethics* opens, in fact, with the question of what is just, *the just* (*to dikaíon*) in friendship.[6] What arises in the first place is precisely the question of the just or of justice, *dikaiosúnē*. Justice characterizes a way of behaving. It consists in behaving in a certain way: in accordance with the just, in harmony with the principle of the just. In its dignity as well as its necessity, this question is immediately equal to that of the beautiful and the desirable in friendship. It arrives, then, also in the first place, immediately following the general opening on the subject of friendship (*peri philías*): What is friendship? How or what is it? What is a friend? Is friendship said in one sense or in several?[7]

The whole task should certainly consist in determining this justice. But that seems possible only by forcing several aporias. We will begin, as always, with the implicit reference to *Lysis* (214–16), with the aporia of a friendship which seems doomed to the similar and to the dissimilar.[8] But even before this first aporia, the just will be said and the passage will be forced only by first aligning oneself on a commonly held opinion. This opinion concerns the *very work of the political*: the *properly* political act or operation amounts to creating (to producing, to making, etc.) the most friendship possible (*tês te gar politikês érgon einai dokei málista poiêsai philían*[9]).

How is this *the most possible* to be understood? How many? Can that be calculated? How can you interpret the possibility of this maximum or this optimum in friendship? How is it to be understood politically? Must the *most friendship* [*plus d'amitié*] still belong to the political?

In all good sense, what you hear above all is *loving*; you must hear loving; you cannot fail to hear it in total confidence when the word friendship resounds: friendship consists in loving, does it not; it is a way of loving, of course. Consequence, implication: it is therefore an act before being a situation; rather, the *act* of loving, before being the state of being loved. An action before a passion. The act of this activity, this intention of loving, the *phileîn*, is more proper to friendship itself (*kata ten philían*) than the situation which consists in letting oneself be loved or inducing love, in any case in being loved (*phileisthai*). Being-loved certainly speaks to something of *philía*, but only on the side of the beloved (*philéton*). It says nothing of friendship *itself* which implies *in itself*, *properly*, essentially, the act and the activity: someone must love in order to know what loving means; then, and only then, can one know what being loved means.

Friendship, the being-friend – what is that, anyway? Well, it is to love *before* being loved. Before even thinking about what *loving, love, lovence* mean, one must know that the only way to find out is by questioning first of all the act and the experience of loving rather than the state or situation of being loved. Why is that? What is its reason? Can we know? Well, precisely by reason of *knowledge* – which is accorded or allied here to the act. And here we have the obscure but invincible force of a tautology. The argument seems, in fact, simple: it is possible to be loved (passive voice) *without knowing it*, but it is impossible to love (active voice) *without knowing it*. Science or self-consciousness knows itself a priori comprehended, comprehended and *engaged* in the friendship of *the one who loves* – to wit, in the friend – but science or self-consciousness is no longer comprehended or engaged, or is not yet so on the side of *the one who is loved*. The friend is the person who loves before being the person who is loved: he who loves before being the beloved, and perhaps (but this is something else, even though the consequence follows) he who loves before being loved. *Engaged* science or consciousness here means conscripted twice over: implicated as in a condition of possibility (theoretical chain) and held in a pledge, a promise, an alliance (performative chain). This view can always fall back on the following analytic evidence: one must start with the friend-who-loves, not with the friend-who-is-loved, if one is to think friendship. This is an irreversible order. One can be loved while remaining ignorant of that very thing – that one is loved – and in this respect remain as though confined to secrecy. It could be said that such a secret is never revealed. But one cannot love, and one must not love, in such a state of ignorance of friendship itself (*ésti gar lanthánein philoúmenon, philoûnta d'oú*[10]). Axiom: the friendship I bear [*porte*] for someone, and no doubt love as well, cannot remain a secret for myself. Even before it is declared (to the other, in a loud voice), the act of love would thereby be, at its very birth, *declared*. It would be in itself declared, given over to knowledge or to consciousness. The declaration would in truth be inscribed upon its act of birth. One loves only by declaring that one loves. Let us call that, for convenience's sake, an axiom: the premiss of this entire line of reasoning seems to appeal to good sense, it is posed as unquestionable. As *incontestable*, in fact: one cannot bear witness against it without being party to it.

But there, in the dark, objections are massing up. We will abandon them to their virtuality for the moment. Being loved – what does that mean? Nothing, perhaps – nothing in any case of friendship itself in which the loved one, as such, has nothing to know, sometimes nothing to do. Being loved therefore remains – with regard to friendship itself, and therefore with regard to the friend – an accident (*to men gar phileisthai sumbebekós*[11]). Friendship, what is proper or essential to friendship, can be thought and lived without the least reference to the be-*loved*, or more generally to the *lovable* – in any case, without having to set out from there, as from a principle. If we trusted the categories of subject and object here, we would say in this logic that friendship (*philía*) is first accessible on the side of its subject, who thinks and lives it, not on the side of its object, who can be loved or lovable without in any way being assigned to a sentiment of which, precisely, he remains the object. And if we do say 'think and love', as we shall see later, life, breath, the soul, are always and necessarily found on the side of the lover or of loving, while the being-loved of the lovable can be lifeless; it can belong to the reign of the non-living, the non-psychic or the 'soulless' (*en apsúkhó*[12]). One cannot love without living and without knowing that one loves, but one can still love the deceased or the inanimate who then know nothing of it. It is indeed through the possibility of loving the deceased that the decision in favour of a certain lovence comes into being.

This incommensurability between the lover and the beloved will now unceasingly exceed all measurement and all moderation — that is, it will exceed the very principle of a calculation. It will *perhaps* introduce a virtual disorder in the organization of the Aristotelian discourse. (This 'perhaps' has already marked the hesitant gait of our reading.) Something trembles, for example, in what Aristotle calls the natural (*phúsei*) hierarchy — that is, the hierarchy inscribed from birth between those inclined to love (to kissing, to caressing), the *philetikoi*, and on the other hand, below them, the last ones, the *philótimoi*. They prefer to be loved; they thus seek honours, distinction, signs of recognition.[13] In addition, even if there were no essentially erotic dimension, no desire at work in the ever-more-dissymmetrical hierarchy of the *philía*, how will its formal structure in the relation between the sublunary world and the Prime Mover be respected?

If Eros and Philia are indeed movements, do we not have here an inverse hierarchy and an inverse dissymmetry? Prime Mover or pure Act, God sets in motion without Himself moving or being moved; He is the absolute desirable or desired, analogically and formally in the position of the beloved, therefore on the side of death, of that which can be inanimate without ceasing to be loved or desired (*apsúkhon*). Now in contrast to what takes place in friendship, no one will contest that this absolute object of desire is also found at the principle and at the summit of the natural hierarchy, whereas He does not allow himself to move or be moved by any attraction.

Let us go back down to the sublunary world. The dissymmetry risks, apparently and at first glance, complicating the egalitarian schema of the *isótēs* or — if I may use the term — the reciprocalist or *mutualist* schema of requited friendship (*antiphileîn*), such as Aristotle seems to insist on privileging them elsewhere.[14] The *phileîn* would therefore be more appropriate to the essence of friendship (*kata ten philían*); the act of loving would better suit friendship, if not the beloved (*philéton*). Aristotle, then, proposes to give proof or a sign (*semeion*) of this suitability. If a friend had to choose between knowing and being known, he would choose knowing rather than being known. Every time he evokes this alternative and determines the choice, Aristotle places himself in the hypothesis in which the two experiences (knowing and being known, loving and being-loved, the lover and the lovable) are not compatible, at the moment when they do not appear possible *at the same time*.[15] Basically it makes little difference. Even if the movement of the act and the passivity of the state were simultaneously possible, if that could take place in fact, the essential structure of the two experiences and the two relations would remain no less different. This irreducible difference is that which counts and permits counting. It is what justifies the intrinsic hierarchy: knowing will never mean, for a finite being, being known; nor loving being loved. One can love being loved, but loving will always be more, better and something other than being loved. One can love to be loved − or to be lovable − but one must first know how to love, and know what loving means by loving. The structure of the first must remain what it is, heterogeneous to that of the other; and that structure, that of loving for the lover, will always − as Aristotle tells us, in sum − be preferable to the other, to that of the being-loved as lovable. Loving will always be preferable to being-loved, as acting is preferable to suffering, act to potentiality, essence to accident, knowledge to non-knowledge. It is the reference, the preference itself.

To make this understood, the *Eudemian Ethics* stages the example of what the women do in Antiphon's *Andromache*. It is a matter of an example of adoption or of a nurse, of prosthetic maternity, of the substitution or the supposition of children, *en tais upobolais*, and here we are already in this *familiarity of election* which will everywhere remain our theme. These mothers confide their children to a nurse and love them without seeking to be loved in return. For to want to be known seems to be an 'egoistic' sentiment, as it is often translated; it is in any case a sentiment turned within oneself, in favour of oneself, for the love of self (*autou éneka*). It is passive, more in a hurry to receive or to enjoy the good than to do it, as Aristotle literally says (*tou páskhein ti agathon alla mē poiein*); but one could just as well say: ready to receive the good that one does not have rather than to give that which one possesses (or even, as Plotinus will one day say − and this is something else − ready to give that very thing that one does not have). The *Nichomachean Ethics* recalls the same example, in order to make the same point. But Aristotle insists at this point on maternal *joy* or *enjoyment* [*jouissance*], in seeing there once again a sign or a proof of the preference (*semeion d'ai metéres tô phileín khaírousai*[16]).

How can you pass from maternal enjoyment to death? This passage is not visible in the immediacy of the text. Naming, cetainly, the enjoyment of maternal love in so far as it renounces reciprocity, the *Nicomachean Ethics* associates it neither with surviving nor with dying. The *Eudemian Ethics* speaks of the renunciation of the mother, in her very love, but without naming enjoyment and in order immediately to go on [*enchaîner*] to death. We have just recalled this logical chain. To want to be known, to refer to self in view of self, to receive the good rather than to do it or to give it – this is an altogether different thing from knowing. Knowing knows in order to do and to love, for love and in view of doing and loving (*to de ginóskein tou poiein kai tou phileîn éneka*), as Aristotle then says, concluding: 'This is why we praise those who continue to love their deceased, for they know but are not known' (*dio kai tous emménontas tó phileîn pros tous tethneótas epainoumen, ginóskousi gár, all' ou ginóskontai*[17]). Friendship for the deceased thus carries this *philía* to the limit of its possibility. But at the same time, it uncovers the ultimate spring of this possibility: I could not love friendship without projecting its impetus towards the horizon of this death. The *horizon* is the limit *and* the absence of limit, the loss of the horizon on the horizon, the ahorizontality of the horizon, the limit as absence of limit. I could not love friendship without engaging myself, *without feeling myself in advance* engaged to love the other beyond death. Therefore, beyond life. I feel myself – and in advance, before any contract – *borne* to love the dead other. I feel myself thus (borne to) love; it is thus that I *feel myself* (loving).

Autology provides food for thought, as always: I feel myself loving, borne to love the deceased, this beloved or this lovable being of whom it has already been said that he was not necessarily alive, and that therefore he was bearing death in his being-loved, smack against his being-lovable, in the range [*portée*] of the reference to his very being-loved. Let us recall it, and let us do so in the words of Aristotle. He explains to us why one can rejoice and why there is a place for rejoicing in loving (*dio to phileîn khaírein*), but one could never rejoice – or at the very least, we would say, not essentially, not intrinsically – in being loved (*all' ou to phileisthai estín*). Enjoyment, the self-rejoicing, is immanent not to the beloved but to the loving, to its act, to its proper *enérgeia*.[18] The criterion of this distinction follows an apparently invisible line. It passes between the living and the dead, the animate and the inanimate, the psychic and the a-psychic. A question of respiration or inspiration: loving belongs only to a being gifted with life or with breath (*en empsúkó*). Being loved, on the other hand, always remains possible on the side of the inanimate (*en apsúkhó*), where a *psukhé* may already have expired. 'One also loves inanimate beings' (*phileitai gar kai ta ápsukha*).[19]

(We are striving to speak here in the logic of Aristotle's two *Ethics*, doing everything that seems possible to respect the conceptual veins of his argumentation. The reader who is familiar with Aristotle may find that the tone has changed, however, along with the pathos and the connotations; he may suspect some slow, discreet or secret drift. Let us ask him – let us ask ourselves – what the law of this drift is and, more precisely, if there is one, and if it be pure, the purely conceptual, logical or properly philosophical law of order. A law which would not only be of a psychological, rhetorical or poetic order. What is taking place here? And what if what is taking place were taking place precisely between the two orders that we have just distinguished, at their very juncture? Let us not forget that in the case of psychology, the question of the *psukhé*, or of animate life, is at the heart of all philosophical reflection on *philía*. For Aristotle, neither rhetoric nor poetics could ever be excluded from this reflection; and poets are quoted, more than once called up to testify, even as judges of truth.)

If *philía* lives, and if it lives at the extreme limit of its possibility, it therefore *lives*, it stirs, it becomes *psychic* from within this resource of survival. This *philía*, this *psukhé* between friends, sur-vives. It cannot survive itself as act, but it can survive its object, it can love the inanimate. Consequently it springs forward, from the threshold of this act, towards the possibility that the beloved might be dead. There is a first and irreducible dissymmetry here. But this same dissymmetry *separates itself*, after a fashion, in an unpresentable topology; it folds, turns inside out and doubles itself at the same time in the hypothesis of *shared* friendship, the friendship tranquilly described as reciprocal. I do not survive the friend, I cannot and must not survive him, except to the extent to which he already bears my death and inherits it as the last survivor. He bears my own death and, in a certain way, he is the only one to bear it – this proper death of myself thus expropriated in advance.

(I say that using the masculine gender {the [male] friend, he, and so forth} – not in the narcissistic or fraternal violence of a distraction, but by way of announcing a question awaiting us, precisely the question of the brother, in the canonical – that is, androcentric – structure of friendship.)

In any case, *philía* begins with the possibility of survival. Surviving – that is the other name of a mourning whose possibility is never to be awaited. For one does not survive without mourning. No one alive can get the better of this tautology, that of the stance of survival [*survivance*] – even God would be helpless.

Here again, the difference between the effective and the virtual, between mourning and its possiblility, seems fragile and porous. The anguished apprehension of mourning (without which the act of friendship would not spring forth in its very energy) insinuates itself a priori and anticipates itself; it haunts and plunges the friend, before mourning, into mourning. This apprehension weeps before the lamentation, it weeps death before death, and this is the very respiration of friendship, the extreme of its possibility. Hence surviving is at once the essence, the origin and the possibility, the condition of possibility of friendship; it is the grieved act of loving. This time of surviving thus gives the time of friendship.

But such a time gives itself in its withdrawal. *It occurs only through self-effacement.* [*Il n'arrive qu'à s'effacer,* also: 'It succeeds only in effacing itself.'] It delivers itself up and withdraws twice and according to two modalities, as we shall see, in two times as incompatible as they are indissociable: firm and stable constancy on the one hand and, on the other, beginning again, renewal, the indefinite repetition of the inaugural instant, always *anew*, once again, the new in re-iteration. And this double *contretemps* delivers up the truth of friendship in the eerie light of a *contre-jour*: the present presents itself there only from within a source of phenomenal light which comes neither from the present (it is no longer the source) nor from the place from which it arises or in which it appears – the place of the gaze, of the self or of the 'subject', if you like. The *contre-jour* of this *contretemps* disjoins the presence of the present. It inscribes both intemporality and untimeliness in at least one of the figures of what Aristotle regularly calls *primary* friendship (*e protè philía*). Primary friendship: primary because it is the first to present itself according to logic and rank, primary according to sense and hierarchy, primary because all other friendship is determined with reference to it, if only in the gap of the drift or the failure. Primary friendship does not work without time, certainly, it never presents itself outside time: there is no friend without time (*oud' áneu khrónou phílos*[20]) – that is, without that which puts confidence to the test. There is no friendship without confidence (*pístis*), and no confidence which does not measure up to some *chronology*, to the trial of a sensible duration of time (*è de pístis ouk áneu khrónou*[21]). The fidelity, faith, 'fidence' [*fiance*], credence, the *credit* of this engagement, could not possibly be a-chronic. It is precisely by taking off from this *credence* [*croire*] that something like a temporalizing synthesis or symbolicity can be apprehended – beyond the letter of Aristotle's text, one might say. Engagement in friendship takes time, it gives time, for it carries beyond the present moment and keeps memory as much as it anticipates. It gives and takes time, for it survives the living present. The paradox of the grieving survival is concentrated in the ever-so-ambiguous value of stability, constancy and firm permanence that Aristotle regularly associates with the value of credence or confidence (*pístis*). In primary friendship, such a faith must be stable, established, certain, assured (*bébaios*); it must endure the test of time. But *at the same time*, if this may still be said, *áma*, it is this faith which, dominating time by eluding it, taking and giving time in *contretemps*, opens the experience of time. It opens it, however, in determining it as the stable present of a quasi-eternity, or in any case from and in view of such a present of certainty. Everything is installed at home, as it were, in this conjunction of friendship, of 'fidence' and stable certainty. There is no reliable friendship without this faith (*ouk ésti d'áneu písteōs philía bébaios²²*),without the confirmed steadfastness of this repeated act of faith. Plato, too, associated *philía* with the same value of constancy and steadfastness. *The Symposium* recalls a few famous examples. A friendship that has become steadfast, constant or faithful (*bébaios*) can even defy or destroy tyrannical power.²³ Elsewhere, as we know – in the *Timaeus*, for example – the value of constancy is quite simply tied to that of the true or the veritable, in particular where it is a question of opinion or belief.

In its sheer stability, this assured certainty is not natural, in the late and current sense of the term; it does not characterize spontaneous behaviour because it qualifies a belief or an act of faith, a testimony and an act of responsible freedom. Only primary friendship is stable (*bébaios*), for it implies decision and reflection: that which always takes time. Only those decisions that do not spring up quickly (*me takhu*) or easily (*mēde radíos*) result in correct judgement (*ten krísin orthēn*).²⁴ This non-given, non-'natural', non-spontaneous stability thus amounts to a *stabilization*. This stabilization supposes the passage through an ordeal which takes time. It must be difficult to judge and to decide. A decision worthy of the name – that is, a critical and reflective decision – could not possibly be rapid or easy, as Aristotle then notes, and this remark must receive all the weight of its import. The time is the time of this decision in the ordeal of what *remains to be decided* – and hence of what has not been decided, of what there is to reflect and deliberate upon – and thus has not yet been thought through. If the *stabilized* stability of certainty is never given, if it is conquered in the course of a stabilization, then the stabilization of what *becomes* certain must cross – and therefore, in one way or another, recall or be reminded of – the suspended indecision, the undecidable *qua* the time of reflection.

Here we would find the difference between spirit (the *nous*) and the animal body, but also their analogy. The analogy is as important as the difference, for it inscribes in the living body the *habitus* of this *contretemps*. It has its place in the very movement and in the possibility of such an inscription. The contretemporal *habitus* is the acquired capacity, the cultivated aptitude, the experimented faculty against the backdrop of a predisposition; it is the *éxis* that binds together two times in the same time, a duration and an omnitemporality at the same time. Such a contretemporality is another name for this *psukhé*, it is the being-animated or the *animation* of this life uniting the human spirit (the *nous*) and animality itself. This unifying feature *conjugates* man and animal, spirit and life, soul and body. It places them under the same yoke, that of the same liability [*passibilité*], that of the same aptitude to learn in suffering, to cross, to record and to take account of the ordeal of time, to withhold its trace in the body. This conjugation will warrant the poetic figure of the analogy which we will quote in a moment and which precisely names the *yoke*, the yoke effect.

It is starting from this analogy that the difference lets itself be thought. In the *passage* of time *through* time. Time exits from time. The ordeal of stabilization, the becoming-steadfast and reliable (*bébaios*), *takes time*. For this ordeal, this experience, this crossing (*peira*), withdraws time, it removes even the time necessary to dominate time and defeat duration. *Bébaios*: the stable but also the reliable. It determines a temporal but also intemporal modality, a becoming-intemporal or omnitemporal of time, *whatever it affects* (certainty, calculability, reliability, 'fidence', truth, friendship, and so forth). But it also marks − or rather, it hides in marking − the passage between two absolutely heterogeneous orders, the passage from assured certainty, calculable reliability, to the reliability of the oath and the act of faith. This act of faith belongs − it *must* belong − to what is incalculable in decision. We know that this break with calculable reliability and with the assurance of certainty − in truth, with knowledge − is ordained by the very structure of confidence or of credence as faith.

Hence of friendship. This structure is both acknowledged and unrecognized by Aristotle. The truth of friendship, if there is one, is found there, in darkness, and with it the truth of the political, as it can be thought in Greek: not only in the word *bébaios* (for example, for we do not think it possible to load such a burden on one word, on this word), but throughout the culture, the technics, the political organization and the Greek 'world' that carry it. In a state of intense philosophical concentration, we have here the whole story of *eidos* all the way up to the Husserlian interpretation of the idealization or production of ideal objects as the production of omnitemporality, of intemporality *qua* omnitemporality. It takes time to reach a stability or a certainty which wrenches itself from time. It takes time to do without time. One must submit, one must submit oneself to time in time. One must submit *it*, but – and here is the history of the *subject* as the history of time – in submitting oneself to it. To conjugate it, to enslave it, to place it under the yoke, and to do so for the spirit of man or of woman as for cattle – under the yoke (*upozúgios*):

> There is no stable friendship with confidence, but confidence needs time (*áneu khrónou*). One must then make trial (*dei gar peiran labein*), as Theognis says: 'You cannot know the mind of man or woman till you have tried (*prin peiratheís*) them as you might cattle (*ósper upozugíou*).[25]

But – as we shall see further on, in the course of one of our sallies to and fro – if *primary* friendship is excluded among animals, excluded between man and animal, excluded between the gods, between man and God, this is because *éxis* itself does not suffice for friendship. The disposition, the aptitude, even the wish – everything that makes friendship possible and prepares it – does not suffice for friendship, for friendship *in act*. Often *éxis* alone remains a simulacrum; it simulates or dissimulates real friendship, and makes the desire for friendship a case of wishful thinking, in which the signs of friendship are mistaken for friendship itself. The nub of the Aristotelian argument, as it can be formalized through development with other examples, certainly amounts to demanding and uncovering *éxis*, to taking into account a concrete and indispensable condition of possibility and describing it not as a formal structure, but – here, in any case – as a sort of existential opening (the power-of-being-a-friend, according to primary friendship, which is given neither to the animal nor to God). Aristotle, however, insists just as much, and with faultless rigour, on the insufficiency of this *éxis*, and thus on all conditions of possibility (liability [*passibilité*], aptitude, predisposition, even desire). The analysis of conditions of possibility, even existential ones, will never suffice in giving an account of the act or the event. An analysis of that kind will never measure up to what takes place, the effectivity – actuality – of what comes to pass – for example, a friendship which will never be reduced to the desire or the potentiality of friendship. If we insist, in turn, on this necessary limitation in the analysis of conditions of possibility, in this thought of the possible, it is for at least *two reasons*.

1. First of all, beyond this singular context (Aristotle on primary friendship), the wake of such a limitation crosses an immense problematic field, that of history, of the event, of the singularity of that which comes to pass in general. It is not enough that something *may* happen for it to happen, of course; hence an analysis of what *makes* an event *possible* – however indispensable it may continue to be, especially in Aristotle's eyes – will never tell us anything about the event itself. But this evidence would still be too simple if one merely deduced from it an *order of good sense*: one that goes from the possible to the real, and from a retrograde *analytic* of the possible to the taking into account of the event, in the novelty of its appearance and the uniqueness of its occurrence. One cannot merely analyse the conditions of possibility, even the potentiality, of what occurs 'once', and then believe – this would be so naive – that one can say something pertinent about it. That which occurs, and thereby occurs only once, for the first and last time, is always something more or less than its possibility. One can talk endlessly about its possibility without ever coming close to the thing itself in its coming. It may be, then, that the order is other – *it may well be* – and that only the coming of the event allows, after the event [*après coup*], *perhaps*, what it will previously have made possible to be thought. To stay with our example: it is the experience of primary friendship, the meeting of its presence in act, that authorizes the analysis of *éxis* and of all predisposition – as well, for that matter, as of the two other types of friendships (derived, non-primary).

Among the immense consequences of this strong logical necessity, we must reckon with those concerning nothing less than revelation, truth and the event: a thought (ontological or meta-ontological) of conditions of possibility and structures of revealability, or of the opening on to truth, may well appear legitimately and methodologically anterior to gaining access to all singular events of revelation – and the stakes of this irreducible anteriority of *good sense* or *common sense* are limitless. 'In fact', 'in truth', it would be only the event of revelation that would open – like a breaking-in, making it possible after the event – the field of the possible in which it appeared to spring forth, and for that matter actually did so. The event of revelation would reveal not only this or that – God, for example – but revealability itself. By the same token, this would forbid us saying 'God, for example'.

Is there an alternative here? Must one choose between these two orders? And is this necessary first of all in the case of the so-called 'revealed' religions, which are also religions of the social bond according to *loving* (love, friendship, *fraternity*, charity, and so forth)? Must one choose between the priority of *revelation* (*Offenbarung*) and that of *revealability* (*Offenbarkeit*), the priority of manifestation and that of manifestability, of theology and theiology, of the science of God and the science of the divine, of the divinity of God?[26] And above all, supposing there were an alternative between these two orders, what difference would it make to introduce this Aristotelian proposition according to which there could never be (primary) friendship between God and man? We shall come across this question again, but it implicitly organizes all reflection on the possibility of a politics of friendship.

2. The thought of the act or the event from which the Aristotelian argument derives its authority is also, rather than a thought of each (good sense and common sense), a thought of 'each one', of individual singularity. It is true that this thought of *each one* can take root, in order to return, in *phrónesis*, in perspicacious judgement and in the prudence of common sense. If the indispensable possibility of *éxis* does not suffice, if for that one must pass to the act and if that takes time while overcoming time, this is because one must choose and prefer: election and selection between friends and things (*prágmata*), but also between possible friends – and this will soon lead us back to the vicinity of an '*O phíloi oudeis phílos*', whose 'O' we shall not determine for the moment, and to its arithmetic lesson. Why are the mean, the malevolent, the ill-intentioned (*phauloí*) not, by definition, good friends? Why do they ignore the sharing or the community of friends (*koina ta phílōn*)? Because they prefer things (*prágmata*) to friends. They stock friends among things, they class friends at best among possessions, among good things. In the same stroke, they thus inscribe their friends in a field of relativity and calculable hypotheses, in a hierarchical multiplicity of possessions and things. Aristotle affirms the opposite: in order to accomplish the antithesis of these mean people or bad friends, I assign (*prosnémō*) relations otherwise, and distribute the priorities differently. I include good things among friends or in view of friends. Here is a preference neglected by the wicked. They invert or pervert this good hierarchy in truth by including their friends among things or in view of things, instead of treating things as things of friendship, as affairs (*prágmata*) belonging to the sphere of friends, serving the cause of friends, assigned first and foremost to friends.[27]

Recommending this preferential attribution, Aristotle speaks, then, of friends rather than of friendship. One must not only prefer friendship, but give the preference to friends. Since it is a question of singularities, this is an inevitable consequence: one must prefer *certain* friends. The choice of this preference reintroduces number and calculation into the multiplicity of incalculable singularities, where it would have been preferable not to reckon with friends as one counts and reckons with things. So the arithmetic consideration, the terrible necessity of reckoning with the plurality of friends (*phíloi*, this plural that we shall come across again later in the two possible grammars for the sentence quoted and examined by Montaigne), still depends on temporality, on the time of friendship, on the essence of *philía* that never works without time (*áneu khrónou*). One must not have too many friends, for there is not enough *time* to put them *to the test* by living with *each one*.

For one must live with each him. With each her.

Is that possible?

Living – this is understood with *with*. Whatever the modalities may later be, living is living with. But every time, it is only one person living with another: I *live*, myself, *with* (*suzao*), and with each person, every time with one person. In the passage we will quote in translation, the conjunction between the test or the experience (*peira*) of time (*khronos*) and of singularity, of each one (*ékastos*) must yet again be underlined. This bond of time and number in the principle of singularity is never separated from the hierarchical principle: if one must choose, then the best must be chosen. A certain aristocracy is analytically encompassed in the arithmetic of the choice:

> The primary friendship (*e philía e prõte*) then is not found towards *many* (*en pollois*), for it is hard to test many men (*kalepon pollôn peiram labein*), for one would have to live with each (*ekásto gar an édei suzêtai*). Nor should one choose a friend like a garment. Yet in all things it seems the mark of a sensible man (*tou noun ékhontos*) to choose the *better* of two alternatives; and if one has used the worse garment for a long time and not the *better*, the better is to be chosen, but not in place of an old friend (*anti tou pálai philou*), one of whom you do not know whether he is *better*. For a friend is not to be had *without trial* (*áneu peíras*) nor in a single day (*mias ēméras*), *but there is need of time* (*alla khrónou dei*) and so 'the bushel of salt' has become proverbial.[28]

The bushel-of-salt proverb recalls simultaneously the test and the parcelling-out, the experience and the part taken: one must have eaten *the whole* bushel of salt *with someone* before one is able to trust him, in a stable, sure, time-tested way, but the time of renewed 'fidence' eludes time, it conquers time in yet another way. Previously, the stable steadfastness of the reliable (*bébaios*) appeared to us in the form of continuity, duration or permanence: the omnitemporality that in time overcomes time. But to pass to the act beyond *éxis*, to be renewed and reaffirmed at every instant, the reliable in friendship supposes a re-invention, a re-engagement of freedom, a virtue (*areté*) that interrupts the animal analogy we were discussing above. This is another way of negating time in time, this time in the form of discontinuity, through the reinvention of the event. But here again the economy of time, even of the 'at the same time' (*áma*), commands that the instant of the act and the plenitude of *enérgeia* be linked to the calculation of number. The test of friendship remains, for a finite being, an endurance of arithmetic. Indeed, the friend must not only be good in himself, in a simple or absolute (*aplôs*) manner, he must be good for you, in relation to you who are his friend. The friend is absolutely good *and* absolutely or simply the friend when these two qualities are in harmony, when they are 'symphonious' with one another. All the more so, no doubt, when the friend is useful to his friend even if he is not absolutely virtuous or good (*spoudaios*). This last passage[29] is famous for its reputed obscurity, but the conclusion seems clear: it is not possible to love while one is simultaneously, at the same time (*áma*), the friend of numerous others (*to de pollois áma einai phílon kai to phileîn kōlúei*); the numerous ones, the numerous others – this means neither number nor multiplicity in general but *too great a number*, a certain determined excess of units. It is possible to love more than one person, Aristotle seems to concede; to love in number, but not too much so – not too many. It is not the number that is forbidden, nor the more than one, but the numerous, if not the crowd. The measure is given by the act, by the capacity of loving *in act*: for it is not possible to be in act (*energein*), effectively, actively, presently at the heart of this 'numerous' (*pros pollous*) which is more than simple number (*ou gar oión te áma pros pollous energein*). A finite being could not possibly be present *in act* to too great a number. There is no belonging or friendly community that is *present*, and first present *to itself, in act*, without election and without selection.

This will have been understood in a flash: if the question of arithmetic seems grave and irreducible here, the word 'arithmetic' remains inadequate. The units in question are neither things, these *prágmata* to which the friend must always be preferred, nor numbers. This restrained multiplicity calls for an account, certainly, and one must not have too many friends, but it nevertheless resists enumeration, counting-off, or even pure and simple quantification.

Why do we insist on this difficulty here and now? First of all, because it announces one of the possible secrets – thus hiding it still – in the cryptic tradition of the apostrophe brought up by Montaigne and so many others. One of the secrets which has remained a secret for the reporters themselves, as if it had to reserve itself for a few people. We will come back to this later. Next, because this secret merges with virtue's (*areté*). We should not pretend to know what this word means without having thought the enigma of *phileîn*. No doubt they are one and the same. And finally, because the quantification of singularities will always have been one of the political dimensions of friendship, of a becoming-political of a friendship which may not be political through and through – not originarily, necessarily or intrinsically. With this becoming-political, and with all the schemata that we will recognize therein – beginning with the most problematic of all, that of fraternity – the question of democracy thus opens, the question of the citizen or the subject as a countable singularity. And that of a 'universal fraternity'. There is no democracy without respect for irreducible singularity or alterity, but there is no democracy without the 'community of friends' (*koína ta philōn*), without the calculation of majorities, without identifiable, stabilizable, representable subjects, all equal. These two laws are irreducible one to the other. Tragically irreconcilable and forever wounding. The wound itself opens with the necessity of having to *count* one's friends, to count the others, in the economy of one's own, there where every other is altogether other.

But where every other is *equally* altogether other. More serious than a contradiction, political desire is forever borne by the disjunction of these two laws. It also bears the chance and the future of a democracy whose ruin it constantly threatens but whose life, however, it sustains, like life itself, at the heart of its *divided virtue*, the inadequacy to itself. Would virtue ever have existed without the chaos opening in silence, like the ravenous mouth of an immeasurable abyss, between one or the other of these laws of the other? There is no virtue without this tragedy of number without number. This is perhaps even more unthinkable than a tragedy. The unthinkable filters through Aristotle's staid treatise, under his worldly-wise counsel, under the wisdom of his precepts: my friends, if you want to have friends, do not have too many.

Note that the counsellor never says *how many*, nor at what number virtue becomes impossible. What knowledge could ever measure up to the injunction to choose between those whom one loves, whom one must love, whom one can love? Between themselves? Between them and the others? All of them?

At stake is virtue, which is no longer in nature, this virtue whose name will remain suspended, without an assured concept, as long as these two laws of friendship will not have been thought. For the reliability of the stable (*bébaios*), that on which virtue depends – therefore of liberty, decision and reflection – can no longer be only natural. No more so than time, which does not belong to nature when it puts primary friendship to the test. In the history of the concept of nature – and already in its Greek history – the virtue of friendship will have dug the trench of an opposition. For it obliges Aristotle himself to restrain the concept of nature: he must oppose it to its other – here to virtue – when he classes friendship among stable things (*tón bebaíōn*), in the same way as happiness belongs to self-sufficient and autarkic things (*tón autárkōn*). It is the same immanence that provides shelter from external or random causalities. And constancy is virtuous only by reason of its autonomy, of the autarky of decisions which renew themselves, freely and according to a spontaneous repetition of their own movement, always new but anew and newly the same, 'samely' new. This is not possible without some naturality, but that is not in nature: it does not come down to nature. Having quoted and approved Euripides' *Electra* (*e gar phúsis bébaios, ou ta khremata*: for nature is stable, not wealth), Aristotle adds that it is much more beautiful (*polu de kállion*) to say virtue (*aretê*) in this case rather than nature (*polu de kállion eipein oti ē aretē tés phúseōs*).[30] Since friendship does not – and above all must not – have the reliability of a natural thing or a machine; since its stability is not given by nature but is won, like constancy and 'fidence', through the endurance of a virtue, primary friendship, 'that which allows all the others to be named' (*di'ēn ai állai légontai*), we must say that it is founded on virtue (*é kat'aretēn estí*).[31] The pleasure it gives, the pleasure that is necessary – this is the immanent pleasure of virtue. There may well be other forms of friendship, those whose name is thereby derived from primary friendship (for example, says Aristotle, with children, animals, and the wicked), but they never imply virtue, nor equality in virtue. For if all the species of friendship (the three principal ones, according to virtue, to usefulness or to pleasure) imply equality or equity (*isótēs*), only primary friendship demands an equality of virtue between friends, in what assigns them reciprocally to one another.

What can such equality in virtue be? What can it be measured against? How do you calculate a non-natural equality whose evaluation remains both immanent, as we have just seen, but at the same time obliged to reciprocity – that is, to a certain symmetry? One wonders what is left of a friendship which makes the virtue of the other its own condition (be virtuous if you want me to love you), but one wonders, too, what would be left of friendship without this condition, and when the number without number intervenes, when virtue is not dispensed in excess. And how can we reconcile this first imperative, that of primary friendship, with what we have begun to uncover: the necessary unilaterality of a dissymmetrical *philein* (you are better off loving than being loved) and the terrible but so righteous law of *contretemps*?

Is there a conflict here in the philosophy of *philein*, in the Aristotelian philosophy of friendship? For other Aristotelian axioms, which we shall consider, seem to forbid or contradict the call of dissymmetry and this law of *contretemps*. For example, the axiom which holds that the friend is another self who must have the feeling of his own existence – an inseparable axiom which makes friendship proceed from self-love, from *philautía*, which is not always egoism or *amour-propre*.

Unless one would find the other in oneself, already: the same dissymmetry and tension of *surviving* in self, in the 'oneself' thus out of joint with its own existence. To be able or to have to be the friend of oneself – this would change nothing in the testamentary structure we are discussing. It would break all ipseity apart in advance, it would ruin in advance that which it makes possible: narcissism and self-exemplarity. We are speaking about anything but narcissism as it is commonly understood: Echo, the possible Echo, she who speaks from, and steals, the words of the other [*celle qui prend la parole aux mots de l'autre*], she who takes the other at his or her word, her very freedom preceding the first syllables of Narcissus, his mourning and his grief. We are speaking of anything but the exemplarity of the Ciceronian *exemplar*. An arche-friendship would inscribe itself on the surface of the testament's seal. It would call for the last word of the last will and testament. But in advance it would carry it away as well.

It would be extraneous neither to the other justice nor to the other politics whose possibility we would like, perhaps, to see announced here.

Through, perhaps, another experience of the possible.

Notes

1. Michel de Montaigne, *The Essays* [trans. M.A. Screech, Allen Lane, Penguin Press, London 1991].

2. Cicero, *Laelius de Amicitia*, [trans. F.O. Copley, *On Friendship*, Ann Arbor Paperbacks, University of Michigan Press 1971], p. 56. For the numerous translations we will henceforth be quoting, the following rule will be followed: no revision or modification (one always says: 'slightly' modified) of any kind, nor additions in parentheses from the original text except when we deem them indispensable for the clarity of our argument.

3. Ibid.

4. *Eudemian Ethics*, 1234b, 18 ff. [Revised Oxford trans.]

5. A fortunate coincidence: in the seminar that I am following here, I believed the

word *aimance* indispensable for the naming of a third or first voice, the so-called middle voice, on the near or far side of loving (friendship or love), of activity or passivity, decision or passion. Now, luckily, I come across this word, invented by a friend, a poet-thinker I admire: Abdelkebir Khatibi, who sings this new word in *Dédicace à l'année qui vient* [*Dedication to the Upcoming Year*], Fata Morgana 1986: 'I will have desired only aimance, lovence', 'our law of lovence', 'on the frontiers of lovence', 'Go and come in the cycle of lovence', 'Lovence, Lovence. . . . The only word I ever invented/In the sentence of my life?'. He recalls the word at the beginning of *Par-dessus l'épaule* [*Over the Shoulder*], Aubier 1988, which presents 'lovence in two sequences, one addressed to women, and the other to men'.

6. *Eudemian Ethics*, 1234b 21.

7. 1234b 18–20.

8. 1235a 5.

9. 1234b 22–3.

10. 1239a 33–4.

11. Ibid.

12. 1237a 35–40.

13. 1239a 27–30.

14. For example, *Eudemian Ethics*, 1239a 4, 20; *Nicomachean Ethics*, 1159b [revised Oxford trans.].

15. *Eudemian Ethics*, 1239a 36; *Nicomachean Ethics*, 1159a 30.

16. *Eudemian Ethics*, 1159a 29.

17. 1239a 40; 1239b 1–2.

18. 1237a 40, 1239b 1–2.

19. Ibid.

20. 1237b 17.

21. 1237b 13.

22. 1237b 10–15

23. Plato, *The Banquet*, 182c.

24. Plato, *Timaeus*, 37b.

25. *Eudemian Ethics*, 1237b 15.

26. For these distinctions marked notably by Heidegger, and for the questions they bring up, allow me to refer to 'Comment ne pas parler' in *Psyché, Inventions de l'autre*, Galilée 1987, pp. 586 ff. ['How to Avoid Speaking', in *Languages of the Unsayable*, ed. Sanford Budick and Wolfgang Iser, trans. Ken Frieden, Columbia University Press, New York.] What I called elsewhere *iterability* might not dissolve this alternative but might at least give access to a structure of experience in which the two poles of the alternative cease to oppose one another to form another node, another 'logic', another 'chronology', another history, another relation to the order of orders.

27. *Eudemian Ethics*, 1237b 30–34.

28. 1237b 34, 1238a 3.

29. 1238a 5–10.

30. 1238a 10–15.

31. 1238a 30.

2

Loving in Friendship:
Perhaps – the Noun and the Adverb

Thy Friendship oft has made my heart to ake
Do be my Enemy for Friendships sake.

Blake

Love of one's enemies? I think that has been well learned: it
happens thousandfold today. . . .[1]
The life of the enemy. He who lives to combat an enemy must
see to it that he remains alive.[2]

Nietzsche

'O my friends, there is no friend': wisdom and last will. The tone of the
address is at first uncertain, no doubt, and we shall try here only one
variation among so many other possibilities.[3]

But on a first hearing, one that lets itself be ingenuously guided by what
some call ordinary language and everyday words, by an interpretation very
close to some common sense (and that is quite a story already!), the sentence
seems to be murmured. Mimicking at least the eloquent sigh, this
interpretation takes on the sententious and melancholy gravity of a
testament. Someone sighs; a wise man, perhaps, has uttered his last breath.
Perhaps. Perhaps he is talking to his sons or his brothers gathered together
momentarily around a deathbed: 'Oh my friends, there is no friend'.

The testament thereby reaches us who also inherit it, beyond its natural
and legitimate heirs, through an unindicated channel and with the meaning
of the inheritance remaining to be deciphered. We are first of all ordered
to understand it correctly. Nothing can justify once and for all my starting
off, as I am in fact doing, from the place of the language and the tradition
in which I myself inherited it – that is to say, the French of Montaigne. It
so happens that we worry over this love of language when, in the place of
the other, it becomes a national or popular cause. Without denying this

26

limit, which is also a chance (for one must indeed receive the address of the other at a particular address and in a singular language; otherwise we would not receive it), I would like to recognize here the locus of a problem – the political problem of friendship.

The apostrophe 'O my friends, there is no friend' states the death of friends. It says it. In its 'performative contradiction' (one should not be able to address friends, calling them friends while telling them that there are no friends, etc.) this saying hesitates between the established fact – it has the grammatical form of such a fact – and the judgement of the sentence: so be it, since it is so; and keep it intact in memory, and never forget it. The address is addressed to memory but also comes to us from memory – and *quoted from memory*, for '*the saying that Aristotle often repeated*', is quoted by Montaigne, as others had quoted it before him; he recites it by heart, where such an event is not attested by any literal document.

The death of friends, as we were saying above: both the memory and the testament. Let us recall, to begin with, that the chain of this quoted quotation ('O my friends, there is no friend') displays the heritage of an immense rumour throughout an imposing corpus of Western philosophical literature: from Aristotle to Kant, then to Blanchot; but also from Montaigne to Nietzsche who – *for the first time*, so it would seem – parodies the quotation by reversing it. In order, precisely, with the upheaval, to upset its assurance.

There is indeed something of an upheaval here, and we would like to perceive, as it were, its seismic waves, the geological figure of a political revolution which is more discreet – but no less disruptive – than the revolutions known under that name; it is, perhaps, a revolution of *the* political. A seismic revolution in the political concept of friendship which we have inherited.

Let us try to hear the ancestral wisdom of the address from within this place of reversal. What is there that is so stunning [*renversant*] here, and what has thereby been reversed? Here we have, for the first time, someone – another witness – coming forward to contest. He refuses even the accepted propriety of its paradox, as if the stakes were, then, to make it avow its other truth. In the history of the quoted quotation, in the incessant workings of its unfurling, Nietzsche's upheaval would arrive as an interruption. It would inscribe in that history the scansion of an unprecedented event; but – hence the upsetting structure of the event – it would interrupt less than recall (and call again for) a rupture already inscribed in the speech it interrupts.

By starting with at least a clue to this event, at the other end of the chain, we would, once again, wish to throw up the question of friendship as the question *of the* political. The question *of the* political, for this question is not necessarily, nor in advance, political. It is perhaps not yet or no longer thoroughly political, once the political is defined with the features of a dominant tradition.

This counter-testimony occurs, as it rightly must, in *Human All Too Human*, when the excess of the beyond itself folds back into immanence, when what is human in man folds into the hem of the '*all too*' of Nietzsche's title, in the hollow of its vague [*vague*] modality, trembling and inscrutable but all the more forceful [*déferlante*, as in '*une vague déferlante*' (breaking wave)]. The irresistible wave of the *all too*, a wave rolling up into itself, the enveloped violence of a wave welling up and falling back on itself. In this turn of the 'all too', around the 'all too' in its very revolution, another sentence begins in fact with a 'perhaps': there will come, *perhaps*; there will occur, perhaps, the event of that which arrives (*und vielleicht kommt*), and this will be the hour of joy, an hour of birth but also of resurrection; in any case, the passage from the dying to the living. Let us prick up our ears, for the moment, towards this *perhaps*, even if it prevents us from hearing the rest:

> *Perhaps* to each of us there *will come* the more joyful hour when we exclaim:
>   'Friends, there are no friends!' thus said the dying sage;
>   'Foes, there are no foes!' say I, the living fool.[4]

Why madness? And why should thought, the thought of friendship to come, lend itself inevitably, maddeningly, to madness? This long sentence should be quoted again, and in its original language. But let us observe in advance: such an event *presents itself*, certainly; *it is*, thus *in the present*, the event of a saying that speaks *in the present*. In the living present. *It is* the living fool that *I am* who is presently speaking to you. I say to you. Shouting, calling out (*ruf ich . . .*). An *I* is speaking to you. *I am* saying *to you*. You. *I am* speaking *to you*. To you, here and now, me: to remind or to announce, certainly; thus to tell you what is not yet, or what is no longer (the wisdom of the dying sage), but speaking to you in a perfectly present way.

If it reaches us none the less with something of a delay – that of a quotation already – this saying of the living fool speaks in the present. It spoke to you, it was in the present speaking to you in order to make a promise. This is not, this was not, just any promise. The promise promises in that fundamental mode of 'perhaps', and even the 'dangerous perhaps' which will open, as *Beyond Good and Evil* prophesies, the speech of philosophers to come.

What is going to come, *perhaps*, is not only this or that; it is at last the thought of the *perhaps*, the *perhaps* itself. The *arrivant* will arrive *perhaps*, for one must never be sure when it comes to *arrivance*; but the *arrivant* could also be the *perhaps* itself, the unheard-of, totally new experience of the *perhaps*. Unheard-of, totally new, that very experience which no metaphysician might yet have dared to think.

Now, the thought of the 'perhaps' perhaps engages the only possible thought of the event – of friendship to come and friendship for the future. For to love friendship, it is not enough to know how to bear the other in mourning; one must love the future. And there is no more just category for the future than that of the 'perhaps'. Such a thought conjoins friendship, the future, and the *perhaps* to open on to the coming of what comes – that is to say, necessarily in the regime of a possible whose possibilization must prevail over the impossible. For a possible that would only be possible (non-impossible), a possible surely and certainly possible, accessible in advance, would be a poor possible, a futureless possible, a possible already *set aside*, so to speak, life-assured. This would be a programme or a causality, a development, a process without an event.

The possibilization of the impossible possible must remain at one and the same time as undecidable – and therefore as decisive – as the future itself. What would a future be if the decision were able to be programmed, and if the risk [*l'aléa*], the uncertainty, the unstable certainty, the inassurance of the 'perhaps', were not suspended on it at the opening of what comes, flush with the event, within it and with an open heart? What would remain to come should the inassurance, the limited assurance of the perhaps, not hold its breath in an 'epoch', to allow what is to come to appear or come – in order to open up, precisely, a concatenation of causes and effects, by necessarily disjoining a certain necessity of order, by interrupting it and inscribing therein simply its possible interruption? This suspension, the imminence of an interruption, can be called the other, the revolution, or chaos; it is, in any case, the risk of an instability. The unstable or the unreliable is what Plato and Aristotle spoke of as that which is not *bébaios* (not firm, constant, sure and certain, reliable, credible, faithful). Whether in its ultimate or minimal form, the instability of the unreliable always consists in not consisting, in eluding consistency and constancy, presence, permanence or substance, essence or existence, as well as any concept of truth which might be associated with them. This inconsistency and/or inconstancy is not an indetermination, but supposes a certain type of resolution and a singular exposition at the crossroads of chance and necessity. The unstable is as required here as its opposite, the stable or the reliable of constancy (*bébaios*), and is indispensable to the Platonic or Aristotelian philosophy of friendship. To think friendship with an open heart – that is, to think it as close as possible to its opposite – one must perhaps be able to think the *perhaps*, which is to say that one must be able to *say* it and to *make* of it, in saying it, an event: perhaps, *vielleicht*, *perhaps* – the English word refers more directly to chance (*hap, perchance*) and to the event of what *may happen*.[5]

Now we know that *this* thought of the *perhaps* – *this one and not any other* – does not occur anywhere or anyhow. Far from being a simple indetermination, the very sign of irresolution, *it just so happens* that it occurs to Nietzsche in the upheaval of a reversing catastrophe: not so as to settle the contradiction or to suspend the oppositions, but at the end of a case pressed against 'the metaphysicians of all ages', precisely at the point where they stop in their 'typical prejudice' and their 'fundamental faith' (*Grundglaube*) – the 'faith in antithetical values' (*Glaube an die Gegensätze der Werthe*)[6] – at that point where they are unable to think their reversal or inversion: that is, the non-dialectical passage from one to the other. This they cannot think, it frightens them; they are not able to endure the contamination coming from what is beyond both antithetical values. Despite the value that must be accorded to the 'true' and to the 'veracious', it is altogether 'possible', 'it might even be possible (*es wäre*)' that *the very thing* constitutive of the 'value of good and honoured things' – and virtue (*areté*) is one of them – is related, knotted, entangled (*verwandt, verknüpft, verhäkelt*) – perhaps (*vielleicht*) identical in its essence – (*wesengleich*) to its antithesis, to wicked things. 'Perhaps!' (*Vielleicht!*)

Before we even reach this exclamation, to this one-word phrase (*Vielleicht!*), a great number of perhapses have rained down. They have multiplied themselves in the writing of Nietzsche before becoming a theme, almost a name, perhaps a category. First of all in defining the 'frog perspective' to which Nietzsche compares metaphysics:

> For it may be doubted, firstly whether there exist any antitheses at all, and secondly whether these popular evaluations and value-antitheses, on which the metaphysicians have set their seal, are not perhaps (*vielleicht*) merely foreground valuations, merely provisional perspectives, perhaps (*vielleicht*) moreover the perspectives of a hole-and-corner, perhaps from below, as it were 'frog-perspectives' (*Frosch-Perpecktiven gleichsam*), to borrow an expression employed by painters.[7]

The transmutation to which Nietzsche submits the concept of virtue –
sometimes, as has often been remarked,[8] also in the Machiavellian sense of
virtù – shudders in the tremor of this *perhaps*. In other words, in what is still
to come, perhaps. This is something other than a reversal. The famous
passage on 'Our virtues' (para. 214) from the same book turns resolutely
towards us, towards ourselves, towards the 'Europeans of the day after
tomorrow' that we are, and, first of all, towards the 'first-born of the
twentieth century'. It invites us, we the 'last Europeans', to be done with
the pigtail and the wig of 'good conscience', the '*belief* in one's own virtue
(*an seine eigne Tugend* glauben)'. And here again, the shudder of the
sentence, the shudder of an arrow of which it is still not known where and
how far it will go, the vibration of a shaft of writing which, alone, promises
and calls for a reading, a preponderance to come of the interpretative
decision. We do not know exactly what is quivering here, but we perceive,
in flight, at least a figure of the vibration. The prediction: 'Alas! if only you
knew how soon, how very soon, things will be – different! – ' (– *Ach!
Wenn ihr wüßtet, wie es bald, so bald schon – anders kommt!*[9]).

What a sentence! Is it a sentence? Do we know that – that things will be
different; and how very soon things will be different? Do we not already
know that? Can that be measured by knowledge? If we knew that, things
would no longer be different. We must not totally know this in order for a
change to occur again. So, in order for this knowledge to be true, to know
what it knows, a certain non-knowledge is necessary. But the non-
knowledge of the one who says he knows that we do not know ('Ah if you
only knew', a ploy or a figure which is neither a question nor an affirmation,
not even a hypothesis, since you are going to know very soon, starting at
the end of the sentence, that which you would know if you knew, and
that therefore you already know: 'Ah if you only knew!') – to wit, what
the person signing the said sentence (which is not a full sentence, but only
an incomplete subordinate) cannot state without attributing to himself
knowledge concerning what the other does not yet know, but already
knows, having learned it in this instant – that is, instantaneously, and so
soon (*so bald*) that it will not wait until the end of the sentence.

The acceleration in the change or the alteration which the sentence in
suspension speaks (*wie es bald, so bald schon – anders kommt!*) is in truth only
its very rapidity. An incomplete sentence rushes to its conclusion at the
infinite speed of an arrow. The sentence *speaks of itself*, it gets carried away,
precipitates and precedes itself, as if its end arrived before the end.
Instantaneous teledromatics: the race is finished in advance, and this is
future-producing. The circle is perhaps future-producing – this is what will

have to be assumed, however impossible it may seem. As with what happens at every instant, the end begins, the sentence begins at the end. Infinite or nil speed, absolute economy, for the arrow carries its address along and implies in advance, in its very readability, the signature of the addressee. This is tantamount to saying that it withdraws from space by penetrating it. You have only to listen. It advances backwards; it outruns itself by reversing itself. It outstrips itself [elle se gagne de vitesse]. Here is an arrow whose flight would consist in a return to the bow: fast enough, in sum, never to have left it; and what the sentence says – its arrow – is withdrawn. It will nevertheless have reached us, struck home; it will have taken some time – it will, perhaps, have changed the order of the world even before we are able to awake to the realization that, in sum, nothing will have been said, nothing that will not already have been blindly endorsed in advance. And again, like a testament: for the natural miracle lies in the fact that such sentences outlive each author, and each specific reader, him, you and me, all of us, all the living, all the living presents.

By way of economy – and in order, in a single word, to formalize this absolute economy of the feint, this generation by joint and simultaneous grafting of the performative and the reportive, without a body of its own – let us call the event of such sentences, the 'logic' of this chance occurrence, its 'genetics', its 'rhetoric', its 'historical record', its 'politics', etc., teleiopoetic. Teleiopoiós qualifies, in a great number of contexts and semantic orders, that which renders absolute, perfect, completed, accomplished, finished, that which brings to an end. But permit us to play too with the other tele, the one that speaks to distance and the far-removed, for what is indeed in question here is a poetics of distance at one remove, and of an absolute acceleration in the spanning of space by the very structure of the sentence (it begins at the end, it is initiated with the signature of the other). Rendering, making, transforming, producing, creating – this is what counts; but, given that this happens only in the auto-tele-affection of the said sentence, in so far as it implies or incorporates its reader, one would – precisely to be complete – have to speak of auto-teleiopoetics. We shall say teleiopoetics for short, but not without immediately suggesting that friendship is implied in advance therein: friendship for oneself, for the friend and for the enemy. We all the more easily authorize ourselves to leave the self of the autos in the wings, since it appears here as the split effect rather than as the simple origin of teleiopoesis [téléiopoièse]. The inversion of repulsion into attraction is, in a way, engaged, analytically included, in the movement of philein. This is a logic that will have to be questioned: if there is no friend elsewhere than where the enemy can be, the 'necessity of the enemy' or the 'one must love one's enemies' (*seine Feinde lieben*) straight away transforms enmity into friendship, etc. The enemies I love are my friends. So are the enemies of my friends. As soon as one needs or desires one's enemies, only friends can be counted – this includes the enemies, and vice versa – and here madness looms. At each step, on the occasion of every teleiopoetic event. (No) more sense [*Plus de sens*]. That which is empty and that which overflows resemble one another, a desert mirage effect and the ineluctability of the event.

(Of course, we must quickly inform the reader that we will not follow Nietzsche here. Not in any simple manner. We will not follow him in order to follow him come what may. He never demanded such a thing anyway without freeing us, in the same move, from his very demand, following the well-known paradoxes of any fidelity. We will follow him here to the best of our ability in order, perhaps, to stop following him at one particular moment; and to stop following those who follow him – Nietzsche's sons. Or those who still accompany him – to them we shall return much later – as his brothers or the brothers of his brothers. But this will be in order to continue, *in his own way again, perhaps*, turning the virtue of virtue against itself; to dig deeper under this 'good conscience' of the 'last Europeans' that continues to impel Nietzsche's statements. This good conscience perhaps leaves on them a mark of the most unthought tradition – and the tradition of more than one tradition – all the way down to the overwhelming thought of friendship. This following without following will be undertaken in several stages, in varying rhythms, but it will also derive its authority from an avowal, however ironic it may be.

In 'Our virtues', Nietzsche continues to say 'we' in order to declare his appurtenance *qua* heir who still believes in his own virtues:

> And is there anything nicer than *to look for* one's own virtues? Does this not also mean: *to believe in one's own virtues*? But this 'believing in one's virtue' – is this not at bottom the same thing as that which one formerly called one's 'good conscience', that venerable long conceptual pigtail which our grandfathers used to attach to the back of their heads and often enough to the back of their minds as well? It seems that, however little we may think ourselves old-fashioned and grandfatherly-respectable in other respects, in *one thing* we are none the less worthy grandsons of these grandfathers, we last Europeans with a good conscience (*wir letzsten Europäer mit gutem Gewissen*): we too still wear their pigtail (*ihren Zopf*).'[10]

This good conscience of the last Europeans might well survive in Nietzsche's head, beyond what he believes, what he thinks he believes, as well as in the heads of his 'philosophers of a new species': those who, in our century and beyond, have not broken any more radically than Nietzsche with the Greek or Christian canon of friendship – that is, with a certain politics, a certain type of democracy.)

These philosophers of a new species will accept the contradiction, the opposition or the coexistence of incompatible values. They will seek neither to hide this possibility nor to forget it; nor will they seek to surmount it. And this is where madness looms; but here, too, its urgency indeed calls for thought. In the same paragraph, *Beyond Good and Evil* opens our ears, and delivers the definition of the fool we need to understand the 'living fool' of *Human All Too Human*, such as he presents himself (I who shout, who exclaim, I the living fool, *ruf ich, der lebende Tor*); at the very moment when he turns the address into its antithesis, when the friends become the enemies or when suddenly there are no more enemies. What in fact does *Beyond Good and Evil* say to us? That one must be mad, in the eyes of the 'metaphysicians of all ages', to wonder how something might (*könnte*) rise up out of its antithesis; to wonder if, for example, truth might be born of error, the will to truth or the will to deceive, the disinterested act of egotism, etc. How is one to ask a question of this kind without going mad? Such a genesis (*Entstehung*) of the antithesis would end up contradicting its very origin. It would be an anti-genesis. It would wage war on its own lineage, as the 'metaphysician of all ages' believes; this would be tantamount to a monstrous birth, an 'impossible' origin ('*Solcherlei Entstehung ist unmöglich*'). Anyone who merely dreams of such a possibility (*wer davon träumt*) immediately goes mad; this is already a fool (*ein Narr*). Here we have yet another way of defining, from the impossible thought of this impossible, both the direct lineage and the dream – and its madness.

> Perhaps! (*Vielleicht!*) But who is willing to concern himself with such dangerous perhapses! For that we have to await the arrival of a new species of philosopher (*einer neuen Gattung von Philosophen*), one which possesses tastes and inclinations opposite to and different from (*umgekehrten*) those of its predecessors – philosophers of the dangerous 'perhaps' (*Philosophen des gefährlichen Vielleicht*) in every sense. – And to speak in all seriousness: I see such new philosophers arising (*Ich sehe solche neue Philosophen heraufkommen*).[11]

Nietzsche renews the call; he puts through – from a different place – this teleiopoetic or telephone call to philosophers of a new species. To those of us who already are such philosophers, for in saying that he sees them coming, in saying they are coming, in feigning to record their coming (further on: *Eine neue Gattung von Philosophen kommt herauf*[12]), he is calling, he is asking, in sum, 'that they come' in the future. But to be able to say this, from the standpoint of the presumed signer, these new philosophers – from the standpoint of what is being written, from where *we* (Nietzsche and his followers) are writing to one another – must already have arrived. Nietzsche makes the call with an apostrophe to his addressee, asking him to join up with 'us', with this 'us' which is being formed, to join us and to resemble us, to become the friends of the friends that we are! Strange friends. What are we doing, in fact, we the friends that we are, we who are calling for new philosophers, we who are calling you to resemble and to join up with us in shared enjoyment (*Mitfreude*, this is what 'makes the friend'; *macht den Freund,* as we read elsewhere,[13] *Mitfreude* and not *Mitleiden,* joy among friends, shared enjoyment [*jouissance*] and not shared suffering)? What are we doing and who are we, we who are calling you to share, to participate and to resemble? We are first of all, as friends, the friends of solitude, and we are calling on you to share what cannot be shared: solitude. We are friends of an entirely different kind, inaccessible friends, friends who are alone because they are incomparable and without common measure, reciprocity or equality. Therefore, without a horizon of recognition. Without a familial bond, without proximity, without *oikeiótēs.*

Without truth? We should wait and see. What truth is there for a friendship without proximity, without presence, therefore without resemblance, without attraction, perhaps even without significant or reasonable preference? How can such a friendship even be possible, except in a figure? Why still call this 'friendship' except in a misuse of language and a diversion of a semantic tradition? How could we not only be the friends of solitude, born friends (*gebornen*), sworn friends (*geschworen*), jealous friends of solitude (*eifersüchtigen Freunde der Einsamkeit*), but then invite you to become a member of this singular community?

How many of us are there? Does that count? And how do you calculate?

Thus is announced the anchoritic community of those who love in separation [who love to stand aloof: *qui aiment à s'éloigner*]. The invitation comes to you from those who can *love only at a distance, in separation* [*qui n'aiment qu'à se séparer au loin*]. This is not all they love, but they love; they love lovence, they love to love – in love or in friendship – providing there is this withdrawal. Those who love only in cutting ties are the uncompromising friends of solitary singularity. They invite you to enter into this community of social disaggregation [*déliaison*], which is not necessarily a secret society, a conjuration, the occult sharing of esoteric or crypto-poetic knowledge. The classical concept of the secret belongs to a thought of the community, solidarity or the sect − initiation or private space which represents the very thing the friend who speaks to you as a friend of solitude has rebelled against.

How can this be? Is it not a challenge to good sense and to sense *tout court*? Is it possible?

It is perhaps impossible, as a matter of fact. Perhaps the impossible is the only possible chance of something new, of some new philosophy of the new. Perhaps; perhaps, in truth, the *perhaps* still names this chance. Perhaps friendship, if there is such a thing, must honour [*faire droit*] what appears impossible here. Let us, then, underscore once again the perhaps (*vielleicht*) of a sentence, the one ending the second section of *Beyond Good and Evil*, entitled 'The free spirit' (para. 44).

After the 'frog perspective', with the eye of the toad − on the same side but also on the other − we have the eye of the owl, an eye open day and night, like a ghost in the immense Nietzschean bestiary; but here too, above all, we have the *scarecrow*, the disquieting simulacrum, the opposite of a decoy: an artifact in rags and tatters, an automaton to frighten birds − the *Vogelscheuchen* that we are and should be in the world of today, if we are to save, with madness and with singularity itself, the friendship of the solitary and the chance to come of a new philosophy. We shall focus on a moment of this clamour − only the conclusion of this long-winded [*au long souffle*] address. It should be allowed to ring out in a loud voice in its entirety, and in its original language. In the light of the night, for this solitude of which we are jealous is that of 'midday and midnight'. Before quoting these few lines, let us recall, however, that this passage begins with an attack on a certain concept of the free spirit, of free thought. Nietzsche denounces the freethinkers, the levellers with their enslaved pens − in the service not of democracy, as they sometimes claim, but of 'democratic taste' and, in quotation marks, 'modern ideas'. It is out of the question to oppose some non-freedom to the freedom of these free spirits (since they are in truth slaves); only additional freedom. These philosophers of the future (*diese Philosophen der Zukunft*) that Nietzsche says are coming will also be free spirits, 'very free' spirits (*freie*, sehr *freie Geister*). But through this superlative and this surplus of freedom, they will also be something greater and other, something altogether other, fundamentally other (*Gründlich-Anderes*). As for what will be fundamentally other, I will say that the philosophers of the future will be at once both *its figure and its responsibility* (although Nietzsche does not put it in this way). Not because *they will come, if they do, in the future*, but because these philosophers of the future *already are philosophers capable of thinking the future*, of carrying and sustaining the future – which is to say, for the metaphysician allergic to the *perhaps*, capable of enduring the intolerable, the undecidable and the terrifying. Such philosophers already exist, something like the Messiah (for the teleiopoesis we are speaking of is a messianic structure) whom someone addresses, here and now, to inquire when he will come.[14] We are not yet among these philosophers of the future, we who are calling them and calling them the philosophers of the future, but we are in advance their friends and, in this gesture of the call, we establish ourselves as their heralds and precursors (*ihre Herolde und Vorläufer*).

This precursivity does not stop at the premonitory sign. It already engages a bottomless responsibility, a debt whose sharing out [*partage*] is differentiated enough to warrant a prudent analysis. Nietzsche sometimes says 'I' and sometimes 'we'. The signatory of the precursory discourses addressed to *you* is sometimes me, sometimes us – that is, a community of solitary friends, friends 'jealous of solitude', jealous of their 'proper and profound solitude of midday–midnight' who call other friends to come.

This is perhaps the 'community of those without community'.[15]

But the declared responsibility, the *Schuldigkeit* thus named, is mine, that of the person saying I. *It* says, *I* say, I must answer *at the same time* before the philosophers of the future to come (before *them*), before the spectre of those who are not yet here, and before the philosophers of the future that we (*we*) already are, we who are already capable of thinking the future or the coming of philosophers of the future. A double responsibility which doubles up again endlessly: I must answer for myself or before myself by answering for us and before us. I/we must answer for the present *we* for and before the *we* of the future, while presently addressing myself to you, and inviting you to join up with this 'us' of which you are already but not yet a member. At the end of the teleiopoetic sentence you, readers, may have already become, nevertheless, the cosignatories of the addresses addressed to you, providing, at least, that you have heard it, which you are invited to do to the best of your ability – which thus remains your absolutely and irreplaceably singular responsibility.

This is a double but infinite responsibility, infinitely redoubled, split in two [*dé-doublée*], shared and parcelled out; an infinitely divided responsibility, disseminated, if you will, for one person, for only one – all alone (this is the condition of responsibility) – and a bottomless double responsibility that implicitly describes an intertwining of temporal ekstases; a friendship to come of time with itself where we meet again the interlacing of the same and the altogether other ('*Gründlich-Anderes*') which orientates us in this labyrinth. The to-come precedes the present, the self-presentation of the present; it is, therefore, more 'ancient' than the present, 'older' than the past present. It thus chains itself to itself while unchaining itself at the same time; it disjoins itself, and disjoins the self that would yet join itself in this disjunction.

Shall we say that this responsibility which inspires (in Nietzsche) a discourse of hostility towards 'democratic taste' and 'modern ideas' is exercised against democracy in general, modernity in general; or that, *on the contrary*, it responds in the name of a hyperbole of democracy or modernity to come, before it, prior to its coming – a hyperbole for which the 'taste' and 'ideas' would be, in this Europe and this America then named by Nietzsche, but the mediocre caricatures, the talkative good conscience, the perversion and the prejudice – the 'misuse of the term' *democracy*? Do not these lookalike caricatures – and precisely because they resemble it – constitute the worst enemy of what they resemble, whose name they have usurped? The worst repression, the very repression which one must, as close as possible to the analogy, open and literally *unlock*?

(Let us leave this question suspended, it breathes the *perhaps*; and the *perhaps* to come will always have anticipated the question. It is a subsidiary question, always late and secondary. At the moment of its formation, a *perhaps* will have opened it up. A perhaps will perhaps always forbid its closing, where it is in the very act of forming. No response, no responsibility, will ever abolish the *perhaps*. The perhaps must open and precede, once and for all, the questioning it suspends in advance – not to neutralize or inhibit, but to make possible all the determined and determining orders that depend on questioning (research, knowledge, science and philosophy, logic, law, politics and ethics, and in general language itself): this is a necessity to which we are attempting to do justice in several ways.

For example:

1. By recalling this acquiescence (*Zusage*) more originary than the question which, without saying *yes* to anything positive, can affirm the possibility of the future only by opening itself up to determinability, thus by welcoming what still remains undetermined and indeterminable. It is indeed a *perhaps* that cannot as yet be determined as dubitative or sceptical,[16] the perhaps of what *remains* to be thought, to be done, to be lived (to death). Now this *perhaps* not only comes 'before' the question (investigation, research, knowledge, theory, philosophy); it would come, in order to make it possible, 'before' the originary acquiescence which engages the question in advance with [*auprès de*] the other.

2. By specifying recurrently: 'if there is one', by suspending the thesis of

existence wherever, between a concept and an event, the law of an aporia, an undecidability, a double bind occurs in interposition, and must in truth impose itself to be endured there. This is the moment when the disjunction between thinking and knowing becomes crucial. This is the moment when one can think sense or non-sense only by ceasing to be sure that the thing ever occurs, or − even if there is such a thing − that it would ever be accessible to theoretical knowledge or determinant judgement, any assurance of discourse or of nomination in general. Thus we regularly say − but we could multiply the examples − the gift, *if there is one*; invention, *if there is any such thing*,[17] and so forth. This does not amount to conceding a hypothetical or conditional dimension ('if, supposing that, etc.') but to marking a difference between 'there is' and 'is' or 'exists' − that is to say, the words of presence. What there is, if there is one or any, *is* not necessarily. It perhaps does not *exist* nor ever *present* itself; nevertheless, there is one, or some; there is a chance of there being one, of there being some. Perhaps − although the French *peut-être* is, perhaps, with its two *verbs* (*pouvoir* and *être*), too rich. Would not the original possibility we are discussing efface itself better in the *adverbs* of other languages (*vielleicht* or *perhaps*, for example)?

I underscore, then, we underscore − more precisely we, in turn, re-mark what the *I* itself (Nietzsche, if you like), will have underlined: its responsibility, *the obligation to answer, the responsibility* which consists in calling as much as in responding to the call, and always in the name of a singular solitude, proper solitude, solitude strictly speaking. In the name of the friend jealous of his solitude, jealous of his secret without secret. Let us then remark, too, the flexions and reflections of personal pronouns, between *I, they, we* and *you*: I feel responsible towards *them* (the new thinkers who are coming), therefore responsible before *us* who announce them, therefore towards *us* who are already what we are announcing and who must watch over that very thing, therefore towards and before *you* whom I call to join us, before and towards me who understands all this and who is before it all: me, them, us, you, etc.

But in saying this I feel I have a duty (I feel I have the responsibility, the debt or the duty: *fühle ich ... die* Schuldigkeit), almost as much towards them as towards us, their heralds and precursors, us free spirits! − to blow away from all of us an ancient and stupid prejudice and misunderstanding which has all too long obscured the concept 'free spirit' like a fog. In all the countries of Europe and likewise in America there exists at present something that misuses this name, a very narrow, enclosed, chained up species of spirits who desire practically the opposite of that which informs our aims and instincts – not to mention the fact that in regard to those *new* philosophers appearing (*heraufkommenden* neuen *Philosophen*) they must certainly be closed windows and bolted doors. They belong, in short and regrettably, among the *levellers* (*Nivellirer*), these falsely named 'free spirits' – eloquent and tirelessly scribbling slaves of the democratic taste and its 'modern ideas', men without solitude one and all, without their own solitude (*allesammt Menschen ohne Einsamkeit, ohne eigne Einsamkeit*), good clumsy fellows who, while they cannot be denied courage and moral respectability, are unfree and ludicrously superficial, above all in their fundamental inclination to see in the forms of existing society the cause of practically *all* human failure and misery: which is to stand the truth happily on its head! (*wobei die Wahrheit glücklich auf den Kopf zu stehn kommt!*) What with all their might they would like to strive after is the universal green pasture happiness of the herd, with security, safety (*Sicherheit, Ungefährlichkeit*), comfort and an easier life for all; their two most oft-recited doctrines and ditties are 'equality of rights' and 'sympathy for all that suffers' – and suffering itself they take for something that has to be *abolished*. We, who are the opposite of this ... [we think that] everything evil, dreadful, tyrannical, beast of prey and serpent in man serves to enhance the species man (*der species Mensch*).[18]

And here, once again, a 'perhaps' arrives to spread disquiet in the opposition itself. The perhaps carries away the extreme alterity, the possibility of this other end, this other term which structures no less the antidemocratic provocation, and results in there never being 'enough to say' or 'enough to silence':

> We do not say enough when we say even that much, and at any rate we are, in what we say and do not say on this point, at the *other* end (at the altogether *other* end, Nietzsche's emphasis: *am* andern *Ende*) from all modern ideology and herd desiderata: as its antipodes perhaps (*als deren Antipoden vielleicht*)?

At each instant the discourse is carried out to its limit, on the edge of silence: it transports itself beyond itself. It is swept away by the extreme opposition – indeed, the *alterity* – by the hyperbole which engages it in an *infinite build-up* [*surenchère*] (freer than the freedom of the free spirit, a better democrat than the crowd of modern democrats, aristocrat among all democrats, more futural and futurist than the modern), swept away by the *perhaps* that arrives to undecide meaning at each decisive moment.

All this (this surplus of democracy, this excess of freedom, this reaffirmation of the future) is not, so we suspect, very promising for the community, communication, the rules and maxims of communicational action. Nietzsche continues, in effect:

Is it any wonder we 'free spirits' are not precisely the most communicative of spirits (*die mitteilsamsten Geister*)? that we do not want to betray in every respect *from what* (*wovon*) a spirit can free itself and *to what* (*wohin*) it is then perhaps driven? And as for the dangerous formula 'beyond good and evil' with which we at any rate guard against being taken for what we are not: we *are* something different (*wir* sind *etwas Anders*) from '*libres-penseurs*', '*liberi pensatori*', '*Freidenker*', or whatever else all these worthy advocates of 'modern ideas' like to call themselves.[19]

And now, for the finishing touch, the owls in full light of day – ourselves again – the scarecrows that we owe it to ourselves to be today; friendship without friendship of the friends of solitude, the surplus of free will, and once again the *perhaps* in which I see you coming, you, the *arrivants* to come, you the *arrivant* thinkers, you the coming, the upcoming (*das Kommenden*), the new philosophers, but you whom I see coming, me, I who am already perhaps a little like you who are perhaps a little like us, a bit on our side, you the new philosophers, my readers to come, who will be my readers only if you become new philosophers – that is, if you know how to read me – in other words, if you can think what I write in my stead, and if you know how to countersign in advance or how to prepare yourself to countersign, always in imminent fashion, what you inspire in me here exactly, teleiopoetically:

curious to the point of vice, investigators to the point of cruelty, with rash fingers for the ungraspable, with teeth and stomach for the most indigestible, ready for every task that demands acuteness and sharp senses, ready for every venture thanks to a superfluity of 'free will' (*dank einen Überschusse von 'freiem Willen'*), with fore- and back- souls into whose ultimate intentions no one can easily see, with fore- and backgrounds to whose end no foot may go, hidden under mantles of light, conquerors even though we look like heirs and prodigals, collectors and arrangers from morn till night, misers of our riches and our full-crammed cupboards, thrifty in learning and forgetting, inventive in schemata, sometimes proud of tables of categories, sometimes pedants, sometimes night owls of labour even in broad daylight (*mitunter Nachteulen der Arbeit auch am hellen Tage*); yes, even scarecrows when we need to be – and today we need to be: in so far, that is, as we are born, sworn, jealous friends of *solitude*, of our own deepest, most midnight, most midday solitude (*unserer eignen tiefsten mitternächt-lichsten, mittäglichsten Einsamkeit*) – such a type of man are we, we free spirits! and perhaps *you* too are something of the same type, you coming men? you *new* philosophers? (*und vielleicht seid auch ihr etwas davon, ihr Kommenden? ihr neuen Philosophen?* –) {Nietzsche's emphasis}.[20]

Community without community, friendship without the community of the friends of solitude. No appurtenance. Nor resemblance nor proximity. The end of *oikeiótēs*? Perhaps. We have here, in any case, friends seeking mutual recognition without knowing each other. One who calls and questions oneself is not even sure that the new philosophers will be part of the free spirits that we are. The rupture will perhaps be radical, even more radical. Perhaps those whom I am calling will be unrecognizable enemies. In any case, I am not asking them to be like me, like us, as the French translation we have quoted puts it. Friends of solitude: this must be understood in multiple fashion: they love solitude, they belong together – that is their resemblance, in a world of solitude, of isolation, of singularity, of non-appurtenance. But in this singular world of singularities, these 'sworn friends of solitude' are conjurers; they are even called to be conjurers by one of the heralds, the one who says *I* but is not necessarily the first, though he is one of the first in our twentieth century to speak this community without community.

To speak to it and thereby – let us not hesitate to clarify this – to form or to forge it. And to do so in the language of madness that we must use, forced, all of us, by the most profound and rigorous necessity, to say things as contradictory, insane, absurd, impossible, undecidable as 'X without X', 'community of those without community', 'inoperative community', 'unavowable community': these untenable syntagms and arguments – illegible, of course, and even derisive – these inconceivable concepts exposed to the disdain of philosophical good conscience, which thinks it possible to hold out in the shade of the Enlightenment; where the light of the Enlightenment is not thought, where a heritage is misappropriated. For us there is no Enlightenment other than the one to be thought.

This secretless conjuration plots itself between day and night, between midday and midnight, in the risk of the *perhaps* – that is, in the already incalculable anticipation of this risk, this thought of risk which will be characteristic of the new philosophy. This *already of the perhaps* acts. We have already undergone the effects of its action; we have this in memory, do we not? It acts within itself – in immanent fashion, we will say – although this immanence consists too in leaving self. Leaving *oneself as of oneself*, which can be done only by letting the other come, which is possible only if the other precedes and informs me – only if the other is the condition of my immanence. Very strong and very feeble, the *already* of the *perhaps* has the paradoxical force of a teleiopoetic propulsion. Teleiopoesis makes the *arrivants* come – or rather, allows them to come – by withdrawing; it produces an event, sinking into the darkness of a friendship which is not yet.

Autobiographical as it remains in the circular movement of its arrow, a boomerang that none the less relentlessly pursues its progress towards changing the place of the subject, *teleiopoesis* also defines the general structure of political allocution, its lure and its truth. We have indeed come into a certain politics of friendship. Into 'great politics', not into the one with which the political scientists and the politicians (sometimes too the citizens of modern democracy) entertain us: the politics of opinion.

For one should not *believe* that our *perhaps* belongs to a regime of opinion. That would be a case of credulousness – just an opinion, and a poor one at that. Our unbelievable *perhaps* does not signify haziness and mobility, the confusion preceding knowledge or renouncing all truth. If it is undecidable and without truth in its own moment (but it is, as a matter of fact, difficult to assign a proper moment to it), this is in order that it might be a condition of decision, interruption, revolution, responsibility and truth. The friends of the *perhaps* are the friends of truth. But the friends of truth are not, by definition, *in* the truth; they are not installed there as in the padlocked security of a dogma and the stable reliability of an opinion. If there is some truth in the *perhaps*, it can only be that of which the friends are the friends. Only friends. The friends of truth are without *the* truth, even if friends cannot function without truth. The truth – that of the thinkers to come – it is impossible to *be it*, to *be there*, to *have it*; one must only be its friend. This also means one must be solitary – and jealous of one's retreat. This is the anchoritic truth of this truth. But it is far from abstaining from afar from the political – and even if the anchorite plays the scarecrow, such a person overpoliticizes the space of the city.

Hence this remarkable redoubling of the *perhaps* (this time in the form of 'in all probability', *wahrscheinlich genug*) which responds to the question of knowing if, on their way or in the imminence of their arrival, the thinkers to come are 'friends of the truth'. These friends of the truth that they will, perhaps, remain begin by denouncing a fundamental contradiction, that which no politics will be able to explain or rationalize, simply because it neither can nor has the right to do so: the contradiction inhabiting the very concept of the *common* and the *community*. For the common is rare, and the common measure is, a *rarity for the rare*, just as, not far from here, Baudelaire's man of the crowds thought it. How many of them are there? How many of us are there? The incalculable equality of these friends of solitude, of the incommensurable subjects, of these subjects without subject and without intersubjectivity.

How can a democrat handle this friendship, this truth, this contradiction? And this measurelessness? I mean the democrat whom we know so well, who is really not familiar with such things? Above all, he is unfamiliar with the practice of putting 'truth' in quotation marks.

Let us listen, then. And first let us put into the present what the standard French translation deemed it necessary to render in a future tense. Those who *are* the future *are on their way*, now, even if these *arrivants* have not yet arrived: their present is not present, it is not in current affairs, but they are coming, they are *arrivants* because they *are going to come*. '*Ils seront*' means: they are what is going to come, and what is to come is in the *present tense*; it speaks (in French) to the presentation of the future, sometimes planned, sometimes prescribed. In paragraph 43 of *Beyond Good and Evil*, the truth of these friends seems to be suspended between quotation marks:

> Are they new friends of 'truth' (and not, as in the French translation, *seront-ils*, [will they be], *Sind es neue Freunde der 'Wahrheit'*), these coming philosophers (*diese kommenden Philosophen*)? In all probability ([*c'est assez vraisemblable* {ou probable}], *Wahrscheinlich genug*, the French translations give here 'probably', thus losing this allusion to the true; for this response to the question of truth, of friendship for the truth, cannot be true or certain, certainly, it can only have a true-semblance [*vrai-semblance*], but already orientated by friendship for the truth): for all philosophers have *hitherto* loved their truths.

I have underlined *hitherto* (*bisher*): we will come across its import again later. Their truths – theirs, without quotation marks this time – this is what the philosophers have loved. Is this not contradictory with truth itself? But if one must love truth (this is necessary, is it not?), how will one love anything other than one's own truth, a truth that one can appropriate? Nietzsche's answer (but how will a democrat handle it?): far from being the very form of truth, universalization hides the cunning of all dogmatisms. Being-common or being-in-common: a dogmatic stratagem, the cunning of the common sense of the community; what is placed in common can reason [*raisonner*] only in order to frame or set [*arraisonner*]. And as for the apparently arithmetical question, the question of the number of friends in which we have begun to perceive the Aristotelian dimension – the question of great numbers *qua* the political question of truth – we shall see that it does not fail to crop up here:

> for all philosophers have hitherto loved their truths (*ihre Wahrheiten*). But certainly (*Sicherlich aber*) they will not be dogmatists. It must offend their pride,

and also their taste, if their truth is supposed to be a truth for everyman, which has *hitherto* (emphasis added) been the secret desire and hidden sense (*Hintersinn*) of all dogmatic endeavours. 'My judgement is *my* judgement: another cannot easily acquire a right to it' – such a philosopher of the future may perhaps (*vielleicht*, once again) say. One has to get rid of the bad taste of wanting to be in agreement with many (*mit Vielen übereinstimmen zu wollen*). 'Good' is no longer good when your neighbour takes it into his mouth. And how could there exist a 'common good' ('*Gemeingut*')! The expression is a self-contradiction: what can be common has ever but little value. In the end it must be as it is and has always been: great things are for the great, abysses for the profound, shudders (*Schuder*, also shivers or quivers or thrills) and delicacies (*Zartheiten*, also fragilities and weaknesses, etc.) for the refined (*Feinen*, the delicate, the subtle, the weak also, the vulnerable, for the aristocracy of this truth of election is both that of force and weakness, a certain manner of being able to be hurt), and, in sum (*im ganzin und kurzen*), all rare things for the rare.[21]

So that is what this philosopher of the future will say, perhaps. That, perhaps, is what he *would say*, the friend of truth – but a mad truth, the mad friend of a truth which ignores both the common and common sense ('I, the living fool'), the friend of a 'truth' in quotation marks that reverses all the signs in one stroke.

Notes

1. '*Seine Feinde lieben? Ich glaube, das ist gut gelernt worden: es geschieht heute tausendfältig.*' Nietzsche, *Beyond Good and Evil* [trans. R. Hollingdale, Penguin, Harmondsworth 1981, 216].

2. '*Das Leben des Feindes. – Wer davon lebt, einen Feind zu bekämpfen, hat ein Interesse daran, dass er am Leben bleibt.*' Nietzsche, *Human All Too Human, A Book for Free Spirits* [trans. R. Hollingdale, Cambridge Unversity Press 1986], 1, 531.

3. The seminar whose first session I am following here will have in fact proposed twelve variations or twelve modalities of reception of the 'same sentence'. Perhaps someday I will prepare this for publication.

4. '*. . . und vielleicht kommt jedem auch einmal die freudigere Stunde, wo er sagt*

"*Freunde, es gibt keine Freunde!* so rief der sterbende Weise;

"*Feinde, es gibt keinen Feind!*" *ruf ich, der lebende Tor.*'

Human All Too Human, 1, '376: Of friends' [trans. R. Hollingdale, Cambridge University Press, 1986, p. 149]. Emphasis added.

5. Beyond the timid prolegomena that we are amassing here with reference to Nietzsche, a systematic study of the 'category', if it is one, should be undertaken, the 'category' or the 'modality' of the 'perhaps' in all languages and in all the world's cultures. In a very fine essay on Heidegger, Rodolphe Gasché begins by recalling the disdain with which classical philosophy considers the recourse to 'perhaps'. He sees in

this disdain – as for Hegel in his awful sarcasms against the unfortunate Krug – a pre-philosophical failure, an empiricist slip back into the approximate formulations of ordinary language. 'Perhaps' would belong to a vocabulary which should remain outside philosophy. That is to say, outside certainty, truth, even outside veracity. In this respect, the philosopher himself echoes the common sense of the German proverb which says: 'Perhaps is practically a lie' (or a half-truth?) (*Vielleicht ist eine halbe Lüge*). Having recalled the German etymology of *vielleicht* (*villithe* in Middle High German gathers the significations of *sehr leicht* (easy), *vermutlich* (probably, conceivably), and *möglicherweise* (possibly), which marked then, more so than now, an expectancy, not a simple possibility and, as Grimm takes note of, the presumed possibility that a statement might correspond to a reality or that something will happen, as Gasché translates: thus perhaps), and before dealing with the abundant use that Heidegger makes of *vielleicht* in one of the essays in *Unterwegs zur Sprache*, Gasché poses the question which is of the utmost interest to us here: 'And what if perhaps modalized a discourse which no longer proceeds by statements (declarations, affirmations, assertions) without being for all that less rigorous than the discourse of philosophy?' ('*Perhaps – a Modality? On the Way with Heidegger to Language*', in *Graduate Faculty Philosophy Journal*, vol. 16, no. 2, 1993, p. 469).

6. Nietzsche, *Beyond Good and Evil*, 1st part, 'On the prejudices of philosophers', 2.

7. Ibid.

8. See Bonnie Honig, *Political Theory and the Displacement of Politics*, Cornell University Press, 1993, pp. 66–9 ('Nietzsche's Recovery of Virtue as *Virtù*').

9. *Beyond Good and Evil*, p. 135.

10. Ibid., para. 214.

11. 'On the Prejudices of Philosophers', para. 2.

12. Ibid., para. 42.

13. "Freund. – *Mitfreude, nich Mitleiden, macht den Freund*', *Human All Too Human*, para. 499: 'Fellow rejoicing, not fellow suffering, makes the friend.'

14. In one of the most blinding passages of *The Writing of Disaster*, Blanchot evokes (with the audacity and prudence required here) 'certain commentators' of 'Jewish messianism', where Jewish messianism 'suggests the relation between the event and its nonoccurrence':

> If the Messiah is at the gates of Rome among the beggars and lepers, one might think that his incognito protects or prevents him from coming, but, precisely, he is recognized; someone, haunted with questioning and unable to leave off, asks him: 'When will you come?' His being there is, then, not the coming. With the Messiah, who is there, the call must always resound: 'Come, Come.' His presence is no guarantee. Both future and past (it is said, at least once, that the Messiah has already come), his coming does not correspond to any presence at all.... And should it happen that, to the question, 'When will your coming take place' the Messiah responds: 'It is today', the answer is certainly impressive: so, it is today! It is now and always now. There is no waiting, although this is as an obligation to wait. And when is now? When is the now which does not belong to ordinary time ... does not maintain but destabilizes it?..., *L'Écriture du désastre*, Gallimard 1980, pp. 214–15 [trans. Ann Smock, *The Writing of Disaster*, University of Nebraska Press, New Bison Book Edition 1995, pp. 141–2 (trans. modified)].

15. It is well known that these words are Bataille's. Why do we quote them here? In order to bear witness – too briefly, shabbily – to the grateful attention that draws me

to those thinkers and texts to which I am bound without ever being their equal. Without hope, then, of ever giving them their due here. These words of Bataille are chosen by Blanchot as an epigraph to *La Communauté inavouable*, Éditions du Minuit, 1983 [*The Unavowable Community*, trans. Pierre Joris, Tarrytown, NY: Station Hill Press 1988], a work which, from the very first lines, is in conversation with an article by Jean-Luc Nancy which later become a book: *La Communauté désoeuvrée*, Bourgois 1986, 1990 [*The Inoperative Community*, University of Minnesota Press 1991]. Like Blanchot's *L'Amitié* (Gallimard 1971), which we will take up later, this is yet another book on friendship, in particular friendship according to Bataille (see, for example, pp. 40 ff.). As those towards which or from which they shine in so singular a fashion, these works are no doubt among those that count the most for me today. Without being able to refer to them here as abundantly and directly as would be necessary, I would at least like to situate my subject with regard to what they have staked out: to pre-name, singularly around the texts of Nietzsche that I am attempting to read here, a seismic event whose 'new logic' leaves its mark on all the necessarily contradictory and undecidable statements that organize these discourses and give them their paradoxical force. A paradigm here might be, for example, this 'community of those without community', 'the inoperative operation of the work', like all the 'X without X' that open up the sense at the heart of these thoughts. These thoughts invent themselves by countersigning, according to the *teleiopoesis* that we have been referring to, the event signed 'Nietzsche'. They belong – but the word is not appropriate – they belong without belonging to the untimely time of Nietzsche. I could have placed the following as epigraph to this entire essay, in any case to that part dealing with Nietzsche, taken from 'The Negative Community' in *The Unavowable Community*:

> For example, Bataille says: 'The community I am speaking of is that which will exist virtually from the fact of Nietzsche's existence (which is the demand for such a community) and that each of Nietzsche's readers undoes by shirking – that is, by not solving the posed enigma (by not even reading it).' But there was a huge difference between Bataille and Nietzsche. Nietzsche had an ardent desire to be heard, but also the sometimes haughty certitude of being the bearer of a truth too dangerous and too superior to be able to be embraced. For Bataille, friendship is a part of the 'sovereign operation'; it is no accident that *Le Coupable* has at the very beginning the subtitle, *Friendship*; friendship, it is true, is difficult to define: friendship for oneself to the point of dissolution, friendship from one to another, as the passage and affirmation of a continuity starting from the necessary discontinuity. But reading – the inoperative operation of the work – is not absent from it . . . (pp. 41–2).

Further on, Blanchot insists on the fact that 'these movements are only apparently contradictory'. 'What is then the case concerning friendship? *Friendship: friendship for the unknown [one] without friends*' (p. 44; original emphasis).

In subscribing in turn, in countersigning, in taking it seriously, as I have always done, the necessity of these 'apparently contradictory' statements, I would like to return (for example, here with Nietzsche) not to some archaeological ground or platform summoned to support them (by definition this ground always gives way, escapes) but to an event that opens up a world in which we must today, now, write in this way, and deliver ourselves over to this necessity. As we are doing.

Then, yes, what I will say – starting from and on the subject of Nietzsche, and in his favour also – will be a salute to the friends I have just quoted or named. What I will say *against* Nietzsche also, perhaps – for example when, later, I will protest against the evidence and the guarantees that he still gives for such fraternization. There is still perhaps some brotherhood in Bataille, Blanchot and Nancy, and I wonder, in the innermost recess of my admiring friendship, if it does not deserve a little loosening up, and if it should still guide the thinking of the community, be it a community without community, or a brotherhood without brotherhood. 'The heart of brotherhood', for example, which, in the last words of 'The Negative Community', still lays down the law: . . . 'not by chance, but as the heart of brotherhood: the heart or the law'. I am also thinking – without being too sure what to think – about all the assembled 'brothers', all the men 'gathered into fraternities,' in *The Inoperative Community*, when 'The Interrupted Myth' is taken up (pp. 109, 111, 112). Must not the interruption of this mythical scene also, by some supplement to the question concerning what transpires 'before the law', at the mythical moment of the father's murder (from Freud to Kafka), reach and affect the figure of the brothers?

16. See my *De l'esprit, Heidegger et la question*, Galilée 1987 [*Of Spirit, Heidegger and the Question*, trans. G. Bennington and R. Bowlby, University of Chicago Press 1989, p. 129.]; and, notably, 'Nombres de oui', in *Psyché*, Galilée, 1987, pp. 644–50 [trans. Brian Holmes, 'A number of yes,' in *Qui Parle*, 2, 2: 120–33].

17. In particular, in *Donner le temps*, Galilée 1991, [trans. Peggy Kamuf: *Given Time*, University of Chicago Press 1992].

18. *Beyond Good and Evil*, 2, para. 44.

19. Ibid. [for the last two quotations].

20. Ibid.

21. Ibid., para. 43.

This Mad 'Truth':
The Just Name of Friendship

It seems to me that the meditations of a man of state must centre
on the question of enemies in all its aspects, and he owes it to
himself to have taken a keen interest in this saying of Xenophon:
'the wise man will profit from his enemies'. Consequently, I
have collected the remarks I have recently made, in approximately the same terms, on this subject, and I will send them to
you. I have abstained as much as possible from quoting what I
had written in my *Political Precepts*, since I see that you often
have this book in hand.[1]

Plutarch

A good-natured hare wanted to have many friends.
Many! you say – that is a major affair:
A single friend is a rare thing in these parts.
I agree, but my hare had this whim and didn't know what
Aristotle used to say to young Greeks upon entering his
    school:
  My friends, there are no friends.
Complacent, assiduous, always driven by zeal,
He wanted to make everyone a faithful friend,
And believed himself loved because he loved them.[2]

Florian

Now. Perhaps we are ready, now, to hear and understand the Nietzschean
apostrophe, the cry of the 'living fool that I am': 'Friends, there are no
friends!' (*Freunde, es gibt keine Freunde!*) Perhaps we are better exposed to it,
there where its destination also depends on us. Its destiny, perhaps, rides on
the event of a response that has come, like the responsibility of a
countersignature, from its addressees. Who will come to countersign?
What? How? How many?

The apostrophe resounds in *Human All Too Human*, in the chapter 'Of friends'.[3] It also plays with a tradition deeper and wider than any of us could fathom: Aristotle, Montaigne, Plutarch, Gracian – *Oráculo manual* – Florian, and so many others awaiting us. Most often they appeal to a wisdom, and this wisdom usually derives its authority from a political experience. In any case, it draws from such experience political lessons, moralities and precepts to be used by wise politicians.

Once again – we will hear it – the provocation strikes and opens with a 'perhaps'. It opens as much as it opens up, it breaks in. The irreducible modality of the 'perhaps' always gives the opening note. 'Perhaps' gives it as a sharp rap is administered. 'Perhaps' gives it with the announcement of a first act or a first scene; but also as the only chance granted to the future. More precisely, the chance of the future as chance itself. Future there is, if there ever is, when chance is no longer barred. There would be no future without chance. The rap of the 'perhaps' not only effects a catastrophic inversion, a reversal of the tradition – already paradoxical ('O my friends, there is no friend') – it provokes the avowal of the opposite, the confession of an error that is not foreign to the truth. This is perhaps truth itself, a superior or more profound truth.

And *perhaps* to each of us there will come the more joyful hour, when we exclaim:
'Friends, there are no friends!' thus said the dying sage;
'Foes, there are no foes!' *say I, the living fool.*

Und vielleicht kommt jedem auch einmal die freudigere Stunde, wo er sagt:
'Freunde, es gibt keine Freunde!' so rief der sterbende Weise;
'Feinde, es gibt keinen Feind!' – ruf ich, der lebende Tor.[4]

Numerous roads promise to open up on a reading of this reversing [*renversante*] apostrophe – an overwhelming one, too, since it converts the friend into the enemy. Someone complains, in sum, about the disappearance of the enemy. Would it already have taken place? In any case, this person fears that it has; he recalls it, announces and denounces it as a *catastrophe*. We shall listen once again, at more or less regular intervals, to a double clamour, the two times and two voices, the two persons of this exclamation: he/I, he exclaimed/I exclaimed, past/present, dying/living, wisdom/madness. But a single *cry* answers the other: this is what the dying sage cried, this is what I cry, I, the living fool, etc.: *so rief der sterbende Weise . . . ruf ich, der lebende Tor.*

'That saying which Aristotle often repeated' is, then, indeed one of someone who is dying – his last will and testament – already speaking from the place of death. A testamentary wisdom to which must be opposed, even at the price of madness, the exclaiming insurrection of the living present. The dying person addresses friends, speaking of friends to them, if only to tell *them* there are none. As for the living person, he addresses enemies, speaking to them of enemies, if only to tell *them* there are none. The dying person dies, turning towards friendship; the living person lives on, turning towards enmity. Wisdom on the side of death, and the past came to pass: the being-past of the passer-by. Madness on the side of life, and the present is: the presence of the present.

This is far from the only time, as we have seen, that Nietzsche associates the thought of the friend-enemy or of the brother-enemy with madness, with sheer madness that begins by inverting all the senses of sense into their opposites. For sheer madness is a priori inscribed in the very sense of sense. The fool is *already* on the premises as a guest who would have preceded his host. He haunts him in advance, his shadow is watching in the darkness of all hospitality: *Human All Too Human* is a fool addressing fools, his friends the fools.

The book is literally dedicated to a corporation of fools (*Narren-Zunft*). The madness is the dedication and the signature at the end. The verse epilogue, the post-lude (*Ein Nachspiel*), is entitled 'Among Friends' (*Unter Freunden*), and it also addresses an apostrophe to them, the friends. He asks neither to be excused nor pardoned for this book of unreason (*diesem unvernünftigen Buche*), only for the kind of hospitality offered to mad *arrivants*. He requests only that they open the doors of their hearts to him, that they listen to him, welcoming him into their selves; that they put him up, honour him – and learn from him, in sum, a history of reason. Only a fool can tell this story, only he can know how to submit reason to reason, how reason becomes what it should have been: finally brought to its senses.

Having said this, we are going to read the book's final lines and the envoy. It, too, is pronounced in the form of a salute or a leavetaking. A moment of separation with friends at last – friends who have become friends – and the testamentary connotation is not absent. All the more so given that in the middle of the epilogue, the epilogual nature of the apostrophe – that is, the beginning of the end – does not fail to appear. We shall have to climb the road separating us from the cemetery: 'Till we reach the grave together. Friends! . . .' *Bis wir in die Grube steigen./Freunde!*

If the address requests that we go beyond excuse and pardon, it still moves in the religious space of benediction or malediction. Unless this space would at last be opened by it. It conjures up malediction (*Fluch*) and pronounces benediction twice (*Amen!, Und auf Wiedersehn!*) in offering the promised coming of the event – in exposing, rather, the arriving stance [*arrivance*] of the question of the *perhaps* ('*So solls geschehn?*'):

> Shall we do this, friends, again? . . . (*Freunde! Ja! So solls geschehn?*)
> *Amen! Und auf Wiedersehn!*
> No excuses! No forgiving!
> You who laugh and joy in living
> Grant this book, with all its follies (*Diesem unvernünftigen Buche*)
> Ear and heart and open door!
> Friends, believe me, all my folly's (*meine Unvernunft*)
> Been a blessing heretofore!
>
> What *I* seek, what *I* discover – (*Was ich suche, was ich finde – ,*)
> Has a book contained it ever?
> Hail in me the guild of fools! (*die Narren-Zunft!*)
> Learn what this fools-book's (*Narrenbuche*) offence is:
> Reason coming to its senses! (*Wie Vernunft kommt – 'sur Vernunft'!*)
> Shall we, friends, do this again? (*Also, Freunde, solls geschehen? –*)
> *Amen! Und auf Wiedersehn!*

The envoy thus confirms that the friend cannot address anything other than a fool's discourse to his friends. The truth of friendship is a madness of truth, a truth that has nothing to do with the wisdom which, throughout the history of philosophy *qua* the history of reason, will have set the tone of this truth – by attempting to have us believe that amorous passion was madness, no doubt, but that friendship was the way of wisdom and of knowledge, no less than of political justice.

Let us return now to 'Enemies, there is no enemy!', at paragraph 376 of *Human All Too Human*, 1. Let us recall only the following for the moment: that the reversal had been prepared by an *avowal*. By a sort of response to self; already, the same 'sage' – the presumed author of 'O my friends' – when he was not yet 'dying', accepted in the prime of life to contradict himself. In any case, he consented to declaring to himself an 'error' and an 'illusion' while appealing, in sum, to responsibility. A responsibility which, following the more or less latent – and thus silent – logic of the argument, can be exercised only in silence – indeed, in secret – in a sort of counterculture of knowing-how-to-keep-silent. As though the sage were speaking silently to himself about silence, answering himself saying nothing – in order to appeal to responsibility. One must know how to reach such silence; 'they' must learn how ('*und Schweigen müssen sie gelernt haben*'):

When one realizes this, and realizes in addition that all the opinions of one's fellow men, of whatever kind they are and with whatever intensity they are held, are just as necessary and unaccountable (*unverantwortlich*) as their actions; if one comes to understand this inner necessity of opinions originating in the inextricable interweaving of character, occupation, talent, environment – perhaps one will then get free of that bitterness of feeling with which the sage cried: 'Friends, there are no friends! (*Freunde, es gibt keine Freunde!*).' One will, rather, avow to oneself (*Er wird sich vielmehr eingestehen*): yes, there are friends, but it is error and deception regarding yourself that led them to you; and they must have learned how to keep silent in order to remain your friend (*und Schweigen müssen sie gelernt haben um dir Freund zu bleiben*); for such human relationships almost always depend upon the fact that two or three things are never said or even so much as touched upon: if these little boulders do start to roll, however, friendship follows after them and shatters. Are there not people who would be mortally wounded if they discovered that their dearest friends actually know about them?

Friendship does not keep silence, it is preserved by silence. From its first word to itself, friendship inverts itself. Hence it says, saying this to itself, that there are no more friends; it avows itself in avowing that. Friendship tells the truth – and this is always better left unknown.

The protection of this custody guarantees the truth of friendship, its ambiguous truth, that by which friends protect themselves from the error or the illusion on which friendship is founded – more precisely, the bottomless bottom founding a friendship, which enables it to resist its own abyss. To resist the vertigo or the revolution that would have it turning around itself. Friendship is founded, in truth, so as to protect itself from the bottom, or the abyssal bottomless depths.

That is why friendship had better preserve itself in silence, and keep silent about the truth. Over the abyss, on the shifting ground of our friendships: 'how uncertain (*unsicher*) is the ground upon which all our alliances and friendships rest, . . . how isolated (*vereinsamt*, solitary, insular-ized, 'solitarized') each man is' (ibid.); that is what you will say to yourself, with so much experience of 'misunderstandings', 'ruptures', 'hostile fleeings' ['*fuites hostiles*']. So you had better keep silent about this truth of truth. The truth of truth is that the truth is there to protect a friendship that could not resist the truth of its illusion. Nietzsche affects a mystical tone when he puts forward aphoristic precepts and sentences (*Sprüche*) that he then names, in Latin, *Silentium*. Asceticism, *kenosis*, knowledge of how to evacuate words to gain breathing space for friendship. Here again, Nietzsche thinks silence from the standpoint of friendship, as though silence itself could not be spoken about, as though *it* could not be spoken elsewhere than in friendship, by friendship. Speech ruins friendship; it corrupts by speaking, degrades, belittles, undoes the speech (*verredet*) of friendship; but this evil is done to it on account of truth. If silence must be kept among friends, concerning friends, this is just as much so as not to tell the truth, a murderous truth. '*Silentium*. One should not talk (*reden*) about one's friends: otherwise one will talk away the feeling of friendship (*sonst verredet man sich das Gefühl der Freundschaft*).'[5]

Not that friends should keep silent, among themselves or on the subject of their friends. Their speech would perhaps have to breathe with an implied silence. This is nothing other than a certain way of speaking: secret, discreet, discontinuous, aphoristic, elliptic, just in disjointed time to avow the truth that must be concealed; hiding it – because it is deadly – to save life. To avow or not to avow – what difference does it make, since the avowal consists in hiding the truth even more safely? What is the truth of a confession? Not the veracity of what it says, but its confessional truth?

At least for the time being, let us speak this moment of avowal, for *perhaps*, perhaps the day of joy will come when the living fool (that I am) will dare to exclaim: 'there is no enemy!'. This day of joy, as we recall, will be one of a shared rejoicing (*Mitfreude*), not fellow-suffering (*Mitleid*). For there would then be two communities without community, two friendships of solitude, two ways of saying to oneself – keeping silent, keeping it hushed – that solitude is irremediable and friendship impossible; two ways for desire to share and to parcel out the impossible: one would be the compassionate and negative way, the other affirmative, which would attune and join two disjointed rejoicings [*jouissances*] conjugated at the heart of the dissociation itself: heterogeneous allies, co-affirmed, perhaps affirmed in total darkness. An ecstatic rejoicing but one without plenitude, a communion of infinite wrenching.

In the meantime, in the course of the first avowal's moment, which still belongs to the community of compassion, you had better keep silence to preserve what remains of friendship. And as the friends know this truth of truth (the custody of what cannot be kept), they had better keep silent together. As in a mutual agreement. A tacit agreement, however, whereby those who are separated come together without ceasing to be what they are destined to be – and undoubtedly what they more than ever are: dissociated, 'solitarized', singularized, constituted into monadic alterities (*vereinsamt*); where, as the phenomenologist says, what is proper to the *alter ego* will never be accessible, *as such*, to an originarily bestowing intuition, but only to an analogical apresentation. These two are not in solidarity with one another; they are solitary, but they ally themselves in silence within the necessity of keeping silent together – each, however, in his own corner. This is, perhaps, a social bond, a contemporaneity, but in the common affirmation of being unbonded, an untimely being-alone and, simultaneously, in joint acquiescence to disjunction. How can you be together to bear witness to secrecy, separation, singularity? You would have to testify where testimony remains impossible. You would have to witness the absence of attestation, and testify in behalf of that absence, as Blanchot says ('Speech still to be spoken beyond the living and the dead, *testifying for the absence of attestation.*'⁶) How can one be silent, one and the other, one the very other [*l'un l'autre même*]?

This '*miteinander Schweigen*' can always come to ruin our ontological assurances, our common sense, our concept of the concept, the One of the common that has always commanded our thought as well as our politics of friendship. How can a politics of separation be founded? Nietzsche dares to recommend separation, he dares to prescribe distancing in the code excluding distance, in this very distance, and as if he were provoking it, in the language that remains as much that of friendship as that of politics, of state, of family (affinity, kinship, *Verwandschaft*, appurtenance, the co-appurtenance of identity: *Zusammengehörigkeit*):

> In parting (*Im Scheiden*). It is not in how one soul approaches another but in how it distances itself from it that I recognize their affinity and relatedness (*Verwandschaft und Zusammengehörigkeit*).⁷

What is keeping silent? Keeping silent among friends, *unter Freunden*, in the rupture (*im Scheiden*), in the interruption that substitutes, as it must (for in silence, everything must be possible), testimony for know-how, faith for the test, 'fidence' for demonstration, the *perhaps* for certainty, the other for the same, friendship for calculation, etc.? The imperative and the enigma of the sense of decency [*pudeur*] are not far off; we shall link them in a moment to the *perhaps*, to the truth and to the question of sexual difference – in Nietzsche's writing, his silence, his erasure without erasure.

Perhaps this is an altogether different way of thinking the 'among', of apprehending the 'among friends', from within the silence of friends – and not the opposite. A particular 'among' would be incommensurable to all others. This is when the end begins, the *incipit* of the epilogue, the advent of the first verses of the *Nachspiel* whose second stanza we quoted. Silence among friends will not work without laughter, and laughter bares its teeth, as does death. And the more evil it is, the better. Doing and laughing, *machen/lachen,* doing evil and laughing at evil, making each other laugh about evil. Among friends. Not laughing evil away, but making ourselves laugh at evil. Among friends.

(You will not, perhaps, have failed to register the fact that we are writing and describing friends as masculine – neuter-masculine. Do not consider this a distraction or a slip. It is, rather, a laborious way of letting a question furrow deeper. We are perhaps borne from the very first step by and towards this question: what is a friend in the feminine, and who, in the feminine, is her friend? Why do 'our' philosophers and 'our' religions, our 'culture', acknowledge so little irreducible right, so little proper and acute signification, in such grammar? In an unpublished passage of *Beyond Good and Evil* – precisely around paragraph 2 on the 'dangerous perhaps' of the 'new philosophers' which we were questioning above – Nietzsche will have bequeathed us a certain number of unerased sentences. They take the movement of truth up into the folds of a veil, and this is always 'truth' suspended between inverted commas, the veiled truth of decency, as Nietzsche often says. But some of these phrases also inscribe the 'perhaps', which is never dissociated from veiled decency, in a staging of feminine seduction where it would be arduous to distribute place, praise, and blame. The veil, and decency too, may signify the absence of courage. In the first draft, in the insistent mode of 'perhaps', and not far from the 'dangerous perhaps', we can read, for example:

> But who has the courage to look on these 'truths' without a veil? *Perhaps* there exists a legitimate decency before these problems and possibilities, *perhaps* we are mistaken about their value, *perhaps* we all thereby obey this will. (emphasis added)

A second draft contains two unerased conclusions:

> 1. But who is willing to concern himself with such 'perhapses'! That violates good taste, especially virtue, when truth becomes scandalous to this point and renounces all decency: one must recommend prudence before that lady.

> 2. Perhaps! But who is willing to concern himself with these dangerous 'perhapses'! That violates good taste, and also virtue. When truth becomes scandalous to this point, when this unscrupulous lady divests herself of her veils to this point and renounces all decency: away! Away with this seductress! May she henceforth go her own way! One can never be too prudent with a lady like

that. You may tell me with a wink that 'one is better off associating with a humble and modest error, with a nice little lie'.[8]

How much of a chance would a feminine friend have on this stage? And a feminine friend of hers, among themselves? See below.)

Among Friends
Epilogue
1
Fine to lie in quiet together
Finer still to join in laughing –
(Schön ists, miteinadander schweigen
Schöner, miteinander lachen, –)
Underneath a silken heaven
Lying back among the grasses
Join with friends in cheerful laughing,
(Lieblich laut mit Freunden lachen)
Showing our white teeth together.

Am I right? let's lie in quiet;
Am I wrong? let's join in laughing
And in being aggravating,
Aggravating, loudly laughing,
(Schlimmer machen, schlimmer lachen),
Till we reach the grave together.
(Bis wir in die Grube steigen.)

Not all silences chime together. Each time the quality, the modality, of the 'keeping quiet together' eludes a common measure. Here, we have just apprehended the moment when the keeping silent of compassion broke into laughter, into a resounding laughter but without a word, still silent, aphonic in the sonority of its break into laughter, into the hysterical laughter of rejoicing among friends.

[The question is one of tonality: Stimmung changes everything. Beyond the concept – even if it is the same one, and even if it becomes undecidable – Stimmung suspends or terrifies oppositions, converts the antithesis into its antithesis (friend into enemy, love into hate, etc.). There is little room for laughter in Heidegger. Nevertheless, if this subject did not result in too long a detour, we might recognize in the very possibility of this silence, the keeping-silent, the discretion, the secret of Schweigen or Verschwiegenheit, which Heidegger, as early as Sein und Zeit [Being and Time] (paras 34 and

60), analyses at the heart of speech. Finding the resource of its own silence in the possibility of speaking, that which thus keeps silent belongs from then on to truth – more precisely, to one of the essential modes (to wit, speech or discourse, *Rede*) of opening or disclosedness (*Erschlossenheit*), disclosedness to truth – that is, of truth 'in which' *Dasein* is, a *Dasein* originarily responsible, indebted or 'responsibilizable' (*schuldig*), but 'in' a truth that is every bit as originarily an 'untruth' ('But *Dasein* is equiprimordially [*gleichursprünglich*] in the untruth').[9] We could demonstrate (and we would like to attempt this elsewhere) that this equiprimordiality of truth and untruth, like that of all the apparently opposite possibilities that are inextricably linked to it, destabilizes all the conceptual distinctions that seem to structure the existential analytic, dooming its logic to an *Unheimlichkeit* marking each of its decisive moments. In truth, it undoes, disidentifies, the identification of every concept. It appeals to a thinking beyond the concept, but *a fortiori* beyond intuition. It surpasses reason, but *a fortiori* the understanding too. This 'thought' – always supposing that the name fits the named and retains its validity beyond these final frontier oppositions; always supposing a proper name could be found for it in any singular language; always supposing that it still speculates – this excessive 'thought' belongs as little to the disinterested or theoretical, even discursive, order of philosophical speculation as the unchained desires of love and hate, friendship and enmity, when they unite in death, at any moment, in the taste of each of our desires. Defying all oppositions, this *Unheimlichkeit* would here suffice to usher in, between friend and enemy, every and all conversion, inversion and revolution [*retournements*]. It lodges the enemy in the heart of the friend – and vice versa. Why do we say it 'lodges' the other, the stranger, or the enemy? Because the word *unheimlich* is not unfamiliar, though it speaks precisely to the stranger, to the intimacy of the hearth and familial lodgings, to the *oikeiótēs*; but above all because it provides a place, in a troubling way, for a form of welcome in itself that recalls the haunt as much as the home – *Unterkunft*, lodgings, shelter, hospitable habitat, said the epilogue we cited above; and in a moment we will hear the voice of the friend as the voice of the spectre. The fact that in its very depth the *keeping silent* of *Sein und Zeit* never laughs will one day indicate to us one of the places for hearing once again the colloquy between Nietzsche and Heidegger, what there is '*among* [those] friends' as well as '*among* [those] enemies'.]

We have just focused our attention on the avowed error, the endured illusion at the beginning of paragraph 376 of *Human All Too Human* – 'Of friends'. The logic of avowal will justify, at the end of the paragraph, the inversion or conversion, the *hour of joy* that will come *perhaps*. This logic prepares the fool's response, my living fool's cry and the clamour of what could be called the *call to the enemy*: 'Enemies, there is no enemy!'

Can an 'alas!', or an 'if only there could be enemies', or again: 'instead of bewailing the friend, bewail the enemy!', be inferred from this call? Perhaps. In all these hypotheses, this call to the enemy *ipso facto* converts the enemy into the friend: you must love your enemies, *seine Feinde lieben*, even if you pretend to love them, but no longer in a Christian fashion. And the friend is asked to convert himself into an enemy. No concept, nor any insurance contract between word and concept, vocable and meaning, is more stable, more reliable (*bébaios*, as Aristotle would say).

This conversion, then, will allow us no respite. We will never have done with it. In a modest book or elsewhere, for this interminability is no accident: one *cannot*, any more than one *must* not, have done with it. This is not a surpassable moment. It remains the structural condition of that which it must yet survive in making it possible: the sentence, the decision, the responsibility, the event, death itself.

Hence, we shall not finish with it. But the first reason that makes us wary of the opposition between the 'dying sage' and the 'living fool', and discourages any dwelling on the stabilized distinction between 'Friends, there is no friend' and 'Enemies, there is no enemy', is that one apostrophe can always feign to be the other. The dying sage can *play fools*, he can *play the fool*, and the fool can pretend to be wiser and deeper in death's throes than the Greek philosopher that he has summoned to bear witness. The face of the fool can be a mask. Behind the mask, a sage wiser than the sage. Fundamentally, from one address to the other, the same person is speaking – him, me; and language liberates this substitution: 'I' is 'me', but an 'I' is a 'him'. One is the other. One guards and guards himself from the other. One does violence to oneself, becoming violence. Here again the infinite build-up [*surenchère*, also a 'raising of the stakes']. A build-up that does not even need an author's intention, or a deliberate decision: it is carried away, it carries itself away, it throws itself into turmoil with the disidentification of concepts and terms that we are analysing right now.

But – no doubt by a stroke of luck – it happens that in another place, rather at one remove from here, Nietzsche himself seems to gloss these two sayings of the sage and the fool, the dying and the living, his saying and mine. He affects, perhaps, to provide us with a key for a reading of the score. Again it is in the *Vermischte Meinungen und Sprüch,* paragraph 246. The French translation of the title of this short section has: 'The sage passing himself off as a fool': *Der Weise sich als Narren gebend*: The sage *giving himself up* as a fool, the sage when he intends to give himself up for a fool, when he agrees to present himself as that which he is not. I prefer to keep, in its literality and playfulness, the reference to the present, the gift, to *giving oneself up as*. For the simulacrum of this sage knows how to offer himself, he makes a gift, he makes himself into a gift, inspired by a generous friendship. He thereby gives the good to avoid doing evil to his *Umgebung*: his entourage, milieu, relatives. And he feigns, lies, disguises or masks himself, out of friendship for mankind, out of *Menschenfreundlichkeit*: philanthropy once again, humanity, sociability. Here is the English translation which we will modify or compare with the words of the original version only when we consider it especially indispensable:

> Paragraph 246. *The wise man pretending to be a fool.* The wise man's philanthropy (*Die Menschenfreundlichkeit*) sometimes leads him to *pose* as excited, angry, delighted (*sich erregt, erzürnt, erfreut zu* stellen), so that the coldness and reflectiveness of his *true* nature (of his *true* essence, *seines* wahren *Wesens*) shall not harm those around him. (original emphasis)

Lie, mask, dissimulation, the simulacrum bestows. It also provokes vertigo: the sage, for friendship's sake – this is what makes him a sage – takes on the disguise of the fool, and, for friendship's sake, disguises his friendship as enmity. But what is he hiding? His enmity, for the coldness and lucidity of his true nature are to be feared only where they may hurt and reveal some aggressivity. In sum, the sage presents himself as an enemy in order to conceal his enmity. He shows his hostility so as not to hurt with his wickedness. And why does he take such pains? Out of friendship for mankind, philanthropic sociability. His pose (*sich stellen*) consists – in the sheer difference between hot and cold, exalted anger and icy lucidity – *in feigning to be precisely what he is*, in telling the truth to conceal the truth and especially to neutralize its deadly effect, to protect others from it. *He loves them enough not to want to do them all the evil he wants for them. He loves them too much for that.*

And what if tomorrow a new political wisdom were to let itself be inspired by this lie's wisdom, by this manner of knowing how to lie, dissimulate or divert wicked lucidity? What if it demanded that we know, and know how to dissimulate, the principles and forces of social unbinding [*déliaison*], all the menacing disjunctions? To dissimulate them in order to preserve the social bond and the *Menschenfreundlichkeit*? A new political wisdom – human, humanistic, anthropological, of course? A new *Menschenfreundlichkeit*: pessimistic, sceptical, hopeless, incredulous?

A new virtue, from that point on?

The Nietzschean thought of virtue will not be simplified here. So very many apparently heterogeneous propositions would have to be not only reread but harmonized. The immense but rigorously *coherent medley* of Zarathustra's addresses to his 'brothers' would also – and this would be an awesome and hitherto unaccomplished feat – have to be taken into account. Addresses to his friends who are also brothers. This consequence, in its shimmering mobility, its untenable instability, appears no less rigorous even though it is not systematic: not philosophical, moral, or theological. Its expository mode can never be reduced to what it nevertheless also is: the discipline of a psychology, a prophecy, a poetics. Our hypothesis is that the 'genre', the 'mode', the 'rhetoric', the 'poetics', and the 'logic' to which Zarathustra's songs belong – 'Of the friend', 'Of the bestowing virtue', 'Of the virtuous', 'Of the belittling virtue' (examples of what interests us here) – could be determined, following old or new categories, only from the place of the very thing that is said *there, in this specific place*, about friendship and virtue, *fraternity*, and the *saying* of what is said *there, in that way*. We shall consider these passages when the time comes.

This said and this saying call for a new type of address. They claim as much, in any case, teleiopoetically. To take saying and the virtue of speaking about virtue seriously is to acknowledge the address of a vocation: the *brothers* (past, present or to come) for whom Zarathustra destines such a harangue on friendship and on virtue, an ever-evil virtue. The brothers? Why the brothers? The addressees, as always, lay down the law of genre. We must meditate upon this: the addressees are brothers, and their coming virtue remains virile. *The Gay Science* (para. 169) says that declared enemies are indispensable for men who must 'rise to the level of their *own* virtue, virility (*Männlichkeit*), and cheerfulness'.

We shall return to this later, then. But to confine ourselves here to the barest schema, let us note that the motive of virtue is never discredited – no more so than the word virtue, in its Greek or Judaeo-Christian cultural context. Virtue is regularly reaffirmed by Nietzsche according to a logic or a rhetoric that can be interpreted in at least three ways (at least three when the question concerns the author of 'Our new "infinite" which never ceased to designate in this way a world that had become infinite again since opening for us onto an "infinity of interpretations."'[10]):

1. the deliberate perversion of the heritage – the opposite meaning under the same word;

2. the restoration of a meaning perverted by the inherited tradition (Greek, Jewish, or Pauline-Christian);

3. or a hyperbolic build-up (more Greek or more Judaeo-Christian than the Greek or the Judaeo-Christian).

For this reason, one must not hesitate to take the 'Path to a Christian virtue' (*Weg zu einer christlichen Tugend*):[11] to learn from one's enemies is the best path to loving them, for it puts us in a grateful mood towards them (one suspects that this is not the most Christian way of going down such a path, nor of thinking the unconscious of virtues). This again is a question of path, of progress along a path, of steps, gait, a way of walking, rather than a question of content. For there are 'unconscious virtues' – this, morality and philosophy could never admit – and like visible virtues, like those that one believes to be visible, these invisible virtues '*follow their own course*' (*gehen auch ihren Gang*, with Nietzsche's emphasis), but a 'wholly different course'.[12] This difference comes to light only under a microscope, a divine microscope capable of perceiving delicate sculptures on the scales of reptiles.

Hence we will not be too surprised, alongside this praise of enmity or these calls to the enemy, to see Nietzsche honouring friendship, the 'good friendship' – even the Greek brand – and sometimes beyond 'the things people call love'.

'Good friendship' supposes disproportion. It demands a certain rupture in reciprocity or equality, as well as the interruption of all fusion or confusion between you and me. By the same token it signifies a divorce with love, albeit self-love. The few lines defining this 'good friendship'[13] mark all these lines of division. 'Good friendship' can be distinguished from the bad only in eluding everything one believed one could recognize in the name friendship. As if it were a question of a simple homonym. 'Good friendship' is born of disproportion: when you esteem or respect (*achtet*) the other more than yourself. Nietzsche points out that this does not mean that one *loves* more than oneself – and there is a second division, within lovence, between friendship and love. 'Good friendship' certainly supposes a certain air, a certain tinge (*Anstrich*) of intimacy, but one 'without actual and genuine intimacy'. It commands that we abstain 'wisely', 'prudently' (*weislich*), from all confusion, all permutation between the singularities of you and me. This is the announcement of the community without community of thinkers to come.

Is such a friendship still Greek? Yes and no. Does this question make sense? Yes and no. If what Nietzsche understands here under the name friendship, if what he wants to *have us hear and understand or give us to hear and understand* for the future still chimes with *philía* but is already no longer Greek, then this is another way of suggesting that this experience, with the help of no other, forbids us to place trust in some presumed unity of Greek culture, with respect to this point as to that of so many others.

Nietzsche knows better than anyone, when he writes 'In honour of friendship',[14] that he is speaking Greek and that his argument, illustrated with a tale, portrays a Greek possibility. He honours it, precisely. But the tale reveals an internal contradiction in the Greek concept of friendship, the Greek virtue of friendship – more precisely, in its philosophical concept, as it could be implemented in a philosopher's life. Nietzsche notes that in Antiquity the feeling of friendship was the highest, more elevated than the most celebrated pride of the sages, who boasted of their independence, autonomy and self-sufficiency. Certainly, this 'unique' feeling seemed to be indissociable from this pride, this freedom of self-determination from which it thus stemmed. Now the tale, setting face-to-face a king and a philosopher, a Macedonian king and a Greek philosopher, tends to mark a split between this proud independence, this freedom, this self-sufficiency that claims to rise above the world, and a friendship which should agree to depend on and receive from the other. The Athenian philosopher disdains the world, refusing as a result the king's gift (*Geschenk*) of a talent. 'What!' demanded the king. 'Has he no friend?' Nietzsche translates: the king meant that he certainly honoured the pride of a sage jealous of his independence and his own freedom of movement; but the sage would have honoured his humanity better had he been able to triumph over his proud self-determination, his own subjective freedom; had he been able to accept the gift and the dependency – that is, this law of the other assigned to us by friendship, a sentiment even more sublime than the freedom or self-sufficiency of a subject. The philosopher discredited himself in his ignorance of one of the two sublime sentiments, in truth 'the more elevated' of the two.

A logic of the gift thus withholds friendship from its philosophical interpretation. Imparting to it a new twist, at once both gentle and violent, this logic reorientates friendship, deflecting it towards what it should have been – what it immemorially will have been. This logic calls friendship back to non-reciprocity, to dissymmetry or to disproportion, to the impossibility of a return to offered or received hospitality; in short, it calls friendship back to the irreducible precedence of the other. To its consideration [*pré-venance*, thoughtfulness of and for that which 'comes before']. But is there more or less freedom in accepting the gift of the other? Is this reorientation of the gift that would submit friendship to the consideration of the other something other than alienation? And is this alienation without relation to the loss of identity, of responsibility, of freedom that is also translated by 'madness', this living madness which reverses, perverts or converts (good) sense, makes opposites slide into each other and 'knows' very well, in its own way, in what sense the best friends are the best enemies? Hence the worst.

What concept of freedom – and of equality – are we talking about? And what are the political consequences and implications, notably with regard to democracy, of such a rupture in reciprocity – indeed, of such a divorce between two experiences of freedom that pride themselves on being respectively the hyperbole of the other?

With regard to democracy *and* with regard to justice? For we would be tempted to match Nietzsche's gesture, as we have just seen it in outline, to the call he seems to be making for *another justice*: the one soon to be within reach of the new philosophers – the *arrivants* – the one already within their reach, since these *arrivants*, who are still to come, *are already coming*: 'But what is needful is a new *justice* (*Sondern eine neue* Gerechtigkeit *tut not!*)',[15] just as we lack – it is the same sentence, the same need, the same exigency – 'new philosophers'. The anchor must be raised with you, philosophers of a new world (for there is more than one [*car il y en a plus d'un*]), in a search for a justice that would at last break with sheer equivalence, with the equivalence of right and vengeance, of justice as principle of equivalence (right) and the law of eye for eye, an equivalence between the just, the equitable (*gerecht*), and the revenged (*gerächt*) that Nietzschean genealogy has relentlessly recalled as the profound motivation of morality and of right, of which we are the heirs. What would an equality then be, what would an equity be, which would no longer calculate this equivalence? Which would, quite simply, no longer calculate at all? And would carry itself beyond proportion, beyond appropriation, thereby exceeding all reappropriation of the proper?

This 'disappropriation' [*dépropriation*] would undoubtedly beckon to this other 'love' whose true name, says Nietzsche in conclusion, whose 'just name' is *friendship* (*Ihr rechter Name ist* Freundschaft).[16] This friendship is a species of love, but of a love more loving than love. All the names would have to change for the sake of coherence. Without being able to devote to it the careful reading it deserves, let us recall that this little two-page treatise on love denounces, in sum, the *right to property*. This property right is the claim [*revendication*] of love (at least, of what is thus named). The vindictive claim of this right can be deciphered throughout all the appropriative manoeuvres of the strategy which this 'love' deploys. It is the appropriating drive (*Trieb*) *par excellence*. 'Love' wants to possess. It wants the possessing. It is the possessing – cupidity itself (*Habsucht*); it always hopes for new property; and even the very Christian 'love of one's neighbour' – charity, perhaps – would reveal only a new lust in this fundamental drive: 'Our love of our neighbour – is it not a lust for new *possessions*? (*Unsere Nächstenliebe – ist sie nicht ein drang nach neuem* Eigentum?)'

This question is doubly important. In contesting the Christian revolution of love as much as the Greek philosophical concept of friendship – and just as much the norms of justice that depend on them – its target is the very value of proximity, the neighbour's proximity as the ruse of the proper and of appropriation. The gesture confirms the warning accompanying the discourse on 'good friendship': not to give in to proximity or identification, to the fusion or the permutation of you and me. But, rather to place, maintain or keep an infinite distance within 'good friendship'. The very thing that love – that which is thus named, 'love between the sexes', egotism itself, jealousy which tends only towards possession (*Besitzen*) – is incapable of doing.

Is this to say that friendship, rightly named, will carry itself beyond Eros? Beyond Eros in general? Or beyond love between two sexes?

Nietzsche does not unfold these questions in this form. But let us not conceal their radicality, which can become disquieting, particularly given the motive of the 'new' or of the 'future' that we perhaps too often trust as if it were univocal, simply opposed to the form of repetition and the work of the arch-ancient. For Nietzsche sees this drive of appropriation, this form always pushing for 'new property', at work everywhere, including where love loves in view of knowledge, of truth, of the novelty of the new, of all new reality in general: 'Our love of our neighbour – is it not a lust for new *possessions*? And likewise our love of knowledge, of truth, and altogether any lust for what is new? (*und überhaupt all jener Drang nach Neuigkeiten?*)'

If 'new' always means, again and again, once again, *anew*, the appropriative drive, the repetition of the same drive to appropriate the other for oneself, the truth, being, the event, etc., what can still take place anew? Anew? What remains to come? And what will become of our just impatience to see the new coming, the new thoughts, the new thinkers, new justice, the revolution or the messianic interruption? Yet another ruse? Once again the desire of appropriation?

Yes. Yes, perhaps.

And you must be coherent with this response. You must acquiesce to this principle of ruin at the heart of the most utterly new. It could never be eluded or denied.

And yet. At the heart of this acquiescence, just when a yes could be proffered to the principle of ruin, beyond knowledge and truth, precisely, an empty place would be left – left by Nietzsche as we would perhaps like to read him: a place open for that which can perhaps still take place – by chance. Favourable to friendship and like friendship, the friendship that would then deserve its just name. More precisely, favourable to the love whose *just name* would be *friendship*.

Because the adequation between the concept, the name, and the event could never be assured. Its appropriateness [*justesse*] would not be regulated by the necessity of any knowledge. Perhaps, one day, here or there, who knows, something may happen between two people in love, who would love each other lovingly (is this still the right word?) in such a way that friendship, *just once*, perhaps, for the first time (another *perhaps*), once and only once, therefore for the first and last time (perhaps, perhaps), will become the correct name, the right and just name for that which would then have taken place, the condition being that it take place between two, 'two people', as Nietzsche specifies. But how can you adjust a name to what could take place only once, perhaps, for the first and last time? In other words – and in a much more general way this time – how can you name an event? For this love that would take place only once would be the only possible event: as an impossible event. Even if the right name for this unique love were to be found, how would you convince everyone else of its appropriateness? And what about the task of convincing the partner, at the moment of the act in which this love would essentially consist, that of giving him or her the name?

There would be no better way of honouring this chance than by quoting Nietzsche: *Was alles Liebe gennant wird*. But let us not quote him without underscoring in advance a point of logic, rhetoric – or onomastics: what might, then, very well happen, by chance, between two, between two in love, would cause no ripple in the calm waters of semantics. There would be no substituting or opposing: of one concept for another, one name for another, a friendship for a non-friendship, a friendship for an enmity, or a friendship for love. No, the 'new' that will perhaps come will be radically new – who knows? – but it might also take on the form of a development or a prolongation (*Fortsetzung*) of love. It would then be a new form of 'lovence', of the becoming-friendship of love, under the same name, but this time under the *right* same name, just for once, just this one time, adjusted rather to an incomparable time, unique and without a concept, at a particular date, between two. The friendship of these friends, if there are any of this kind, should their friendship take place one fine day, in the chance of a moment, an instant, with no assurance of duration, without the firm constancy of Aristotelian *philía* – this would be the condition of an improbable alliance in the thought of the *perhaps*. And since this thought to come is not a philosophy – at least, not a speculative, theoretical or metaphysical philosophy – not an ontology and not a theology, neither a representation nor a philosophical consciousness, at stake would be another *experience* of the *perhaps*: of thought as another experience of the *perhaps*. Hence another way of *addressing*, addressing oneself to the possible. Such a possible would no longer belong to the space of this possible, to the possibility of the possible whose concept would have assured its constancy, through so many mutations, from Aristotle to Hegel and Bergson. In order to open oneself to this other possibility of the possible, the word experience itself would have to refer to another concept. And attempt to translate itself, if this other possibility were possible, into a political language. The price to pay, if this were necessary, would be having to change the meaning of the word 'political' – in other words, one would have to change politics.

Such a change to come is perhaps under way. But let us not be blind to the aporia that all change must endure. It is the aporia of the *perhaps*, its historical and political aporia. Without the opening of an absolutely undetermined possible, without the radical abeyance and suspense marking a *perhaps*, there would never be either event or decision. Certainly. But nothing takes place and nothing is ever decided without suspending the *perhaps* while keeping its living possibility in living memory. If no decision (ethical, juridical, political) is possible without interrupting determination by engaging oneself in the *perhaps*, on the other hand, the same decision must interrupt the very thing that is its condition of possibility: the *perhaps* itself. In the order of law, politics or morality, what would rules and laws, contracts and institutions indeed be without steadfast (*bébaios*) determination, without calculability and without violence done to the *perhaps*, to the possible that makes them possible? We insist on the decision in order to introduce the aporia in which all theory of decision must engage itself, notably in its apparently modern figures – for example, that of Schmittian decisionism, of its 'right-wing' or 'left-wing' or even neo-Marxist heritage, which we will take up later. Such a decisionism, as we know, is a theory of the enemy. And the figure of the enemy, condition of the political as such, takes shape in this century against the backdrop of its own loss: we would be losing the enemy, and thereby the political. But since when?

The aporia of the *event* intersects with, but also capitalizes or overdetermines, the aporia of *decision* with regard to the *perhaps*. There is no event, to be sure, that is not preceded and followed by its own *perhaps*, and that is not as unique, singular and irreplaceable as the decision with which it is frequently associated, notably in politics. But can one not suggest without a facile paradox, that the eventness of an event remains minimal, if not excluded, by a decision? Certainly the decision makes the event, but it also neutralizes this happening that must surprise both the freedom and the will of every subject — surprise, in a word, the very subjectivity of the subject, affecting it wherever the subject is exposed, sensitive, receptive, vulnerable and fundamentally passive, before and beyond any decision — indeed, before any subjectivation or objectivation. Undoubtedly the subjectivity of a subject, already, never decides anything; its identity in itself and its calculable permanence make every decision an accident which leaves the subject unchanged and indifferent. *A theory of the subject is incapable of accounting for the slightest decision.* But this must be said *a fortiori* of the event, and of the event with regard to the decision. For if nothing ever happens to a subject, nothing deserving the name 'event', the schema of decision tends regularly — at least, in its ordinary and hegemonic sense (that which seems dominant still in Schmittian decisionism, in his theory of exception and of sovereignty) — to imply the instance of the subject, a classic, free, and wilful subject, therefore a subject to whom nothing can happen, not even the singular event for which he believes to have taken and kept the initiative: for example, in an exceptional situation. But should one imagine, for all that, a 'passive' decision, as it were, without freedom, without that freedom? Without that activity, and without the passivity that is mated to it? But not, for all that, without responsibility? Would one have to show hospitality to the impossible itself — that is, to what the *good sense of all philosophy* can only exclude as madness or nonsense: a *passive decision*, an originarily affected decision? Such an undesirable guest can intrude into the closed space or the home ground of common sense only by recalling, as it were, so as to derive authority from it, an old forgotten invitation. It would thus recall the type or the silhouette of the classic concept of decision, which must interrupt and mark an absolute beginning. Hence it signifies in me the other who decides and rends. The passive decision, condition of the event, is always in me, structurally, another event, a rending decision as the decision of the other. Of the absolute other in me, the other as the absolute that decides on me in me. Absolutely singular in principle, according to its most traditional concept, the decision is not only always exceptional, *it makes an exception for/of me*. In me. I decide, I make up my mind in all sovereignty – this would mean: the other than myself, the me as other and other than myself, *he makes or I make* an exception of the same. This normal exception, the supposed norm of all decision, exonerates from no responsibility. Responsible for myself before the other, I am first of all and also *responsible for the other before the other*. This heteronomy, which is undoubtedly rebellious against the decisionist conception of sovereignty or of the exception (Schmitt), does not contradict; it opens autonomy on to itself, it is a figure of its heartbeat. It matches the decision to the gift, if there is one, as the other's gift. The aporetic question 'what can "to give in the name, to give to the name of the other" mean?'[17] could translate into the question of the decision, the event, the exception, sovereignty, and so on. To give in the name of, to give to the name of, the other is what frees responsibility from knowledge – that is, what brings responsibility unto itself, if there ever is such a thing. For yet again, one *must* certainly *know, one must know it*, knowledge is necessary if one is to assume responsibility, but the decisive or deciding moment of responsibility supposes a leap by which an act takes off, ceasing in that instant to follow the consequence of what is – that is, of that which can be determined by science or consciousness – and thereby *frees itself* (this is what is called freedom), by the act of its act, of what is therefore heterogeneous to it, that is, knowledge. *In sum, a decision is unconscious* – insane as that may seem, it involves the unconscious and nevertheless remains responsible. And we are hereby unfolding the classic concept of decision. It is this act of the act that we are attempting here to think: 'passive', delivered over to the other, suspended over the other's heartbeat. For a few sentences earlier on, 'its heartbeat' had to be necessarily accorded thus: as the heartbeat of the other. Where I am helpless, where I decide what I cannot fail to decide, freely, necessarily, receiving my very life from the heartbeat of the other. We say not only heart but heartbeat: that which, *from one instant to another*, having come again from an other of the other to whom it is delivered up (and this can be me), this heart receives, it will *perhaps* receive in a rhythmic pulsation what is called blood, which in turn will receive the force needed to arrive.

The reader will have sensed that this is what I would be tempted to call 'lovence': love *in* friendship, lovence beyond love and friendship following their determined figures, beyond all this book's trajectories of reading, beyond all ages, cultures and traditions of loving. This does not mean that lovence itself can take place figurelessly: for example, the Greek *philía*, courtly love, such and such a great current (as we call it) of mysticism. But a lovence cuts across these figures.

Providing you open yourself, trembling, on to the 'perhaps'.

(We shall undoubtedly return to this point, directly or indirectly.)

That is what can take place, if one thinks with a minimum of coherence the logic of the *perhaps*. This is, rather, what can happen *to logic* following the experience of the *perhaps*. That is what may happen to experience, perhaps, and to the concept of experience. That is what could happen, if hope for such a thing were possible, among friends, between two, between two or more (but how many?), who love each other.

(In speaking like this, saying that love or friendship is improbable, I am saying nothing, I am neither stating nor describing anything. First of all because it is not *certain* that something of the sort exists, that anything ever exists outside of what I have to say about it, which you are reading perhaps in your own way; and this is precisely what I mean in drawing the *perhaps* into this free zone – where we can rely on nothing, nor count how many of us there are. Next, because no predication, no judgement of attribution – we have now seen this in sufficient depth – can measure up to what lets itself be thus marked – indeed, signed – by such a *perhaps*.

I am saying nothing, then, that can be said or is sayable.

And yet my saying, the declaration of love or the call to the friend, the address to the other in the night, the writing that does not resign itself to this unsaid – who could swear that they are consigned to oblivion simply because no said can speak them exhaustively?

The response no longer belongs to me – that is all I wanted to tell you, my friend the reader. And without knowing any longer if the rare or the numerous is preferable.

I assume responsibility for speaking rightly, justly, on this point, *up until now*, up to the point when I am no longer responsible for anything. Hence the point from which all responsibility is announced.)

This is undoubtedly only an active and hazardous, perhaps momentary, interpretation, of what Nietzsche thus said one day about chance, about the unknown factor, the 'here and there' of favour, of a sort of species of love, of the continuation or the follow-up to love, of a future for love the like of which it is not known if anyone will have ever had the experience. This is the conclusion of 'The things people call love' and, like a certain Aristotle, an Aristotle whose oligarchical recommendations no one, not even Nietzsche or Blanchot,[18] will ever have disavowed, this conclusion pronounces something of a sentence on number. One must think and write, in particular as regards friendship, against great numbers. Against the most numerous who make language and lay down the law of its usage. Against hegemonic language in what is called public space. If there were a community, even a communism, of writing, it would above all be on condition that war be waged on those, the greatest number, the strongest and the weakest at the same time, who forge and appropriate for themselves the dominant usages of language – leaving open the question of knowing if the greatest force – in a word, hegemony or dynasty – is on the side of the greatest number; and if, as always according to Nietzsche, the greatest force be not on the side of the weakest – and vice versa. Cicero, as we recall, also explained in his own way this transmutation of weak into strong, dead into living, etc., and precisely as a history of friendship. This commutability is never alien to that which destabilizes the friend/enemy opposition. What, then, can the true name be? Of what 'friendship' can it be the 'right name'? Is it only a name? Is it nameable, that which it is wearing itself out trying to name?

As we were saying, it would be better now to quote Nietzsche, to honour this chance:

> At this point linguistic usage has evidently been formed (*haben . . . den Sprachgebrauch gemacht*) by those who did not possess but desired {the unfulfilled, those that covet out of need: *die Nichthesitzenden und Begehrenden*}. Probably, there have always been too many of these (*immer zu viele*). Those to whom much possession and satiety were granted in this area have occasionally (*hier und da*) made some casual remark about "the raging demon", as that most gracious and beloved of all Athenians, Sophocles, did; but Eros has always laughed at such blasphemers; they were invariably his greatest favourites (*seine größten Lieblinge*). – Here and there (*hier und da*) on earth we may encounter a kind of continuation of love (*eine Art Fortsetzung der Liebe*) in which this possessive craving of two people for each other (*bei der jenes habsüchtige Verlangen zweier Personen nacheinander*) gives way to a new desire and lust for possession (*einer neuen Begierde und Habsucht*), a *shared* higher thirst [Nietzsche's emphasis: *einem gemeinsamen* höheren *Durste*] for an ideal above them. But who knows such love? Who has experienced it? Its right name is *friendship* (*Ihr rechter Name ist Freundschaft*).

Questions remain. In this semantic upheaval, why these words and not others? And what do 'reciprocal' and 'common' and 'ideal' and 'higher' and 'right' mean? What does the adjective 'just' or 'right' mean for all these words? Friendship as a just name? Or enmity – supposing, precisely, that is its opposite?

To take an example and to put these questions differently, what does Blake mean? Heartbroken, let down in a friendship he believes betrayed,[19] he asks or pretends to ask Hayley, his friend, to become his enemy (*Do be my enemy*): but he ordains it also, since the phrase is in the imperative voice, in the name of friendship, for love of friendship (*for Friendships sake*).

A last fidelity to some spectre of lost friendship? A living enemy, the friend would remain today more present, and more faithful in sum than under his misleading features, in the figure or the simulacrum of the unfaithful friend. There would be more attentive friendship, singular attention and consideration in a tension full of hatred. The enemy is then my best friend. He hates me in the name of friendship, of an unconscious or sublime friendship. Friendship, a 'superior' friendship, returns with the enemy. There would be an enemy's fidelity.

The two concepts (friend/enemy) consequently intersect and ceaselessly change places. They intertwine, as though they loved each other, all along a spiralled hyperbole: the *declared* enemy (Blake declares the enemy by ordering him to declare himself: *be* my enemy), the true enemy, is a better friend than the friend. For the enemy can hate or wage war on me in the name of friendship, *for Friendships sake*, out of friendship for friendship; if in sum he respects the true name of friendship, he will respect my own name. He will hear what my name should, even if it does not, properly name: the irreplaceable singularity which bears it, and to which the enemy then bears himself and refers. If he hears my order, if he addresses me, me myself, he respects me, at hate's distance, me beyond me, beyond my own consciousness. And if he desires my death, at least he desires it, perhaps, him, mine, singularly. The declared friend would not accomplish as much in simply declaring himself a friend while missing out on the name: that which imparts the name both to friendship and to singularity. That which deserves the name.

Every time, then, the issue involves the name. The name borne. The name which is imparted. The person imparting the name to the person to whom the name is handed down. The issue involves reference and respect. Each time, it involves what 'declaring' means: war, love, friendship. The difference between the two declarative regimes hesitates at this point between two truths, two logics of negation and denial, as between a logic of lying and a logic of the unconscious. These two logics cannot help but haunt one another. And share and separate even the concept of this haunting at work in the language of our time.

Hence, every time, a concept bears the phantom of the other. The enemy the friend, the friend the enemy.

In order to hear and understand this Blakeian vocative (*Do be my Enemy for Friendships sake*), one would have to do justice one day to the incessant return of his ghosts – of which there are so many in Blake – as well as to the infinite partition of all his divided spectres. Respect for the spectre, as Mary Shelley would say.

Singularly, to all the spectres of *Jerusalem*: '*Half Friendship is the bitterest Enmity . . .*' '*his Spectre also divided. . . . But still the Spectre divided, and still his pain increas'd!/In pain the Spectre divided. . . . And thus the spectre spoke: Wilt thou still go on to destruction? Till thy life is all taken away by this deceitful Friendship?*'[20]

Notes

1. *Comment tirer profit de ses ennemies* [*How to Take Advantage of One's Enemies*], trans. P. Maréchaux, Payot 1993, pp. 33–4.

2. *Le Lièvre, ses Amis et les Deux Chevreuils, Fables* [*The Hare, His Friends, and the Two Roebucks, Fables*], Book III, Fable VII.

3. *Human All Too Human*, 2, para. 376.

4. Ibid.; emphasis added.

5. Ibid., 2, para. 252.

6. *Le Pas au-delà*, Gallimard 1973, p. 107.

7. *Human All Too Human*. 2, para. 251.

8. [These passages have not, to my knowledge, been published in English translation. Derrida cites them from: *Par-delà bien et mal*, Oeuvres philosophiques complètes, Gallimard 1971, vol. VII, pp. 362–3 – Trans.]

9. *Being and Time*, trans. John Macquarrie and Edward Robinson. New York: Harper & Row 1962, para. 62, p. 356.

10. *The Gay Science*, trans. W. Kaufmann, New York, Vintage 1974, para. 374.

11. *Human All Too Human*, 2, para. 248.

12. *The Gay Science*, 1,8, 'Unconscious virtues'.

13. *Human All Too Human*, 2, 'Assorted opinions and maxims', para. 241.

14. *The Gay Science*, para. 61.

15. *The Gay Science*, 4, para. 289.

16. *The Gay Science*, 1,14, 'The things people call love'.

17. *Mémoires – for Paul de Man* [trans. by Cecile Lindsay, Jonathan Culler, Eduardo Cadava and Peggy Kamuf, Columbia University Press, New York, second edition, 1989, p. 150].

18. See Blanchot, *The Unavowable Community*, pp. 17, 78.

19. See '*To forgive Enemies H{ayley} does pretend/Who never in his Life forgave a friend*,' William Blake, *Complete Poems*, Penguin Classics, p. 617. See also, pp. 617–18, '*On H{ayley}s Friendship*' and '*To H{ayley}*': '*Thy Friendship oft has made my heart to ake/Do be my Enemy for Friendships sake.*'

20. William Blake, *Jerusalem, The Emanation of the Giant Albion*, ibid., pp. 635, 642,

643. Everything would have to be reread. For example: '*Each man is in His Spectres power/Until the arrival of that hour/When his Humanity awake/And Cast his own Spectre into the Lake,*' p. 494; or this: '*Never shalt thou a [lover] true love find/My Spectre follows thee Behind,*' p. 495. Is Stirner so far off? Spectral affinities, the friendship of ghosts. And Marx?

4

The Phantom Friend Returning
(in the Name of 'Democracy')

Friends as ghosts (Die Freunde als Gespenster)
If we greatly transform ourselves, those friends of ours who have
not been transformed become ghosts of our past: their voice
comes across to us like the voice of a shade [in a frightfully
spectral manner (*schattenhaft-schauerlich*)] – as though we were
hearing ourself, only younger, more severe, less mature.[1]

Nietzsche

we may wonder why democracy was unable to forge a specific
language for itself ... nowhere else is the dissociation between
the reality and name of democracy carried as far.... So,
attacking democracy with its own weapons. ...[2]

Nicole Loraux

We would, however, hesitate on the edge of a fiction. The world would
be hanging on a sort of elementary, borderless hypothesis; a general
conditionality would spread over all certainties. The virtual space and time
of the 'perhaps' would be *in the process* of exhausting the force of our
desires, the flesh of our events, the uttermost life of our lives. No, they
would not be *in the process* of exhausting us, for the very *presence* of such a
process would be reassuring and still too effective; no, they would be on
the verge of success, and this imminence would suffice for their victory. It
would suffice, not in the task of standing in opposition to this force and
this life, nor in that of contradicting them – or even harming them – but,
worse still, of making them possible, thereby making them simply virtual.
From this virtuality they could never escape, even after their effectuation;
this would, then, by the very fact, render them impossible, to the point of
rendering their presumed reality simply possible. The modality of the
possible, the unquenchable *perhaps*, would, implacably, destroy everything,

by means of a sort of self-immunity from which no region of being, *phúsis* or history would be exempt. We could, then, imagine a time, this particular time – in any case we would not have any other at our disposal – but we would hesitate to say 'this particular time', for its presence, here and now, and its indivisible singularity, would give rise to doubt. We would want to reappropriate for ourselves, here and now, even this hesitation, even the virtualizing, suspenseful abeyance of this epoch, in order to do it in, to open it in a single stroke on to a time that would be ours, and only ours: the *contemporary*, should such a thing ever present itself. But we would not dare to give it a name. For fear of virtualizing even more – both our desires and our events – precisely on account of this abeyance. Nothing there could any longer be recognized, neither a moment nor a state, not even a transition. This would be an unprecedented time; a time which, reserving itself in the unique, would then remain without relation to any other, without attraction or repulsion, nor living analogy. Without even this friendship for itself, nor this enmity: without the love or the hate that would make this time appear as such. But absolutely without indifference. A time said to be contemporary that would be anything but contemporary – anything, except proper to its own time. It would resemble nothing, nor would it gather itself up in anything, lending itself to any possible reflection. It would no longer relate to itself. There would, however, be absolutely no indifference; it *would not be* – in other words, it would not be *present* – either *with* the other or *with* itself. Should it present itself, should it with some word, say 'I', its speech could only be that of a madman; and if it described itself as living, this would again be – and more probably than ever – a sign of madness.

One would then have the time of a world without friends, the time of a world without enemies. The imminence of a self-destruction by the infinite development of a madness of self-immunity. And anyone who would say 'O my friends, there are no friends', and again, *or* again, 'O enemies, there is no enemy', would convince us, following a cool, directly logical analysis of his statements, that he does not yet have a friend, but already no longer has an enemy. Or conversely, at the present time. This would be, perhaps, as if someone had lost the enemy, keeping him only in memory, the shadow of an ageless ghost, but still without having found friendship, or the friend. Or a name for either.

If we were not wary, in determining them too quickly, about precipitating these things towards an excessively established reality, we might propose a gross example, among an infinity of others, simply to set a heading: since what a naive scansion dates from the 'fall-of-the-Berlin-Wall', or from the 'end-of-communism', the 'parliamentary-democracies-of-the-capitalist-Western-world' would find themselves without a principal enemy. The effects of this destructuration would be countless: the 'subject' in question would be looking for new reconstitutive enmities; it would multiply 'little wars' between nation-states; it would sustain at any price so-called ethnic or genocidal struggles; it would seek to pose itself, to find repose, through opposing still identifiable adversaries – China, Islam? Enemies without which, as Schmitt would have said – and this is our subject – it would lose its political being; it would purely and simply depoliticize itself [*se dépolitiserait*].

These are questions we therefore murmur to ourselves – the whisper of the aforementioned fiction, just for a start; without an enemy, and therefore without friends, where does one then find oneself, *qua* a self? [*où se trouver, où se trouver soi-même*]? With whom? Whose contemporary? Who is the contemporary? When and where would we be, ourselves, *we*, in order to say, as in Nietzsche's unbelievable teleiopoesis, 'we' and 'you'? Let us call these questions fictive questions, to recall an evidence of common sense: I can address them – these anguished, but abstract and fleshless questions – only to an addressee; I can only throw them out towards a reader, whoever he may be; I can only *destine* them with the precipitative supposition of a *we* that, by definition and by destination, has not yet arrived to itself. Not before, at the earliest, the end and the arrival of this sentence whose very logic and grammar are improbable. For the 'I' that feigns to address these fictive questions *finds itself* comprised and determined in advance by the fact that it belongs to the most suspended '*we*' of this supposed contemporaneity. It is the arrow of this teleiopoesis that we have been following, waiting for, preceding for such a long time – the long time of a time that does not belong to time. A time out of joint.

Let us start again. We had just attempted, in the preceding chapter, a first interpretation. One among an infinite number of other possible ones, as Nietzsche himself said one day, an interpretation of one of his sayings, the exegesis of a fiction or an apostrophe, in memory of Montaigne, who said it himself as the heir of Aristotle and Cicero, in the great unending maieutic tradition of *Lysis* (*è perì philías, maieutikós*).

Let us not forget that *Lysis* begins with the scene of a proper name which cannot at first be pronounced: who is the loved one? Will his name be cited? Will he be called by his name for the first time? Everything in the political question of friendship seems to be suspended on the secret of a name. Will this name be *published*? Will tongues be untied, and will the name be delivered over to public space? Will a public space be opened up?

Centuries later, as we shall see, between Montaigne and La Boétie, the birth of friendship, the knowledge of the name and the question of public space will be caught up in the same knot. Here, the proper name to be quoted, Lysis, is not just any name. And it involves a knot. Maieutic as an effect of *analysis* [in English in the original], the Lysis quotes within itself its homonym, thereby tying itself to the common name (*lysis*) which designates, as if by chance, unbinding, detachment, emancipation, untangling, the tie undone or dissolved by *analysis*, solution – indeed, absolution, even solitude. Here we have an inaugural dialogue on friendship. Now, what is it called? Have we given it a thought? Its title quotes a proper name which commonly describes a knot undone, while engaging you in the analysis of what it means to be solitary.

Quoted quotations, then, on the subject of the possibility of quoting great friends, the true ones. Even if there are more than two of them, the model (*exemplar*) will most often be furnished by a twosome, by some great couples of friends. Always men. Well, more often than not, and that is what counts; it is of *them* that one speaks – the *two of them*, it is the *twosome* that is kept in memory and whose legend is archived. Our culture, our school, our literature are the theatre of these couples – and the posterity of these great friends. La Boétie knew that in advance; that is what he promised for the two of them, before evoking 'a secret pact of nature', 'the paternal sap' and the change 'in name':

> Should destiny so desire, be assured that posterity
> Will place our names on the list of celebrated friends.[3]

The interpretation involved here remains – there can be no doubt about it – insufficient and preliminary with regard to so many heritages, notably with regard to the Nietzschean corpus – an abundant, aphoristic and apparently unstable body of work. Our approach remains prudent and modest before this boundless provocation. We remain almost speechless before this demanding but, in its successive or simultaneous postulations, elusive indictment. Now, despite or on account of these precautions, such a reading may perhaps seem too philological, micrological, *readerly* – complacent, too, with the time it allows itself when matters are urgent, at just the moment when one should no longer wait. At a moment when our world is delivered over to new forms of violence, new wars, new figures of cruelty or barbarity (and not always to this 'just' and necessary barbarity that Benjamin sometimes called for against the other, the barbarity of the old culture), at a moment when hostilities are breaking out, no longer resembling the worst that we have ever known, the political and historical urgency of what is befalling us should, one will say, tolerate less patience, fewer detours and less bibliophilic discretion. Less esoteric rarity. This is no longer the time to take one's time, as a number of our well-intentioned contemporaries must no doubt think – as if we had ever been allowed to take our time in history, and as if absolute urgency were not the law of decision, the event and responsibility, their structural law, which is inscribed a priori in the concept. Centuries of preparatory reflection and theoretical deliberation – the very infinity of a knowledge – would change nothing in this urgency. It is absolutely cutting, conclusive, decisive, heartrending; it must interrupt the time of science and conscience, to which the instant of decision will always remain heterogeneous. It is, nevertheless, true that we feel called upon, 'live', to offer answers or to assume immediate responsibilities. It is also true that these answers and responsibilities seem to be inscribed more naturally in the space of political philosophy. This is true – it will always be true – and in this respect we will always be in a state of lack [en défaut]. Our answers and our responsibilities will never be adequate, never sufficiently direct. The debt is infinite. Urgent because infinite. A priori infinite for a finite being, as soon as a duty, if there is one, presents itself to it.

Without pretending to offer a defence or an adequate justification of our approach in this matter, let us nevertheless risk a limited hypothesis: questioned at once for itself and as a symptomatic effect, the event of the text signed 'Nietzsche' appears to us to mark, in already being a part of it, a mutation in the field of the political and of the community in general. No doubt Nietzsche is not the only one to have signalled this mutation. This is why we precisely speak, at least provisionally, of a *field*, even if the identity and closure of this field constitute precisely what is, from now on, most problematic. But who more or better than Nietzsche, who more thematically than he, would have called the politics and history of the world a history of the political (as political history), *in its link to loving*, precisely, to friendship as well as to love – more precisely, to the Greek, Jewish and Christian history of this link, of the binding and unbinding of this link? And thus to enmity, hatred, hostility and war? In other words, who would have better named our history, our memory, our culture, if there is one and if it is one? Who will have better *represented* what is happening to our world, what is happening to us, what is happening to us by affecting even the possibility of saying *we* – and precisely, concerning the political example of the friend/enemy opposition? Who better than he, from this point of view, will have *represented* the massive and molecular movement which, at the end of the last century, set out to agitate all the atoms – conceptual ones or not, the more or less semantic elements – of this unclosed ensemble? Who, if not Nietzsche, set out to overturn, to contest, even their elementary identity, to dissolve what is irreducible to analysis in them, to show the ineluctable necessity of this perversion which made opposites pass into one another: the friend into the enemy, the strong into the weak, the hegemonic into the oppressed, and so forth? And who brought it off, then, in an ensemble (or 'field', but one henceforth without an assignable limit, without assured and reassuring ground, but all the more finite for this very fact) – perhaps in a world, but *in* a world which suddenly no longer holds together, which has split asunder, no longer closes, is no longer *within* it, and appears to be delivered over to what resembles a chaotic madness, to disorder and randomness?

Certainly this mutation does not belong only to the order of discourse or to that of the text, in the narrow, ordinary and outdated sense of these terms. It is not only philosophical, speculative or theoretical. Multiple, expandable and protean as it may be, the corpus of a singular individual named 'Nietzsche' could not be its sole witness, even less contain it. As is the case in any mutation, this one is never exempt from repetition, but according to us, it would have affected the unity of this field, its closure as well as all the organizing concepts of something like a political community. Although this affirmation does not rely on any assured contemporaneity, we *belong* (this is what we take the risk of saying here) to the time of this mutation, which is precisely a harrowing tremor in the structure or the experience of *belonging*. Therefore of property. Of communal belonging and sharing: religion, family, ethnic groups, nations, homeland, country, state, even humanity, love and friendship, lovence, be they public or private. We belong to this tremor, if that is possible; we tremble within it. It runs through us, and stops us dead in our tracks. We belong to it without belonging to it. Within it we hear the resonant echo of all the great discourses (we have already named those of Bataille, Blanchot and Nancy, for example, but there are others, still so many others, far removed and quite close to us) where they assume the risk and the responsibility, but also where they *give themselves over to* the necessity of thinking and formalizing, so to speak, absolute dislocation, borderless disjoining; when these thinkers point to these obscure plights, sometimes according to the time without duration of a thunderbolt, sometimes following the regular revolutions of a watchtower, always emitting mad and impossible pleas, almost speechless warnings, words that consume themselves in a dark light, such as these typical and recurrent syntagms: 'relation without relation', community without community ('the community of those without community'), 'inoperative' community, 'unavowable' communism or community, and all the 'X without X' whose list is, by definition, endless, finite in its infinitude. Yes, these warnings turn endlessly. Yes, like searchlights without a coast, they sweep across the dark sky, shut down or disappear at regular intervals and harbour the invisible in their very light. We no longer even know against what dangers or abysses we are forewarned. We avoid one, only to be thrown into one of the others. We no longer even know whether these watchmen are guiding us towards another destination, nor even if a destination remains promised or determined.

We wish only to think that we are on the track of an impossible axiomatic which remains to be thought. Now, if this axiomatic withdraws, from instant to instant, from one ray of the searchlight to another, from one lighthouse to the next (for there are numerous *lighthouses*, and where there is no longer any home these are no longer homes, and this is what is taking place: there are no longer any homes here), this is because darkness is falling on the value of value, and hence on the very desire for an *axiomatic*, a consistent, granted or presupposed system of values.

Now, what would a 'history', a science, or a historical action purporting to be resolutely and ingeniously extradiscursive or extratextual *actually do*? What *would* a political history or philosophy, at last *realistic, in truth do*, if they did not assume – so as to be confronted by and to account for the extreme formalization, the new aporias, the semantic inconstancy – all the disquieting conversions that we have just seen operating in these signals? What else could they do without attempting to read all the apparently contradictory possibles ('relation without relation', 'community without community', etc.) that these 'sophisticated discourses' impose on our memory? Let us answer: they could do very little, almost nothing. They would miss the hardest, the most resistant, the most irreducible, the othermost of the 'thing itself'. Such a political history or philosophy would deck itself out in 'realism' just in time to fall short of the thing – and to repeat, repeat and repeat again, with neither consciousness nor memory of its compulsive droning.

For in the end, what does the fact that we may henceforth speak of and with these signals say about what is taking place in the world? The fact that we must speak in this way? The fact that the convincing, rigorous, ineluctable voice of necessity – its most responsible voice, too – resounds in just this way? For example, what has become of the *real* structure of the political – that of political forces and domination, the relations of strength and weakness, the 'social bond', the marks and the discourse that give it form – to *allow* us to speak of them in such a way today, *seriously* and *solemnly*? What has this *reality* become; but what was it in the first place, if that which goes beyond the understanding may now be heard and understood? Better yet, for it now to appear the most *consistent*? For it to be *necessary* for us to speak in this manner? For us to feel obliged to speak precisely in such a *paradoxical, aporetic, impossible manner* of community, law, equality, the republic and democracy? Fraternity? Of friendship, in sum, or enmity, given that the meaning of this 'thing' is implicit throughout, in each of these words?

Were we even to trust the still so crude concepts of *effect* or *symptom*, in speaking of 'those sorts of things', it should not be forgotten that these 'things-texts' consist precisely in a radical contestation of the traditional schemes of causality and signification, confronting us ceaselessly with the irreducibility of that which lies beyond this very discourse: the other, the event, singularity, power/weakness, differential force, the 'world', and so forth. How can one read these discourses as discourse, these writings, if you like (those of Bataille, Blanchot, Nancy, and others, all those whose advent Nietzsche's text – this is what we have wished to demonstrate – announces, or rather calls for, bringing law and disorder into the secret of this call, already bringing about what has yet to come, in the same teleiopoetic sentence)? Even if they were considered as derivable effects or symptoms, we would still have to analyse and formalize that possibility pertinently. Pertinently, and if possible – but that is exactly what the question is all about – exhaustively. Its complete formalization would be necessary not only to determine of what these texts are the symptomatic effect, but one would have to know of what this supposed cause, the thing, the 'real' itself, will have been *capable*. To account for a symptom-effect from within that of which it is supposed to be the symptom-effect, one must, first of all, attempt to read it in the language in which it speaks, even if the account is not limited to such a reading. Reading also consists in not being thus limited, from one trace to the next. Otherwise, the 'reality' of this real or the 'history' of this thing that one is claiming or that one has distinguished in the reading would remain both undetermined and imaginary. We know only too well how often this happens in the discourse – for let us not forget that theirs is a discourse as well – of countless 'realistic' champions of the historical referent and actuality [*effectivité*].

It is, therefore, with this concern in mind that we embark on what looks like a long detour, the first step of which was taken long ago. With this concern in mind we shall outline once again a more directly political reading, if you like, of Nietzsche's vocative phrase ('O enemies . . .'), as the teleiopoesis that regularly turned the friend into an enemy, and vice versa, with the risk of spectralizing – others would say: of losing – both.

– We have lost the friend, as it is said in this century.

– No, we have lost the enemy, another voice says, in this same waning century. Both voices speak of the political, and that is what we wish to recall. They speak, in sum, of a political crime of which it is no longer known – this is a question of borders – if it is to be defined *in the order of the political* (for instance, when there is assassination, torture, or terrorism in a given political state for political reasons) or if it is a crime *against the political itself*, when in one way or another it puts to death that without which a political crime could no longer be defined or distinguished from other sorts of crimes, when appeal to political reason or to some critique of political reason would no longer be possible. Following this hypothesis, losing the enemy would not necessarily be progress, reconciliation, or the opening of an era of peace and human fraternity. It would be worse: an unheard-of violence, the evil of a malice knowing neither measure nor ground, an unleashing incommensurable in its unprecedented – therefore monstrous – forms; a violence in the face of which what is called hostility, war, conflict, enmity, cruelty, even hatred, would regain reassuring and ultimately appeasing contours, because they would be *identifiable*. The figure of the enemy would then be helpful – precisely as a figure – because of the features which allow it to be *identified* as such, still identical to what has always been determined under this name. An identifiable enemy – that is, one who is *reliable* to the point of treachery, and thereby familiar. One's fellow man, in sum, who could almost be loved as oneself: he is acknowledged and recognized against the backdrop of a common history. This adversary would remain a neighbour, even if he were an evil neighbour against whom war would have to be waged.

Among all the possible political readings of Nietzsche's phrase, we are on the verge of giving precedence to one, specifically where – at least apparently – it would lead back to a tradition, a tradition already in modernity. One which the twentieth century would certainly have replayed; and would replay again under new conditions, between two world wars and from one mutation to another of its postwar periods.

But it would lead back to a tradition of modernity which, in a naturally differentiated and complicated fashion, goes back at least to Hegel.

This tradition takes on systematic form in the work of Carl Schmitt, and we believe it is necessary to dwell temporarily on it here. At length, but temporarily. Certainly on account of the intrinsic interest of Schmitt's theses – their originality, where they seem, however, as ragingly conservative in their political content as they are reactive and traditionalist in their philosophical logic. But also on account of their heritage. Their paradox and equivocality are well known. Is it fortuitous that the same filiation unites several right-wing and left-wing (Marxist, post-Marxist, and neo-Marxist) families?[4]

First reminder: for Schmitt, it is indeed nothing more and nothing less than the political as such which would no longer exist without the figure of the enemy and without the determined possibility of an actual war. Losing the enemy would simply be the loss of the political itself – and this would be our century's horizon after two world wars. And today, how many examples could be given of this disorientation of the political field, where the principal enemy now appears unidentifiable! The invention of the enemy is where the urgency and the anguish are; this invention is what would have to be brought off, in sum, to repoliticize, to put an end to depoliticization. Where the principal enemy, the 'structuring' enemy, seems nowhere to be found, where it ceases to be identifiable and thus reliable – that is, where the same *phobia* projects a mobile multiplicity of potential, interchangeable, metonymic enemies, in secret alliance with one another: conjuration.

Here is the Schmittian axiom in its most elementary form: the political itself, the being-political of the political, arises in its possibility with the figure of the enemy. It would be unfair, as is often done, to reduce Schmitt's thought to this axiom, but it would nevertheless be indispensable to his thought, and also to his decisionism, his theory of the exception and sovereignty. The disappearance of the enemy would be the death knell of the political as such. It would mark the beginning of depoliticization (*Entpolitisierung*), the beginning of the end of the political. Facing this end, at the eschatological edge of this imminent death, at the moment when the political has begun to expire, the Christian sage or the fool might say, with a sighed *alas*: 'there is no enemy! (*es gibt keinen Feind!*)' But then, to whom would he address himself ('Enemies . . .!' '*Feinde . . .!*'), to which enemies? Perhaps to his political enemies with whom he would still share that love of war outside the horizon of which, according to Schmitt, there is no state. But perhaps he would also be addressing the enemies *of the* political, the ultimate enemies, the worst of them all, enemies worse than enemies.

At any rate, the Schmittian axiom is also posited in a 'Nietzschean' posterity. The fact that it is attuned to a fundamentally Christian politics is certainly not insignificant even if in many respects this is considered secondary. In *The Concept of the Political*,[5] Schmitt (whose massively attested Nazism remains as complex and overdetermined as his relation to Heidegger, Benjamin, Leo Strauss,[6] etc.) claims to have pinpointed the determining predicate, the specific difference of the political. He writes, for example: 'The specific political distinction (*die spezifisch politische Unterscheidung*), to which political actions and notions can be reduced, is the distinction (*Unterscheidung*) *between* friend and enemy.'[7]

If the distinction or the differential mark (*Unterscheidung*), if the determination of the political, if the 'political difference' itself (*die politische Unterscheidung*) thus amounts to a discrimination (*Unterscheidung*) between friend and enemy, such a dissociation cannot be reduced to a mere difference. It is a determined opposition, opposition itself. This determination specifically assumes opposition. Should that opposition erase itself, and war likewise, the regime called 'politics' loses its borders or its specificity.

Schmitt draws a great number of consequences from this axiom and these definitions, notably with regard to a certain depoliticization. There would be an essential risk for modern humanity *tout court*, which, *qua* *humanity*, ignores the figure of the enemy. There is no enemy of humanity. A crime against humanity is not a political crime. Alas, for humanity *qua* humanity, there is not yet, or already no longer, any enemy! Anyone who takes an interest in humanity *qua* humanity has ceased, according to Schmitt, to talk about politics, and should realize it.

Is the person levelling this warning at us too much the sage or too much the fool? Schmitt claims that he has awakened a tradition that was beginning to lull. Whether we can substantiate them or not, some of his remarks must claim our attention here. We should underscore two of them. They deal on the one hand with the opposition public/private, and on the other with a certain concept of ethics. Let us begin with the first. The second will be taken up much later.

Although he does not propose equivalence or symmetry for the friend, one of the opposing terms of the discrimination (*Unterscheidung*), Schmitt considers that the enemy has always been esteemed a 'public' enemy. The concept of a *private* enemy would be meaningless. Indeed, it is the very sphere of the public that emerges with the figure of the enemy:

> One may or may not share these hopes and pedagogic ideals. But, rationally speaking, it cannot be denied that nations continue to group themselves according to the friend and enemy opposition, that this opposition still remains actual today, and that it subsists in a state of real virtuality (*als reale Möglichkeit*) for every people having a political existence.
>
> Hence the enemy is not the competitor or the adversary in the general sense of the term. Neither is he the personal, private rival whom one hates or feels

antipathy for. The enemy can only be an ensemble of grouped individuals, confronting an ensemble of the same nature, engaged in at least a virtual struggle, that is, one that is effectively possible (*Feind ist nur eine wenigstens eventuell, d.h. der realen Möglichkeit nach* kämpfende *Gesamtheit von Menschen die einer ebensolchen Gesamtheit gegenübersteht*).[8]

We have cited the letter of the last sentence of the original (slightly abused in the French translation) because the most obscure zone of the difficulty is enclosed therein. This last sentence points up in fact – but furtively, almost elliptically, as if it were self-evident – the innermost spring of this logic: the passage from possibility to eventuality (which is here specified as *minimal eventuality*) and from eventuality to effectivity-actuality (which in the sentence is named real possibility, '*reale Möglichkeit*'). This passage takes place, it rushes into place, precisely where the abyss of a distinction happens to be filled up. The passage consists in fact in a denial of the abyss. As always, the tank is replenished in the present, with presence [*le plein se fait au présent*]: in the name of a present, by allegation of presence – here, in the form of a present participle (*kämpfende*). Schmitt emphasizes this present participle, as if to point to the sensitive spot of the operation, with an attentiveness which the translation, unfortunately, has passed over. As soon as war is possible, it is taking place, Schmitt seems to say; presently, in a society of combat, in a community presently at war, since it can present itself to itself, as such, only in reference to this possible war. Whether the war takes place, whether war is decided upon or declared, is a mere empirical alternative in the face of an essential necessity: war is taking place; it has already begun before it begins, as soon as it is characterized as *eventual* (that is, announced as a non-excluded event in a sort of contingent future). And it is *eventual* as soon as it is *possible*. Schmitt does not wish to dissociate the quasi-transcendental modality of the possible and the historico-factual modality of the eventual. He names now the eventuality (*wenigstens eventuell*), now the possibility (*Möglichkeit*), without thematizing the crite- rion of distinction. No account of this distinction is taken in the French translation.[9] As soon as war is possible-eventual, the enemy is present; he is there, his possibility is presently, effectively, supposed and structuring. His being-there is effective, he institutes the community as a human community of combat, as a *combating* collectivity (kampfende *Gesamtheit von Menschen*). The concept of the enemy is thereby deduced or constructed a priori, both analytically and synthetically – in synthetic a priori fashion, if you like, as a political concept or, better yet, as the very concept of the political. From then on, it is important that the concept be purified of all other dimensions

– especially of everything opposed to the political or the public, beginning with the private: anything that stems from the individual or even the psychological, from the subjective in general. In fact, this conceptual prudence and rigour are bound to imply, as is always the case, some sort of phenomenological procedure. Following what resembles at least an eidetic reduction, all facts and all regions that do not announce themselves *as* political must be put in parentheses. All other regional disciplines, all other knowledge – economic, aesthetic, moral, military, even religious knowledge – must be suspended, although the theological-political tradition has to remain in operation for essential reasons – this is well known, but we shall return to it later – in this apparently secular thought of the political.[10] This prudence, at once phenomenological and semantic, is often difficult to respect, but the stakes involved, for Schmitt, are decisive. This prudence sometimes receives authorization, at least in *The Concept of the Political*, from a distinction first marked in two languages, Latin and Greek (*hostis/inimicus*, *polémios/ekhthrós*), as though the distinction of the political could not be properly formulated in more than two idioms; as if other languages, even the German language, could not have as clear an access to the distinction. But whether Schmitt allows himself this linguistic reference or whether it is used as a convenient pedagogic tool is difficult to say. He may well do both at the same time, as though the whole history of the political – that is, the rigorous determination of the enemy – sealed here or there, in a linguistic felicity, a universal necessity forever irreducible to it. In fact, following the publication of his book in 1932, Schmitt more than once returned to re-examine this linguistic limitation, in a context we shall specify in a moment.

Would the question still be, as it always is, that of the 'right name', as Nietzsche would say? The question of the right name of friendship or of its supposed antithesis, enmity? We, speakers of Latin that we are, would have to understand, in adjusting our language on this point, that the antithesis of friendship *in the political sphere* is not, according to Schmitt, *enmity* but *hostility*. First consequence: the political enemy would not inevitably be inimical, he would not necessarily hold me in enmity, nor I him. Moreover, sentiments would play no role; there would be neither passion nor affect in general. Here we have a totally pure experience of the friend-enemy in its political essence, purified of any affect – at least of all personal affect, supposing that there could ever be any other kind. If the enemy is the stranger, the war I would wage on him should remain essentially without hatred, without intrinsic *xenophobia*. And politics would begin with this purification. With the calculation of this conceptual purification. I can also wage war on my friend, a war in the proper sense of the term, a proper, clear and merciless war. But a war without hatred.

Hence a first possibility of semantic slippage and inversion: the friend (*amicus*) can be an enemy (*hostis*); I can be hostile towards my friend, I can be hostile towards him publicly, and conversely I can, in privacy, love my enemy. From this, everything would follow, in orderly, regular fashion, from the distinction between private and public. Another way of saying that at every point when this border is threatened, fragile, porous, contestable (we thus designate so many possibilities that 'our time' is accentuating and accelerating in countless ways), the Schmittian discourse collapses. It is against the threat of this ruin that his discourse takes form. It defends itself, walls itself up, reconstructs itself unendingly against what is to come; it struggles against the future with a prophetic and pathetic energy. But it is also from within this threat, from within the dread that it seems to provoke in this traditionalist and Catholic thinker of European law, that he is able to see coming, better than so many others, the force of the future in this threatening figure. This reactive and unscrupulous dread is often presented in the rigour of the concept, a vigilant, meticulous, implacable rigour inherited from the tradition – from a tradition, moreover, that this entire discourse intends to serve and repeat, in order to put it up against the novelty of what is coming and to see, so it would seem, that it carries the day. With the energy of a last-ditch effort. If one is not to lose the enemy, one must know who he is, and what, in the past, the word 'enemy' always designated – more precisely, what it must have designated. No, what it *should have* designated:

> The enemy is solely the *public* enemy (*nur der* öffentliche *Feind*), because everything that has a relationship to such a collectivity of men, particularly to a whole nation, becomes *public* by virtue of such a relationship. The enemy is *hostis*, not *inimicus* in the broader sense; *polémios*, not *ekhthrós*. As German and other languages do not distinguish between the private and political enemy, many misconceptions and falsifications are possible. The often quoted 'Love your enemies' (Matt. 5:44; Luke 6:27) reads *diligite hostes vestros, agapâte tous ekhthrous umôn* and not *diligite inimicus vestros*. No mention is made of the political enemy. Never in the thousand-year struggle between Christians and Moslems did it occur to a Christian to surrender rather than defend Europe out of love toward the Saracens or Turks. The enemy in the political sense need not be hated personally, and in the private sphere only does it make sense to love one's enemy, that is, one's adversary.[11]

(We could say a great deal today, among so very many other analogous indications that abound in Schmitt's text, on the choice of this example: Islam would remain an enemy even though we Europeans must love the Muslims as our neighbours. At a determining moment in the history of Europe, it was imperative not 'to deliver Europe over to Islam' in the name of a universal Christianity. You are obliged, you will always have been obliged, to defend Europe against its other without confusing the genres, without confusing faith and politics, enmity and hostility, friendship and alliance or confusion. However, a coherent reading of this example should go further: today more than ever such a reading should take into account the fact that all the concepts of this theory of right and of politics are European, as Schmitt himself often admits. Defending Europe against Islam, here considered as a non-European invader of Europe, is then more than a war among other wars, more than a political war. Indeed, strictly speaking, this would be not a war but a combat with the political at stake, a struggle for politics. And this holds even if it is not necessarily a struggle for democracy, which is a formidable problem in any reading of Schmitt. From then on the front of this opposition is difficult to place. It is no longer a thoroughly political front. In question would be a defensive operation destined to defend *the* political, beyond particular states or nations, beyond any geographical, ethnic or political continent. On the political side of this unusual front, the stakes would be saving the political as such, ensuring its survival in the face of another who would no longer even be a political enemy but an enemy of *the* political – more precisely, a being radically alien to the political as such, supposing at least that, in its purported purity, it is not Europeanized and shares nothing of the tradition of the juridical and the political called European.)

Although it can never be reduced to a question of language or discourse, the differentiated rooting of this friend/enemy opposition in certain idioms could never be considered accidental or extrinsic. It recalls the too-evident fact that this semantics belongs to a culture, to structures of ethnic, social and political organization in which language is irreducible. One would then have to follow closely[12] all the difficulties encountered by Schmitt in the justification of his terminological distinctions. Schmitt returns to this difficulty as if in passing, but regularly, in footnotes that one may be tempted to read as second thoughts, or at least as signs of worry. The Greek distinction (*polémios/ekhthrós*) is sustained only with a brief reference to the *Republic* (V, 470), where Plato opposes war strictly speaking (*pólemos*) to civil war, to rebellion or to uprising (*stásis*).[13] Without specifying what type

of relationship or connection this is, Schmitt recalls Plato's insistence on
the distinction 'bound' (*verbunden*) to that of two sorts of enemies (*polémios*
and *ekhthrós*) – that is, the distinction between *pólemos* ('war') and *stásis*
('riot, uprising, rebellion, civil war'). He adds:

> In Plato's eyes, only a war between Greeks and barbarians ('natural enemies') is
> actually a war (*wirklich Krieg*), whilst struggles (*die Kämpfe*) between Greeks are
> of the order of *stásis* (internecine quarrels). The dominant idea here is that a
> people cannot wage war on itself and that a 'civil war' is never but a rending of
> self but would perhaps not signify the formation of a new State, or even of a
> new people.[14]

This last hypothesis seems hardly Platonic. In any case, it would seem to us,
not literally so and not in this context. Plato does say, in fact, that the
Greeks, where there is a disagreement [*différend*] (*diaphorá*) between themselves, consider it an internal discord (*stásis*), since it is quasi-familial (*ōs
oikeíous*), but they never bestow on it the name of war (*pólemos*) (471a). It
is true that between themselves, the Greeks always end up in reconciliation
(a theme that reappears in *Menexenus*), and never seek either to subjugate
or to destroy. They attack only the 'causes', the authors of the disagreement
– that is (a specification upon which, from different points of view, we
shall not cease to insist) *the few in number*. But if Plato indeed says that the
barbarians are natural enemies and that, as we will read, the Greeks are 'by
nature friends among themselves', he does not conclude, for all that, that
civil war (*stásis*) or enmity between Greeks is simply outside of nature. He
invokes an illness, which is something else again. Above all, far from being
satisfied with the opposition on which Schmitt relies so heavily, the *Republic*
indeed *prescribes* its erasure. In this case, it is indeed recommended that the
Greeks behave towards their enemies – the barbarians – as they behave
today among themselves. This prescription is *laid down* like a *law*:

> I, he said, agree that our citizens ought to deal with their Greek opponents in
> this wise [*semblable doit être*, 'their policy must be similar'] (*omologó outō dein*),
> while treating barbarians as Greeks now (*ōs nun*) treat Greeks. Let us then lay
> down this law also (*tithómen dē kai touton ton nómon*), for our guardians, that they
> are not to lay waste the land or burn the houses. Let us so decree (*thomen*), he
> said, and assume that this and our preceding prescriptions are right. (471bc
> [translation modified])

Although Schmitt, to my knowledge, does not do so – never with sufficient
precision, in any case – it must also be recalled that we are dealing with the

very famous passage in which, in view of what is proper to justice (*diakaiosúnē*) and to injustice (*adikía*), Plato excludes the possibility of realizing this ideal State as long as philosophers do not reign over it, as long as the kings and sovereigns, the 'dynasts' who dispose of power, are not philosophers (473cd) – that is, as long as *philosophía* is not bound to political power, synonymous, if you will, with *dúnamis politiké*: in other words, as long as justice is not bound to power, as long as justice is not one with force. As long as this unity remains out of reach – that is, for ever – the conceptual unities that depend on it – in fact, every one that Plato proposes or recalls – remain ideal entities. No empirical language is in fact fully adequate to it. This improbability does not rule out, on the contrary, it commands, as we know if we follow Plato – the perfectly rigorous description of these pure structures of the ideal State; for they give their meaning, legitimately and on principle, to every concept, and hence to every term, of political philosophy. It is no less the case that the distinction *polémios/ekhthrós*, considered precisely in its purity, already implies a discourse on *nature* (*phúsis*) that makes us wonder how Schmitt, without looking into the question more closely, could incorporate it into his general theory. Let us never forget that the two names that Plato is intent on keeping should name rigorously, in their ideal purity, two things that are in nature. These two names (*pólemos* and *stásis*) are in fact assigned to two kinds of disagreement, contestation, disaccord (*diaphorá*). The disagreement (*diaphorá*) between those who share kinship ties or origins (*oikeion kai suggenés*: family, household, intimacy, community of resources and of interests, familiarity, etc.) is *stásis*, the discord or war that is sometimes called civil. As for the *diaphorá* between foreigners or foreign families (*allótrion kai othneion*), it is sheer war (*pólemos*). The naturalness of the bond uniting the Greek people or the Greek race (*Hellénikon génos*) always remains intact [*inentamée*], in *pólemos* as well as in *stásis*. The Greek *génos* (lineage, race, family, people, etc.) is united by kinship and by the original community (*oikeion kai suggenés*). On these two counts it is foreign to the barbarian *génos* (*tó de barbarikó othneión te kai allótrion*) (470c). As in every racism, every ethnocentrism – more precisely, in every one of the nationalisms throughout history – a *discourse* on birth and on nature, a *phúsis* of genealogy (more precisely, a discourse and a phantasm on the genealog-ical *phúsis*) regulates, in the final analysis, the movement of each opposition: repulsion and attraction, disagreement and accord, war and peace, hatred and friendship. From within and without. This *phúsis* comprises everything – language, law, politics, etc. Although it defines the alterity of the foreigner or the barbarian, it has no other. 'We shall then say that Greeks fight and wage war with barbarians, and barbarians with Greeks, and are enemies *by nature* (*polemíous phúsei einai*), and that war is the fit name for this enmity and hatred (*kai pólemon tēn ékhthran taútēn klētéon*)' (ibid.). But even when Greeks fight and wage war among themselves, we should say that they are no less naturally friends (*phúsei phílous einai*). Sickness is what then emerges, an equally natural sickness, an evil naturally affecting nature. It is divided, separated from itself. When such an event occurs, one must speak of a pathology of the community. In question here is a clinic of the city. In this respect the *Republic* develops a nosological discourse; its diagnostic is one of ill health and dissension, a faction inside Greece (*nosein d'en tō toioutō tēn 'Helláda kai stasiásein*). *Stásis*, the name that should apply to this hatred or to this enmity (*ékhthra*), is also a category of political nosography.

In following a certain logic staged by *Menexenus*, this accident, evil or sickness[15] that internal dissension (*stásis*) is could not be explained, even, in the last instance, by hatred, enmity (*ékhthra*) or malice. One would have to spot in this *stásis* a fatal disorder, a stroke of bad luck, misfortune (*dustukhía*) (244a). The question whether this staging is ironic (we shall return to this point[16]), whether the most common logic and rhetoric, the most accredited eloquence of *epitáphios*, is reproduced by Plato in order to belittle it, only gives that much more sense to the fictive contents of the discourse attributed to Aspasia, that courtesan who, moreover, plagiarizes another funeral oration and mouths once again the 'fragments' of a discourse by Pericles (236b). We have here a gold mine of commonplaces. The fact that the satirical character of this fiction-in-a-fiction has been ignored so often and for such a long time can hence be explained. Among the commonplaces, then, there is the assiduity with which Greeks hasten to reunite with Greeks. This ease in reconciliation has no other cause than actual kinship, *suggéneia*, which produces a solid friendship founded on *homogeneity*, on *homophilia*, on a solid and firm affinity (*bébaion*) stemming from birth, from native community. This kinship nurtures a constant and homophilial friendship (*philían bébaion kai omóphulon*) not only in words but in fact, in deeds (*ou lógō all' érgō*). In other words, the effectivity/actuality of the tie of friendship, that which assures constancy beyond discourses, is indeed real kinship, the reality of the tie of birth (*è tō onti suggéneia*). Provided that it is real – and not only spoken or set by convention – this syngenealogy durably guarantees the strength of the social bond in life and according to life.

(We insist on this condition: a *dreamt* condition, what we are calling here a phantasm, because a genealogical tie will never be simply real; its supposed reality never gives itself in any intuition, it is always posed, constructed, induced, it always implies a symbolic effect of discourse – a 'legal fiction', as Joyce put it in *Ulysses* on the subject of paternity. This is true also – as true as ever, no matter what has been said, down to and including Freud – of maternity. All politics and all policies, all political discourses on 'birth', misuse what can in this regard be only a belief, some will say: what can only remain a belief; others: what can only tend towards an act of faith. Everything in political discourse that appeals to birth, to nature or to the nation – indeed, to nations or to the universal nation of human brotherhood – this entire familialism consists in a renaturalization of this 'fiction'. What we are calling here 'fraternization', is what produces symbolically, conventionally, through authorized engagement, a *determined politics*, which, be it left- or right-wing, alleges a real fraternity or regulates spiritual fraternity, fraternity in the figurative sense, on the symbolic projection of a real or natural fraternity. Has anyone ever met a brother? A uterine or consanguine (distantly related) brother? In nature?)

Return to *Menexenus*. The supplementary proof of the ease with which the Greeks achieve reconciliation and pardon among themselves, the sign showing that *stásis* does not in any way originate in hatred but in misfortune (*dustukhía*), is us. We say so, and that is enough. The logic of testimony, the becoming-proof of a testimony that should never become equivalent to proof, can be found at work here in its privileged place: in kinship. We can testify, we the living, we the survivors who share this homophilia and who, therefore, are qualified to speak of it from within: 'And that such was the fact we ourselves are witnesses, we the living (*mártures . . . oi zôntes*): are of the same race with them, and have mutually received and granted forgiveness for what we have done and suffered.'[17] Aspasia's discourse draws all the political consequences of proper birth [*bonne naissance*], of a eugenicism (*eugéneia*) that is nothing but – has no other function than that of – autochthony. The homage to the earth and to the mother goes hand in hand with the eulogy of fraternization – more precisely, of fraternal democracy, which no way excludes the aristocracy of virtue and of wisdom. It is equality of birth (*isogonía*), 'natural' equality (*kata phúsin*), that *necessarily demands* the search for 'legal' equality (*isonomía kata nómon*) – that is, an equality compatible with an aristocracy founded upon the reputation of virtue and wisdom (*ê aretês dóxê kai phonéseôs*). Nature commands law; equality of birth founds *in necessity* legal equality. Having quoted this passage,[18] we shall come back to the modality of this *necessity*.

It comes as no surprise that such a discourse should have its privileged resource in the testimonial, testamentary fervour of the heir – in other words, in the funeral oration.

(Our hypothesis here is that no great discourse on friendship will ever have eluded the major rhetoric of *epitáphios*, and hence of some form of transfixed celebration of spectrality, at once fervent and already caught in the deathly or petrified cold of its inscription, of the becoming-*epitaph* of the oration. The great examples awaiting us, from Montaigne to Blanchot, will not make us change our mind. But there would be so many, an infinite number, of other examples. What discourse does not call up the deceased? Does not appeal to the deceased? The becoming-epitaph of *epitáphios*, the impression in space of a funeral speech, is what the first word dedicated to the deceased promises. At the beginning of this *lógos*, there is the promise of epitaph.)

Aspasia's discourse is a summons to appear before the dead. You must answer for the dead, you must respond to them. Here and now. But this responsibiity can be called for only by first of all summoning the dead. They are, after a fashion, made to be *bom again*; they are convoked in an invocation, once again, of their birth. The oath of this co-engagement thus resembles a fraternal conjuration:

> A word is needed which will duly praise the dead and gently admonish the living, exhorting the brethren and descendants (*ekgónois men kai adelphois*) of the departed to imitate their virtue, and consoling their fathers and mothers and the survivors, if any, who may chance to be alive of the previous generation ... And first as to their [noble] birth. Their ancestors were not strangers, nor are these their descendants sojourners only (*en tē khóra* [*métèques dans le pays*]), whose fathers have come from another country, but they are the children of the soil, dwelling and living in their own land (*tô onti en patrídi oikountas kai zóntas*). And the country which brought them up is not like other countries, a stepmother to her children, but their own true mother (*all'upo mētros tēs khóras en é ókoun*); she bore them and nourished them and received them, and in her bosom they now repose. It is meet and right, therefore, that we should begin by praising the land which is their mother, and that will be a way of praising their noble birth (*eugéneia*).[19]

After the eulogy of the authentic or veritable mother – that is, having reversed the order of precedence betweeen earth and mother (the latter imitates the former, and not the other way round (238a)) – the political consequence follows as a matter of course: the aristo-democracy of brothers according to virture. The name 'democracy' has less import, as we shall see, than the concept aimed at here: the right of the best, starting from equality at birth, from natural, homophilial, autochthonous equality. In truth, it is less a question of consequence than of political principle. It is the *politeía* that forms men, from the moment it regulates itself, in its laws, on *phúsis*, on eugenics and on autochthony, giving them food and education (*trophē*) – not the other way round. This is what must be enunciated, this is what must *be recalled*, for at stake is an act of memory – this is what must engage memory in the present, *in the presence of the dead*, if that can be said; for however difficult this remains to say (Cicero will agree: *difficilius dictu est, mortui vivunt*), the dead live and the absent are present. They still keep watch over those who keep watch over them. And the given word [the 'pledge', *la parole donnée*] before the living dead, before 'the dead here present', rushes up *here and now*, in the first person plural, in the faithful and present tradition of *our* politics:

> Thus born into the world and thus educated, the ancestors of the departed lived and made themselves a government (*politeían* [political regime]), which I ought briefly to commemorate. For government is the nurture of man (*politeía gar trophē anthrṓpōn estín* [*le régime politique qui forme les hommes*]), and the government of good men is good, and of bad men bad. And I must show that our ancestors were trained under a good government (*en kalē politeía etráphēsan* [*(ils) ont été nourris sous un bon gouvernement*]), and for this reason they were good, and our contemporaries are also good, among whom our departed friends are to be reckoned (*ōn oíde tugkhánousin óntes oi teteleutēkótes*). Then as now, and indeed always, from that time to this, speaking generally, our government was an aristocracy (*aristokratía*) – a form of government which receives various names, according to the fancies of men, and is sometimes called democracy (*dēmokratía*), but is really an aristocracy or government of the best which has the approval of the many (*met'eudoxías pléthous aristokratía*). For kings we have always had, first hereditary and then elected, and authority is mostly in the hands of the people, who dispense offices and power to those who appear to be most deserving of them. Neither is a man rejected from weakness or poverty or obscurity of origin, nor honored by reason of the opposite, as in other states, but there is one principle – he who appears to be wise (*sophos*) and good (*agathos*) is a governor and ruler (*kratei kai árkhei*). The basis of this our government is equality of birth (*ē ex isou génesis*), for other states are made up of all sorts and unequal conditions of men, and therefore their governments are unequal – there are tyrannies and there are oligarchies, in which the one party are slaves and the others masters. But we and our citizens are brethren, the children all of one mother (*mias mētros pántes adelphoi phúntes*), and we do not think it right to be one another's masters or servants, but the natural equality (*kata phúsin*) of birth compels us to seek for

legal equality (*isonomían anagkázei zētein kata nomon*), and to recognize no superiority except in the reputation of virtue and wisdom.[20]

(The brothers have just been named in this passage (*adelphoi*). They have called themselves − *themselves*, reflexively − 'brothers', 'we and ours'. They have named themselves with the name 'truly fair and full of love' − that is, the 'name of brother', as Montaigne will say in 'On Friendship', this 'soldering that binds brothers together', this 'brotherly harmony'). Brothers have named themselves brothers in so far as they issue from one and the same mother: uterine brothers. But what will one say of brothers ('distantly related' or 'consanguine') who are thus called because they issue from the same father? And what about the sister? Where has she gone?

Since the question of brother and sister will play for us, as the reader has already sensed, a determining role, let us refer immediately to Emile Benveniste's indispensable information on the 'two Greek words for "brother", *adelphós* and *kasígnētos*', as well as those on the 'notion of *phrátēr*' and *phrātría*.[21] On this point as on so many others, this information sets out for us the immensity and complexity of the tasks at hand. If it were still necessary, it would be enough to recall us to prudence and modesty. The present essay risks only − I must insist on this once again − a barely preliminary step into these still so obscure regions. Benveniste's article would have to be quoted in its entirety, and what stems from the most precious knowledge − but also what it sometimes introduces, in the apparent neutrality of its metalinguistic presentation, by way of unquestioned axioms − would have to be carefully analysed. I shall retain here only that which will be of the greatest import, from the vantage point of its contents as much as that of its methodology, to the outcome of my argument, notably with regard to a Christian semantics of fraternity or sorority. At stake would be, in short, the Christianization of fraternization, or fraternization as the essential structure of Christianization:

> Such is this complex history in which we see that, when a culture is transformed, it employs new terms to take the place of traditional terms when they are found to be charged with specific values. This is what happened to the notion of 'brother' in Ibero-Romance. As a term of kinship, Latin *frater* has disappeared, and it has been replaced by *hermano* in Spanish and *irmão* in Portuguese, that is to say by Latin *germanus*. The reason for this is that in the course of Christianization, *frater*, like *soror*, had taken on an exclusively religious sense, 'brother and sister in religion'. It was therefore necessary to coin a new term for natural kinships, *frater* and *soror* having become in some way classificatory terms, relating to a new classificatory relationship, that of religion.[22]

This passage points up an example of decisions made by the author of *Indo-European Language and Society*, but left in the dark: why are these two kinships (said to be 'natural' or of an 'exclusively religious' nature) still kinships or classificatory kinships? What is the analogy? How does the tropical or homonymic passage from one register to the other take place? In what manner is it or is it not a question of rhetoric or of linguistics? Why should that force us to question again the concept of institution, of proof, indication, and linguistic testimony operating in this study (one of the exemplary places with regard to this, as we will attempt to demonstrate elsewhere, would be the chapter on '*ius* and the oath in Rome' and everything concerning testimonial semantics)? What does 'religious' mean? And what does 'natural' mean, when one knows that no classificatory kinship is devoid of all religiosity? The rest of Benveniste's article thus renews contact with the non-natural equivalent (Benveniste says *mystical* as in Joyce's *Ulysses*, where paternity, as we have said, is named a *legal fiction* and the entire mystique of kinship is restaged) of pre-Christian religiosity in a phratry which this time has issued from 'the same father' and not, as in *Menexenus*, from one and the same mother. 'Apparently slight facts', indications of a 'profound transformation', Benveniste rightly concludes:

> Similarly in Greek it was necessary to distinguish two types of kinship, and *phrátēr* now being used solely as a classificatory term, new terms for consanguineous 'brother' and 'sister' had to be forged.
>
> These lexical creations often overturn the ancient terminology. When Greek used for 'sister' the feminine form (*adelphḗ*) of the term for brother (*adelphós*), this instituted a radical change in the Indo-European state of affairs. The ancient contrast between 'brother' and 'sister' rested on the difference that all the brothers form a phratria *mystically* [Derrida's emphasis] descended from the same father. There are no feminine 'phratriai'. But when, in a new conception of kinship, the connection by consanguinity is stressed – and this is the situation we have in historical Greek – a descriptive term becomes necessary, and it must be the same for brother and sister. In the new names the distinction is made only by morphological indication of gender (*adelphós, adelphḗ*). Apparently slight facts, like this one, throw light on the profound transformation which the Greek vocabulary of kinship has undergone.

We have been taking our semantic bearings in the immense space of an adventuresome questioning, and we should like to question this 'profound transformation' in its intrinsic relation to the transformation that can affect the *philía*. This, then, is perhaps the place to quote, to doubly heuristic ends, Benveniste's analogous conclusion, this time at the end of an article on *phílos*. It deals in a first stage with the genealogy of *cīvis* (fellow citizen) in a familial group which is a group of friends as well. The social value of *phílos* is linked to hospitality. The guest is *phílos*. *Phileîn* is to 'hospitize'. *Phileîn, philótēs* imply the exchanged oath, *phílēma* the embrace hailing or welcoming the guest. In Homer, *phílos* is not only the friend, it has possessive value, at times without apparent friendly affect ('*his* knees', '*his* son') and 'without distinction'. At the end of a long article whose rich and detailed insights defy description, here is the conclusion which is of the greatest import for us:

> It would take many chapters to list and analyse with the necessary care all the examples of *phílos* where it is said to be 'possessive'. We believe, however, that we have interpreted the most important. This re-examination was necessary to expose a long-standing error, which is probably as old as Homeric exegesis, and has been handed down from generation to generation of scholars. The whole problem of *phílos* deserves a full examination. We must start from uses and contexts which reveal in this term a complex network of associations, some with institutions of hospitality, others with usages of the home, still others with emotional behaviour; we must do this in order to understand plainly the metaphorical applications to which the term lent itself.

Although he seems to have no doubts (where we would be more inclined to entertain them) about the possibility of 'understanding plainly the metaphorical applications', and first of all, of 'plainly understanding' what 'metaphor' means in this context, Benveniste concludes – and these are the final words of the article:

> All this wealth of concepts was smothered and lost to view once *phílos* was reduced to a vague notion of friendship or wrongly interpreted as a possessive adjective. It is high time we learned again how to read Homer.
>
> As to the etymology of *phílos*, it is now clear that nothing which has been proposed on this subject holds good any longer [an allusion here to an interpretation proposed in 1936 at the 'Société de Linguistique' that appeared in *BSL* 38, 1937, p. x]. We now know that the protohistory of the word belongs to the most ancient form of Greek: Mycenean already had proper names composed with *phílos*-: *pi-ro-pa-ta-ra* (=Philopatra), *pi-ro-we-ko* (=Philowergos), and so on. The discussion about its origins is thus not finished. It is more important to begin to see what it signifies.[23]

'To begin to see what it signifies'? Indeed.

In the passage from *Menexenus* that we were analysing, three points still have to be noted. The first concerns the *necessity* of equality, the next the tie linking *Greek fraternity* to itself in *pólemos* as well as in *stásis*. The last point has to do with the suspended usage of the word '*democracy*'.

1. *Necessity*. Everything seems to be decided where the decision does not take place, precisely in that place where the decision does not take place *qua* decision, where it will have been carried away, where it will have got carried away in what has always-already taken place: at birth, in other words the day before birth, in this necessity which makes obligatory (*anagkázei*), at birth, in noble birth, in eugenic birth, the search for an equality before the law *in conformity* with equality of birth. We were saying above that nature commands law, that equality at birth founds *in necessity* legal equality. It is difficult to decide here if this foundation in necessity is a just foundation, just according to nature or just according to the law. If there is a justification to this foundation (this would be *Begründung* in German, or *Rechtfertigung*), it is to the extent that the justification strictly speaking, nomological justification, is founded firmly on the physio-ontological ground of what *is* in *nature*, revealing itself in truth at birth. The same relation would thereby tie birth in general to what is *noble* in *noble* birth [*ce qu'il y a de bon dans la bonne naissance*] (*eugéneia*). Everything called democracy here (or aristo-democracy) founds the social bond, the community, the equality, the friendship of brothers, *identification qua fraternization*, and so forth, in the link between this isonomic and the isogonic tie, the natural bond between *nómos* and *phúsis*, if you like, the bond between the political and autochthonous consanguinity. This is also a bond between a (theoretical or ontological) report and a performative commitment (promise, oath, fidelity to dead ancestors, and so forth). This bond between the two ties – this synthetic a priori necessity, if we can speak of it thus – ties what is to what must be, it obliges, it connects the obligation to the tie of birth which we call natural; it is the *obligatory* process of a natural law, the embedding of an 'it is necessary' in the filiation of what is, of what is born and what dies. It is the place of fraternization as the symbolic bond alleging the repetition of a genetic tie. Responsibility must imperatively answer for itself before what is, at birth and at death. In more modern terms, one might speak of the foundation of citizenship in a nation. Such a bond between two structurally heterogeneous ties will always remain obscure, *mystical*, essentially foreign to rationality – which does not mean simply irrational, in the equally modern sense of the term. It will always be exposed, to say the least, to the 'sophistications', mystifications, and perversions of rhetoric. Sometimes to the worst symptoms of nationalism,

ethnocentrism, populism, even xenophobia. It is not sufficient to free the concept of public enemy of all private hatred – indeed, of all psychology of the passions, as Schmitt would have it – to exclude the xenophobic exclusion of this 'logic'. Are we certain that throughout all the mutations of European history (of which, of course, the most rigorous account must be taken), no concept of the political and of democracy has ever broken with the heritage of this troubling necessity? Made a radical, thematic break with it? This is the question we are concerned with here.

2. *Fraternity.* Since the distinction between *polémios* and *ekhthrós* (enemy of war, political enemy and hated enemy, object of hatred in general, and so on), and then, between *pólemos* and *stásis* (war/internal dissension, inter-ethnic, interstate or international war/internal or civil war, and so on) is so important to us in the deconstructive problematization of a certain Schmittian discourse, let us also emphasize that this same 'obligatory necessity' binds the Greeks one to another *at the same time* in the war they wage on Greeks and in their war with barbarians. As long as they remain faithful to the memory of their dead, to the fathers of their dead – that is, to the spectres of their fathers of noble birth – they are bound by this testamentary tie which, in truth, is nothing other than their originary patrimony. A monumental memory begins by instituting them in telling them who they really are. The memory of their dead – their fathers of noble birth – recalls nothing less than their truth, their truth *qua* political truth. This memory inaugurates as much as it recalls or reproduces truth. The obligatory necessity of this bond of memory forms the condition of their political freedom. It is the element of their freedom, the sense of their world as the truth of their freedom. It is their freedom – indeed, for them, the only imaginable freedom. Truth, freedom, necessity, and equality come together in this politics of fraternity. One can hardly see how a *perhaps* could ever stand a chance in such a politics, the chance of an absolute housebreak or hospitality, an unpredictable decision or *arrivance*. Except by accident or fortuitously – and this is why we are speaking of chance – a *perhaps* always delivers itself to chance; thus one cannot, one *must* not, hope – for the *perhaps* – some essential or necessary possibility, or a non-accidental condition. On the contrary, perhaps the *perhaps* will have opened for this configuration (the bond between the two necessities, the two equalities, freedom, truth, fraternity: in a word, 'the epitome' of Greek politics) the possibility of configuring itself in a forgetting of the *perhaps*. This forgetting of the *perhaps*, this amnesia of the decision without decision, of the absolute *arrivant* – that is what is perhaps hidden in the Greek act of memory. Forgetting or memory, the Greek son or brother recalls them to

himself in his combat for freedom *on the outside and from within*. This is how we might read the follow-up of Aspasia's discourse:

> And so their and our fathers, and these too, our brethren, being nobly born and having been brought up in all freedom, did both in their public and private capacity (*kai idía kai dēmosía*) many noble deeds famous over the whole world. They were the deeds of men who thought that they ought to fight both against Hellenes for the sake of Hellenes on behalf of freedom (*tēs eleutherías*), and against barbarians in the common interest of Hellas. (239ab)

3. *The name 'democracy'*. The hesitation, even the indifference as to the name of 'democracy' will have been noted earlier on. One person calls it 'democracy', someone else will give it another name 'according to his fancy' (*an khaírē*). It is not the name but the thing or the concept that counts 'in truth': aristocracy, the power of the best (the most virtuous and the most wise) with the 'approbation' of the multitude (*plēthos*), the right opinion (*eudoxía*) of the crowd, as it is sometimes translated, of the masses, the people, one could also say of the majority. Let us say of *number* − that is, the greatest number.

(Among all the questions of number that should attract an essay on the politics of friendship, let us never give short shrift to what is called demography. It has always been a sensitive and classic stake of the democratic tradition. How far beyond a certain number of citizens can a republic still claim to be a democracy? If this becomes problematic well before the canonical examples of Athens, Corsica, Geneva or Poland, if this begins with number itself, with the supplement of 'one more [*plus un*, also 'no more']', what will be said, beyond the billions, of a universal democratic model which, if it does not regulate a world State or super-State, would still command an international law of European origin?)

If the word 'democracy' allies itself or competes with that of aristocracy, it is because of number, of the reference to the required approbation of the greatest number. We are giving preference to this translation by 'number' − legitimately, we believe − the better to highlight the arithmetical dimension that will mark the entire history of the concept of friendship, at least since Aristotle, and that will later determine our way of listening to '*O philoi, oudeis philos*' (in the way we are for the moment transcribing it: without accents and without breathing, for the question of number will arise again with this grammatical choice and reading decision). Must friends be *in number*? Numerous? In great numbers? How many will there be? At what point do 'great numbers' begin? What does 'a friend' mean? 'A friend' in the feminine? 'Some friends' in the masculine or feminine? 'No friend', in either gender? And what is the relationship between this quantum of friendship and democracy, as the agreement or approbation of number? We are saying here number as the greatest number, to be sure, but in the first place number as the deployment of countable unity, of the 'one more' and of this calculable form of presentable unity, the voice of the subject.

Let us put these questions aside for the moment, but not before registering this nominalist or conventionalist style of hesitation of the subject of the name 'democracy'. This hesitation, even this indifference, is relative; it does not fall into arbitrariness. It limits itself by itself in keeping an irreducible bond to conceptual necessity. This necessity amounts twice over to number – that is, to presumed calculability: once in the form of decision (no democracy without the decided and declared approbation of the greatest number) and once in the form of that which passes, predicts and makes the decision possible: birth – this is the so-equivocal concept of double equality (isonomy founded on isogony).

But providing these conceptual traits are maintained, providing they are associated with eugenics (autochthony plus consanguinity) on the one hand, and with the aristocracy of virtue on the other, the name could, if one wished, be changed.

There is a strategy here whose stakes are limitless, even if we situate its effect in a quite particular place: in a text, one of Plato's dialogues whose authenticity used to be called into question (but this, it would seem, is no longer the case today,[24] and it is of little import to our subject) and, within this dialogue, in the form of an *epitáphios* put, to satiric ends, in the mouth of a courtesan and plagiarizer. Even if we took into account its irony, and underwrote it here (and why shouldn't we? Who would deny it? Let us say that *to this extent at least*, our critical or 'deconstructionist' worries still belong to a certain Platonic heritage of this irony: they participate in the heritage or share it, perhaps, therefore divide it), let us not forget that Plato is dealing with a thematics and an eloquence corresponding to the most stable structures, the dominant, most accredited *topoi* of a Greek discourse. This is not to say to a homogeneous Greek discourse or people, identical to themselves – we do not believe so – but, let us say, to what in them represents the 'greatest number' precisely, whether it be a matter of the political in general or of democracy in particular. If an orator is all the more eloquent in praising his listeners, as Socrates suggests in *Menexenus* (235d), in listening to him the 'exemplary' image (in the Ciceronian sense of which we have already spoken) or the 'ideal self' of the people applauding can be determined. This image can either pre-exist the orator or form itself, reform itself, in the mirror thus held out. In both cases, it is a matter of a people in so far as it can *identify itself*, in so far as it is what it is or would wish to be. And it would be easy to show that under the eloquence of the *epitáphios* that *Menexenus* seems to denounce, and at the very moment when Socrates belittles Aspasia, who knows precisely how to say 'what should be delivered' (236b) to flatter the expectations of the orator's public, one meets again, precisely for this very reason, the axioms, the conceptual veins, the oppositions and associations which structure not only dominant Greek discourse but, *on the other hand, elsewhere*, Plato's least ironic political discourse, in the most numerous places of the Platonic 'corpus', especially in the *Republic*, with regard, precisely, to the political enemy *qua pólemos* or *stásis*.

To be sure, we cannot thereby absolutely justify the privilege of this reference to *Menexenus*. There will never be an absolute justification to such a limit. We shall attempt only this: an appeal to another reason to explain our choice in part. This reason intersects with the preceding reasons, and one has already sensed what it is: the genre of *epitáphios*, of the funeral oration, of the discourse of mourning in general, of heritage and testament, whose theme has preoccupied us for quite some time. Our reflection on friendship, where it will have intersected the political thing [*la chose politique*], will regularly pass through this moment of *political mourning*. It seems to us to be constitutive, with the figure of the brother, of the model of friendship that will have dominated, in all its canonical authority, the Greek or Christian *discourses*. One should, more prudently, say 'Greek, Christian, and beyond', to designate those places towards which we are still timorously advancing: Judaism and Islam, at the very least, where the figure of the brother accumulates so many virtues, of course, but above all starting from and *still* in Nietzsche's wake, and the entire passage *beyond* whose movement bears his name. That is to say, everywhere (it is 'our time', the out-of-jointness proper to our time, if it is one, to our experience of being '*out of joint*' [in English in the text]), in every place where a tradition thus tends of itself to break with itself, not being able to do so, by definition, in anything but an irregular and a trembling fashion.

Nevertheless, considered in itself, beyond the ruses and irony that may mark *Menexenus*, this hesitation over the name 'democracy' will always provide food for thought. If, between the name on the one hand, the concept and the thing on the other, the play of a gap offers room for rhetorical effects which are also political strategies, what are the lessons that we can draw today? Is it still *in the name of democracy* that one will attempt to criticize such and such a determination of democracy or aristo-democracy? Or, more radically — closer, precisely, to its fundamental *radicality* (where, for example, it is *rooted* in the security of an autochthonous foundation, in the stock or in the genius of filiation[25]) – is it still in the name of democracy, of a democracy to come, that one will attempt to deconstruct a concept, all the predicates associated with the massively dominant concept of democracy, that in whose heritage one inevitably meets again the law of birth, the natural or 'national' law, the law of homophilia or of autochthony, civic equality (isonomy) founded on equality of birth (isogony) as the condition of the calculation of approbation and, therefore, the aristocracy of virtue and wisdom, and so forth?

What remains or still resists in the deconstructed (or deconstructible) concept of democracy which guides us endlessly? Which orders us not only to engage a deconstruction but to keep the old name? And to deconstruct further in the name of a *democracy* to come? That is to say, further, which enjoins us still to inherit from what – forgotten, repressed, misunderstood, or unthought in the 'old' concept and throughout its history – would still be on the watch, giving off signs or symptoms of a stance of survival coming through all the old and tired features? Would there be in the concept of *eudoxia* (reputation, approbation, opinion, judgement), and in the concept of equality (equality of birth, *isogonia*, and equality of rights, *isonomia*) a double motif that might, interpreted differently, exclude democracy from autochthonous and homophilic rooting? Is there another thought of calculation and of number, another way of apprehending the universality of the singular which, without dooming politics to the incalculable, would still justify the old name of democracy? Would it still make sense to speak of democracy when it would no longer be a question (no longer in question as to what is essential or constitutive) of country, nation, even of State or citizen – in other words, *if at least one still keeps to the accepted use of this word,* when it would no longer be a political question?

This last hypothesis may lead to two types of rejoinder to the Schmittian project or, if you prefer, to two distinct sides of the same answer to *The Concept of the Political,* that is, to the reconstruction of the political. On the one hand, we seem to be confirming – but not by way of deploring the fact, as Schmitt does – an essential and necessary depoliticization. This depoliticization would no longer necessarily be the neuter or negative indifference to all forms of the social bond, of the community, of friendship. On the other hand, through this depoliticization, which would apply only to the fundamental and dominant concept of the political, through this *genealogical* deconstruction of the political (and through it to the democratic), one would seek to think, interpret and implement another politics, another democracy. One would seek to say it, to thematize it, to formalize

it in the course of a deconstruction – the course of the world – under these
old names. Saying, thematizing, formalizing are not neuter or apolitical
gestures, arriving after the fact from above [*en surplomb*]. These gestures are
positions staked out in a process. Calling this *experience* (for it is an
experience that crosses through and ventures out before being a philosophical, theoretical or methodological statement) '*genealogical* deconstruction'
would here no longer be naming, as was often done, an operation
proceeding only through genealogical analysis, retrospection and reconstitution. At stake would thus be a deconstruction *of the* genealogical schema,
a paradoxical deconstruction – a deconstruction, at once genealogical and
a-genealogical, *of the* genealogical. It would concern, by way of a privilege
granted – thus its attribute – the *genealogical*. Wherever it commands in the
name of birth, of a national naturalness which has never been what it *was
said to be*. It would concern confidence, credit, credence, *doxa* or *eudoxia*,
opinion or right opinion, the approbation given to filiation, at birth and at
the origin, to generation, to the familiarity of the family, to the proximity
of the neighbour – to what axioms too quickly inscribe under these words.
This is not to wage war on them and to see evil therein, but to think and
live a politics, a friendship, a justice which *begin* by breaking with their
naturalness or their homogeneity, with their alleged place of origin. Hence,
which begin where the beginning divides (itself) and differs, begin by
marking an 'originary' heterogeneity that has already come and that alone
can come, in the future, to open them up. If only unto themselves.

Saying that to keep this Greek name, democracy, is an affair of context,
of rhetoric or of strategy, even of polemics, reaffirming that this name will
last as long as it has to but not much longer, saying that things are speeding
up remarkably in these fast times, is not necessarily giving in to the
opportunism or cynicism of the antidemocrat who is not showing his cards.
Completely to the contrary: one keeps this indefinite right to the question,
to criticism, to deconstruction (guaranteed rights, in principle, in any
democracy: no deconstruction without democracy, no democracy without
deconstruction). One keeps this right strategically to mark what is no longer
a strategic affair: the limit between the conditional (the edges of the context
and of the concept enclosing the effective practice of democracy and
nourishing it in land [*sol*] and blood) and the unconditional which, from
the outset, will have inscribed a self-deconstructive force in the very motif
of democracy, the possibility and the duty for democracy itself to de-limit
itself. Democracy is the *autos* of deconstructive self-delimitation. Delimitation not only in the name of a regulative idea and an indefinite perfectibil-
ity, but every time in the singular urgency of a *here and now*. Precisely

through the abstract and potentially indifferent thought of number and equality. This thought certainly can impose homogenizing calculability while exalting land and blood, and the risk is as terrifying as it is inevitable – it is the risk today, more than ever. But it perhaps also keeps the power of universalizing, beyond the State and the nation, the account taken of anonymous and irreducible singularities, infinitely different and thereby indifferent to particular difference, to the raging quest for identity corrupting the most indestructible desires of the idiom.

But we have undoubtedly just given in to precipitation. We will now have to decelerate slightly, and again take up a patient reading of Schmitt. We were drawn into this detour – as the reader will perhaps recall – by the highly elliptical justification that Schmitt gives in a few lines to the choice of his words, sometimes to his concepts: private enemy/public or political enemy (*ekhthrós/polémios, inimicus/hostis*), war and internal dissension, war and civil war (*pólemos/stásis*). The detour was necessary in order to try to understand what 'enemy', 'on our side, on the home front', has meant over the centuries. And in what respect, if Schmitt is to be believed, politics could never be thought without knowing *what* 'enemy' means, nor a decision made without knowing *who* the enemy is. That is to say: without the *identification* by which the enemy is identified, himself, and by which one is identified, oneself.

We shall try to show further on in what respect this *double identification* engages in privileged fashion both brother friends and brother enemies in the same process of fraternization.

Henceforth, things have begun to appear a little more complicated than Schmitt has it. In any case, in the Platonic justifications he finds for a semantics without which his discourse would become dangerously fragile. We shall take them into account in making a few more steps in our reading of *The Concept of the Political* (1932) and in the singular itinerary that this work will have begun, down to the *Théorie du partisan. Note incidente relative au concept du politique* (1962).

Notes

1. *Human All Too Human*, 2, *Assorted opinions and maxims*, 242, p. 274.
2. 'As for the name ... that is called democracy', in *L'Invention d'Athènes. Histoire de l'oraison funèbre dans la 'cité classique'*, 1981, second edition, Payot, 1993, pp. 225, 227. [*The Invention of Athens: The Funeral Oration in the Classical City*, trans. Alan Sheridan, Harvard University Press, Cambridge, MA and London, 1986, pp. 217, 219.]

3. La Boétie, 'To Michel de Montaigne'.

4. In order to limit at least one inevitable ambiguity, let us say immediately and straightforwardly that the deconstructive reading of Schmittian thought that we shall attempt here will keep two convictions in view.

The first concerns the undeniable link between this thinking of the political and political thought on the one hand and, on the other, Schmitt's political commitments, those which led to his arrest and conviction after the war. In many respects, these commitments often appear more serious and more repugnant than those of Heidegger (see, for instance, his anti-Semitic declarations on the 'Jewish falsifications of the concept of spirit' quoted by Habermas in 'German Idealism and its Jewish Thinkers', *Profiles philosophiques et politiques*, TEL, Gallimard 1974, p. 83; and, more recently, 'Le besoin d'une continuité allemande. Carl Schmitt dans l'histoire des idées politiques de la RFA ['The Need for German Continuity. Carl Schmitt in the History of Political Ideas in the GFR] in *Les Temps modernes*, no. 575, June 1994).

But the second conviction is that this should not distract us from a serious reading, nor keep us from taking up a thought and a work so deeply rooted in the richest tradition of the theological, juridical, political and philosophical culture of Europe, in that of a European law of which this Catholic thinker (who probably remained a Nazi for a much longer period of time than he publicly confessed, and no doubt remained anti-Semitic for the rest of his life – and the forms of his anti-Semitism were extremely virulent) claimed to be the last – fervent – advocate. To exactly this extent this thought and this work repeatedly presaged the fearsome world that was announcing itself from as as early as the 1920s. As though the fear of seeing that which comes to pass take place in effect had honed the gaze of this besieged watchman. Following our hypothesis, the scene would be thus: lucidity and fear not only drove this terrified and insomniac watcher to anticipate the storms and seismic movements that would wreak havoc with the historical field, the political space, the borders of concepts and countries, the axiomatics of European law, the bonds between the tellurian and the political, the technical and the political, the media and parliamentary democracy, etc. Such a 'watcher' would thereby have been more attuned than so many others to the fragility and 'deconstructible' precariousness of structures, borders and axioms that he wished to protect, restore and 'conserve' at all costs. This lucidity – that is, the courage of his fear – also led him to multiply, in the panic of a defensive strategy, the most paradoxical of alliances, thereby revealing formal combinations whose possibility is still today in the greatest need of meditation: how does the most uncompromisingly conservative discourse, that of Schmitt, manage to affirm, in certain respects, so many affinities with what are apparently, from Lenin to Mao, the most revolutionary movements of our time? Who would have been their common enemy? And how can one explain the interest in Schmitt shown by a certain extreme-left-wing movement, in more than one country? How is this still-active influence to be explained, despite so many trials? There is more to be learned from these equivocations than from many right-minded denunciations that take shelter behind a chronic wave of contagious or objective alliances. These indolent denunciations often use this disquiet and the empirically established fact of 'evil influences' as a pretext, without having anything else to say on the matter, for shirking and for deterring others from the task of reading, from the work and from the question. Those who are satisfied with mere denunciation too often conceal their apathy and misapprehension – indeed, their denial of the very thing that

Schmitt at least, in his own way, through his reactive panic, apprehended. Which way was that? This is what we would like to consider temporarily.

5. Under this title, we will be referring regularly to *Der Begriff des Politischen* (1932), reissued in 1963, and once again in 1974, by Duncker & Humblot, Berlin, with the subtitle 'Text von 1932 mit einem Vorword und drei Corollarien', as well as to the French translation, *La Notion du Politique, Théorie du Partisan*, trans. M.-L. Steinhauser, with a preface by J. Freund, Flammarion 1992. We have again slightly modified this translation, at several points. We will indicate each time the page number of the original followed by the page number of the translation. [Translated into English by George Schwab as *The Concept of the Political*, Rutgers University Press, New Brunswick, New Jersey 1976; hereafter CP. The page numbers following those of the original will be from this edition.]

6. On the relationship between Schmitt and Strauss, see Heinrich Meier, 'Carl Schmitt, Leo Strauss und "Der Begriff des Politischen". Zu einen Dialog unter Alwesenden.' This work contains Strauss's paper on *The Concept of the Political* [which is found in English translation at the end of the English edition of Schmitt's work] and three unpublished letters of 1932–33.

7. Ibid., p. 26; p. 26.

8. Ibid., p. 29; p. 28 [translation modified].

9. Ibid., pp. 33–5; pp. 34–7. Further on, to warn against the confusion that may ensue, Schmitt recalls the profound analogy between theological and political postulates. He then speaks, concerning the friend–enemy distinction, of 'effectivity-actuality or of real possibility' (*die reale Wirklichkeit oder Möglichkeit der Unterscheidung von Freund und Feind*). This distinction would be presupposed by 'pessimistic' theoreticians of the political, such as Machiavelli, Hobbes, and even Fichte (p. 64; p. 65). We shall see below what makes these pessimistic theoreticians, in Schmitt's eyes, the only authentic thinkers of the political.

10. See *The Crisis of Parliamentary Democracy*, trans. Ellen Kennedy, MIT Press, Cambridge, MA, and London, 1985; and *Théologie politique*, trans. and presented J.-L. Schlegel, Gallimard, 1988, p. VII [English translation, *Political Theology*, by George Schwab, MIT Press, Cambridge, MA and London 1985].

11. pp. 29–30; pp. 28–9.

12. We shall attempt to do so elsewhere, especially around several examples from the Old Testament which, to us, appear difficult to incorporate into Schmittian logic.

13. p. 29, n. 5; tr.p. 28, n. 9. On the theme of *stásis*, as on so many related themes, we already refer here, and shall do so again, to the original and indispensable works of Nicole Loraux. For the moment, let us simply note this sensitive place where Loraux points out the suspension of the opposition *stásis/pólemos*. When citizens are 'killed by other Athenians' while they were coming to the rescue of democracy against oligarchy, 'their death actually transgresses the opposition of *stásis* and *pólemos*, the norm of all organized political life, thereby creating an exceptional situation' (*The Invention of Athens*, p. 201].

Long after *The Concept of the Political* (1932), in 1969, Schmitt went back to this notion of *stásis*, and devoted several truly pregnant pages to it. Their starting point is Gregory of Nazianzus's argument according to which any *stásis* in the Trinity would be unthinkable, whereas 'the One – *to hen* – is always in revolt – *stasiázon* – against itself –

prós heautón'. Schmitt thus notes that the word *stásis*, meaning revolt, appears 'at the heart of the most irreproachable formulation of the thorny dogma'. He recalls not only Plato (*Sophist*, 249–54), and the passage from the *Republic* that we are dealing with here, but also the Greek Church Fathers, neo-Platonism and Plotinus. He goes on:

> *Stasis* means in the first place *repose*, state of rest, position, arrest (*status*); the opposite notion is *kinesis*: movement. But secondly, *stasis* also means (political) unrest, movement, revolt and civil war. Most Greek lexicons juxtapose with no further ado the two opposed meanings, without attempting to explain them, something which, moreover, could never be legitimately demanded of them. However, even the simple juxtaposition of numerous examples of such an opposition is a gold mine for the knowledge of political and theologico-political phenomena. In this case, a veritable theologico-political *stasiology* emerges from the heart of the doctrine of the Trinity. The problem of enmity and of the enemy could never be eclipsed. In the linguistic usage of the modern world, a significant fact has been recently added in the Anglo-American linguistic zone: the word *foe*, judged outdated and of only 'rhetorical' value since Shakespeare, has a new lease of life since the Second World War (*Théologie politique*, 1922, 1969, pp. 127, 173–5).

On the modern rehabilitation of the word *foe*, see also the end of the preface to the French reissue of *Le Concept du politique* (1963). On the difficulties in maintaining these distinctions in the etymology of the German *Feind*, see the unwieldy development in *Corollaire* II (3), 1938. We shall return to this later, in the next chapter, around the figure of the brother.

Schmitt's usage of *status* here should be set beside that which he emphasizes elsewhere, on the first page of *The Concept of the Political*: the State is Status, status *par excellence*, sheer status (*der Status schlechthin*). As for the stasiology evoked therein (which would be working either at the heart of the One, or in the centre of a Trinity or Holy Family), this is a motif which – in different words, in another style and in view of other consequences – could very well describe one of the subterranean but utterly continuous themes of this essay: how the One divides and opposes itself, opposes itself by posing itself, represses and violates the difference it carries within itself, wages war, *wages war on itself, itself becoming war [se fait la guerre], frightens itself, itself becoming fear [se fait peur]*, and *does violence to itself, itself becoming violence [se fait violence]*, transforms itself into frightened violence in guarding itself from the other, for *it guards itself from, and in, the other [il se garde de l'autre]*, always, Him, the One, the One 'different from itself'.

14. Schmitt adds a specification that he judges analogous to the opposition between *hostis* (public enemy) and *inimicus* (private enemy); this does not mean – let us note the dissymmetry of which Schmitt does not seem to take account – that *ekhthrós*, who can be the enemy in a 'civil war' (*stásis*), is a 'private' enemy: can one not have 'private' (therefore political) enemies in a civil war (*stásis*)? As for the Latin, Schmitt's reference is as follows: '*Hostis is est cum quo publice bellum habemus . . . in quo ab inimico differt, qui est is, quocum habemus privata odia. Distingui etiam sic possunt, ut inimicus sit qui nos odit; hostis qui oppugnat*' (Forcellini, *Lexicon totius Latinitatis*, III, 320, 511), pp. 29, 196.

15. '. . . absolute evil', writes Nicole Loraux, but also 'a parasitical evil grafted on to the proper nature of the city' (*The Invention of Athens*, pp. 198, 199).

16. Ibid.., pp. 175, 189, 310, 312–13.

17. *Menexenus*, 244ab [in *Plato, The Collected Dialogues*, ed. Edith Hamilton and Huntington Cairns, Princeton University Press 1961, p. 194].

18. Ibid., 239a.

19. Ibid., 326e, 237b.

20. This passage from *Menexenus* is also evoked by Nicole Loraux, in particular in *Les Enfants d'Athéna. Idées athéniennes sur la citoyenneté et la division des sexes*, Maspero, 1981, p. 41 [*The Children of Athena: Athenian Ideas about Citizenship and the Division Between the Sexes*, trans. Cardine Levine, foreword Froma I. Zeitlin, Princeton University Press, Princeton, NJ, 1993], precisely in one of her priceless chapters on 'Autochthony, an Athenian Topic', and 'the required theme of the *epitáphioi*' (p. 41) and in a footnote to her *Les Mères en deuil* [Mothers in Mourning], Le Seuil 1990, p. 128, n.29. On most of these questions, I naturally refer back – and, as is meet and fitting, with much gratitude – to all the works of Nicole Loraux, to those just mentioned and to *Façons tragiques de tuer une femme*, Hachette 1985 [*Tragic Ways of Killing a Woman*, trans. Anthony Forster, Harvard University Press, Cambridge, MA, and London, 1987].

To my knowledge this has never been done, but it would undoubtedly be interesting to compare the two lines of research – so different in so many respects – of Nicole Loraux and Paul de Man on the laws, genre, poetics and rhetoric, and also the paradoxes, of the epitaph. See in particular Paul de Man, 'Autobiography as De-Facement' (around Wordsworth's *Essays upon Epitaphs*) in *The Rhetoric of Romanticism*, New York 1984. See also 'Mnemosyne', in *Mémoires – for Paul de Man*, in which I also followed through this motif of the discourse of mourning, the funeral oration and the epitaph (Galilée, 1988), especially pp. 43 ff. [trans. Cecile Lindsay, Jonathan Culler, Eduardo Cadava and Peggy Kamuf, Columbia University Press, New York 1986, 1989, pp. 21 ff.].

21. *Le Vocabulaire des institutions européennes*, Minuit, 1969, vol. 1, pp. 220 ff. [*Indo-European Language and Society*, trans. by Elizabeth Palmer, London: Faber & Faber 1973].

22. Ibid., trans., p. 179.

23. Ibid., pp. 335 ff., pp. 352–3; trans. p. 288.

24. See Loraux, *The Invention of Athens*, pp. 312–13.

25. As we have indicated from the epigraph on, and then repeatedly, the argument of this chapter intersects in its own way, in paying homage to it, the reflection that Nicole Loraux entitles, in *The Invention of Athens*, 'For the name ... It is Called Democracy'. The particular orientation of this essay on friendship, in discussing the name of democracy and the deconstruction of a certain concept of democracy in the name of democracy, could take the following form today, still today and perhaps more than ever: how do you deconstruct the essential link of a certain concept of democracy to autochthony and to eugenics without, for all that, giving up the name of democracy? Nor its historicity? But how do you think this historicity to which no history has ever been able to measure up? Such a question would resemble at least that of the 'immemorial' or the relations between 'myth' and 'history' as it is formulated, for example, in these following lines by Nicole Loraux:

> It is not only in the temporal unfolding of the text that *demokratía*, annexed to autochthony and flanked by noble exploits, is linked to *eugéneia*, but also, in absolute terms, the time of the myth is for the orator the moment of democracy. In other words, it has no origin; it is immemorial: 'they were thus the first and only ones of that time who abolished kingdoms among themselves and established democracy' (*Lysias*, 18), *en ekeínōi tôi khrónōi* referring *either* to the first birth of the autochthons, that is, to the origin of mankind, *or*, beyond the passage on autochthony, to

the period of the great mythical exploits. So there is, to say the least, a tension between myth and history in this passage. (p. 194)

'Either . . . or': I have underlined these words. A question, then: is it possible, will it ever be possible, *for us* to keep the name democracy beyond this alternative, in excluding it *both* from history as the history of autochthony or eugenics *and* from myth? In order to confide it to or open it to another memory, another immemoriality, another history, another future?

5

On Absolute Hostility:
The Cause of Philosophy and
the Spectre of the Political

The two fundamental principles of Empedocles – *philía* and *neikos* – are, both in name and function, the same as our two primal instincts, *Eros* and *destructiveness*, the first of which endeavours to combine what exists into ever greater entities, while the second endeavours to dissolve these combinations and to destroy the structures to which they have given rise. . . . And no one can foresee in what guise the nucleus of truth contained in the theory of Empedocles will present itself to later understanding.[1]

Freud

By overturning the address attributed to Aristotle ('O friends, no friend', to: 'O enemies, no enemy'), Nietzsche's 'living fool' intensified a first seizure of vertigo. With this second stanza, this second apostrophe, one's head spins even faster.

This is not due only to the structure of the sentence, with which we have certainly not finished, not by a long shot. It is first of all due to a sort of *hyperbolic* build-up that is perhaps the very origin of good and evil, both beyond being (the *Republic* once defined the Good by this hyperbole that ranges beyond being): a hyperbole at the origin of good and evil, common to both, a hyperbole *qua* the difference between good and evil, the friend and the enemy, peace and war. It is this infinite hyperbole common to the two terms of the opposition, thereby making them pass into one another, that makes one's head spin. Is there any hope for the person addressing his friends or his enemies in this way? An interviewer of the 'dying sage' and the 'living fool' would have asked them: 'Are you "pessimistic" or "optimistic"?'. For where is the ultimate in optimism? Its hyperbole? In still addressing oneself to friends to inform them of such a sombre piece of news (their nonexistence or their disappearance)? Or in announcing to one's enemies that there is no enemy? And what, on the contrary, is the ultimate in pessimism, if that can be said? Declaring that there is 'no friend', or still bemoaning the fact that there is no enemy? Would the ultimate of the ultimate be a theory of absolute ambivalence, in the Empedoclean tradition of Freud – that is, one hospitable to the death instinct? Herein, perhaps, lies the shared secret of the 'dying sage' and the 'living fool'. It will have been understood that they have never stopped speaking an initiatory language. And to hit it off, laughing at one another: like fellows, companions, as thick as thieves.

While declaring: The question is not settled by psychological comments on "optimism" or "pessimism"[2] – words he deliberately leaves in quotation marks – Schmitt resolutely affirms, more than once, that only 'pessimistic' thinkers of human nature are systematic, authentic, and coherent thinkers of the political fact [la chose politique] (Machiavelli, Hobbes, etc.[3]). But would these thinkers have recognized themselves better in the sentence of the 'dying sage' or in that of the 'living fool'? Their pessimism, from the moment there is no longer anything 'psychological' or moral about it, nevertheless consists only in the fact that they 'presuppose (voraussetzen) in truth ... only the actuality/effectivity or the real possibility of the distinction of friend and enemy (die reale Wirklichkeit oder Möglichkeit der Unterscheidung von Freund und Feind)'.[4]

We shall have to question the logic of this presupposition. What is this 'actuality/effectivity'? This 'possibility'? Here, in one case as in the other, in one case or the other, what does 'real' mean? Under what conditions, from within what axiomatic, can Schmitt be assured that a knowledge is 'right' or 'correct' (richtige) in acknowledging – as does Hobbes, for example – that the conviction of possessing the truth, the good, the just, is what sparks the worst hostilities, or that 'the war of all against all' is neither the unchained monstrosity of a delirious imagination nor the 'free competition' of bourgeois capitalism, but 'the fundamental presupposition of a specific political philosophy'?[5]

Let us retrace our steps. Schmitt thinks there would be a difference between two forms of disagreement (diaphorâ). He believes he can substantiate this when he defines the enemy – in other words, the political – when he thinks he can appeal so briefly to Plato to describe, explain and illustrate this divide. One has the impression that sometimes the appeal to Plato serves as its justification. Attempting to take a closer look at the question, we were intent on emphasizing, among other points, that such a difference amounts to the same thing, that it belongs to the same. The two different forms of the disagreement are both natural, 'physical'. They remain natural even if one of them, civil war (*stásis*), sometimes takes on the figure of de-naturalization. For this would then be a de-naturalization of nature *in* nature: an evil, an illness, a parasite or a graft – a foreign body, in sum, within the body politic itself, in its own body. The body politic should, no doubt – but it never manages to – identify correctly the foreign body of the enemy outside itself. The purity of the distinction between *stásis* and *pólemos* remains in the *Republic* a 'paradigm',[6] accessible only to discourse. Occasionally, as we have seen,[7] Plato recommends, from a certain vantage point, that this paradigmatic limit be erased, and that the enemies from outside be handled *as* the enemies within. Whether one claims to respect or to erase this limit, in any case its *purity* cannot be put into practice. It is impossible to *implement* the rigour of such a conceptual limit. One cannot do what one says. Neither what one says one will do nor what should be done. No *práxis* can correspond to indications contained in a *léxis*. Plato emphasizes this limit of the limit, this inevitable bastardization of opposed terms. In other words, marking in sum the inaccessibility of the *border* (the line of separation between concepts, as much as the one between the inside and outside of the body politic, the city, State or country), he sharpens all the more the cutting edge of this difference between *práxis* and *léxis* in the difference between the two sorts of disagreement: *this difference is also in nature*. This is a law of *phúsis*: practical implementation does not get as close to truth as does discourse.[8]

Practical conclusion: in practice, in other words, in this political practice that history is – this difference between the disagreements never takes place. It can never be found. Never *concretely*. As a result, the purity of *pólemos* or the enemy, whereby Schmitt would define the political, remains unattainable. The concept of the political undoubtedly corresponds, as concept, to what the ideal discourse can *want* to state most rigorously on the ideality of the political. But no politics has ever been adequate to its concept. No political event can be correctly described or defined with recourse to these concepts. And this inadequation is not accidental, since politics is essentially a *práxis*, as Schmitt himself always implies in his ever-so-insistent reliance on the concept of *real, present possibility* or *eventuality* in his analyses of the formal structures of the political.

Here we have another way of marking the paradox: the inadequation to the concept happens to belong to the concept itself. This inadequation of the concept to itself manifests itself pre-eminently in the order of the political or political practice, unless this order – or rather, its possibility –

would situate the very place, the phenomenon or the 'reason' of an inadequation of any concept to itself: the concept of disjunction *qua* the conceptual being of the concept. It follows that even what is called politics, an ideal politics, a regulative and programmatic aim – indeed, an idea of politics in general – could never regulate (itself on) such a 'concept of the political'.

What makes us so sensitive to this problem? And why is it – precisely in a Schmittian-style discourse – something other than a methodological, epistemological, theoretical, speculative, even simply discursive problem, like an equivocation which logico-rhetorical precautions could easily eliminate? Because, in the remarkable effort of what can be called a modern 'political expert' to recover possession of the concept opening and commanding the field of his own discourse, the effect of this limit is capitalized '*en abyme*'. We are saying 'political expert' here, for if Schmitt is a jurist-historian-of-the-theological-political, and so on, he would offer *de jure* its conceptual foundations, its phenomenogical and semantic axioms to a *science of the political as such*: he is a political expert who would acknowledge no other regional knowledge, no other experience than the 'political', the right to found a political discourse [polito*logie*]: an ontology or an epistemology of the political. Only the purely political can teach us how to think and formalize what is purely political. From the very first words of the 1963 preface to the second edition of *The Concept of the Political*, this concern is recalled: concern for the *tableau*, spatial and taxonomic concern, methodological and topological concern. A concern which cannot last without hierarchical classification. The assigned task, the duty, is to frame and to enframe (*encadrieren*), to put into order (*orden*), to propose 'a theoretical framework for a measureless problem.' Hence a framework (*ein Rahmen*) had to be given also to the problematic of the theory of right, to order its 'entwined thematic', and to discover 'a topology of its concepts'.

Despite or on account of such an aim, Schmitt tirelessly claims *concrete*, living and relevant pertinence for the *words* of political language. Among these words, first and foremost for the word 'political'. These vocables must not and cannot remain, in their 'ultimate consequence', the correlate of ideal or abstract entities. Now this necessity of concrete determination would stem from the 'polemical sense' that always determines these terms. It is therefore all the more troubling that the meaning of *pólemos* remains, as we have just suggested, both natural and blurred, naturally and irreducibly blurred. And precisely where Schmitt would exclude politics from natural-ness. This blurred impurity stems from the fact, recalled by Schmitt, that all political concepts have a 'polemical sense', in two respects, as we shall see: these are concepts *of the* polemical, and they are never implemented except in a polemical field. These concepts *of the* polemical have a strictly *polemical use*.

There are moments when the form of this paradox can be judged pathetic. Schmitt goes to great lengths – in our judgement totally in vain, a priori doomed to failure – to exclude from *all other* purity (objective, scientific, moral, juridical, psychological, economic, aesthetic, etc.) the purity of the political, the *proper and pure impurity* of the concept or the meaning of the 'political'. For he wants, moreover – he will never renounce this – the polemical sense of this purity of the political to be, in its very impurity, still pure. Failing this, it could not be distinguished from anything from which it distinguishes itself. Schmitt would like to be able to count on the pure impurity, on the impure purity of the political as such, of the properly political. He would wish – it is his Platonic dream – that this 'as such' should remain pure at the very spot where it is contaminated. And that this 'as such' should dissipate our doubts concerning what 'friend' and 'enemy' mean. More precisely – and this difference is important here – the doubts must disappear not so much relative to the meaning of friendship or hostility but, above all, relative to *who* the friend and enemy are. If *the* political is to exist, one must know who everyone is, who is a friend and who is an enemy, and this knowing is not in the mode of theoretical knowledge but in one of a *practical identification*: knowing consists here in knowing how to identify the friend and the enemy. The practical identification of self – and from one self to another – the practical identification of the other – and from other to other – seem to be sometimes conditions, sometimes consequences, of the identification of friend and enemy (we shall have to come back to the logic of *philautía* or narcissism – even the fraternal double – working obscurely away at this discourse).

Schmitt wants to be able to count on the opposition, and reckon with it. Even if no pure access to the *eîdos* or essence is to be had, even if, in all conceptual purity, it is not known what war, politics, friendship, enmity, hate or love, hostility or peace are, one can and must know – first of all practically, politically, polemically – *who* is the friend and *who* is the enemy. This, it would seem to us, is the singular torsion marking, for example, the passage we shall quote shortly. The weight of the semantic or conceptual determination is carried in this passage, as we shall point out, by the word 'concrete'. Schmitt's entire discourse posits and supposes in fact, as we shall verify, *a concrete sense of the concrete* which he opposes – as if only in passing, and without the word being kept in the French translation – to the spectral (*gespenstisch*). In this analysis, the spectral is evoked in passing – as if in passing, like a passer-by – as a synonym of 'abstract' or 'empty'. But why would they be synonyms? Would there be no difference between emptiness, the abstract, and the spectral? What are the political stakes of this figure? On the other hand, the unending insistence here on what would be the *opposite* of the spectral – the concrete; the compulsive and obsessional recurrence of the word 'concrete' as the correlate of 'polemical' – does indeed provide food for thought. What thought? Perhaps that the concrete finally remains, in its purity, out of reach, inaccessible, unbreachable, indefinitely deferred, thereby inconceivable to the concept (*Begriff*); consequently as 'spectral' (*gespenstisch*)[9] as the ghost on its periphery, which one opposes to it and which could never be set apart. We shall see how this concretion of the concrete, this ultimate determination to which Schmitt ceaselessly appeals, is always exceeded, overtaken – let us say haunted – by the abstraction of its spectre. Is it not for this reason that so much effort must be exerted – vain effort – to find an intuition and a concept adequate to the concrete?

These efforts create the very tension of this strange book. They are remarkably at work in the passage devoted to the polemical sense of the political. It will not be a matter of the polemological contents of the concept of the political, in so far as it implies the enemy, war, *pólemos*, hence *qua* concept of the polemical. It will be a matter, as we have announced, of only the polemical *use* of this concept of the political, its concrete use, the practical and effective modality of its implementation – let us say its very performativity. Such a necessity cannot leave intact a so-called theoretical discourse on it, a meta-discourse, a meta-polemical or meta-political discourse, a polemico-*logical* or politico-*logical* discourse. Can one conclude that Schmitt's discourse claims this pure theoreticity? In certain respects, we believe, the answer is yes, and this is to a large extent what makes his project interesting: it offers a pure and rigorous conceptual theory of the political, of the specific region of that which is properly and without polemical rhetoric called *the* 'political', the politicity of the political. Within this region, in the enclosure proper to a *theoretical* discourse, all examples, all facts, all historical contents should thus issue in *knowledge*; indeed, in those forms of disinterested theoretical reports called *diagnostics*.[10] But would Schmitt say, for all that, that his discourse on politics is of a *theoretical* nature, and that it is not affected by the polemical modality, and therefore by the performativity, whose incessant contamination he has, on the other hand, described? Would he refuse his theorems the signification of taking sides, an act of war, a certain war? We are not sure that he would. His attitude around this subject would undoubtedly be unstable and wily, and his cunning all the more significant. What appears to us more certain, on the other hand, is that the polito*logical* or polemo*logical* project and the political-polemical engagement are indissociable. It cannot be denied that their respective purity is a priori inaccessible. This is tantamount to saying that it can *only* be denied. This structural disavowal informs and constructs the *political* discourse and the discourse *on* the political. One like the other, one *qua* the other. We shall neither determine nor denounce here the fatality of this performative disavowal as a logical fault, even less as a symptom that could be dissolved in analysis. It inscribes again, and at the same time, a principle of ruin and affirmation at the heart of the most coherent gestures, when their greatest force simultaneously takes on the figure of a performative contradiction, or – and this may amount to the same thing – the figure of a tautology that we were earlier calling teleiopoetic. We have already given many examples of this. Here, then, is another, one that we have just announced (we emphasize in the passage the word 'concrete'; all other emphasis is Schmitt's, even if the English translation we are quoting [which will be slightly modified] does not always point it out):

> But the fact that the substance of the political is contained in the context of a *concrete* antagonism (*konkrete Gegensätzlichkeit*) is still expressed in everyday language (*der landläufige Sprachgebrauch*), even where the awareness of the extreme case (of 'a case of war': *das Bewusstsein des 'Ernstfalles'*) has been entirely lost.
>
> This becomes evident in daily speech and can be exemplified by two obvious phenomena. First, all political concepts, images and terms have a *polemical* meaning (*einen polemischen Sinn*). They are focused on a *concrete* conflict (*eine konkrete Gegensätzlichkeit*) and are bound to a *concrete* situation (*an eine konkrete Situation gebunden*); the result (which manifests itself in war or revolution) is a friend–enemy grouping (*Freund–Feindgruppierung*), and they turn into empty and ghostlike (spectral) abstractions (*werden zu leeren und gespenstischen Abstraktionen*) when this situation disappears. Words such as state, republic, society, class, as well as sovereignty, constitutional state, absolutism, dictatorship, economic planning, neutral or total state, and so on, are incomprehensible if one does not know *concretely* (*in concreto*) who is to be affected, combated, refuted, or negated by such terms. Above all the polemical character determines the usage by language of the word *political* itself, regardless of whether the adversary is designated as 'apolitical' ('*unpolitisch*') (in the sense of: foreign to the world [*weltfremd*], who is lacking the [sense of the] *concrete* [*das Konkrete verfehlend*]), or vice versa if one wants to disqualify or denounce him as political in order to portray oneself as 'apolitical' (in the sense of: purely objective (*rein sachlich*)

purely scientific, purely moral, purely juristic, purely aesthetic, purely economic, or on the basis of similar purities) and thereby superior.[11]

This would be the first of the two announced phenomena. One may already wonder whether Schmitt places his own discourse – and within it this very passage, precisely – in the order of the 'purely objective' or that of the 'purely scientific'. The doubts we have already formulated relative to his theoretical neutrality would not be dissipated by the allusion to 'everyday language'. This language must not mystify. Schmitt cannot analyse an 'everyday language' from the standpoint of a discursive instance that would be superior or foreign to it. The words and syntax forming the framework of his book forever belong to 'everyday language'. No refinement can extract them from it, if only because of the natural language in which they are found, which forbids any absolute formalization. A single indication would suffice to confirm this once again: Schmitt constantly considers it indispensable to justify his choice of terms – beginning with the words 'friend', 'enemy', 'war', or 'civil war' – by reference to everyday or predominant usage in such and such a natural European language: Greek, Latin, English. There is no other criterion for these quotations, and no other guarantee, than the statistical reference to the ordinary usage of the natural language.

The second of the two announced phenomena belongs to the logic already evoked in parentheses, when Schmitt names war and revolution as the *two* manifestations of the friend/enemy figure. This alternative had already marked a sort of logical contradiction in Schmitt's development, to the extent that he claimed to align his definition of the political on the possibility of exterior war, and then referred to Plato, to *pólemos* so sharply distinguished from *stásis*. Now, though, in order to describe the second phenomenon, Schmitt must transport the entire polemical necessity of the discourse analysed hitherto *in general* to the order of *domestic* politics. But instead of presenting this alternative (foreign affairs/domestic politics) as a pair of symmetrical possibilities, he considers the interiorization, as it were, the becoming-civil of this polemic, as a weakening of the political unity of the State. Not of the political in general, but of this *State* form of the political that Schmitt intends to distinguish, whereas he often uses it as the *télos* or guiding thread of his definition of the political. But for all that, it would be a mistake to neglect the initial warnings of the work. On the very first page, there is a reminder that the concept of the State presupposes the concept of the political, not the other way round, even if the State – this particular modality of the mode of existence of the people (*Volk*) – lays down the law in 'decisive' moments and even if, therefore, it constitutes, with regard to all thinkable 'statuses', the Status itself, the Status *par excellence* (*der Status schlechthin*), the stasis or the irreducible static stance [*statique*] that we have linked back up – on a suggestion from Schmitt himself, and at the price of considerable difficulties – with *stásis*.[12] The State is the Status. Only the State can bestow status on the political, supposing that should be necessary. For even if he denounces the inadequacy of the vicious circle (*ein unbefriedigender Zirkel*), the errors and meanderings induced by this equation (the State = the political), can it not be said that at the precise moment when he distinguishes them, Schmitt continues to make one the teleological pole of the other? Does he not see the State as the political *par excellence*, that which serves as an exemplary guide for the definition of the political? If this were the case, despite the precautions we have just evoked and the wealth of differentiated analyses that such prudence and carefulness allow, Schmitt would still belong (and he would undoubtedly admit to this readily, at least concerning this particular point) to what he himself identifies as the German tradition of the doctrine of the State in its Hegelian form. With regard to society, this doctrine considers the State other than and superior to it (*qualitativ verschieden und etwas Höheres*).[13] Our hypothesis is that the path, at once continuous and discontinuous, coherent and – willy-nilly – self-critical (or auto-critical?), separating *The Concept of the Political* (1932) from *The Theory of the Partisan* (1962) is thoroughly informed by this logical matrix: the State presupposes the political, to be sure, hence it is logically distinguished from it; but the analysis of the political, strictly. speaking, and its irrreducible core, the friend/enemy configuration, can only privilege, from the beginning and as its sole guiding thread, the State form of this configuration – in other words, the friend or enemy *qua* citizen.

In 'everyday language' a second signal could be found to confirm that everything in politics is said in the polemical mode. It is that 'in the modes of expression of the polemic everydayness interior to state affairs (*In der Ausdrucksweise der innerstaatlichen Tagespolemik*) [the English translation gives: 'in usual domestic polemics'], the adjective 'political' is most often used today in the sense of 'party politics' ('*parteipolitisch*'). This does mark the absence of 'objectivity' ('*Unsachlichkeit*') of all political 'decisions'; it can provide only the 'reflection' (*Reflex*) of the discriminations between friend and enemy in so far as it is 'immanent' to all political behaviour. The 'depoliticization' at which some of these manoeuvres aim is but a ruse designed to promote and impose a party politics. Schmitt's diagnostic is one of a weakening of the State. When the thought of the 'political unit' ('that of the State', specifies Schmitt in parentheses), 'loses its force (*seine Kraft verliert*)', internal antagonisms win out in terms of 'intensity' over the unit or the community on which the foreign affairs are based. From this point the 'real possibility of combat' (*die reale Möglichkeit des Kampfes*), which should be ever-present (*vorhanden*) 'when one is talking about the political', no longer refers to war between units of peoples organized into States or Empires but, 'logically', 'coherently', to civil war.[14] This weakening of the State calls for 'internal pacification' and attends the rise of the concept of the 'domestic, [or internal], enemy', a public enemy for which public law had a name in the Greek democracies as well as in Rome, as Schmitt recalls (*polémios* or *hostis*[15]).

We must attempt to shed light here on at least two concepts and emphasize several typical problems. At stake each time is the obscure status of a possibility or eventuality said to be 'real' and 'present'. It is only under the condition of this 'real possibility' (*reale Möglichkeit*), under the condition that it 'remain present' (*vorhanden bleiben*), that the 'concept of the enemy has its meaning'. We have already alluded to this, and must return to it now.

How can Schmitt, at one and the same time, privilege the State (even if he does not reduce the political to it), base the concept of enemy on the possibility of war between States, and nevertheless symmetrically align, as he does, exterior war and civil war – as if the enemy were sometimes the foreigner, sometimes the fellow citizen? The answer to this question would seem to lie in the prevailing determination of civil war in this analysis. At once both a paradox and a piece of good sense, this determination establishes civil war as a war between two States, a war in view of the State, a war between a weakened State and a potential State to be constituted, a war for the seizure or reconstitution of State power. War within a State would be but one case of war in general, war in the proper sense – that is, war between States. This specification is given in passing, in parentheses, when Schmitt seems to be aligning symmetrically the two concepts of the enemy with the two concepts of war, civil or domestic war and exterior war. In truth, there is only one concept of war, and the notion of *real possibility* as present (*vorhanden*) ensures the synthetic mediation between the two predicates:

> For to the enemy concept belongs the ever present possibility of combat (*im Bereich des Realen liegende Eventualität eines Kampfes*). All peripherals must be left aside from this term, including military details and the development of weapons technology. War is armed combat between organized political entities; civil war

is armed combat within an organized unit (*but called up into question again by this very fact*). (We emphasize this last phrase in parentheses: *dadurch aber problematisch werdenden.*)[16]

In both cases, it is an armed combat. In view of killing. 'Weapon' designates here, in the concept of its essence, the means in view of 'physical' death, as the killing of a man (*ein Mittel physischer Tötung von Menschen*). The death of a *human being*, thus implied in this concept of the enemy – that is, in all war, exterior or civil war – is neither natural death, since the enemy must be killed, nor murder, for wartime killing is not seen as a crime. The war crime is something else again; it would consist in transgressing this law to revert to the savageness of a violence that no longer respects the laws of war and the rights of people (Schmitt doesn't like that at all, although he is quicker to denounce this transgression on the part of the stranger or enemy). What is said here of the enemy cannot be indifferent to what is said of the friend, since these two concepts co-determine one another. But the correlation can formally follow *three logical chains*:

1. One can infer symmetrically that there is no friend without this possibility of killing which establishes a non-natural community. Not only could I enter into a relationship of friendship only with a *mortal*, but I could love in friendship only a mortal at least exposed to so-called violent death – that is, exposed to being killed, *possibly by myself*. And by myself, in lovence itself, in an essential, not an accidental, manner. To love in love or friendship would always mean: I can kill you, you can kill me, we can kill ourselves. Together or one another, masculine or feminine. Therefore, in all cases, we *already* are (*possibly*, but this possibility is, precisely, real) dead for one another. We shall later question in several ways this possibility that intersects with the one Freud analyses in his own style, under the heading of ambivalence, during a war and exactly in 'Thoughts for the Times on War and Death' (1915).[17]

2. But to this logic one can, precisely, *oppose opposition*: what is true of the enemy (I can or I must kill you, and vice versa) is the very thing that suspends, annuls, overturns or, at the very least, represses, transfigures or sublimates friendship, which is therefore simultaneously the same (repressed) thing and *something altogether different*. What is said of the enemy is not symmetrical and cannot be said of the friend, even under the heading of structural or shared conditions of possibility. Friendship would consist in the suspension of this structure of possibility. To love in love or in friendship (unless the distinction which interests us would pass at this exact place between the two, and 'killing' would be an affair of love, not of

friendship), would precisely be the opposite of killing, of this putting to death, this putting of death (*mise de mort*), this deadly stake – even if, as Freud recalls, the most categorical, the most unconditional 'thou shalt not kill' confirms, and hence *says*, the real possibility that the *interdict* orders to be interrupted while expressing it.

3. Let us not forget that the political would precisely be that which thus endlesly *binds* or *opposes* the friend–enemy/enemy–friend couple in the drive or decision of death, in the putting to death or in the stake of death. We were speaking of the political enemy at the beginning of this analysis. A hypothesis, then: and what if another lovence (in friendship or in love) were bound to an affirmation of life, to the endless repetition of this affirm- ation, only in seeking its way (in loving its way, and this would be *phileín* itself) in the step beyond the political, or beyond *that* political as the horizon of finitude, putting to death and putting of death? The *phileín* beyond the political or another politics for loving, another politics to love, for love (*à aimer*)? Must one dissociate or associate altogether differently *pólis*, *politeía*, *philía*, *Érōs*, and so forth? If a choice between these three hypotheses and these three logical chains were simply or clearly possible, we would make that choice, we would choose one immediately. In this very place.

Hence we must be patient at the crossroads and endure this *undecidable trivality*. Without it – and this is the thesis and the decision – no decision would be possible, nor ever any friendship. There are we. In this very place? No, there.

Let us return to Schmitt, who names this putting to death unequivocally. He sees in it a sense of ontological origination (*im Sinne einer seinsmässigen Ursprünglichkeit*) that one must recognize in the words 'enemy' and 'combat'; but first of all and on the backdrop of a fundamental anthropology or ontology of 'human life': it is a 'combat' (*'Kampf'*), and every person is a 'combatant' (*'Kämpfer'*), says Schmitt, with the inverted commas necessary in the ontological distinction of this definition. This does not so much mean that the being-for-death of this human life cannot be separated from a being- for-putting-to-death or for-death-in-combat. One may induce the natural- ness of this determination (it is the plight of all 'beasts' who would ignore the law and eat each other from one species to another), as well as the indispensable rupture with naturalness (laws of war and non-cannibalistic respect for individuals of the same species). One would say, in a Hegelian sense, that a being-for-death that would not be a being-for-putting-to- death would still be too natural or simply biological.[18] As for this originary and ontological sense, war between enemies cannot be reduced either to competition or intellectual discussion, nor to a simply symbolic struggle.

Just as hostility is entirely dependent on the *real possibility* of this putting-to-death, so also, correlatively, there is no friendship independent of this deadly drive – which is not necessarily to say, this criminal drive. The deadly drive of the friend/enemy proceeds from life, not from death, not from some attraction of death by death or for death. This deadly necessity could not be purely psychological, although it is anthropological. Impossible as it may seem and, in truth, remain for us, what would have to be thought is a hostility without affect or, at least, without an individual or 'private'[19] affect, a purified aggressivity, with all passion and all psychology removed: a pure hostility and, ultimately, a purely philosophical one. As we shall see below, Lenin is, for Schmitt, an illustrious representative – and a radical one, too – of such a pure hostility, but in a tradition whose first moment, in *The Theory of the Partisan*, is extremely difficult to determine.

This possibility can remain a possibility, and this is why it becomes the object of an analysis and a report which make a claim to *neutrality* – indeed, to some kind of positivism in the diagnostic: Schmitt says it is not bellicist, pacifist, militarist or imperialist – it is, all in all, purely theoretical. (We have just expressed doubts about this kind of theoreticity which can be nothing else but a cunning or a strategy indissociable from the political practice of Schmitt himself.) But even if this possibility remains a possibility, it must already be, or still be, *concrete*, 'real', and, to this extent, 'present'. The realization is but the passage to the limit, the extreme accomplishment, the *éskhaton* of an *already real* and *already present* possibility. The realization is not the actualization of a possible but something altogether different: the radicalization of a possible *reality* or a *real* possibility. Here we are no longer in the conventionally Aristotelian opposition of potentiality and act. This is why *Realisierung* should not be translated, as it has been, by 'actualization':

> The friend, enemy and combat concepts receive their real meaning (*ihren realen Sinn*) precisely because they refer to the real possibility of physical killing (*auf die reale Möglichkeit der physischen Tötung*). War follows from enmity, for war is the existential negation of the enemy (*seinsmässige Negierung eines anderen Seins*). It is the most extreme realization of enmity (*die äußerste Realisierung der Feindschaft*). It does not have to be common, normal, something ideal, or desirable. But it must nevertheless remain *present as a real possibility* (*als reale Möglichkeit vorhanden bleiben*) for as long as the concept of the enemy remains valid.[20]

The logic of this discourse implements a strategy that is at once original (a displacement of the traditional concept of possibility) and classic (in the recourse to a condition of possibility in a transcendental-ontological type of analysis). This logic *is* this strategy. It consists in a sophisticated (or ingenuous or naive) oscillation between two *situations*, two *stratifications* of the political: sometimes the political is a particular and grounded stratum (with the following consequence: you may very well live something other than politics, or, if you will, beyond politics, and you may love your (political) enemy; but you will not love him politically, you will love him from another angle: as friend, lover, neighbour, human being – the political should not be confused with something else, etc.); sometimes the political, *qua real possibility*, invades the entire fundamental or grounding stratum of existence, whether individual or communal. All the eventualities we have just summarily considered would then be excluded or contaminated in advance by the real possibility of the very thing from which they are cut. This fundamentalist stratification makes the political *at once* both a regional stratum, a particular layer, however grounding the layer is, *and* the supplementary or overdetermining determination cutting through all other regions of the human world or of the cultural, symbolic, or 'spiritual' community. This is what allows Schmitt to affirm that 'all of the concepts of the spiritual sphere (*der geistigen Sphäre*), including the concept of spirit (*Geist*)' must be 'understood in terms of concrete political existence'. They cannot be neutral or neutralizable, nor can they be reduced to unity; they are 'pluralistic': 'each nation has its own concept of nation', and so forth. One can see what such a warning frees for the differentiated analysis of all these concepts. But one can also sense to what alliance of politicism and empiricism it can expose itself.

This is the strategy of presupposition (*Voraussetzung*). In some of its features, it could be analogous to Heidegger's existential analytic. This said, it always demands that the presupposition of *real possibility* or *eventuality* be *present* in a determined (*vorhanden*) mode. And this presupposed presence is that of political decision: the decision deciding who the enemy is. The question 'who' is at the heart of the principle, it summons and commands [*mande et commande*]. The major moments of political decision are those of the response to the question: 'who is the enemy?'. Cromwell is exemplary here in his jubilant denunciation of '*The Enemies to the very Being of these Nations*': '*Why, truly, your great Enemy is the Spaniard. He is a natural enemy. He is naturally so; he is naturally so throughout – by reason of that enmity that is in him against whatsoever is of God . . . enmity is put into him by God.*' He is '*the natural enemy, the providential enemy*' [in English in the text], 'and he who considers him to be an "*accidental enemy*" is "not well acquainted with Scripture and the things of God".'[21]

Victorious war and revolution belong neither to the 'social' nor to the 'ideal'. Military combat is not the pursuit of politics by other means, as in the Clausewitzian definition, 'generally incorrectly cited'. War has its own rules and perspectives, its strategies and tactics, but they presuppose (*voraussetzen*) a political decision (*politische Entscheidung*). They presuppose, in fact, that this decision, naming 'who is the enemy' (*wer der Feind ist*), is preliminary (*bereits vorliegt*). It is no easy task to determine the place assigned by Schmitt to this pure preliminary decision, nor is it easy to know if, *qua* free act, it breaks with or is in accord with the state of belonging to a people, group, class, etc. In short, it is no easy task to decide whether this decision supposes, rends, undermines or produces the community; or to decide what binds it to itself in a friendly attraction or a self-conservation which resembles *philía* or *philautía*. The fact remains that this allegation of presupposition, always present as real possibility, allows at one and the same time for war to be waged as the political's condition of possibility without it being for all that, in any respect, the aim, the finality or even the content of the political!

Let us read Schmitt emphasizing the word 'presupposition':

> War is neither the aim nor the purpose nor even the very content of politics. But as a real possibility it is an ever present *presupposition* (*die als reale Möglichkeit immer vorhandene* Voraussetzung) which determines in a characteristic way human action and thinking and thereby creates a specifically political behaviour.[22]

This is neither the time or the place to follow up the decisive occurrences of this surprising and strategically precious concept of 'real possibility'. It would also be possible to see it as a rhetorical ploy in a disguised polemic. Let us be content with situating the play with the sensitive notion of neutrality which the ploy, for example, allows, simultaneously in the theoretical sense (a scientific, phenomenological or ontological discourse which analyses or describes without taking sides) and in the polemico-political sense (a State that has not declared war). The real possibility of 'real possibility', as one might say, enables two contradictory propositions to be held successively or simultaneously: yes, neutrality is always possible, but no, it is impossible, unless it be the end of the political. And the enemy (O enemies, there is no enemy!'). And thereby, the end of the friend ('O my friends, there is no friend!'). The very concept of neutrality, as we shall see, is swept away by its own possibility; it contradicts itself and is destroyed in itself. There is a neutrality of the neutral, but it cannot be found politically. One would be friend or enemy, friend and enemy before all possible neutrality, yet that would not keep neutrality from being possible. How is this; how could this be possible? This question has especial import to us in that a certain thought of the neutral (which is certainly not political neutrality, but cannot, in any case, remain foreign to its grammar) will, in this century, notably in the work of Blanchot, have been bound to an experience and a thought of friendship that we shall strive to hear later.

For Schmitt, the criterion of the friend/enemy distinction does not in fact entail that a 'determined people' should have to be for all eternity the friend or the enemy of another. This suggests that the 'decision' we have been talking about is not linked to communal appurtenance, is not caused by it, even though the decision reaffirms appurtenance. Nor does it mean that 'a state of neutrality is not possible (*möglich*) or could not be politically meaningful (*politisch sinnvoll*)':

> As with every political concept, the neutrality concept is also subject to the ultimate presupposition of a real possibility of a friend–enemy grouping (*unter dieser letzten Voraussetzung einer realen Möglichkeit der Freund-und Feindgruppierung*). Should only neutrality prevail in the world, then not only war but also neutrality would come to an end. The politics of avoiding war terminates, as does all politics, whenever the possibility of fighting disappears. What always matters is the possibility of this decisive eventuality taking place (*die Möglichkeit dieses entscheidenden Falles*), the actual war (*des wirklichen Kampfes*), and the decision whether this eventuality is or is not the given case (*die Entscheidung darüber, ob dieser Fall gegeben ist oder nicht*).[23]

(Such a singular decision that decides if it is the case or not, if an eventuality is or is not 'given' – is this an active or a passive decision? Conscious or unconscious? Free or not? Responsible or not? A decision as to what is given, and to whom, relative to knowing who, 'who is who,' etc.? One does not know, with this decision, whether a decisionism informs it in depth or, on the contrary, whether it does not negate such a decisionism, sweep it away, forget it, unless the decision would always be linked to oblivion itself.)

The exception is the rule – that, perhaps, is what this thought of real possibility thinks. The exception is the rule of what takes place, the law of the event, the real possibility of its real possibility. The exception grounds the decision on the subject of the case or the eventuality. The fact that the case or situation (*dieser Fall*) arises only exceptionally (*nur ausnahmsweise*) does not suspend, sublate or annul (*hebt . . . nicht auf*) its 'determining character'. On the contrary, this exceptionality grounds (*begründet*) the eventuality of the event. An event is an event, and a decisive one, only if it is exceptional. An event as such is always exceptional.

As for war, this is a paradoxical consequence, concerning killing also, which here is not just one example among others: it is because killing is exceptional that it remains the decisive ordeal. And, one might say, the more exceptional, unusual, improbable it is, the more it weighs decisively on decision. A diagnostic for our times: today, notes Schmitt, if wars are less frequent, less usual and *more* exceptional (if that can be said of the exception) than in former times, the 'total' purchase of their power has increased in the same proportion. The real possibility of killing tends to be infinite. That means that today war, the state of war, the case of war (*der Kriegsfall*), still remains the decisive ordeal, the serious thing, the major critical affair, the *krinein* of crisis, the very seriousness of the decision, which in German is called '*Ernstfall*', which also means, in military language, the 'case of war'. The serious decision is the case of war, the absolute hostility which, therefore, always decides between the friend and the enemy. The decision discriminates, we will say, recalling that in Latin *discrimen* is at once separation, distinction, difference and the moment of decision, *instance* in the two senses of the term. Schmitt plays with this word '*Ernstfall*' in inverted commas when he says that 'yet today' the case of war is the 'case of war': '*Auch heute noch ist der Kriegsfall der "Ernstfall"*.'

It is, then, the improbable situation, the exceptional case (*der Ausnahme-fall*), the 'perhaps', perhaps, which carries 'a particularly determinating signification' (or discriminating, decisive: *eine besonders entscheidende . . . Bedeutung*); but it is the improbable situation, and no other, which, exceptionally, *qua* exception, unveils the essence, the centre and the heart of things. It is that which may not happen, that which happens only in so far as it might just as well not happen, this undecidable eventuality *qua* real possibility, that informs decisions and forms truth [*fait la décision et fait la vérité*]. This undecidable decision bestows the force of unveiling. This deciding signification which unveils the kernel of things (*den Kern der Dinge enthüllende Bedeutung*) accrues to the decision. The unveiling of things, of the heart of things in the coming asunder of decision, is perhaps accomplished not in the act of war which bears death, but surely in the asundering possibility, of a killing, in this possibility *qua* real and present possibility. The latter can uncover the heart of things only in undressing the other, in uncovering the possibility of what Schmitt called above 'physical killing'.

Hence the oscillation and the association between actuality/effectivity and possibility. As if it were sufficient that an event be possible for it to happen, for it to have already actually taken place in its very perhaps, at the end of the sentence naming its possibility (this is perhaps the spring of the teleiopoetic or quasi-messianic logic that we were analysing above in terms of Nietzschean statements, whose possibility, however, verily haunts all statements. Yes, haunts them. For what is this 'real possibility' haunting Schmitt if not the very law of spectrality?). Oscillation and association, the conjunctive disjunction binding real actuality/effectivity and possibility – that is how the conjunction conjuncts and disjuncts at one and the same time. It is found at the end of the paragraph speaking to the 'case of war' as 'case of war' (we stress actual/effective and possibility):

> For only in actual/effective combat (*im wirklichen Kampf*) is revealed the most extreme consequence (*die äusserste Konsequenz*) of the political grouping of friend and enemy. From this most extreme possibility (*Von dieser extremsten Möglichkeit her*) human life gains (*gewinnt*) its specifically political tension (*Spannung*).[24]

This tension is to be conquered: it is not a given fact, it is conquered like a place to which one gains access; it is won as a victory is, when a resistance must be overcome; it is conquered as an intensity which can always increase and gain *on itself* out to its extreme limit.

The extreme consequence of these propositions, the one which would seem to us as unavoidable as it is properly disastrous, is of course not drawn by Schmitt, at least not in this form, but we must draw it: if it is true, as has been said above, that the rarer or the more improbable the situation of exception or of decision (war, hostility, the political event as such, etc.), the more decisive, intense and revealing it is, and in the end the more it politicizes (as would be the case in the modernity of the rarefaction of wars, according to the Schmitt of 1932), then one must conclude that rarefaction intensifies the tension and the revealing power (the 'truth' of the political): the less war there is, the more the hostility, etc. This is less a default of 'common sense' than it would appear, to be sure, but it does inevitably lead to a change in all the signs, *and therefore to having to measure politicization in terms of the degree of depoliticization.*

What would the symptom of neutralization and depoliticization (*Entpolitisierung*) that Schmitt learnedly denounces in our modernity reveal? In truth, an over- or hyperpoliticization. The less politics there is, the more there is, the less enemies there are, the more there are. The number of friends increases according to exactly the same proportion and in the same proportion. Hence the inversion and the vertigo, hence the mirror reflection in which the 'dying sage' and the 'living fool' reflect themselves. This is in fact the same number and the same calculation. The inversion and the vertigo are not sophisms. These enunciations unfold a structure of decision and of the event, and account for any logic purporting to calculate their incalculable singularity. We are simply formalizing a principle of ruin or spectrality at the heart of this discourse on the political, a discourse of madness allied to an excess of common sense. A double hyperbole, a chiasmus of double hyperbole. When we suggested above that Schmitt did not draw this consequence himself, we specified 'at least not in this form'. For *The Theory of the Partisan* can be considered the intrepid exercise of this paradoxical consequence. Through an exploration of the future of the Second World War and of everything preceding it over centuries, Schmitt analyses a general hyperbolization of the political. But the unleashing of pure hostility appears to him, gives itself over to his diagnostic, through all the phenomena of depoliticization, through everything that is destructive of the classical limits of the political.

Consequently, depoliticization, the 'without politics' which is not necessarily the 'withdrawal of the political',[25] could characterize a world which would no longer be a world, a 'world without politics', reduced to a 'terrestial globe' abandoned by its friends as well as its enemies; in sum, a dehumanized desert. And this is indeed what Schmitt literally says – we shall quote him again. But he could say exactly the opposite (and he will say it later, willy-nilly). In both cases, the 'possibility' of combat remains the arbiter: 'A world in which the possibility (*die Möglichkeit*) of war is utterly (without a remainder: *restlos*) eliminated, a completely pacified globe, would be a world without the distinction of friend and enemy and hence a world without politics.'[26]

This 'world without politics' may present all manner of oppositions, contrasts and competitions, but no enemy (and thus no friend) will be found there, nor this antagonism which 'authorized to shed blood, and kill other human beings'.[27] The allusion to blood is anything but secondary and rhetorical (no more so than in Rosenzweig, or Benjamin – precisely on the theme of state violence). To kill without bloodshed, with the help of new techniques, is perhaps already to accede to a world without war and without politics, to the inhumanity of a war without war. Regardless of whether this 'world without politics' is an ideal (and Schmitt's decision on this subject is clear, even though he pretends to be interested only in the theoretical and neutral determination of political non-neutrality), the only conclusion *The Concept of the Political* purports, then, to hold after this properly phenomenological neutralization of the two 'ideals' is that the 'phenomenon of the political' cannot be grasped or apprehended (*begreifen*) without this reference to the 'real possibility (*die reale Möglichkeit*) of the friend and enemy grouping'.[28] Whatever consequences may be drawn from this 'real possibility' – that is, from the structure of the political – whether these consequences be moral, religious, aesthetic, or economic, they will not be able to reduce the properly political phenomenality of this 'real possibility'. We believe it is necessary to insist on the recurrence of this call to a 'real possibility'. Not only because its concept remains obscure, but because the haunting nature of this recurrence confirms both a difficulty and a necessity. We have just referred to phenomenology (and it is indeed a matter of a phenomenology of the friend as well as of the enemy) because at stake is indeed the 'phenomenon of the political', as Schmitt himself says, and the sense of this phenomenon, the presentation of its presence after the eidetic reduction of everything it is not; but also because what is at stake in the same stroke is indeed a phenomenalization as revelation, manifestation, unveiling.

The three criteria (*reality*, *possibility*, *presence*) intertwine here at the heart of the same 'eventuality'. At the heart of a selfsame eventness of the event. How does the friend/enemy grouping *manifest itself*, how does it *present itself*? How is their 'real possibility' presented or realized, either as possible or as real? How can this reality mark sometimes presence, sometimes possibility itself? In war. In any case in war as an extremity, as the extreme limit of a state of exception, as 'extreme eventuality' (*als extreme Eventualität*). It is on this account that this reality is revealing; it constitutes a fact from which an essence can be read – surely – but read first of all from an uncommon, non-empirical fact, exemplary in a teleological (the *telos* as extreme limit) and paradigmatic sense. The 'presence' (*Vorhandenheit*) thereby manifested in the real possibility, this real or possible presence, is not that of the fact or example, it is that of a *telos*. Not that of a political *telos*, of one or another political end, of one or another politics, but that of the *telos* of the political (life opposed to itself, and not to death, as we recalled above, spirit opposed to itself, the life of spirit opposing itself to itself: there is only life, and this is why, in sum, there are enemies). War, *qua* the 'most extreme (*extremste*) of political means, manifests (*offenbart*) the possibility of this friend/enemy discrimination which 'founds' all political representation; and it has no meaning, it is '*sinnvoll*', as long as this discrimination is 'actually present' (*real vorhanden*), or at least actually possible (*oder wenigstens real möglich*). 'The sole remaining question', Schmitt then concludes, is that of knowing if the friend/enemy grouping which determines the opposition as purely and solely political (not religious, moral, or economic) 'is or is not present as possibility or as real actuality/ effectivity (*als reale Möglichkeit oder Wirklichkeit vorhanden ist oder nicht*)'. The syntax of this question, which we have already cited, does not admit of a decision on whether the double alternative (*oder . . . oder*) is of the order of presence (*vorhanden ist oder nicht*) or of the order of modalities of this presence (real *or* effective/actual possibility, *real* possibility or *real* effectivity/ actuality: *reale Möglichkeit oder Wirklichkeit*). In the first case the grouping of the political (friend/enemy) would always be present, in one mode or another; in the other, it could be present or not. The consequences of these two distinct alternatives – certain, but apparently subtle and fragile – indeed seem limitless: what does 'politically' 'present' mean? And present in this mode (*Vorhandenheit*)? On this subject there is no need to refer to a Heideggerian style of questioning (for example, regarding the *Vorhandenheit*) to recognize the necessity, be it political or not, of these interrogations. Sometimes it is presence itself that seems spectral, a disappearing virtuality of apparition. Sometimes the sole presence (at once permanent and recurrent) figures that to which a call must be made, a despairing call, in order to resist the return of the spectral – in a word, to exorcize, to conjure, to 'repress' the returning ghost [*le revenant*]. As for the meaning of war, and the question of knowing under what condition a war is *sinnvoll*, Schmitt never hesitates: he judges it indubitable that war always has a meaning; war has a meaning, and no politics, no social bond *qua* social bond, has meaning without war, without its real possibility. But this does not necessarily mean that in his eyes war is good, useful, that it has meaning in the moral or religious sense of an ideal or of a *telos* to be attained. It simply means that in order for the concept of war (and hence politics) to have meaning, for the phenomenological and semantic determination of the discourse on war, conditions of possibility must be ascertained. And this is what *The Concept of the Political* purports to do. If it is not a *telos* in the sense of a moral or religious ideal, nor even in the sense of a determined political ideal, this semantico-teleological content is nevertheless intrinsi- cally teleological. Its structure is teleologically immanent, auto- and tauto- teleological (war aims at the death of the enemy, etc.), even if – or, rather, because – this political *telos* is irreducible to any other. But it does seem that, as a conscious or unconscious strategy, the Schmittian phrase strives to dissociate the two teleological values (war is not good in view of another end, moral, religious, etc., but it has its end in itself) while constantly oscillating from one to the other, going so far, in the operation of a 'partisan', as to smuggle in one for the other. This seems to be made possible – and easy – by the constant *presence*, by the surviving presence – in any case by the presence of war 'yet today' – as 'real possibility'. Even if today, in the form of 'the very last war of humanity', wars are waged in a particularly inhuman manner, morally discrediting the enemy to the point of making him an inhuman monster and thereby pretending to 'exceed the political' (über das Politische hinausgehend [Schmitt's emphasis]), making the enemy someone who must be 'annihilated', not only driven back and 'led back within its boundaries' (Schmitt's emphasis, and one wonders what difference he sees between 'physical killing', whose aim he judges indispensable, and the annihilation which he seems to condemn. He would no doubt answer that physical killing concerns the individual life of soldiers but not the annihilation of a people or a State); well, this war 'yet today' attests, despite everything, to the presence of the political as 'real possibility': 'The possibility of such war is particularly illustrative (besonders deutlich) of the fact that war as a real possibility (als reale Möglichkeit) is still present today (heute noch vorhanden ist), and this fact is crucial for the friend-and-enemy antithesis and for the knowledge [or recognition, the determinating identification, the accounting, Erkenntnis] of the political.'[29]

We have already sensed and suggested that when Schmitt says that this is clear (deutlich) he is relying on a logic of inference, of proof, of indication and of testimony which allows him always to decide for the presence of the political. He decides thus either in terms of positive and univocal signs of the presence of the political, or in terms of what the disappearance of these signs witnesses of their possible and permanent presence – indeed demonstrates it, a contrario, through a denegation which would indiscernibly be in the things themselves, in real history and in the Schmittian discourse – in truth, in the entire tradition which he represents and repeats with so much cunning as authority. This disavowal potentializes a logic of negativity that will always allow, from The Concept of the Political to The Theory of the Partisan, for the multiplication of refined intuitions – so crucial for an analysis of our times – while at the same time diagnosing a depoliticization which, in sum, would be but the supplementary and inverted symptom, the abyssal hyperbole, of a hyperpoliticization. This depoliticization would apparently blur the criteria for boundaries of the political; it would neutralize them only to expand the control of the political to the point of absolute hostility, in its most pristine philosophical purity.

We shall see how absolute hostility would then be the affair of philosophy, its very cause.

Notes

1. *Die endliche und die unendliche Analyse*, 1937, GW, Bd XVI [trans., *Analysis Terminable and Interminable*, Standard Edition 23, p. 246].

2. CP, p. 63; p. 63 [The English translation has omitted the quotation marks.]

3. For example, ibid., p. 64; p. 65.

4. Ibid. [Translation modified.]

5. Ibid., p. 64; p. 65.

6. 472e.

7. See above, pp. 90–91. This would suffice to justify circumspection in having recourse to this opposition, and especially to the single word *stásis*. But there is more. Recalling that 'Plato shares with all his contemporaries' the 'logic' of the opposition of complementarity between *pólemos* and *stásis*, Nicole Loraux adds, by way of drawing interesting consequences, the following point: 'But the insistence on emphasizing that, in the case of civil war, *stásis* is a name is especially Platonic. Only a name: a simple appellation, indeed, as a passage from *Laws* suggests, an inaccurate appellation. Defining "the worst scourge for a city", the Athenian-nomothete is at great pains to contest the pertinence of the standard appellation of civil war, "whose right name would indeed be rather *diastasis* than *stásis*."' 'Cratyle à l'épreuve de *Stásis*', in *Revue de philosophie ancienne*, no. 1, 1987, pp. 56–7.

8. 473a.

9. For Benjamin, spectral (*gespenstische*) is the force of law in the figure of the police, such that it can assure politics and protect the State in 'the life of civilized States'. We have analysed the implications of this passage of Benjamin's 'For a critique of violence' in *Force de loi* (Galilée 1994) ['Force of Law: The "Mystical Foundation of Authority"', in *Deconstruction and the Possibility of Justice*, ed. Drucilla Cornell, Michel Rosenfeld and David Gray Carlson, Routledge, New York and London 1992].

10. Whether by polemical strategy or not, whether or not he was sincere (that is the whole question), Schmitt did not fail, here or there, to present such and such of his incriminated political discourses as acts of knowledge, as the *neutral diagnostics* of an analysis, not as Nazi or anti-Semitic interventions or position-takings. This was the case, in exemplary fashion, in the course of his interrogation by Professor Robert Kempner, a German immigrant and American prosecutor at Nuremberg after the war. Asked if he had intended to contribute to the 'institution' of a new international order of right in conformity with the ideas of Hitler, Schmitt answered that he did not do this in conformity with Hitler's ideas, and that he was not searching to *institute* [*instituer*], only to *diagnose*. This did not prevent him from presenting himself elsewhere as an adventurer of intelligence who had always assumed the risks of his actions and never sought to avoid paying their price. The same ruse – the same answer, in any case – before a sentence refusing 'Jewish authors' responsibility not only in the development of the theory of space (*Raum*) but in 'the creation of anything at all'. 'Do you deny', Kempner then inquires, 'that this passage is in the purest Goebbels style?' Schmitt denies it, of course, in its form and content. He requests that the 'serious scientific context' of the passage be taken into consideration: 'in its intent, method, and formulation, it is a pure diagnosis. . . . Everything I stated, in particular in this passage, was intended as scholarship, as a scholarly thesis I would defend before any scholarly body in the world'

(pp. 98–100 of the English translation of this interrogation, presented by Joseph W. Bendersky: 'Schmitt at Nuremberg', in *Telos*, New York, special issue, 'Carl Schmitt: Enemy or Foe?' no. 72, Summer 1987).

11. CP, pp. 30–32; ibid.

12. See above, pp. 108–9, n. 13.

13. CP, p. 25, p. 24.

14. Ibid., p. 32; p. 32.

15. A long note gives numerous historical details on this point: pp. 44–7 (the English translation has excised them). For example, this phrase of the Comité de salut public (10 October 1793), quoted in E. Friesenhahn, *Le Serment politique* (*The Political Oath*): 'Since the day the French people manifested its will, everything opposed to it is outside the sovereign; everything outside the sovereign is an enemy.... Between the people and its enemies there is nothing left in common but the sword.'

16. CP, p. 33; p. 32 [translation modified].

17. An attentive reading of 'Thoughts for the Times...' in this context would undoubtedly be necessary. To my knowledge, Schmitt never showed much interest (no more than Heidegger in any case, and this fact is by no means without import) in someone he could have classed, according to his own criteria, among the authentic thinkers of the political – that is, those beginning with a pessimistic vision of mankind. Man is not originally good – according to Schmitt, this is the fundamental thesis of a theory of the political. It is also the resigned thesis of 'Thoughts for the Times on War and Death', which, in addition, on the subject of the essential violence of the State, piles up statements of a Schmittian or Benjaminian sort. Freud indeed insists on the fact that if the State forbids the individual from having recourse to injustice, it is not in order to suppress injustice but to maintain a monopoly on it. Concerning the 'optimistic' answer to the question of man ('man is born noble and good'), Freud declares it 'of no value': 'we do not have to concern ourselves with it here'. The interdict 'thou shalt not kill' confirms that we descend from a generation of murderers. Not to speak of the law of ambivalence inscribing hatred in the very mourning of our friends, and of a love which is as old as the drive to murder. The epitaph and the funeral oration are a theme of Chapter 2. To this fundamental violence, Freud never proposes (nor does Schmitt, for that matter) anything but compensations in the name of a life which, however, does not know death, and does not have to deal with it as such (we shall clarify this paradoxical point concerning Schmitt). The *si vis vitam, para mortem* that Freud proposes as a substitute for the *si vis pacem para bellum* at the end of 'Thoughts for the Times' only confirms this fundamental political pessimism. That could be verified on every page of *Group Psychology and the Analysis of the Ego*, and is illustrated by the Schopenhauerian fable that Freud enjoys quoting in this context: some porcupines give up cuddling each other to ward off the cold: their quills hurt them. Obliged one cold winter day to huddle together, they end up, finding a mean distance between attraction and repulsion.

18. Proximity to Heidegger. Does the being-for-death of *Dasein* include, in the structure of its essence, war and combat (*Kampf*) or not? We have taken up this point in 'L'oreille de Heidegger' ['Heidegger's Ear, Philopolemology (Geschlecht IV),' in John Sallis (ed.) *Reading Heidegger*, trans. John P. Leavey, Jr, Bloomington: Indiana University Press 1991]. Among the many themes of the chiasmus through which the Heideggerian and Schmittian discourse intersect in a distancing and an opposition, there is not only the theme of technics (which, according to both thinkers, seems only to

depoliticize or neutralize – and this only within certain limits, limits we are approaching in this century which we, however, believe to be delivered over to technics), there is also the theme of death. But here divergence prevails. This may seem paradoxical, but the real possibility of putting-to-death (execution), which is an irreducible condition of the political, and indeed the ontological structure of human existence, means for Schmitt neither an ontology of death or of dying nor a serious consideration of a nothingness (*néant*) or of a *Nichtigkeit*; nor, in another code, the position of a death principle or instinct. Execution indeed proceeds from an oppositional negativity, but one which belongs to life through and through, in so far as life *opposes itself in affirming itself*. Not to life against death, but to life against life, to spirit against spirit, as *The Concept of the Political* concludes, here again, in Hegelian *and* anti-Hegelian expressions (Hegel would not have affirmed as easily as Schmitt that spirit, or life as the life of the spirit, does not confront death itself). This affirmation of life (in the war *of life against life*) culminates precisely in a condemnation of modern technologism which would strive to neutralize the political (and the politicity of technics) by relying on the antithesis mechanical/organic *qua* the antithesis the dead/the living: 'A life confronted with nothing more than death is no longer life; it is pure impotence and distress.' Life can only love life, even when it is opposed to itself. One should therefore (Schmitt does not say so) 'love' one's enemy, at least in so far as he is living. To be put to death, the enemy must precisely be a living being. 'The person knowing no other enemy than death, and who sees in this enemy but an unhinged mechanism, is closer to death than to life, and the facile antithesis that opposes the organic to the mechanical stems itself from a primitive mechanism (*etwas Roh-Mechanisches*)' (p. 95). We shall come across the logic of this evaluation of the 'technicized earth' and economic planning once again, in *Ex Captivitate Salus* (Greven Verlag, Cologne 1950), with a pathos more marked by history, and a stress that is not so far from that of Heidegger.

19. But what would a purely collective or communal affect be without the least individual or 'private' dimension, a purely public affect? Yet it is essential to Schmitt to have this undiscoverable limit. He is hopelessly seeking the signs of such an affect everywhere – linguistic clues, testimonies that would at least come to mark the desire or the need of this impossible distinction. This is why he would undoubtedly judge our indistinct usage illegitimate and lacking in rigour (but who does not use them in this way? And why, fundamentally, are they thus used? What is the shared root, the analogy, of such use?) of words such as *philía*, 'friendship', 'love', 'enmity', 'hostility', and so forth, as long as we do not specify if it is a matter of feeling or not, of a universal or political feeling (that is, from one community to the other), of private or public feeling, one being heterogeneous to the other. *Phileîn* or *amare*, for example, would not mean 'to love' in the Christian sense of love of one's neighbour. A footnote to the 1963 edition of *The Concept of the Political* (p. 118) recalls that in the New Testament, enemy in Latin is *inimicus*, not *hostis*; to love is *diligere*, not *amare*; in Greek, *agapán*, not *phileîn*. The concept of hatred, as a feeling, would have not juridical or political meaning, and the concept of enemy (juridical or political: *hostis*) in no way implies hatred. Alvaro d'Ars: '*hate is no term of law*' [in English]. Spinoza, in the *Theological-Political Treatise*: '*hostem enim imperii non odium sed jus facit*' (ch. XVI).

20. CP, p. 33; p. 33. Derrida's emphasis [translation modified].

21. CP, p. 67; p. 68.

22. CP, pp. 34–5; p. 34. [The English translation has been modified (including,

above all, the restitution of the stress on 'presupposition', absent in translation) to follow Derrida's modifications of the French translation of the German original.]

23. CP, p. 35; pp. 34–5.

24. CP, p. 35; p. 35.

25. We are evidently thinking here of another delimitation and of another beyond-the-political in its traditional form, of another 'withdrawal of the political'. I refer the reader to the rewarding volume with this title (*Le Retrait du politique*, Galilée 1983) which, after *Rejouer le politique* (Galilée 1981), brought together remarkable papers given at the Centre for Philosophical Research on the Political at the Ecole normale supérieure, under the direction of Ph. Lacoue-Labarthe and J.L. Nancy. If my memory serves me well, there is no mention of Schmitt, nor of his concept of depoliticization, in these papers. My work here would be, as a sign of gratitude, a modest and belated contribution to work that was important for my own.

26. CP, p. 35.

27. Ibid.

28. Ibid.

29. Ibid., pp. 36–7.

6

Oath, Conjuration, Fraternization
or the 'Armed' Question

Following its meaning in German (as in so many other
languages), 'friend' is originally only the person to whom a
genealogical bond unites. Originally the friend is but the friend
of blood, the consanguine parent or again the 'parent by alliance'
through marriage, oath of fraternity, adoption or other corresponding institutions.[1]

Carl Schmitt

If, then, you two are friendly to each other, by some tie of
nature (*phúsei pē oikeioí*) you belong to each other.[2]

Plato

We have become attuned to a certain effect of haunting. Where it seems
inaccessible to intuition and concept, the purely concrete starts to resemble
the ghost, just when you start to believe that you can tell them apart. This
is the tormented experience of the inversion of signs. Such an experience
allows itself, then, to be revealed in Schmitt's obsessional insistence on the
'concrete' and on 'real possibility', at the very point at which these values
were opposed to the 'spectral' (*gespenstisch*). We are constantly reminded
that only a *concrete, concretely determined* enemy can awaken the political;
only a real enemy can shake the political out of its slumber and, as we
recall, out of the abstract 'specularity' of its concept; only the concrete can
awaken it to its actual/effective life (as 'the *living* fool that I am', when it
bemoans the fact that there is no longer, or not yet, an enemy). But there
is the spectre, lodged within the political itself; the antithesis of the political
dwells within, and politicizes, the political. The spectre might well be – it
might well already have been, in 1932 – this 'partisan' who no longer
respects the normal conditions and the juridically guaranteed boundaries of

war. And this has not begun today, nor did it begin yesterday, or the day before.

Negativity, disavowal and politics, haunting and dialectics. If there is a politicism in Schmitt, it lies in the fact that it it is not enough for him to define the political by the negativity of polemics or opposition. He defines antagonism or opposition (oppositional negativity in general) – which is not at all the same as defining the political – as teleologically political. The political is all the more political for being antagonistic – certainly, but opposition is all the more oppositional – supreme opposition, *qua* the essence and *telos* of opposition, negation, and contradiction – when it is political. It is impossible here – as it is impossible in any absolute proposition of speculative idealism, and hence of ideal dialectics – to distinguish between subject and predicate. Schmitt does not so much define the political by oppositional negation as define the latter by the political. This inversion stems from a teleological law of power or intensity. The stronger a contradiction or oppositional negativity, the more its intensity tends towards a limit, the more political it is. Example: 'Political antagonism (*der politische Gegensatz*) is the most intense (*intensiviste*) and extreme (*äusserste*) antagonism, and every concrete antagonism (*Gegensätzlichkeit*) becomes that much more political the closer it approaches the most extreme point (*sich dem äussersten Punkte . . . nähert*), that of the friend–enemy grouping.'[3]

It will come as no surprise when this politicism of oppositional negativity calls on Hegel. The discrimination between friend and enemy would also be, in Hegelian terms, an 'ethical difference' (*sittliche Differenz*), the first condition of ethical determination, which does not mean moral determination. The modern definition of hostility, perfectly distinct from enmity, would be due to Hegel and Marx (despite the economistic and hence depoliticizing tendency that would make the latter a nineteenth-century thinker[4]). And if Schmitt evokes this debt to Marx and Hegel, it is not simply to stress that this concept of hostility – in his view the only purely political concept of the political – is also an ethical concept. He is intent on already denouncing the misunderstanding in which modern philosophers begin to apprehend this logic of the political. They tend to avoid it – *qua* the political in sum – in so far as it is linked to a certain concept and to a certain practice of war. Although Hegel may at times show a 'double face', he must be inscribed in the great tradition of 'specifically political' thinkers (Machiavelli, Hobbes, Bossuet, de Maistre, Donoso Cortés, Fichte – 'as soon as he forgets his humanitarian idealism!') who knew how to break with an optimistic anthropology ('Man would be fundamentally and originally good'). In this discourse on Man, on his original innocence or on his accidental or extrinsic corruption, Schmitt denounces a strategy too often enrolled in the service of anti-State liberalism. 'Authentic' political theories, on the other hand, all presuppose a Man essentially 'evil', 'dangerous', a 'dynamic' and 'problematic' being:

> Hegel . . . remains everywhere political in the decisive sense. . . . Of a specifically political nature also is his dialectic of concrete thinking. . . .
>
>   Hegel also offers the first polemically political definition of the bourgeois. The bourgeois is an individual who does not want to leave the apolitical riskless private sphere. He rests in the possession of his private property, and under the justification of his possessive individualism he acts as an individual against the totality. He is a man who finds his compensation for his political nullity in the fruits of freedom and enrichment and above all in the total security of its use. Consequently he wants to be spared bravery and exempted from the danger of a violent death. { *Wissenschaftliche Behandlungsarten des Naturrechts (The Methods of the Science of Natural Right*), 1802, Lasson edn p. 383; Glockner 1 edn p. 499.} Hegel has also advanced a definition of the *enemy* which in general has been evaded by modern philosophers. 'The enemy is the ethical difference [*die sittliche Differenz*] (not in the sense of morality [*nicht im moralischen Sinne*], but in the perspective of 'absolute life' in the 'eternal being of the people'), as the Foreigner to be negatived in his living totality (*als ein zu negierendes Fremdes in seiner lebendigen Totalität*). 'A difference of this sort is the enemy, and this difference, posited in its ethical bearing, exists at the same time as its counterpart, the opposite of the being of its antithesis, i.e., as the nullity of the enemy, and this nullity, commensurate on both sides, is the peril of battle. For ethical life (*für des Sittliche*) this enemy can only be an enemy of the people and itself only a people (*nur ein Volk*). Because single individuality comes on the scene here, it is for the people that the single individual abandons himself to the danger of death.' . . . 'This war is not a war of families against families, but between peoples, and hatred becomes thereby undifferentiated and freed from all personal elements (*von aller Persönlichkeit frei*)'[5]

To remain consistent with itself, this homage to a Hegelian paternity must reach out and embrace Hegel's Marxist posterity. This consistency plays no small role in the notable sympathies this hyper-traditionalist jurist of the Catholic right wing will always have inspired in certain circles of leftist political thought. These 'friends' on the left do not correspond to a fortuitous or psychological formation born of some interpretative confusion. In question is an immense historico-political symptom the law of which remains to be thought. Be this as it may, Schmitt regrets that Hegel's spectre has deserted Berlin to reappear elsewhere: with those of Lenin and Marx in Moscow:

The question is how long the spirit of Hegel (*der Geist Hegel*) has actually resided (*residiert hat*) in Berlin. In any event, the new political tendency which dominated Prussia after 1840 preferred to avail itself of a conservative philosophy of state, especially one furnished by Friedrich Julius Stahl, whereas Hegel wandered to Moscow via Karl Marx and Lenin. His dialectical method became established there and found its *concrete* expression in a new *concrete*-enemy concept, namely that of the international class enemy, and transformed itself, the dialectical method, as well as everything else, legality and illegality, the state, even the compromise with the enemy, into a weapon of this battle. The actuality of Hegel is very much alive in Georg Lukács. [*History and Class Consciousness*, trans. Rodney Livingstone, Merlin Press, London 1971; *Lenin: A Study of the Unity of his Thought*, trans. Nicholas Jacobs, New Left Books, London 1970][6]

The salute to Lenin forms the link between the two texts that we have been distinguishing, opposing and comparing, in order to understand how the second (*The Theory of the Partisan*) confirms the first (*The Concept of the Political*) precisely at that point where the former seems to contradict the latter.

We are unable to follow in detail the argument of a work which, in its time, multiplies in an impressive and often pointed fashion valuable insights into the many transformations taking place in the political space of modernity. Regarding the classical European *jus belli* (interstate war between regular armies), and to the extent that its regulation was ever respected, the partisan remains a marginal figure until the First World War. The preferred example of Schmitt, as it was for Clausewitz, is first the Spanish guerrilla fighting against the Napoleonic army. The modern partisan, on the contrary, leaves this initial marginality, expecting from his enemy no respect for the rights of conventional warfare. In the course of civil war, as of colonial war, the partisan transforms the concept of conventional hostility and blurs its boundaries. Apparently the partisan is no longer an enemy, and has no enemy in the classical sense of the term. Real hostility henceforth extends, through terrorism and counter-terrorism, all the way to extermination. Yet the definition of the partisan will long maintain the tradition of autochthony, the telluric dimension on which we have insisted so much. It is, for example, the autochthony of the Russian partisans against the Napoleonic army, then the readaptation of this 'myth of the national and autochtonomous partisan' by Stalin in the course of the Second World War. This 'myth' serves a worldwide communist politics. With Mao Tse-tung it represents a new stage in the history of the partisan, and therefore in the process of rupture with the classical criteriology of the political and that of the friend/enemy grouping. The partisan not only simply transgresses, he confuses the two classical distinctions (regular/irregular, legal/illegal from the standpoint of constitutional or international law). One of the numerous advantages of these analyses is the precise and differentiated account of the relation to space (land, sea, or aerial space) – that is, *first of all to technics* or to tele-technology (the speed and expanse of transmission, mobilization and motorization) – as one of the essential factors in the mutation of the classical concept of the enemy and even in what had become the 'classical concept' of the partisan.

This question of technics appears *doubly* decisive.

On the one hand, although he does not say so explicitly in this form, the question is found to be at the heart of what Schmitt calls 'a process of concept dissolution', 'a remarkable sign of the times'.[7] Such a dissolution of concepts induces a 'metaphoric' but not necessarily improper use of the partisan concept. Schmitt himself acknowledges having recourse to it. This uncontrollable extension is due in particular to the criteria chosen for the definition of the partisan. These criteria authorize a limitless generalization ('every human being is a being who struggles'; thus he is found to be 'his own partisan', which is practically meaningless). Indispensable as they may be, these criteria are false ones, quasi-concepts, criteria of degree of intensity – that is, indefinitely extensive. Now, along with (1) irregularity and (2) the intensity of political engagement, we find (3) 'the high degree of mobility of active combat'[8] – that is, the appropriation of space by the science of the tele-technical prosthesis.

On the other hand, and as a consequence, this speed of motorization, and hence that of tele-technical automation, produces a break with autochthony. This rupture cuts the telluric roots characteristic not only of the classical enemy but of the first form of the partisan guerrilla war. It must be specified that telluric autochthony, ground warfare, the consideration of geographical configurations, and the lay of the terrain no doubt persist throughout this mutation; Schmitt takes note of this and gives numerous examples: Mao Tse-tung, whose revolution has a 'better telluric base than that of Lenin',[9] Ho Chi Minh, Fidel Castro, the war for independence in Algeria, the Cypriot war, and so forth. But also – and first of all – this means that this territorial drive has itself always been contradicted, tormented, displaced and delocalized. *And that this is the very experience of place.* That is what Schmitt does not acknowledge explicitly. In any case, he draws no visible and conceptually rigorous consequence from it. He shows no interest in the fact that telluric autochthony is *already a reactive response to a delocalization and to a form of tele-technology*, whatever its degree of elaboration, its power, or its speed. This law undoubtedly governs historically different events, places and contents. But what Schmitt is right in saying of the modern partisan, whose agrarian autochthony is driven by technical and industrial progress, whose mobility is reinforced by a motorization which interrupts the 'local bond' and destroys the 'telluric character', could have been said of the most 'classical' combatant. We should not consider this a simple problem of dating or periodization. At stake are the relations between the history of the political and the structure of theoretical concepts which one claims to articulate upon it. For this is not without effect on the two axes of the *Theory of the Partisan*. First of all on the juridical axis (the critical examination of 'equivocations', 'floating concept' and the 'default of clarity' in the concepts of the Hague Agreement (1907) and the Geneva Conventions (1949);[10] an examination highly 'motivated', let us say, by the example of the indictment of German generals after the Second World War). Secondly, the properly political axis which is our main interest here. The case made against the four Geneva Conventions in fact introduces this political axis. Having paid them exaggerated insistent homage (they are admirable for their sense of justice and humanitarian virtue, as well as their respect for the tradition of international law of European origin), Schmitt accuses them of having 'weakened' – indeed, compromised – the 'system of essential distinctions': war and peace, the military and the civilian, enemy and criminal, interstate war and civil war. From that point, the road was clear for a form of war which 'deliberately destroys these clear-cut distinctions'. The normalizations of compromise that the law then proposed would be, for Schmitt, but fragile gangways above the 'abyss'.[11]

The abyss occasions vertigo, which engulfs, in sum, the conceptual banks of these 'clear-cut distinctions'. It is definitively sweeping away the reassuring littoral on which it was believed possible to discern, in a word, Man, the humanity of Man, Man as 'political animal'.

(We shall not multiply the glosses on the edge of this abyss. First of all because to speak of the abyss can be done only from the shore, and there we have a first immoderateness, sometimes even an unbearable indecency. We shall not take advantage of this pretext for pathetic eloquence over the bottomless depths of a chaos which is ours today, this great yawning mouth which cannot 'talk politics' without screaming, shouting hunger or suffering, without swallowing in one gulp all the assurances of 'clear-cut distinctions' to remain, finally, 'voiceless'.

To be ready to *listen* to this screaming chaos of the 'voiceless', one has only to lend an ear to any 'news item'. At the very instant when I am rereading the previous sentence, *all* points in the world, all the places of the *human* world, and not only *on the earth*, and not only in Rwanda and in Italy, in ex-Yugoslavia and in Iran, in Israel and in Palestine, Cambodia and Ireland, Tahiti and Bangladesh, Algeria and France, Ukraine and the Basque Country, etc., are – and will always have been – just so many forms of the abyss for Schmitt's 'clear-cut distinctions' and his nostalgia. Still to give them country names is to speak a language without an assured foundation. *To be ready to listen,* we were saying: at the very instant when I reread this, a new stage has opened up (but have we not known that for such a long time?) with the 'Clipper' chip, a new bugging device – that is, a new stage in modern technics to lose the 'distinction' between private and public in the abyss. Why does Schmitt take no account of the fact that the police and spy network – precisely, the police *qua* spy network (the 'spectre' of the modern State of which Benjamin speaks in *'For a Critique of Violence'*) – points to what, precisely in the service of the State, ruins in advance and *from within* the possibility of the political, the distinction between private and public? What would he have thought of the new cryptographies, and of the unassignable 'political' status that is the singular institution of psychoanalysis – of which he never speaks? And what about *cybercrime*, consisting today in breaking into the electronic files of the State, the army, the police, banks, hospitals and insurance companies? A debate (of course, a hopeless one) is under way today (in the United States, naturally) between the State and citizen associations (all assuredly 'democrats' and 'liberals') concerned over the right to initiative, invention, communication, commerce, and safeguarding privacy. The citizens contest the state monopoly on the production and control of the 'Clipper' chip, designed to protect the secrecy of private communication in an age when, capable of intercepting and recording everything, the highways of numeric transmission leave no leeway or chance to the heart of hearts. Today we have a State just as 'liberal' and 'democratic', just as concerned over its responsibilities, as its citizens, but *providing* it can maintain its hold on the means of protecting internal security and national defence – that is, the possibility of bugging *everything* every time it deems it necessary – politically necessary – to do so (internal and external security).

– Fundamentally, one will say that there is nothing new here, despite the leap of technological mutation which also produces structural effects.

– Certainly, but the novelty of these structural effects must not be neglected; this is the entirety of the 'concrete' in politics.

The choice of this topical example, among an infinity of others, is designed only to recall that a reflection on the politics of friendship should not be distinguishable from a meditation on secrecy, on the 'meaning', the 'history', and the 'techniques' of what is still called today, with the old Latin word, *secret*. We shall return to this later – with Kant.)

Let us return to Schmitt, supposing that we ever left his company. When did this abyss open up? Schmitt claims to know. He believes he is able to determine bearings, events, dates. However worthwhile these determinations may be, however interesting and instructive these historical soundings are, they always admit of some counter-example or of an anterior example in an infinite regression. When Schmitt accuses specialists of *the right of European peoples* with 'repression' (these specialists are said to have repressed from consciousness the image of transformations visible from the beginning of this century[12]) this accusation can be levelled against Schmitt himself. What does he himself do? Does he not situate in this century the mutation whose premises – and the premises of those premises – he is obliged, retreating step by step, to admit without admission? For example: the Bismarckian moment of the *acherontic* (*Acheronta movere*, as Bismarck used to say: to foment revolution and to take control at any price of the national forces pitted against the adversary) had a precedent in 1812–13, when an elite corps of Prussian officers sought to mobilize, with all the means at their disposal, the national forces hostile to Napoleon. Even if this was not, strictly speaking, a partisan war, 'this brief revolutionary moment nevertheless has incredible importance for the theory of the partisan'.[13] Then Schmitt quotes Clausewitz's *On War*, and also an edict of the king of Prussia calling, in sum, for partisan war. Schmitt cannot conceal his admiration for these ten pages signed by a legitimate king. Without hesitation he classes them, in a fervent tremor, 'among the most extraordinary pages of the world's collections'. These pages were made to seduce and to fascinate Schmitt: the paradox of a military legality, political legitimacy, Prussian nationality regularly enrolled in the service of the irregularity of a revolutionary war, of a partisan war – against the French emperor! Against, in sum, the occupying forces whose expansionism masked in 'humanitarian ideology'[14] *The Concept of the Political* had already revealed thirty years earlier. Is it not on account of Napoleon that Fichte and Hegel restored Machiavelli to a place of honour, to allow the German people to resist such an enemy? Along with the Spaniards and all the Europeans, Prussia, the Prussian king, invented partisan war against the French occupying forces. He wrote a 'kind of *Magna Carta* of the partisan'.

At the end of the book, at the other end of the same tradition, in the same lineage as Clausewitz, Lenin and Mao, in 1962, it is General Salan – yes, General Salan – who, in the eyes of a Schmitt alternately convincing and hardly credible, comes to reincarnate the concept and the determination of this struggle – once again against the French State, even if it be in the name of its former colonial empire.

But let us stay with what is most important to us, from the vantage point we have chosen to privilege here: the question of philosophy. Friendship *qua* philosophy, philosophy *qua* friendship, philosophical-friendship, friendship-philosophy, will always in the West have been a concept indissociable within itself: no friendship without some *philosophía*, no *philosophía* without *philía*. Friendship-philosophy: from the outset we have been inspecting the political *next* to this hyphen. Now, here is Schmitt asking us – and it is perhaps not different, since it is still a matter of the political itself – to think war, hence killing, and finally what he calls *absolute hostility*, as philosophy's thing. Although this move belongs to the end of the *Theory of the Partisan*, to an essay registering the evolution of the concept of the political and an evolution contradictorily described in one place as a 'dissolution',[15] in another as an 'upheaval',[16] the reader of *The Concept of the Political* should not be surprised by this call to philosophy. Philosophy represents the properly productive agency of the purely political, and hence of pure hostility – and this, from within the historical process that develops the concept and the practice of the partisan: that is, that which calls into question the classical and stabilized, the regular concept of the political. Despite certain signs of ironic distrust in the areas of metaphysics and ontology, *The Concept of the Political* was, as we have seen, a philosophical type of essay to 'frame' the topic of a concept unable to constitute itself on philosophical ground. But in the *Theory of the Partisan*, it is in the same areas that the topic of this concept is both radicalized and properly uprooted, where Schmitt wished to regrasp *in history* the event or node of events that engaged this uprooting radicalization, and it is precisely there that the philosophical as such intervenes again. Quite precisely at the moment of the partisan's *Magna Carta*, at the moment of Prussian, Spanish, and Russian resistance to the Napoleonic armies and their 'humanitarian ideology'. But why does the philosophical discovery of the partisan occur only in Berlin? Because however Prussian it is, and uniquely Prussian, it owes something to the 'French philosophy of the Enlightenment' and to the French Revolution. The Spanish guerrilla war, just like the 1809 uprising in Tyrol and the Russian partisan war of 1812, were, Schmitt says, insurrections of an 'underdeveloped people'. Catholic or Orthodox culture remained untouched by the Revolution and the Enlightenment. But the latter, on the contrary, are very much present in Berlin, in the age of the philosopher Fichte, the poet Kleist, and even those soldiers 'of genius and vast culture': Scharnhorst, Gneisenau, Clausewitz, 'witnesses to the enormous spiritual potential of Prussian intelligence prepared for action in this critical moment'. Such a nationalism was not one of a simple, illiterate people: 'The philosophical discovery of the partisan and the historical possibility of its theory took place in this atmosphere, in which an aggravated national feeling united to a philosophical culture.'[17]

This properly philosophical theory of the partisan could not fail to feature a doctrine of war. Clausewitz had given courses on guerrilla warfare at the Berlin School of War in 1810–11 and had also written in 1809, as an anonymous soldier, a letter to Fichte, author of a study on Machiavelli, author of *The Art of War*. Yet this philosophical event, this unique and decisive invention of the partisan, was also, to Clausewitz's great disappointment, an abortive attempt, a semi-failure. On this subject Engels spoke of a semi-insurrectional war. This unaccomplished event betrayed at once both a philosophical default and a political one. Philosophy, here, was not yet philosophical enough; it had failed to realize itself outside of discourse and representation. It remained a still-abstract 'theoretical form' and, as such, a spark, a bolt in the dark, a flame, a witness awaiting its heir: 'The spark which, flashing out in Spain in 1808, had reached the North found in Berlin a theoretical form allowing the flame to be conserved for transmission to other hands.'[18] The Acheron was hidden in the canals of state order: the dominant philosophy of Hegel, and the conservative reconciliation between the State and revolution. But the 'ideological arm' remained available, even in Hegel, and always 'more dangerous than the philosophy of Rousseau in the hands of the Jacobins'. Its immediate heirs, Marx and Engels, were still too purely philosophers, thus by no means philosophical enough: thinkers rather than activists of revolutionary war. A 'professional revolutionary' was still awaited: Lenin. The first authentic heir of the Prussian *Magna Carta*, he is in turn followed and radicalized by Mao. He would replace the classical concept of the political founded in the eighteenth and nineteenth centuries on the State based on the right of European peoples, and on interstate war, with the revolutionary war of parties. The latter assumes, certainly, in its Clausewitzian form, the friend/enemy distinction, but it becomes radicalized by carrying hostility to its absolute limit. 'In the eyes of Lenin, only revolutionary war is true war, for it is born of absolute hostility.'[19] Only this absolute hostility confers upon war 'its meaning and its justice'.[20] Only this absolute hostility repoliticizes space throughout a modern depoliticization which will have neutralized political oppositions in the classical age. A single question then remains to be asked, and it is the coincidence of the purest philosophy and the most intense concrete determination: who, *in concreto*, is the absolute enemy? Response: the class enemy, the Western bourgeois and capitalist, wherever he imposes his social order.

Such was the passage between possible reality, real reality, and philosophical consciousnesss; this was, *at present*, the 'alliance (*Bündnis*) of philosophy and the partisan'. This alliance frees new and unexpected explosive forces, and sets off 'the splintering of this entire Eurocentric world which Napoleon had hoped to save, which the Vienna Congress had hoped to restore'.[21] In this absolute present, in this parousia of the political, the identification of the two movements – depoliticization and overpoliticization – still necessarily leaves some leeway. A diastemic inadequation gives history its chance. For example: if at last, and in turn, Lenin determines the absolute enemy in a way that is still 'too abstract and intellectual',[22] Stalin, then Mao ('the greatest practitioner of subversive war' and its 'most famous theoretician'), know how to provide this same war with its telluric rooting. Here would be the absolute accomplishment, the philosophical and historic concretization of absolute hostility.

From this re-tellurization and its analysis given by Schmitt, we shall retain, in the economy of our argument, only one clue. It is of the utmost importance to us, even if it seems non-apparent, or seems to disappear as soon as it appears. We deem it important, in truth, for this very reason and because Schmitt points it out furtively – twice – as if in passing, like a passer-by who would go unnoticed. The double passage of a brother, in effect.

How could a brother be the *subject* of absolute hostility? The hypothesis will have to be inverted. There can be absolute hostility only *for* a brother. And the history of friendship is but the experience of what in this respect resembles an unavowable synonymy, a murderous tautology.

The absolute war Schmitt talks about, the revolutionary war that drives the theory of the partisan to its extremity, the war that violates all laws of war, can be a *fratricidal* war. And thereby have the fraternal figure of the friend return. As a brother enemy. This is an immense tradition, biblical and Greek. The first allusion refers to a Stalinian moment (the 'fratricidal' struggle of Tito, 'helped by Stalin', against Mihailovič, his 'enemy from within', supported by the English).[23] The second allusion recalls the Maoist moment ('race' hostility, 'class' hostility, 'national hostility opposed to the Japanese invader of the same race, hostility regarding the brother of the same nation, growing stronger throughout fierce, interminable civil wars'[24]).

If, in what is worse than civil war, worse than an unleashing of modern *stásis*, *absolute* hostility can aim at the brother and convert, this time, interior war into true war, into absolute war, hence absolute politics, does not this vertiginous reversal in the truth of the political occur at the moment when it touches its limit – to wit, itself or its double, the twin, this absolute friend who always returns with the features of the brother? And if the brother is also the figure of the absolute enemy, what does fraternization mean?

(– But, I ask you, what is a brother?
– Yes, what is a brother? Is one born a brother?
– The question seems ridiculous, dear friend. Of course.
– Not likely. Have you encountered brothers in nature? In nature and in so-called animal births? Fraternity requires a law and names, symbols, a language, engagements, oaths, speech, family and nation.
– It is difficult, however, to erase this memory of 'real', perceptible birth, and birth of an identical, hence identifiable,[25] mother. The memory of an identifiable birth, nature or nation.
– Perhaps it is just the opposite. Well, it is indeed the same thing, if you prefer, but it is perhaps the opposite: instead of saying 'difficult to erase this memory', I would prefer to say 'difficult not to remember'. Now that changes everything. To find the brother, the unfindable brother who is never found in an experience of perception, should you not start from memory's injunction, and thus from some oath? Do you not think, dear friend, that the brother is always a brother of alliance, a *brother in law* or an adoptive brother, a *foster brother*?
– And the sister? Would she be in the same situation? Would she be a case of fraternity?)

It seems to me that Schmitt never speaks of the sister. He speaks little of the brother, but always in a significant and serious way: the originary friend as a brother of alliance or brother by oath, 'sworn brother'[26] (fraternization or fraternity according to the *Schwurbrüderschaft*, in the passage quoted in our epigraph), but also – and this is the same one – the friend killed in absolute war: the absolute political enemy. Much later, as we shall soon see, to the question 'Who can be my enemy?' Schmitt will answer: 'Myself or again my brother'; 'My brother is found to be my enemy'. But he responds in this way to what, in effect, is in the form of a question; he responds to an *enemy question*, to the question of an enemy, as if he were speaking to the other *qua* enemy ('O enemy . . .'), to the enemy present in the very form of the question, to what calls the questioner into question. The enemy would then be the figure of our own question, or rather, if you prefer this formulation, our own question in the figure of the enemy. We will hear Schmitt quoting: '*Der Feind ist unser eigne Frage als Gestalt*' – 'The enemy is our own question as figure'.

There would be not a question of the enemy, or of the brother. The brother or the enemy, the brother enemy, is the question, the questioning form of the question, this question that I ask because it is first of all put to me. I ask it only from the moment it descends upon me with blunt violence, in an offensive and in offence. In crime or in complaint. The question injures me; it is a wound within myself. I pose this question only, I pose it effectively, only when I am called into question by the question. Aggression, traumatism, war. The enemy is the question, and through the brother, the brother enemy, it originarily resembles, indiscernibly resembles, the friend, the original friend (*Freund*) *qua* brother of alliance, sworn brother, according to the 'oath of fraternity' (*Schwurbrüderschaft*). The question is armed. It is an army, a friend enemy army.

It would be easy to show – but we will not spend too much time doing so – that the history of the question, starting with the question of being, likewise for the entire history governed by it (*philosphía*, *epistémē*, *istoría*, research, inquest, appeal, inquisition, requisition, and so forth), could not have taken place without polemical violence, without strategy and without arms techniques. This should be known, this can be known, without concluding that the question should be disarmed, or that only disarmed questions should be addressed. But without renouncing any question, hence any knowledge, and in order to keep investigating with vigilance, *before and outside all war*, what enables the deployment of this question of which Heidegger said one day that it was the 'piety of thought',[27] perhaps once again it will be necessary – and this would, *perhaps*, be the friendship of the *perhaps*, the *perhaps* 'prior to' the question, even 'prior to' the affirmation that opens it up and of which we were speaking above – to move back up the question, to move back along the question, further back than it, with and without it, next to it before it – at least before it takes form, when the friend and the enemy pass into one another through the figure of the brother. Before any question, before the question mark, an exclamation mark would then have to be heard. And this double clamour would have to be heard again, addressed to the friend who is no longer or who is not yet ('O my friends, there is no friend!'), as well as to the enemy who no longer is or who is not yet ('O enemies, there is no enemy!').

'"Enemies, there is no enemy!" shouts the living fool that I am' – would this reversing apostrophe, this *cat'apostrophe*, be ours? Can we at least dream of reappropriating it as an event of our times – 'modern or postmodern', as some would say? Nothing is less clear. To believe it, we should have, at least, to be convinced that it both affects and characterizes, at its edges, a modernity *against which* it rises up in indignation, to be sure (modernity, you are losing the enemy and deserting grand politics!, it seems to say; you neutralize and depoliticize; you must find the absolute enemy again!) but *against which* it also rises up like a figure against a ground. Rising up like a figure against a ground to which it belongs, this cat'apostrophe thus also marks and delimits a landscape, that of a political age for which it is so difficult, as we have seen, to mark off the limits. The 'living fool' could certainly want to say, among many other things at least as enigmatic as this one: there is no more politics, there is no more 'great politics' – the same news Nietzsche shouts elsewhere. In complaining rather than rejoicing. Deploring, in sum, what Schmitt will call 'neutralization' and 'depoliticization'. But, as we have just seen, this depoliticization broaches and conditions the build-up of an overpoliticization. The figure of the absolute enemy, in this reversing passage, starts to resemble that of the absolute friend: the deadliest tragedy of fratricide.

(We could look for our examples in the Bible, which in sum speaks of nothing else, starting with Cain and Abel, whose ghosts we will see haunting Schmitt in his prison cell. Let us choose Atreus and Thyestes instead. In what is thus doomed to incest and to anthropophagy (to have the sons eaten by the father rather than the father by the sons), the stakes are, *among brothers*, those of politics, heritage, sharing out and assumption of power. In the absence of the father or the king. This is a matrix for a more strictly political rereading, a conjoined reading of 'The Purloined Letter' and the *Theory of the Partisan*, even the *Ex Captivitate Salus*. Such a reading would not play on the fact that Dupin introduces himself as a 'partisan', and that a certain feminization of the rivals seems to be on the programme. Before copying these lines from Crébillon: '"*Un dessein si funeste/S'il n'est digne d'Atrée, est digne de Thyeste.*" *They are to be found in Crébillon's Atrée.*' Dupin had *talked politics*, he had declared his *'political prepossessions'* ('*In this matter, I act as a partisan of the lady concerned*'); he had predicted the end, in truth the political suicide of his rival, the self-destruction of his brother enemy. The latter will vouch for himself, if that can be said, to disappear, he will doom himself to his own political destruction ('*Thus will he inevitably commit himself, at once, to his political destruction*'). But what is it that you do in designating the self-destruction that resembles you like a brother? There are so many contradictory perversions, so many monstrosities (with all these words we are speaking here, of course, of *truth* as *monstrosity*). These *monstrous truths* call up the equivocal admiration of the brother enemy, of the double or the rival; they excite his pitiless sympathy; for if he refuses him all compassion, Dupin has trouble rejecting this feeling so close to, even indissociable from, pity: sympathy. A pitiless sympathy: this would be the most striking figure of war and death among brothers. War to death according to the phantasm of the symbiotic, not far from the genius, the congeneric and the congenital: '*In the present instance I have no sympathy – at least no pity – for him who descends. He is that* monstrum horrendum, *an unprincipled man of genius.*')

Schmitt has been reproached for making the enemy rather than the friend the 'properly positive conceptual criterion (*das eigentlich positive Begriffsmerkmal)*' of his definition of the political. In the preface to the 1963 edition of *The Concept of the Political* he responds to this objection, which he considers a 'stereotype'. In his apparently classical role as logician or dialectician – as didactician too – intent on methodically teaching the topic of concepts, Schmitt invokes the privilege that negation must be maintained in a dialectical determination of the 'life of law' and the 'theory of law'; but also, let us recall, in the life of the living in general. The law of killing (the enemy, war, politics, etc.) no more presupposes a 'philosophy of death' – indeed, the essential existence of something like death (for Schmitt, paradoxically *there is no death*) – than the unceasing insistence on the enemy would in any way imply a prevalence of the negative, or at least the 'primacy' of what is thereby 'negated'. It is as if – in a language which is not literally his own, but which seems to me to impose his own logic – Schmitt responded, in sum: I insist *first of all* on the enemy rather than the friend, and this is proper strategy because it is correct method. Should I have to start from the friend, as you invite me to do, I would first have to provide its preliminary definition. Now, such a definition would be possible only in reference to the opposed term: the enemy. I must therefore start from this oppositional negativity, hence from hostility, in order to attain the political. 'To start from the enemy' is not the opposite of 'to start from the friend'. It is, on the contrary, to start from the *opposite* without which there is neither friend nor enemy. In short, hostility is required by method and *by definition* – the very definition of the definition. By the dialecticity or diacriticity, by the necessity of the *topic* as well, which cannot function without the possibility of war. There is no space, nor is there any place –

neither in general nor for a thought, for a definition or for a distinction – without the real possibility of war.

No doubt Schmitt's language is, in appearance, more strictly juridical than this, but his response to the objections moves back up to the very genesis of a juridical concept as such. Hence his response affects the non-juridical or pre-juridical origin of the juridical. It is a question of knowing what to put at the beginning if one wishes to go about things in the right way:

> The objection claiming that I give primacy to the enemy concept is a quite generally widespread cliché (*allgemein verbreitet und stereotyp*). It fails to understand that any development of a juridical concept (*jede Bewegung eines Rechtsbegriffs*) issues, by dialectical necessity, from negation (*aus der Negation*). In the life of law as in the theory of law, to include the negation means anything except a 'primacy' of the negated contents (*alles andere als ein 'Primat' des Negierten*). A trial *qua* legal action is conceivable only once a right has been negated. It is not a fact (*Tat*) but a wrongdoing (*Untat*) that penal action and penal law pose (*setzen*) at their commencement (*an ihren Anfang*). Would this, for all that, be a 'positive' conception of wrongdoing and a 'primacy' of crime?[28]

Like the Aristotelian discourse on friendship, this argument could also be inscribed in the logic – at least, in one of its moments – of the unsettling logic of *Lysis*: once the enemy had disappeared, the friend would disappear at once. He would vanish in the same stroke, actually/effectively and virtually, in his very possibility. The possibility, the meaning and the phenomenon of friendship would never appear unless the figure of the enemy had already called them up in advance, had indeed put to them the question or the objection of the friend, a wounding question, a question of wound. No friend without the possible wound. The tension between friendship and enmity would be pharmacological. Friendship to remedy a wrongdoing, friendship to answer a possible wrongdoing or crime, friendship of consolation or of mourning, friendship of reparation – in the hypothesis that there could ever be another. But it is true – there are quite a number of differences – that this passage from *Lysis* represents only a stage in a process. It is equally true that *Lysis* names the friend rather than the enemy. And, what is more, the enemy is *ekhthrós*, not *polémios*:

> For if there is nothing any more to hurt us, we have no need whatever of any assistance (*oudemias ōphelías deoímetha*). And thus you see it would then be made apparent that it was only on account of evil that we felt regard and affection for good (*dia to kakon tagathon egapômen kai ephiloumen*), as we considered good to

be a medicine (*ōs phármakon*) for evil, and evil to be a disease. But where there is no disease, there is, we are aware, no need of medicine (*nosḗmatos de mē óntos ouden dei phannákou*). . . . It follows, then, I think, that the original thing to which we are friendly, that wherein all those other things terminate to which we said we were friendly for the sake of another thing, bears to these things no resemblance at all. For to these things we called ourselves friendly for the sake of another thing to which we were friendly, but that to which we are really friendly (*to de tô ónti phílon*) appears to be of a nature exactly the reverse of this, since we found that we were friendly to it for the sake of a thing [we could go so far as to translate: by reason of, in view of, indeed by virtue of the enemy, thanks to the enemy, *ekhthrou éneka*] to which we were unfriendly, and, if this latter be removed, we are, it seems, friendly to it no longer.[29]

Here the analogy between the foregoing argument and Schmitt's would end – or so it would seem. After this logic of contradiction (the friend as the adverse response to the enemy, the friend as the rejoinder to the enemy) *Lysis* seeks another reason to love, another cause of loving and being loved (*alle tis aitia tou phileîn te kai phileisthai*). In order to prevent the foregoing from becoming 'idle talk', a kind of 'lengthy poem', the hypothesis of desire (*épithumia*) is then put forward: the friend is the friend of what he desires, but if he can desire only that which he lacks, and if what is lacking can be only that of which he has been deprived (that which has been taken away), then one must indeed imagine that before this feeling of privation, and precisely in order to experience it, friendship (*philía*), *qua érōs* and *epithumía*, must indeed be found to be linked to what is proper, suitable, appropriate and familiar (*oikeios*) to it.

The value of *oikeiótēs* dominates the end of the dialogue. It is most often translated as 'suitability'. It frequently qualifies the bond of friendship itself, an always natural bond (we necessarily recognize in *phileîn* some kinship or natural familiarity, *to men dē phúsei anagkaion ēmin péphantai phileîn*,[30] but it forms an indissociable network of significations which are of import to us here, a semantic locus totally assembled, precisely, around the hearth (*oikos*), the home, habitat, domicile – and grave: kinship – literal or metaphorical – domesticity, familiarity, property, therefore appropriability, proximity: everything an *economy* can reconcile, adjust or harmonize, I will go so far as to say *present*,[31] in the *familiarity* of the *near* and the *neighbour*.

(If the *hearth* is found within the semantic locus of *philía*, and if *philía* cannot function without *oikeiótēs*, then little would stand in the way of saying that the central question of this essay – and we have already seen why this 'question' comes 'before' the question – indeed, 'before' the affirmation that precedes it, from the moment of the *perhaps* that they both presuppose – would be that of a friendship without hearth, of a *philía* without *oikeiótēs*. Ultimately, a friendship without presence, without resemblance, without affinity, without analogy. Along with presence, truth itself would start to tremble. Like this prayer which, as Aristotle reminds us, could be neither true nor false. Is an *aneconomic* friendship possible? Can there be any other friendship? Must there be another? Can one answer this question otherwise than with a 'perhaps' – that is, by suspending in advance the very form of a 'question', and the alliance of the 'yes' – in order to think and to dream before them? And must not this reflection account for a certain end of *Lysis*, in its final leavetaking? Must not this question take as its starting point this place where it is avowed, after the ordeal and the experience of *oikeiótēs*, after the so strong distinction between 'oikeion' and 'hómoion': between the familiar and the proper on the one hand and the homogeneous and the like on the other: 'we have not as yet been able to discover what we mean by a friend'. Departure after the departure of certain 'pedagogues', these 'demons' who speak 'bad Greek' (*upobarbarizontes*). They have, then, departed, those who seemed 'hardly fit to talk':

> We owned ourselves vanquished, and broke up the party. However, just as they were leaving, I managed to call out, Well, Lysis and Menexenus, we have made ourselves rather ridiculous today, I, an old man, and you children. For our hearers here will carry away the report that though we conceive ourselves to be friends with each other – you see I class myself with you – we have not as yet been able to discover what we mean by a friend.

The structure of this conclusion announces the reported statement of Aristotle – such, at least, as it is most often translated. Here, too, someone is addressing friends. He speaks to them to tell them, in the vocative *élan* of the apostrophe: we who are, *among ourselves*, friends, my friends, we who call ourselves friends, we do not know what a friend is. And we should have to imagine, we should never exclude the possibility, that perhaps, therefore, there are none. Or perhaps so few. . . . Exactly how many friends, if there are any, are there, my friends?)

Let us return to Schmitt, and expand our perspective. That which a macroscopic view is able to align, from afar and from high above, is a certain desert. Not a woman in sight. An inhabited desert, to be sure, an absolutely full absolute desert, some might even say a desert teeming with people. Yes, but men, men and more men, over centuries of war, and costumes, hats, uniforms, soutanes, warriors, colonels, generals, partisans, strategists, politicians, professors, political theoreticians, theologians. In vain would you look for a figure of a woman, a feminine silhouette, and the slightest allusion to sexual difference.

At any rate, this seems to be the case in the texts that deal with the political, with the political as such (*The Concept of the Political* and the *Theory of the Partisan*). Granted, there are indeed these two allusions to fratricide, but they are so brief. They lead to no reflection on the difference between a brother and a sister. Sisters, if there are any, are species of the genus brother. In this Christian space (we will speak later of the Christian scansion in the history of fraternity), one remembers that letter of the great and good Saint Francis of Assisi, who could not help but write to a nun: 'Dear Brother Jacqueline'.

Granted, there is this remark that we picked up on a 'stasiology' that was to deal with civil war within the Holy Family or with a conflict interior to the Trinity − and it seems to us potentially ripe with the most serious consequences. But Schmitt does seem to give it short shrift − at least, in so far as it concerns sexual difference. Granted, too, there is this essay on *Hamlet or Hecuba*, but that deals more with 'the queen's taboo' and with being an accomplice, perhaps, to a fratricide.[32]

What could, then, be massively evident in this immense, modern and ageless procession, in this theory of the political working its way in the middle of the desert, what *strikes* us in this philosophy of merciless war, in this staging of 'physical' killing, in this implacable logic of absolute hostility, what should be massively evident but goes as unnoticed as absence itself, what disappears in becoming indiscernible in the middle of the desert, is the woman or the sister. Not even a mirage. Nothing. Desert and absolute silence, it would seem. Not even a woman-soldier. Not even in the theory of the partisan is there the least reference to the role played by women in guerrilla warfare, in the wars[33] and the aftermath of wars of national liberation (in Algeria today, for example − for another liberation, since Schmitt speaks of the Algeria of Salan). Never a word for the action of women in resistance movements (Schmitt is then more eloquent, let it be said in passing, when he evokes the resistance against the Napoleonic empire, against French imperialisms in general; and he remains so discreet on the subject of those women whom the Nazi occupation forces encountered not so long ago; they could nevertheless have provided him with interesting examples at the time of the theory of the partisan). If the woman does not even appear in the theory of the partisan − that is, in the theory of the absolute enemy – if she never leaves a forced clandestinity, such an invisibility, such a blindness, gives food for thought: what if the woman were the absolute partisan? And what if she were the absolute enemy of this theory of the absolute enemy, the spectre of hostility to be conjured up for the sake of the sworn brothers, or the other of the absolute enemy who has become the absolute enemy that would not even be recognized in a regular war? She who, following the very logic of the theory of the partisan, becomes an enemy all the more awesome in not being able to become a female enemy (*une ennemie*); in his blurring, in her blurring and interference with the reassuring limits between hostility and hatred, but also between enmity and its opposite, the laws of war and lawless violence, the political and its others, and so forth.

Is this a question? Is it a question in the form of an objection?

Nothing is less certain.

If it were the rhetorical ploy of an objection – a 'rhetorical question', as it is called in English – it would be so foreseeable, so massive (which does not mean, for all that, unjustified), that it would undoubtedly issue in an amused and condescending protestation on the part of Schmitt. He would hardly put himself out, he would hardly lift his little finger, to start up the argumentative machine which has proved its worth. 'Of course,' he would say, 'there is reason to be worried about the absence of woman in this analysis; one can even find therein what you are calling her clandestinity. One may, on the subject of woman, pursue sociological or psychoanalytical explanations. You can even protest in the name of morals, justice, or the universal equality of the Rights of Man. This may all be legitimate, even urgent, and I would be ready, under certain conditions, to join you, and to share in your interest in the cause of women – who, moreover, are indeed indispensable in the formation of enemy groups and peoples without which there would be no politics. But mind you, such a cause may derive from all these disciplines: psychoanalysis, morals, law, even religion; and you may even deal with the question from the vantage point of economics. But it remains the case that all this has no political pertinence as such. All this is undoubtedly – like love or friendship in general, between men, between women, between men and women – a universal human cause, but I have shown that what concerns humanity in general, and as such, had no political significance. Reread the sixth chapter of my *Concept of the Political*. I explain that the concept of humanity is an efficient "ideological instrument of imperialist expansion"; and, "in its ethico-humanitarian form, a specific vehicle of economic imperialism". The universal concepts of humanity, the earth, or the world are, by definition, foreign to the political. What you call "globalization" is a strategy of depoliticization enrolled in the service of particular political interests. What is more, the analysis I propose – in which, in effect, sexual difference plays no part, and the women never appears – is above all a diagnosis. It is a matter of saying what is: the subject of the political is genderless; moreover, it has always been, in fact and as such, a man, a group of men determining his or their enemy and determined to "physically kill him", as you have just explained. I never do anything but diagnose.'

How are we to respond to this rejoinder? We have already called into question this pretension to diagnosis and to the pure delimitation of regions, the very topic of this discourse. We shall not return to that, although we could now add the hypothesis according to which Schmittian strategy – as well as his topology, perhaps – has as its clandestine finality only this sealing away, this clandestine house arrest, this phallogocentric neutralization of sexual difference. In question would not be waging war on this being called a woman – or the sister – but repeating and consolidating in the diagnosis a general structure keeping under control and under interdiction the very thing which constitutes it – and which has for so long been called the political – indeed, the theologico-political.

There would, then, remain only one choice, and it would call for a decision:

1. *Either* to admit that the political is in fact this phallogocentrism in act. Schmitt would record the fact; and we could not fail to recognize that indeed, so many indications attest to it in all European cultures, in the Bible and in the Koran, in the Greek world and in Western modernity: political virtue (the warrior's courage, the stakes of death and the putting to death, etc.) has always been *virile virtue* in its androcentric manifestation. *Virtue* is *virile*. Woman's slow and painful access to citizenship would go hand in hand with the symptoms of depoliticizing neutralization noted by Schmitt. This structure can be combated only by carrying oneself beyond the political, beyond the name 'politics'; and by forging other concepts, concepts with an altogether different mobilizing force. Who would swear that this is not in progress?

2. *Or else* keep the 'old name', and analyse the logic and the topic of the concept differently, and engage other forms of struggle, other 'partisan' operations, and so forth.

If there were a single thesis to this essay, it would posit that there could be no choice: the decision would once again consist in deciding without excluding, in the invention of other names and other concepts, in moving out *beyond this* politics without ceasing to intervene therein to transform it.

For example, here. This double gesture would consist in not renouncing the logic of fraternization, *one* fraternization rather than *such and such another*, therefore one politics rather than some other, all the while working to de-naturalize the figure of the brother, his authority, his credit, his phantasm. The preference given to one or another fraternization (the democratic one) presupposes such work, presupposes that the brother figure not be a natural, substantial, essential, untouchable given. This same work would affect, in changing it, democratic fraternization – everything which, in democracy, still presupposes this natural fraternity, with all the risks and limits it imposes.

To be consistent with this de-naturalization of fraternal authority (or, if you prefer, with its 'deconstruction'), a first necessity, a first law, must be taken into account: there has never been anything *natural* in the brother figure on whose features has so often been drawn the face of the friend, or the enemy, the brother enemy. De-naturalization was at work in the very formation of fraternity. This is why, among other premisses, one must recall that the demand of a democracy to come is already what makes such a deconstruction possible. This demand is deconstruction at work. The relation to the brother engages from the start with the order of the oath, of credit, of belief and of faith. The brother is never a fact.

Nor any bond of kinship. Thus when Schmitt classes the 'oath of fraternity or the fraternity of the oath (*Schwurbrüderschaft*)' among bonds of birth or alliance implied in the 'originary' concept of the friend, when he sees it only as a case or an example, he still argues for a distinction between the bond of alliance and the natural bond, between the structure of credit (or of faith) and a 'natural' attachment which would go beyond credit. Now, such a distinction, however powerful its effects, remains a phantasm. It rises up on the background of that phantasmatics or that general symbolics in which, in particular, all bonds of kinship are determined. If, elsewhere, Schmitt privileges the brother, even in the fatality of fratricide, it is still in the vigilance of the frightened watchman. A watchman on edge [*aux aguets*] would still protect himself: in his watchtower, in the fort of a fortress, from the tower or the loophole, he would remain in this logic of the political that we think is deconstructible, in the process of deconstruction.

'Wisdom of the prison-cell':[34] after the war, through his prison experi-ence, Schmitt recalls Max Stirner. Stirner is convoked like the phantom of Schmitt's childhood. Like a brother as well, an admirable but estranged brother. '*Max Stirner kenne ich seit Unterprima.*' For he had read Stirner in his public-school years, this ghost, this childhood friend, this same Stirner whose spectres *The German Ideology* was already conjuring up. Schmitt then acknowledges his debt, knowing that Stirner had prepared him for what would happen to him today, which would otherwise have surprised him. 'Poor Max', he notes just before 1948, belongs part and parcel to 'what is exploding today' and to what 'was in preparation before 1848'. And now Stirner 'pays him a visit' in his prison cell, the spectre of the man who invented 'the most beautiful title in German literature: *Der Einzige und sein Eigentum*'. Schmitt cites *The Ego and its Own*; he paraphrases it, he plays in its wake with the words *Pan* and *Plan*, 'this beautiful example of the oracular power immanent in our German language'. Having meditated on nakedness and on its opposite, on economic planning, productivity, technics, the 'technologized earth', the new Man and the new paradise, he takes up the theme of deceit or imposture – more precisely, of illusion about oneself, the 'deceiving oneself' (*Selbstbetrug*), of this Narcissus victim of the 'dupery of self proper to solitude', of this 'poor Self who can only marry his own Echo' (as if Echo could not have been able to speak in turn, and Schmitt quickly forgets his *Metamorphoses*; yes, as if Echo had not invented the necessary ruse for speaking in its own name, for reclaiming the floor, for calling the other while feigning to repeat the ends of sentences). The prisoner evokes, then, the terrible anxiety of Descartes pursued by the evil genius, the deceitful one *par excellence*, by the other spirit, the *spiritus malignus*. In the anxiety of dupery, the philosopher masks himself, he shields himself from nakedness. *Larvatus prodeo*. Schmitt quotes and echoes, in the first person: he speaks of himself in taking on the mask of Descartes. From one end to the other of these red-hot and despairing pages – haughty ones, too – whose rhetoric does not always avoid, with a certain pride, a landscape and commonplaces only too familiar today, they are the confession of one who confesses his doubts about confession. The anxiety is all the more terrifying, he admits, when it gives birth to new impostures. He throws himself headlong into this anxiety, having imagined himself, in order to conjure it away, confronting deceit head-on: 'Imposture of feeling and understanding, imposture of the flesh and the spirit, imposture of vice and virtue, imposture of husband and wife.' These *vis-à-vis* are all equivalent. Then comes death: '*Komm, geliebter Tod*', 'Come, beloved death'. These words appear to close a chapter; they follow immediately the sigh of the deceit of man and woman (*Betrug des Mannes und des Weibes*).

Yet another chapter, for there is more: 'death can also abuse us'. It is the next-to-last chapter; a 'fraternal kiss' will be spoken of. The phantom of the friend, Stirner's phantom, has returned, the phantom of the thinker of phantoms. Everything the latter will have done to shield and to barricade himself is but the 'greatest deceit of self'. 'As anyone is mad with self, mad with the I (*Ich-verrückte*)', mad with me – sick of me, as we say – 'he sees the enemy in the non-I (*sieht er im Nicht-Ich den Feind*)'. 'Then the whole world becomes his enemy.' For now we have him imagining that the world should let itself be caught when, 'guarding its freedom, it offers him the fraternal kiss (*den Bruderkuss*)'. He then hides from the 'dialectical dissociation' of the ego, and seeks to escape from the enemy in the very time of deceit. 'But the enemy is an objective force.' It is impossible to escape him: 'the authentic enemy will not brook deceit'.

This last phrase then opens a brief meditation, a few lines, on the enemy. *The enemy in the figure of the brother.* We see Schmitt, the thinker of the enemy, he who in this century will have become famous for having made the enemy his theme, his concept, his theatre, in his prison putting his head in his hands and beginning the final anamnesis. He is ready to put himself in question, precisely on the subject of the enemy. He will not do so, he will never do it, no more than he will ever avow or disavow his Nazism.[35] But he will attempt to say – on the subject of what calls into question, of what calls *me* into question – something that will still be called the enemy, the brother enemy. The question that resounds in this cell is not the converse of the question in *Lysis* (Who is the friend?), nor even the general or ontological question (*What is* the enemy? *What is* hostility or the *being*-hostile of the enemy?). No, it is the question 'who?' as the concrete question *I put to myself*, and for which I will have to conclude that with this question the enemy puts me in question. It is the question 'who', to be sure, but first of all or simply 'who for me?' '*Wer ist denn mein Feind?*' Who, then, is *my* enemy, mine, here, now? 'Is it my enemy, he who feeds me in my cell? He even dresses and houses me (*Er kleidet und behaust mich sogar*). The cell is the piece of clothing that he has offered to me. I therefore ask myself: who can finally be my enemy? '*Wer kann denn überhaupt mein Feind sein?*'

Before this question, the jurist finds a second wind; he is willing to confess, but he recalls, across general considerations, that he is a jurist, not a theologian. These general conditions redialecticize the question. A dialectic of recognition (*Anerkennung*): in order to identify my enemy, I must recognize him, but in such a way that he recognizes me also: 'In this reciprocal recognition of recognition resides the grandeur of the concept.' That is hardly a fitting piece for an 'age of the masses' and its 'pseudo-theological myths of the enemy'. 'The theologians tend to define the enemy as something which must be annihilated (*vernichtet*). But I am a jurist, not a theologian.'

Oh really? What does he mean, exactly? That contrary to what certain 'theologians' claim, the 'enemy', the concept of enemy, must not be annihilated? This, indeed, is exactly what he has always maintained. Or else that the enemy *himself* would not be 'something which must be annihilated'? But had he not defined the enemy in these terms, and more than once? Had he not repeated that the enemy is first and foremost he who must be 'physically' killed? And as for his refusal to be a theologian, one wonders who said — and often in so convincing a manner — that all the concepts of the modern theory of the State are secularized theological concepts, and that one must start from theology if one is to understand them, and if one is to understand the concepts of decision, exception and sovereignty.[36] What game is this man playing, then, when he says he is a 'jurist', not a 'theologian'? Should he not be the first to smile at this distinction?

After this dialectical exercise (a Hegelian one, it must be said), the question returns, more or less identical, literally. One simply passes from being-enemy to the recognition of the enemy — that is, to his identification, but to an *identification* which will carry me to my identification, finally, myself, with the other, with the enemy whom I identify. Previously, the sentence was: 'I wonder, then, who can finally *be* my enemy?'; now it is: 'Whom may I finally *recognize* as my enemy?' Response: 'Manifestly, he alone who can put me in question (*der mich in Frage stellen kann*). In so far as I recognize him as my enemy, I recognize that he can put me in question. And who can effectively put me in question? Only myself. Or my brother. That's it. The other is my brother. The other is revealed as my brother, and the brother reveals himself as my enemy.'[37]

The power and the sleepwalking levity of this progression. The prudence and the sureness of a rhetoric. The prisoner gropes about in the night, from one corner of his cell to another. He hazards a step, then another, then stops to meditate.

1. We first went from a question (Whom can be my enemy? Whom can I recognize as such?) to the preinscription of the question itself, as a calling into question, in the 'who' to be identified, in the enemy as he who calls into question. Who is my enemy? How is he to be recognized but in the very question, which puts me in question? The question is no longer a theoretical question, a question of knowledge or of recognition, but first of all, like recognition in Hegel, a calling into question, an act of war. The question is posed, it is posed to someone; someone puts it to himself like

an attack, a complaint, the premeditation of a crime, a calling into question of the one who questions or interrogates. It is posed to oneself in terms of a break into the other, or its breaching. One cannot question oneself on the enemy without recognizing him – that is, without recognizing that he is already lodged in the question: this is what the 'wisdom of the cell' teaches the solitary prisoner. The enemy is properly unavoidable for the person who thinks a little – if, at least, thinking begins with the question. The quotation of a verse by Däubler will express this in a moment: the enemy has the figure of the question, of our question – he is 'our own question as figure (*als Gestalt*)'.

2. Another step in the night – we then went from 'calling into question' to 'calling oneself into question'. The enemy in question is he who calls into question, but he can call into question only someone who can call *himself* into question. One can be called into question only in calling oneself into question. The enemy is oneself, I myself am my own enemy. This concept of 'one's own enemy' at once confirms and contradicts everything Schmitt has said about the enemy up to now. It confirms the necessity, so often stressed, of correctly determining, concretely, one's enemy; but it contradicts the same necessity, for nothing is less proper, proper to self, than one's enemy. The solution to this problem – the response that comes from a word like a key found inside the home, whereas it was being sought outside – is '*Oder mein Bruder*'. The 'or', the 'or else', oscillates between the oscillation of the alternative or the equivalence of the equation (*aut* or *vel*). Who can put me into question? Myself alone. 'Or my brother.' *Oder mein Bruder*.

This is an a priori synthesis of the following sequence (I am, myself, the other who puts me in question, puts myself in question, the other is my brother, my brother is my enemy, and so forth). The a priori synthesis, the armed tautology, the genetic pleonasm comes down to making the enemy he who is at one and the same time the closest, the most familiar, the most familial, the most proper. *Oikeiótēs* would gather up the totality of these values to define the friend in *Lysis*. But now *oikeiótēs* characterizes the enemy, my own enemy, in the brother figure, myself as my brother: myself or, if it is not me, my brother.

Such would be the originary complaint. We shall abandon as of little interest the question of knowing if that reverses or repeats Platonism. One does not exclude the other, since thanks to my brother, on his account, I am the other, and the closest is the most removed, the most proper is the most foreign.

Why do we suspend the question of Platonism or its reversal? To some extent because for some time now it has been slightly wearisome. But above all because what follows and finishes this brief meditation brings together in the filiation of the brother a biblical lineage and a Greek lineage. And we are all the more intent on marking off this genealogical bifurcation, which will divide the history of friendship *qua* the history of fraternity, given that it announces the argument of subsequent chapters of this work. Which brother are we talking about? Who are these brother enemies? And which one is their father? Where were they born? On biblical or Hellenic ground? In a finite family or an infinite one? And what if these two families of brothers were precisely giving birth (procreating) the brother enemies, the *true* brothers *truly* enemies? And what if both, twice two − what if these two couples of brother enemies had exactly in common the fact that they never renounce either belonging (to a natural ethnic group or to a group of choice, to the family and to the fatherland, to the phratry, to the nation, to blood and to the earth) or the universalism for which they claim responsibility ('all men are brothers'[38]), a responsibility that is always, of course, exemplary?

The powerful and traditional logic of exemplarity would allow all the brothers in the world to reconcile the two imperatives. To believe it possible, in any case, to allow it or to have it believed. A brother is always exemplary, and this is why there is war. And among all the meanings of this exemplarity we do not exclude that of the *exemplar*, this Ciceronian *model* of friendship with which we decided to begin, a model at once both the original and the copy, the face and its mirror, one and the other.

In the very next paragraph, Schmitt grafts one family on to another. And again dialecticizes. Deliberately or not, he names Cain and Abel, then a 'father of all things' who cannot not cite a certain Heraclitean *pólemos* ('*Pólemos pantōn men patér esti*').[39] The Bible and Greece:

'Adam and Eve had two sons, Cain and Abel. Thus begins the history of humanity. That is how the father of all things appeared. It is the dialectical tension that maintains the history of the world in movement, and the history of the world is not yet over.'

Between the Greek family and the biblical family appears the thinker of the infinite − the thinker of the 'true infinite', not the 'false infinite'. He has the features and bears the name of 'philosopher'. We recognize the spectre of Hegel, even though he is not explicitly named. Schmitt ventriloquizes once again, to recall that the infinite passes through the annihilation of self. An allusion to all the exterminators face to face with one another; we are in the aftermath of the war, Schmitt writes from his prison:

Prudence, then, one does not write in levity of the enemy. One is classed according to one's enemy. One situates oneself according to what one recognizes as enmity (hostility, *Feindschaft*). The exterminators are assuredly sinister, who justify themselves in the allegation that the exterminators must be exterminated. But all extermination is but self-extermination. The enemy, on the other hand, is the other. Remember the formidable propositions of the philosopher: the relation to oneself in the other – there we have the true infinite. The negation of the negation, says the philosopher, is not neutralization; what is truly infinite on the contrary depends on it. But what is truly infinite is the fundamental concept (*der Grundbegriff*) of his philosophy.

Then he quotes Theodor Däubler's verse: 'The enemy is our own question *qua* figure': '*Der Feind ist unser eigne Frage als Gestalt.*'[40]
Immediately afterwards, just before the epilogue, a double echo resounds in this prison cell. The 'wisdom' of the solitary one lets two apostrophes ring out: one attributed to Aristotle, the 'dying sage', and the one that Nietzsche cried out, in the name of the 'living fool'. Two grievances, two complaints and two warnings name here the friend, there the enemy; each time the friend or enemy one *has not*. A double echo, to be sure, both wise and mad, but yet another language – that of the man who is undoubtedly awaiting judgement:

> Woe to him who has no *friend*, for his enemy will sit in judgement upon him.
> Woe to him who has no enemy, for I *shall myself be* his enemy on judgement day.

Epilogue. Here everything is in the form of epilogue and epitaph. Everything chimes with this *dying voice* [in English] of which Schmitt speaks so much in his *Hamlet or Hecuba*. Will it be said once again, in conclusion, that the sister is altogether mute in this interminable and eloquent dialectic of inimical brothers? And Antigone between all these families, finite or infinite, of inimical brothers.[41] No, one would do better to become attentive to several enigmatic signs in the epilogue of this '*Weisheit der Zelle*'. Something of a eulogy to Echo can be heard; her name appears twice. It is true that she speaks German, and celebrates her belonging to the German language. 'Such is the wisdom of the cell', Schmitt notes. 'I lose my time and gain my space.' He then pulls up short on the word space: *Raum*. The same word as *Rom*. He is admiring the marvels of 'the German language', its potential and its powers, its spatial energy and its generating force, its spatial and germinal dynamic (*die Raumkraft und die Keimkraft der deutschen Sprache*). In his own language speech and place rhyme (*Wort und Ort*). His language was able to safeguard in the word 'rhyme' its spatial sense and its space-of-sense (*seinen Raum-Sinn*), while bestowing on its poets the 'obscure play' that brings together, untranslatably, *Reim* and *Heimat*, rhyme and the motherland, rhyme and the 'at-home' [*le chez-soi*] (let us not attempt to translate the assonance, for that would be to translate what should not be translated: precisely the untranslatable, that which does not have the good fortune of echo in another language, another nation, especially France, as we shall see).

And here it is: no, not yet Echo's sister, but already the kinship of brother-and-sister: in the very rhyme in which the word seeks the fraternal resonance (*den geschwisterlichen Klang*) in its sense [*à son sens*] (*Im Reim sucht das Wort den geschwisterlichen Klang seines Sinnes*). But *geschwisterlich* qualifies the fraternal *qua* kinship between brother and sister. And the fraternity of this rhyme is German, 'German rhyme', not the 'traffic signal' (*Leuchtfeuer*) or the 'fireworks' of a 'Victor Hugo'! 'She is Echo (*Er ist Echo*), the clothing and the finery' (the heart of the text is the theme of nakedness and clothing); she is the 'witch's broomstick' for the place (*Ort*) of sense – its location and its dislocations.

Schmitt then evokes the speech of 'sibylline' poets, his 'friends', in fact, Theodor Däubler and Konrad Weiss. 'The obscure play of their rhymes becomes sense and prayer.'

This is the obscure friendship of rhyme: alliance, harmony, assonance, chime, the insane linking [*appariement*] of a couple. Sense is born in a pair, once, randomly and predestined.

The friendship of these two friends (and that makes three) would opportunely remind us that a friendship should always be poetic. Before being philosophical, friendship concerns the gift of the poem. But sharing the invention of the event and that of the other with the signature of a language, friendship engages translation in the untranslatable. Consequently, in the political chance and risk of the poem. Would there not always be a politics of the rhyme?

The prisoner lends an ear to the speech of his poet friends; he is suffering, and sees that he is not naked but 'dressed and on the way home' (*bekleidet und auf dem Weg zu einem Haus*).

The last words are those of a poem. As untranslatable as its rhymes. Naming Echo, it calls out to her as, naturally, she is born, grows or matures (*wächst*), like *phúsis*, in front of each word, before all speech; and she in effect comes first, she is the first word of the poem.

Echo wächst vor jedem Worte.

Everything begins with Echo. But only in a language, for a people, and for a nation. Rhymes sign, and in cadence seal a belonging. Rhymes attune the word of a language with place, then with a place's gate, an 'open place', but 'our gate'. And the stamp of the rhyme, like the hammer of a storm, bestows on Echo − we will be hearing it − an accent as exalted as it is sinister:

> *wie ein Sturm vom offnen Orte*
> *hämmert es durch unsre Pforte.*

A sinister exaltation, for one would have had to remind Schmitt − among so many other things, so as to warn him, if it were not too late − that in all languages − all languages − and therefore for all peoples, a rhyme can become a 'traffic signal'. And sometimes worse still. Such a risk is inscribed flush with the structure of rhyme, in the insane couple it forms with itself, in the *philautie* of its linkage. It is also a technique, and can become mechanized to serve the law of the worst. To speak, soberly, only of traffic signals − all languages fall prey to them, as do the great poets of all languages. And nothing looks more like the traffic signals of one country than those of another, in Europe or elsewhere: this is the law.

On another occasion, we shall say something different to honour Echo − the Echo of the *Metamorphoses*, in any case. This is not the place.

Here, in its 'obscure play' − yes, in what such play recalls of what is most sombre − a particular German Echo retains the power to make both those who agree to hear her and those who prefer to remain deaf tremble.

We shall therefore translate neither for the former nor for the latter:

> *Echo wächst vor jedem Worte*
> *wie ein Sturm vom offnen Orte*
> *hämmert es durch unsre Pforte.*

Notes

1. '*Nach deutschem Sprachsinn (wie in vielen anderen Sprachen) ist "Freund" ursprünglich nur der Sippengnosse. Freund ist also ursprünglich nur der Blutsfreund, der Blutsverwandte, oder der durch Heirat, Schwurbrüderschaft, Annahme an Kindes Statt oder durch entsprechende Einrichtungen "verwandt Gemachte"*' (*The Concept of the Political*, Corollary II, p. 104 of the German edition).

2. '*Umeis ára eí philoei eston allélois, phúsei pē oikeioi esth'umin autois*' (*Lysis*, 221e).

3. CP, p. 29.

4. Ibid., pp. 74–5.

5. Ibid., pp. 62–3. [Hegel's definition of the enemy, which Schwab has not included in his translation of this section of CP, is from the *System of Ethical Life*, trans. H.S. Harris and T.M. Knox, Albany, State University of New York Press 1979, p. 147.]

6. Ibid., p. 63 (Derrida's emphasis).

7. *Theorie des Partisanen, Zwischenbemerkung zum Begriff des Politischen*, Duncker & Humblot, Berlin 1963. p. 25 [henceforth abbreviated TP. Page references are to the German edition, and all English translations of this work are my own – Trans.]

8. TP, pp. 25–6.

9. (*'Tellurischer fundiert als die Lenins.'*) Ibid., p. 61.

10. Ibid., pp. 29, 41.

11. (*'die dünne Brücke über einem Abgrund.'*) Ibid., p. 37.

12. *'aus ihrem Bewusstsein verdrängt.'* Ibid., p. 41.

13. TP, p. 46.

14. Ibid.

15. *'Begriffsauflösung'*. Ibid., p. 25.

16. *'eine umstürzende Wendung.'* Ibid., p. 53.

17. TP, p. 49.

18. Ibid., p. 52. Thanks to the spectral 'evocation' (*Beschwörung*) of the partisan.

19. Ibid., p. 56.

20. Ibid.

21. Ibid., p. 57.

22. Ibid., p. 65.

23. (*'Bruderkampf.'*) Ibid., p. 59.

24. (*'gegen den eigenen, nationalen Bruder.'*) Ibid., p. 63.

25. On this question, that of surrogate mothers – in sum, well before the surrogate mother – on its 'classical and modern' stakes, on the ineradicable phantasm of an identifiable mother on the basis of the testimony of the perceptible (the identity of the father, a 'legal fiction' as it is called in Joyce's *Ulysses*, remaining inferred in a judgement), on the phallogocentric blindness of Freud, among others, who sees, in the *Rat Man*, patriarchy as the condition of progress in human reason and culture, I would like to refer the reader to my essay: *Le concept d'archive, une impression freudienne*, Galilée 1996.

26. The tradition that Schmitt refers to, that of the oath of fraternity or the sworn brother, is no doubt not foreign to the rich strands of the tradition found in the Icelandic sagas. *'Föstbrodir'* means foster brother or sworn brother. The *Saga of the Sworn Brother* and that of *Gisli Súrsson* describe a friendship formed in rituals and sacred liturgies. The concept of sworn brother has wide application. It also determines adoptive fraternity between so-called natural or legitimate brothers and brothers welcomed into the same family, following the usage of *fóstri* (no doubt of Celtic origin), often intended to increase clan power or to save an inheritance. See *La Saga des frères jurés* or *La Saga de Gisli Súrsson*, in *Sagas islandaises*, texts translated, introduced and annotated by Régis Boyer, Gallimard, 'Bibliothèque de la Pléiade', 1987.

27. On this point see *De l'esprit, Heidegger et la question*, Galilée 1987, pp. 147 ff. [*Of Spirit. Heidegger and the Question*, trans. Geoffrey Bennington and Rachel Bowlby, University of Chicago Press, Chicago and London 1989, pp. 129–36.]

28. CP, pp. 14–15. [The preface to the 1963 edition of CP has not been translated. I have done so from the French – Trans.]

29. *Lysis*, 220ce.

30. Ibid., 222a.

31. I hope I have not stretched too far the limits of the semantic field generally ascribed to *oikeiótēs*. I refer the reader here, as I should do more often, to Jean-Claude Fraisse's fine study, *Philía, La notion d'amitié dans la philsophie antique* (Vrin 1984). In the chapter devoted to an analysis of *Lysis*, to its place in the Platonic corpus and to the idea of *oikeiótēs*, the analysis provides an enlightening definition, but one which I would like to expand slightly, while suspending the values of 'personality' and 'interiority', which are perhaps difficult to fit into this Greek context. The definition is as follows: 'in a rather rich ambiguity, the adjective *oikeios* connotes, in Plato as in common language, that which is one's own, personal, even intimate and interior, as well as that which is close, from the parent or the friend to the compatriot. It thus takes on all the original signification of the term *phílos*, while undoubtedly stressing more than that word the relation to personality and to interiority. Plato will play on this ambiguity to designate the good as our *oikeion*, to the extent to which it is always simultaneously exterior and intimately present for us. . . .' And a quotation from the *Symposium* (205e) confirms this result, yet introduces – Fraisse makes no note of it – a distinction, perhaps a veritable disjunction generating desire, between what belongs, as one's own, and the good, designated as *oikeion*: 'Love longs for neither the half nor the whole of anything except the good. . . . Indeed, I think we prize our own belongings only in so far as we say that the good [is our own] (*oikeion*), belongs to us, and the bad belongs to someone else (*allotrion*)' (pp. 143–4).

Is it not this last difference, as important as that which disjoins the what is one's own and distinguishes it from the homogeneous (*oikeion*/*homoion*), a difference stressed in the last page of *Lysis*?

32. *Hamlet oder Hekuba. Der Einbruch der Zeit in das Spiel*, Stuttgart, Klett Verlage 1985. We will attempt elsewhere to take up this essay in its own right. It conducts a dialogue in passing with Benjamin (Schmitt recalls Benjamin's debt to his own definition of the sovereign decision, which the latter acknowledged in a letter of 1930). Beyond ancient tragedy and the Atreides, through the themes of vengeance, of the brother and of election, this essay also questions the political destiny of the 'European spirit'. If the latter has been 'demythologized' since the Renaissance, how is it that Hamlet (or the process of a 'Hamletization of the avenger') has become a myth? Among the three major works of European literature, among the three symbolic figures that have marked a reversal – indeed, a deranging and derailing of the spirit, a madness of the spirit that becomes out of joint or is derailed (*'Alle drei sind vom Geist aus der Bahn geworfen'*): Don Quixote, 'Spanish and purely Catholic'; Faust, 'German and Protestant'; finally Hamlet, occupying the middle position between the two (the German and the Spaniard, let us remember, the two Resistance fighters, the two inventors of the war of partisans against the State, the Napoleonic army and its 'humanitarian ideology'), Hamlet would connote this between-the-two, the fission or the division of this milieu, this *Spaltung* which has 'determined the destiny of Europe' (*Hamlet steht zwischen beiden mitten in der Spaltung, die das Schicksal Europas bestimmt hat*', p. 54).

But – a well-known theme (see Heidegger) – this between-the-two as a rending is also a name for Germany. Recalling that in Hamlet has been recognized the figure of 'the German people', a people 'torn and divided within itself', Schmitt quotes several times from the poem 'Hamlet', written shortly before the liberal revolution of 1848 by Ferdinand Freiligrath. The poem begins: '*Deutschland ist Hamlet!*'.

33. Since he calls upon the *Republic* when he needs to explain his concept of *pólemos*, Schmitt might have remembered that Plato, in precisely these same passages, has a word to say for women in war. He tries his best, a little, in his own way, to do right by them, whether they fight on the front or remain behind to frighten the enemy. Having noted that the warriors would be all the more successful in war for knowing each other 'by the names of brothers, fathers, sons', Plato adds: 'And if the females should also join in their campaigns, whether in the ranks or marshalled behind to intimidate the enemy, or as reserves in case of need, I recognize that all this would make them irresistible.' *Republic*, V, 471d.

34. 'Weimsheit der Zelle', in *Ex Captivitate Salus, Erfahrungen der Zeit 1945/47*, pp. 80–87.

35. 'According to a remark by a commentator in the immediate post-war period, Schmitt "could be neither nazified nor denazified" ('Der Fall Carl Schmitt: Charaktermord', *Der Fortschritt*, 4, 25 January, 1952', J.-W. Bendersky, 'Carl Schmitt at Nuremberg', *Telos* 72, Summer 1987, p. 96.

36. This is the central and organizing affirmation of his *Political Theology*, 1922, 1969. As for these problems, particularly the way they are posed in Schmitt, I refer the reader to a remarkable article by Jean-François Courtine, 'A propos du "problème théologico-politique"', in *Droits, Revue française de théorie juridique*, 18, 1993, pp. 109–18.

37. '*Und wer kann mich wirklich in Frage stellen? Nur ich mich selbst. Oder mein Bruder. Das ist es. Der Andere ist mein Bruder. Der Andere erweist sich als mein Bruder, und der Bruder erweist sich als mein Feind*', *Ex Captivitate Salus*, p. 89.

38. On this theme ('*All men are brothers*' or '*All human beings are siblings*') see Marc Shell's rich and recent *Children of the Earth, Literature, Politics and Nationhood*, Oxford 1993.

39. Heraclitus, fragment 53. We shall take up the Heideggerian reading of this fragment later. We shall mention a letter that Heidegger, still rector, sent in August 1933 to Schmitt, who had just sent him the second edition of *The Concept of the Political* and had no doubt, in the dedication or in an accompanying letter, quoted this fragment of Heraclitus.

40. *Sang an Palermo*. In August 1946, Schmitt dedicated a text to 'two Berlin graves', Kleist's and Däubler's. This and the following verse ('*Und er wird uns, wir ihn zum selben Ende hetzen*') form the epigraph of a recently published book on which I regret that I am not able to comment: Heinrich Meier, *Die Lehre Carl Schmitts*, Metzler, Stuttgart/Weimar 1994.

41. On Antigone, Hegel, and Greek, Jewish, or Christian families, on the speculative thought of the Holy Family, I refer the reader to *Glas* [trans. John P. Leavey, Jr and Richard Rand, University of Nebraska Press 1986 (1974)].

He Who Accompanies Me

Amor enim, ex quo amicitia nominata est . . .

Ex quo exardescit sive amor sive amicitia. Utrumque enim ductum est ab amando . . .[1]

Cicero

nature, the minister of God and the governor of men, has made all of us in the same form, in the same mould as it were, so that we should recognise each other, as *fellow-beings – or rather, as brothers*. . . . Rather must we believe that in giving greater shares to some and less to others, she wanted to leave scope for the exercise of *brotherly love*, with some people being in a position to offer assistance and others needing it. Since then our good mother nature has given all of us the whole world as our dwelling, and has, so to speak, lodged us all in the same house, and has designed us on the same pattern so that each of us could see himself reflected in others and recognise himself in others, and has given us all the great gift of speech so that we could come to a still deeper acquaintance and brotherhood, and acquire a common will by sharing our thoughts one with another, and has striven by every possible means to bind us together in the tight embrace of kinship and companionship, and has shown in everything she does that her intention was not so much to make us united as to make us one – we cannot doubt that we are by nature free, since we are companions of each other. And nobody can imagine that nature has placed anyone in a position of servitude, since she has made each of us *the companion of all others*.[2]

La Boétie

But there is no example yet of woman attaining to it.

Montaigne

And the brother is revealed as my enemy, Schmitt said. My own enemy. The suitability [*convenance*: also affinity, correspondence, appropriateness, convenience] of the enemy. The suitability of the enemy at one's own convenience. The enemy had indeed to be there already, so near. He had to be waiting, lurking close by, in the familiarity of my own family, in my own home, at the heart of resemblance and affinity, within parental 'suitability', within the *oikeiótēs* which should have lodged no one but the friend. This enemy was a companion, a brother, he was like myself, the figure of my *own* projection; but an *exemplarity* more real and more resistant than my own shadow. My truth in painting. The enemy did not *rise up*; he did not come *after* the friend to oppose or negate him. He was already there, this fellow creature, this double or this twin; I can identify and name him.

The proof? He has disappeared, he has slipped off and I must call him back. The proof, above all others, is that I am still able to address him, him as well as them ('Enemies, there is no enemy!') for there immediately are, *and by this very token, more than one of them*, for the enemy, by definition, includes me. ... To the point of madness: how many of them, of us, are there? Are we going to count the enemies now? And suddenly, how many brothers? I can call the enemy to appeal to him. I can do so owing to him, owing to his being the origin as well as the destination of the call. When did this begin? Who began?

'"Friends, there are no friends!" cried the dying sage;
"Enemies, there is no enemy" shouts the living fool that I am.'

A moment ago, we were saying that I can call the enemy. The friend too. Theoretically, I can talk to both. But between talking *to them* and speaking *of them* there is a world of difference. In the apostrophe, there are first of all the friends *to whom* the dying sage was talking, and the enemies *whom* the living fool addresses. This is in each case the first part of the sentence, the vocative moment of the interjection. Then come the friends and enemies – the second part of the sentence – *of whom* the sage and the fool speak, *on the subject* of whom they pronounce a verdict. On the subject of whom something is said in the form of assertion, predication, judgement. And as if by chance, from the moment they are spoken of instead of being spoken *to*, it is to say that they are no longer, or not yet, there: it is to register their absence, to *record* [*constater*] after having *called*. They are summoned to be spoken to, *da*, then dismissed, *fort*, saying to them, speaking *of them*, that they are no longer there. One speaks *of them* only in their absence, and *concerning* their absence.

We are now going to deal with this difference. We are going to speak of it while speaking to you, through several detours. In English, this would be *to address* the possibility of this question. The question lies clandestinely on the threshold of our sentence, restlessly occupying the grammatical secret of its first word, a single letter, ω. We are going to speak *of it*, talk *with it*, talk *to it*, across several philological debates around the unstable status of this initial *ōméga*. Everything, in effect, begins with the last letter; everything begins in a certain undecidability of the *ōméga*. But before saying even one word about it, we can divine a certain friendship towards the enemy *to whom* we are talking, and sometimes this friendship is more intense than the one with the friend *of whom* we speak. But nothing is ever certain.

When you speak to someone, to a friend or an enemy, does it make any sense to distinguish between his presence or absence? In one respect, I have him come, he is present for me; I *presuppose* his presence, if only at the end of my sentence, on the other end of the line [*au bout du fil*], at the intentional pole of my allocution. But in another respect, my very sentence simultaneously puts him at a distance or retards his arrival, since it must always ask or presuppose the question 'are you there?'. This drama of presupposition is at work in the *messianic sentence* we were speaking of above[3] (the incredulous believer who presently addresses the Messiah, while the latter, in rags in one of the capital's suburbs, moves about, as always, incognito: 'When will you come?', thereby removing or deferring into the future the very thing whose coming he verifies, calls for, salutes and perhaps fears). There is nothing fortuitous in the fact that this same *contretemps* also dictates, being itself just as insane and inevitable, the *teleiopoetic sentence*, an example of which we recognized in the Nietzschean promise of philosophers to come, philosophers of the *perhaps* who may perhaps come but who are already, perhaps, at the end of the sentence promising them – providing your friendship for me lets you hear it.

In both cases, appealing to the other presupposes his advent. By this very gesture the other is made to come, allowed to come, but his coming is *simultaneously* deferred: a chance is left for the future needed for the coming of the other, for the event in general. For, furthermore, who has ever been sure that the expectation of the Messiah is not, from the start, by destination and invincibly, a fear, an unbearable terror – hence the hatred of what is thus awaited? And whose coming one would wish both to quicken and infinitely to retard, as the end of the future? And if the thinkers of the 'dangerous perhaps' can be nothing other than dangerous, if they can signify or bring nothing but threat and chance at one and the same time, how could I desire their coming without simultaneously fearing it, without going to all ends to prevent it from ever taking place? Without going to all ends to skip such a meeting? Like teleiopoesis, the messianic sentence carries within it an irresistible disavowal. In the sentence, a structural contradiction converts a priori the called into the repressed, the desired into the undesired, the friend into the enemy. And vice versa. I must, by definition, leave the other to come (the Messiah, the thinker of the dangerous 'perhaps', the god, *who*ever would come in the form of the event – that is, in the form of the exception and the unique) free in his movement, out of reach of my will or desire, beyond my very intention. An intention to renounce intention, a desire to renounce desire, etc. 'I renounce you, I have decided to': the most beautiful and the most inevitable in the most impossible declaration of love. Imagine my having thus to command the other (and this is renunciation) to be free (for I need his freedom in order to address the other *qua* other, in desire as well as in renunciation). I would therefore command him to be capable of not answering – my call, my invitation, my expectation, my desire. And I must impose a sort of obligation on him thereby to prove his freedom, a freedom I need, precisely in order to call, wait, invite. What I thus engage in the double constraint of a *double bind* is not only myself, nor my own desire, but the other, the Messiah or the god himself. As if I were calling someone – for example, on the telephone – saying to him or her, in sum: I don't want you to wait for my call and become forever dependent upon it; go out on the town, be free not to answer. And to prove it, the next time I call you, don't answer, or I won't see you again. If you answer my call, it's all over.

'Enemies, there is no enemy.' The enemy is not given. Nietzsche's *cat'apostrophe* was long since prepared, as we have seen, by such an avowal of hostility in self, within oneself. Not necessarily by a declaration of hostility but in the avowal of enmity – and in that of an enmity within the very intimacy of friendship. Prepared before Hegel, whose powerful heritage we have just recognized in *The Concept of the Political*, older than him in the patrimony, the ancestral interlocutor is once again he whose paternity Hegel was most inclined to invoke at every turn: Aristotle the grandfather. We must then return once more – and it will not be the last time we do so – to the one who will have been credited with these four incredible words that we are still transcribing without accent and without breathing, in an approximative spelling (*O philoi, oudeis philos*). We must return to the one to whom will have been lent, with so much interest, in a doubtful syntax, the indestructible capital of what, one day, one time, he would have given up to be heard 'by the young Greeks admitted into his school' – that is, this time citing Florian's quotation:

'My friends, there are no friends.'

The epigraph of the preface (1963) to *The Concept of the Political*, prior even to its first word, also convokes Aristotle. It does not relate at that point what Aristotle said about friendship or war. Nor what is said of what he said. But what he is said to have reported. For though his sayings are sometimes reported (like 'O my friends, there is no friend'), Aristotle also reported the sayings of other sages. Schmitt's epigraph, then, reports what Aristotle is said to have reported of what numerous sages declare and want to say, what they think of friendship as well as war, institution as well as destruction. It is said that Aristotle subscribed and spoke in unison with these sages (*und spricht es mitsambt in*). Like them, he believed that the cause (*Ursache*) of the institution (*Stiftung*) – hence the cause of the social and political bond, but also that of destruction (*Störung*) – is friendship on the one hand, war on the other.

Now for the epigraph, again a quotation: 'Aristotle reports what numerous sages say and think, and he speaks with them: friendship and war are the origin of all institutions and all destruction.'[4]

If something *is converted* or *inverted* in the two Nietzschean apostrophes, this is perhaps not so much because of the *content* of the utterances: the reversal of friendship into enmity. Once again, a reversal would perhaps leave things unaltered. What is of more import is what is inscribed rather, earlier [*plutôt, plus tôt*], prior to their contents, in the *modalities* of the uttering. Here and now, the quotation in the past tense (*so rief*), the exclamation *attributed* to a dying sage (*der sterbende Weise*), is replaced by a quotation – or rather, by the performative uttering of an exclamation in the present tense (*ruf ich*). A first-person singular responds to it, a person presented precisely as a living fool (*ruf ich, der lebende Tor*), a fool and living by that very token – and perhaps, too, because the loss of the enemy no longer leaves him either enough reason or enough force to identify himself, to pose himself in opposing himself, to present himself in the present or to *gather himself as himself* (*ego cogito, ego sum*, 'the I think' which *accompanies* all my representations, transcendental consciousness, *Jemeinigkeit* of *Dasein*, etc.). Without an enemy, I go mad, I can no longer think, I become powerless to think myself, to pronounce '*cogito, ergo sum*'. For that I must have an evil genius, a *spiritus malignus*, a deceitful spirit. Did not Schmitt allude to this in his cell? Without this absolute hostility, the 'I' loses reason, and the possibility of being posed, of posing or of opposing the object in front of it; 'I' loses objectivity, reference, the ultimate stability of that which resists; it loses existence and presence, being, *logos*, order, necessity, and law. 'I' loses the thing itself. For in mourning the enemy, I have not deprived myself of this or that, this adversary or that rival, this determined force of opposition constitutive of myself: I lose nothing more, nothing less, than the world.

How will reason be safeguarded in such a mourning? How is the enemy *to be mourned*? How is that to be worked out, however timidly? But at this point, how will you avoid thinking that reason is intimately linked to enmity, that reason is the friend of the enemy?

Philosophy is at stake here, and this is what the cry of the living fool gives up to be heard. This is the piece of news brought forth on the winds of rumour, in its direct and continuous propagation ('O my friends . . .') or in inverted form ('Enemies . . .').

Hence a first question: in what respect does Nietzsche here reverse a Greek and properly philosophical tradition of *philía*? In what respect, in a context which would rather be *Zarathustra*'s, does he denounce, instead, the Christian mutation that prefers the neighbour, to the Greek friend? And the neighbour, *this other brother* – is he not something else again than the Greek friend, than the near one of *oikeiótēs* or – to speak Ciceronian – the near one of *propinquitas*, the proximity of neighbourhood and familial alliance? Would this neighbour be something altogether different from my relatives, something else again in being simply altogether other, the trace or the son or the brother of the altogether other?

At the origin there is a rumour, an 'it is said', an 'it is said that he is supposed to have said'. The origin of a rumour is always unknown. Indeed, this is how a rumour is identified. To say 'the origin is not known and never will be' is always – let us not doubt the importance of this risk – to open up the space of rumour and to license the 'it is said', 'idle talk', and the myth. But the question 'Who signs a rumour?' does not necessarily amount to the question 'Who becomes responsible for its proverbialization?'.

If the author of these four words, their very first signatory, is a matter of conjecture, can you at least trust the *letter* of the reported remark? The very spelling and grammar of the transcription? Nothing is less certain. From quotation to quotation, from glosses to glosses, from poems to philosophemes, from fables of morality to precepts of wisdom, from Montaigne to

Deguy and Blanchot, including Florian, Kant, Nietzsche, and so many others, an impressive convoy of Western culture has perhaps opted, at one particular marshalling yard, for a mistake on the part of a copyist or specialist in hermeneutics. Perhaps: there can be no testament without the possibility of a philological sidetracking. A testament is read, offers itself to readings, but also ordains readership; the testament is the Bible of hermeneutics. The fable would then not be *The Hare, its Friends and the two Chipmunks* but, rather, *what* the storyteller accuses the hare of not knowing: what Aristotle is reported to have said:

> . . . but my hare had this whim / and didn't know what Aristotle / Used to say to young Greeks upon entering his school: / My friends, there are no friends . . .

Come now, would Aristotle ever have said that? And what if it were a fable? And even supposing he said it, what could he have meant by it?

Let us first take note of this: the citational rumour does not seem to have any origin. It would never have begun, but would have simply alleged the simulacrum of its inauguration. In his *Lives of Eminent Philosophers*, Diogenes Laertius does not himself quote the sentence Aristotle is reported to have said. He is already playing the spokesperson for what Favorinos reports in his *Memoirs*.

Everything here seems to issue from a last will and testament. Explicit arrangements were entrusted to lawful authorities by a mortal. The reference to Aristotle's testament (*diathéké*) is its tone-imparting context. Friendship will never be described differently. Its description requires the last will and testament. Diogenes Laertius describes the contents of the testament like a public notary, a friend of the family, sharing in their mourning. He is, as it were, one of the legatees. As if he were conducting an inventory, he first reports the fine sentences and attractive apophthegms attributed to the philosopher. He is said to have answered the question 'what is a friend?' (*ti esti phílos*) through the *economic* figure of *habitat*. The body houses the soul, offers its hospitality, inviting it to stay over. But how is this topology of habitat in friendship to be thought? 'What is a friend?' Response: 'One soul in twin bodies'.[5]

Dislodging the logic and identity of the territory in general, designating a principle of errancy, the letter of this response might well leave no one at peace. It would provide food for thought: a friend, having more than one place ['twin bodies'], would never have a place of his own. He could never count on the sleep or nourishment of the economic intimacy of some 'home'. The body of the friend, his body proper, could always become the body of the other. This other body could live in his body proper like a guest, a visitor, a traveller, a temporary occupant. Friendship would be *unheimlich*. How would *unheimlich, uncanny,* translate into Greek? Why not translate it by *atópos*: outside all place or placeless, without family or familiarity, outside of self, expatriate, extraordinary, extravagant, absurd or mad, weird, unsuitable, strange, but also 'a stranger to'? Fundamentally, 'unsuitable' would be the most ominous, since friendship was so often defined by that suitability (*oikeiótēs*) fitting to familiarity, as in a bonding affinity. And here we have madness rising up on the premisses. If we are stressing this strange *atopia* of the friend, the reason lies in the irreducible tension that may ensue in its confrontation with the principle, at once topical and familial – precisely the principle of suitability – which elsewhere defines the political, but in its bond to the bond of friendship.

[A digression here, remaining between square brackets, on suitability, unsuitability. Montaigne draws the most audacious and the most uncontestable consequence of this – if you like – *doubly singular* definition of the friend: the friend *qua* one soul (singularity) but in two bodies (duplicity). Here again quoting Aristotle, keeping to the letter of his discourse, Montaigne nurtures this double singularity. He maintains its rigour to the point of the most troubling paradoxes in the logic of gift, loan, debt or duty – indeed, in the logic of gratitude – and therefore in the genealogy of morals. For any and all calculations are impossible, and these very words lose their meaning if it is true that friends are 'one soul in bodies twain following that most apt definition of Aristotle's'. The impossibility of this calculation, the ruin of the ordinary meaning of words, the avalanche of logical and grammatical absurdities, are the signs that allow the difference between 'sovereign and masterful' friendship and 'other ones' to be determined. The *philía* most devoted to the other, the most heterotopical or heterophilial, is no other, finally, than the friendship of self, *philautia*, if not narcissism – and that's not bad for a start. No more gifts or debts or duties between friends. If someone is to say thank you, it is the person giving to the person accepting. Montaigne has just quoted Aristotle ('O my friends, there is no friend!'), and he then moves on:

> In this noble relationship, the services and good turns which foster those other friendships do not even merit being taken into account: that is because of the total interfusion of our wills. For just as the friendly love I feel for myself is not increased – no matter what the Stoics may say – by any help I give myself in my need, and just as I feel no gratitude for any good turn I do to myself: so too the union of such friends, being truly perfect, leads them to lose any awareness of

such services, to hate and to drive out from between them all terms of division and difference, such as good turn, duty, gratitude, request, thanks and the like. Everything is genuinely common to them both: their wills, goods, wives, children, honour and lives; their *correspondence* is that of one soul in bodies twain, according to that most apt definition of Aristotle's, so they can neither lend nor give anything to each other. (I emphasize '*correspondence*' [*convenance*]; earlier Montaigne had defined friendship as the 'correspondence of wills' [*convenance des volontez*].)]

Such is the ineluctable communal and communist consequence (stylistically at once both Platonic and Aristotelian) of this absolute community *qua* the community of souls. But a communism dreaming in secret of the secret, as we shall see, a political and apolitical communism which does not count – no further than to 'one', and therefore not even up to 'one'. (Not even 'Against One', to cite the second title given to *On Willing Slavery* by the Protestants, which Montaigne, at the outset of his chapter 'On Friendship' – on this great testamentary stage – recalls. The allusion to 'our civil wars' at the beginning of the chapter gives us the clue: we are going to speak again of *stásis* and fraternity, of *stásis* among brothers.) What is, in fact, the inevitable conclusion of this 'correspondence', this so-beautiful word often used to translate *oikeiótēs*? If *correspondence* is another name for an *indivisible* community of the soul between lovers, why should it harbour this taste of death, of the impossible, of the aporia? When friends *correspond*, when they suit one another, are a good match, when they match, *one* matching *the other*, when they agree to come to each other, then *division* would affect only their bodies, it would not harm the soul of those who thus love each other in sovereign friendship. In a moment Montaigne will draw from this *indivisibility* ('For the perfect friendship which I am talking about is indivisible') still other consequences – dangerous and abyssal ones! They will interest us under the heading of *number, secrecy,* and *brotherhood* [*confrérie*].

For the moment let us follow the *economy of the gift*, the gift without gift that Montaigne deduces from this joint ownership of the soul. In this gift without gift consequent upon the joint ownership of the soul, Montaigne recognizes not so much an indistinction, a confusion or a communion but, rather, a disproportionate inversion of dissymmetry: the 'liberal' is the one who consents to receive, the debtor the one who gives. The gift is not impossible, but it is the receiver who gives, and from this point on neither measure nor reciprocity will legislate in friendship. Neither synchrony nor symmetry. As if friends were never contemporaries. Broaching this passage, we shall be wondering whether the model of this friendship with neither measure nor reciprocity, this break with the *mutuality* of exchange, still derives from the Greek paradigm of *philía*, from which Montaigne still literally seeks inspiration. And whether this question makes sense, whether there is such a paradigm – *if it is one* – which would be an example of one (an *exemplary* model or artifact) and would be *one*.

The person who gives is therefore the one who receives, as we are told in 'On Friendship'. The former thus gives only on condition that he does not have what he gives. The great but discreet tradition of this 'giving what one does not have' – which is bequeathed from Plotinus to Heidegger, then to Lacan (they do not return or give the gift back, of course; thus no one is in possession of it) – would now have to include Montaigne.

But we should underscore the fact that Montaigne, by presenting marriage, as he typically does,[6] as that which bears only an 'imaginary resemblance' to this 'holy bond' of sovereign friendship, silently dismisses heterosexual friendship, excluding a holy bond that would unite anyone other than two men, two male 'companions', in the *figure* and the *oath* of friendship, if not in so-called natural fraternity. The bond between female companions or between a woman-friend and her companion could never be equal to its model: the bond of two male companions. *The person who accompanies me*, if he is the friend of the friend that I am, *is a man*. In any case, it indeed seems as if friendship between a man and a woman cannot be, in Montaigne's view, 'sovereign' and capable of joint ownership:

> That is why those who make laws forbid gifts between husband and wife, so as to honour marriage with some imagined resemblance to that holy bond, wishing to infer by it that everything must belong to them both, so that there is nothing to divide or to split up between them. In the kind of friendship I am talking about, if it were possible for one to give to the other it is the one who received the benefaction who would lay an obligation on his companion. For each of them, more than anything else, is seeking the good of the other, so that the one who furnished the means and the occasion is in fact the more generous, since he gives his friend the joy of performing for him what he most desires. When Diogenes the philosopher was short of money he did not say that he would ask his friends to give him some but to give him some back! And to show how this happens in practice I will cite an example – a unique one – from Antiquity. (p. 214; emphasis added)

Once again, it is always the example of a testament: poor Eudemus bequeathes nothing to his two rich companions, nothing but a responsibility, a duty, a debt: to provide for his mother until her death, and to provide the dowry for his daughter's marriage. He is the liberal, since he 'bestows a grace and favour on his friends when he makes use of them in his necessity. He left them heirs to his own generosity, which consists in putting into their hands the means of doing him good.' But for Montaigne, this is only a pretext for posing the question of number. This example supposes 'more than one friend' (at least two, since Eudemus made one of the heirs the potential heir of the other). How are you going to reconcile 'more than one friend' with what 'perfect friendship' maintains of the 'indivisible'? Each 'gives himself so entirely' to his friend that he has nothing left to share with another, to 'share elsewhere'. But arithmetic defies arithmetic. Here indivisibility permits and interdicts counting. Yes, indivisibility, that of the soul and of friendship, but the perfect friend that I am, totally united in my soul to my friend, I wish to give him so much that I would prefer to see this singularity multiply to give him even more. I give of myself entirely, but this is not enough – I wish, so great is my love (in fact it is infinite), to multiply, to double, triple, quadruple my very entirety, so as to give myself entirely more than once:

> For the perfect friendship I am talking about is indivisible: each gives himself so entirely to his friend that he has nothing left to share with another: on the contrary, he grieves that he is not twofold, threefold or fourfold and that he does not have several souls, several wills, so that he could give them all to the one he loves. Common friendships can be shared.

We touch here on the most sensitive spot, the fragile and indispensable distinction, once again, between two kinds of fraternities, the natural one and the other. Natural fraternity (Montaigne, like Schmitt and so many others, seems to believe in the existence of such a thing) is not indispensable to perfect friendship; it would even be improper to it, as is natural paternity, for there can be no correspondence in the factual family ('Father and son can be of totally different complexions: so can brothers'[7]). Likewise natural friendship can be only one of the attributes which I appreciate in the other, one among others in those 'common, customary friendships' which are by definition divisible. Whereas the fraternity of alliance or election, the figure or the oath, the correspondence of convention, the fraternity of the 'covenant' as one would say in English, the fraternity of spiritual correspondence, is the indivisible essence of 'perfect friendship'. Natural fraternity is only an attribute; spiritual fraternity is a full-fledged essence, the very indivisibility of the soul in the coupling of sovereign friendship:

Common friendships can be shared. In one friend one can love beauty; in another, affability; in another, generosity; in another, a fatherly affection; in another, a brotherly one; and so on. But in this friendship love takes possession of the soul and reigns there with full sovereign sway: this cannot possibly be duplicated. If two friends asked you to help them at the same time, which of them would you dash to? If they asked for conflicting favours, who would have the priority? (p. 215)

Not only the indivisibility, nor the uniqueness of the soul, but the singularity of the couple. Montaigne seems perfectly certain that one friend, one true friend, can never demand 'conflicting favours' of you (this contradicts – at least – the desire for 'several souls and several wills', a desire properly immanent to the one [true friend] and recognized as such by Montaigne). Montaigne, above all, marks off the simultaneously political and apolitical, or a-civic, structure of a perfect friendship which assumes the impossibility of honouring multiple demands and doing one's duty beyond the couple of friends. This tension between politicism and apoliticism is all the more paradoxical since the model of the fraternal couple for such comparisons is regularly engaged in an extremely politicized scene. Here we have an invariant feature of which the friendship with the author of *Against the One* is only an example. Yet Montaigne also seems to mark off a certain transcendence of friendship with respect to the public or civic realm. Not without a subtle equivocation for which we shall have to account. It occurs at least twice in 'On Friendship'.

1. The first time when Montaigne insists on the *exceptional* nature of this *sovereign* friendship. If it is exceptional, it depends on fortune, on what *happens*: *túkhē*; and if 'it is already something if Fortune can achieve it once in three centuries',[8] no political project can predict, prescribe or programme it. No one can legislate on the matter. A passive decision, an unconscious one, the decision of the other in myself. Exceeding all generality. If Aristotle tells us that 'good lawgivers have shown more concern for friendship than for justice', this is precisely because the former should be placed above the latter, and even that such legislation is perhaps no longer of a juridical or political order. (Michelet will say in his *Journal* – and we shall come back to this – 'Fraternity is the law above the law'.[9]) The law of friendship here seems – at least for the Montaigne who refers in his own way to Aristotle's authority – heterogeneous to political laws. Better yet, its universality being only one of exceptional singularities, it would be *heterogeneous* to genericity, to all law – indeed, to all concepts that would not form the genus of the non-genus, the genus of the unique. The unique

must be, every time, as is said of genius, a genus: in its own unique respect its own genus. The condition for the outburst of the 'I love you' of love or friendship. Hence the obligatory conclusion that spiritual fraternity is a-generic and a-geneological. There is no law of the genus for such unique brothers:

> thus preparing for that loving-friendship between us which as long as it pleased God we fostered so perfect and so entire that it is certain that few such can even be read about, and no trace at all of it can be found among men of today. So many fortuitous circumstances are needed to make it, that it is already something if Fortune can achieve it once in three centuries.
>
> There seems to be nothing for which Nature has better prepared us than for fellowship – and Aristotle says that good lawgivers have shown more concern for friendship than for justice.[10] Within a fellowship the peak of perfection consists in friendship; for all forms of it which are forged or fostered by pleasure or profit or by public or private necessity are so much the less beautiful and noble – and therefore so much the less 'friendship' – in that they bring in some purpose, end or fruition other than the friendship itself.
>
> Nor do those four ancient species of love conform to it: the natural, the social, the hospitable and the erotic. (p. 207)

Friendship *at the principle* of the political, to be sure, but then – and to this very extent – friendship beyond the political principle – is that right? Is that the good (beyond being)? The friendship of a justice that transcends right [*le droit*], the law [*la loi*] of friendship above laws – is this acceptable? Acceptable in the name of what, precisely? In the name of politics? Ethics? Law? Or in the name of a sacred friendship which would no longer answer to any other agency than itself? The gravity of these questions finds its examples – endless ones – every time a faithful friend wonders whether he or she should judge, condemn, forgive what he decides is a political fault of his or her friend: a *political* moment of madness, error, breakdown, crime, whatever their context, consequence, or duration.

2. The second time, in praising the response of Blosius when he declares his allegiance to the orders of Gracchus – an apparently unconditional fidelity, since it would have held even if Gracchus had ordered him to set fire to the temples. But, perhaps things are not so clear:

> They were more friends than citizens; friends, more than friends or foes of their country or friends of ambition and civil strife. Having completely committed themselves to each other, they each completely held the reins of each other's desires; granted that this pair were guided by virtue and led by reason (*without*

which it is impossible to harness them together), Blosius' reply is what it should have been.[11]

The dividing line between the political and the apolitical is no longer assumed as soon as the *unconditional* engagement (and therefore the apparently transcendental engagement with respect to the public realm) with the friend supposes a priori reason and virtue. They could never incite wrongdoing, nor even allow something harmful to the public sphere to be done. Friendship can exist only between good men, repeats Cicero.[12] Reason and virtue could never be *private*. They cannot enter into conflict with the public realm. These concepts of virtue and reason are brought to bear in advance on the space of the *res publica*. In such a tradition, a virtuous reason or a rational virtue that would not be in essence homogeneous to the best reason of State is unthinkable. All the couples of friends which serve as examples for Cicero and Montaigne are citizen couples. These citizens are men whose *virile virtue* naturally tends, however successful or unsuccessful the attempt, to the harmonization of the measure of friendship – unconditional union or affection – with the equally imperative reason of the State.

The friendship between these two men who are *as brothers* is also the passion of a love. At least love is its origin, for Cicero never fails to recall the affinity of friendship and love which gives the former its name ('*Amor enim, ex quo amicitia nominata est.*'[13]) There is no secret capable of separating two experiences in which sometimes, in the singularity of an occurrence, what is fundamentally the same *socius*, the same friendship, the same virtue, the same reason, is revealed. This identity is *sometimes* revealed, it is *perhaps* bestowed by fortune and in a state of wonder: the *túkhē* of what *happens* to a virile couple of friends, 'once every three centuries'.

Yet Montaigne seems to continue to dream of a fundamental apoliticism or transpoliticism, which would command secrecy, an equally unconditional secrecy. Placing the law of secrecy above the laws of the city, this apolitical drive divides reason or virtue. The apolitical drive allows the essence of secrecy – or the interdiction of perjury – *and*, simultaneously, the essence of the political, to be read. Essences not *qua* facts or orders, but *qua* two oaths, two engagements, two responsibilities. Here again, this *double bind* does not happen to fraternity like an accident, but draws an interior and tragic structure out to its limit. One must choose between the sovereign fraternity of secrecy between two, in the friendship of exception, and, on the other hand, the brotherhood or the conjunction of political secrecy, which begins with three:

If one entrusted to your silence something which it was useful for the other to know, how would you get out of that? The unique, highest friendship loosens all other bonds. That secret which I have sworn to reveal to no other, I can reveal without perjury to him who is not another: he is me. It is a great enough miracle for oneself to be redoubled: they do not realize how high a one it is when they talk of its being tripled. The uttermost cannot be matched. If anyone suggests that I can love each of two friends as much as the other, and that they can love each other and love me as much as I love them, he is turning into a plural, into a confraternity, that which is the most 'one', the most bound into one. One single example of it is moreover the rarest thing to find in the world. (p. 215)

In each feature of this sovereign friendship (exception, improbable and random unicity, metapolitical transcendence, disproportion, infinite dissymmetry, denaturalization, etc.), it might be tempting to recognize a rupture with Greek *philía* – a testamentary rupture, as some would hasten to conclude, a palaeo- or neo-testamentary rupture. How easy that would be! The irruption of the infinite! A reassuring principle would thereby be found, the diachronic order of a scansion, a periodization which the painstaking historian would then have to refine or overdetermine. But the fact is here before us: we have just verified that this new 'paradigm' is not the coherent and applied consequence of a Greek principle of correspondence or suitability (*oikeiótēs*). This logical concatenation could rightly, even literally, place itself under the aegis of Aristotle, under that of his argument reported by Diogenes Laertius – that 'correspondence' is but one 'of one soul in bodies twain, according to that most apt definition of Aristotle's'; that therefore friends 'can neither lend nor give anything to each other'. If this continuity spreads across a logic, a rhetoric, and a politics of 'spiritual' friendship, then it would be difficult indeed, more reckless than might be believed, to oppose a Christian fraternity to some form of Greek fraternity. Not that the discrepancies are negligible – they are undoubtedly profound and irreducible – but they do not follow from a principle of distinction or opposition. Therefore their analysis demands other protocols. We are here in the vicinity of a generative graft in the body of our culture. 'Our' 'culture' is such an old body, but such a young one too. It is a child's body, the body of so-called European culture, between all these testaments, between Greek philosophy and the so-called Religions of the Book. A patriarch, born yesterday, who knows but forgets, too young and too old to remember that his own body was grafted at birth. There is no body proper without this graft. This body 'begins' with this prosthesis or this supplement of origin. Among other consequences, endless political consequences should follow from this law. Furthermore, this is the exact locus of what is happening today, today more than ever, and will continue endlessly.

One last word to close this long parenthesis on 'one soul in bodies twain'.

'One soul in bodies twain, according to that most apt definition of Aristotle's': between Aristotle and Montaigne, among all the discourses setting off a powerful historical tremor, there is not only Cicero, but so many others. In the tortured landscape of these geological folds, on the crests of another massif rising out of it to leave on it an immense and singular signature, there is Saint Augustine. On the friend, the couple of friends, on mourning and the testament, the flow and the economy of tears on the death of a friend, the Christian infinitization of friendship or of spiritual fraternity which continues, beyond all 'conversion', to implement, in their translations, Greek and Roman schemata, Book IV of his *Confessions* would here deserve, for itself alone, an interminable meditation. We will, however, have to limit ourselves to a sort of preliminary topology.

In the first place, Augustine adopts, without quoting it, the 'most apt definition of Aristotle's': 'one soul in bodies twain'. But he does so in surprise at having survived his friend. If he is one with the deceased, if their soul is indivisible, how could survival be possible? Augustine knew his Aristotle; thus he could write: 'Still more I wondered that he should die and I remain alive, for I was his second self (*ille alter eram*). How well the poet put it when he called his friend the half of his soul. I felt that our two souls had been as one, living in two bodies.' From this admirable and rightly erroneous calculation, Augustine first draws – this will be a first stage to his move – a cunning, profound, troubling consequence, which bears both his inimitable signature and a form of universal revelation. He avows 'horror', and confesses to a double terror: that of surviving and not surviving, of surviving with half his soul amputated – the ineluctable arithmetical consequence of the Aristotelian axiom – but also that of not surviving, that is, of *perhaps* (*forte*) not keeping within himself, in what is left of self, at least a little of the beloved. 'Perhaps' signs the wager, and signs the calculation as well: 'Life to me was fearful because I did not want to live with only half a soul. Perhaps (*forte*) this, too, is why I shrank from death, for fear that one whom I had loved so well might then be wholly dead.'[14] This is an abyssal calculation: do you desire to survive for yourself or for the person whom you are mourning, from the moment the two of you are as one? The paradoxes concerning the gift we were evoking above (concerning what would come down to giving in the name of the other [*donner au nom de l'autre*, also: 'giving to the other's name']) in this case translate as follows: 'to survive, or not, the name of the other [or: 'in the name of the other']', for self or for the other, for the other in self, in a narcissism which is never related to itself except in the mourning of the other. Augustine can be suspected of offering his own egotistical interest in the conservation of the ideal pretext of the other's survival in self. Let us not proceed too quickly. For Saint Augustine will have preceded us on this path, and he will perhaps have been mistaken to accuse himself so quickly: later on – in his *Retractations*, in fact – he will beat his breast in a retrospective denunciation of the 'declamation' and 'ineptitude' of the *Confessions*, when he presumed to desire survival in order to have his friend survive in him. But here he is assigning all the weight of the excuse – in truth, the chance of mitigation, of an extenuating circumstance if not of an exoneration – to a modest adverb, the one to which we have entrusted so much, on which we have wagered so much, the adverb *perhaps*: 'This declaration appears to me as flimsy as the confession is grave, although the ineptitude is in some fashion tempered by the *perhaps* added to it.'[15]

In the second place, an *economy without reserve is unleashed*, announcing literally what we were calling above, with Montaigne, the arithmetical challenge of arithmetic, the indivisibility that induces a desire for an *infinite* multiplication of the subject. Hence a desire that aggravates all the more, to the point of vertigo, the originary guilt born with friendship. There is nothing fortuitous here, nothing necessarily indicating the path of a historical influence. For it is due to the internal logic of the indivisibility of the soul in the couple of friends: 'This is what we cherish in friendship, and we cherish it so dearly that in conscience we feel guilty if we do not return love for love (*si non amaverit redamantem*), asking no more of our friends than these expressions of goodwill (*praeter indicia benivolentiae*). This is why we mourn their death . . . and life becomes a living death because a friend is lost.'[16]

Lastly, *in the third place*, the infinitization *qua* conversion *in God*, if this can be said, of this model of fraternal friendship. Here, one would then have to call on the testimony of the entirety of the *Confessions*, for this is the very law of their movement. In following our lead, we will limit ourselves to this *point* of passage where that which is turned towards God, towards His face, entrusted to God, trusting in God, assembled in and affected by God, in the dwelling place of *God*, in the home – that is, in the family or in the filiation of God, in this 'God of virtues' whom we pray to *convert* us and to *turn* us towards Him ('*Deus virtutum converte nos et ostende faciem tuam*'[17]), is not only the friendship of the friend but the enmity of the enemy. The enemy, too, must be loved according to God. The friend should be loved *in God*; the enemy must be loved not – to be sure – in God, but *because of* God. The question is not loving the enemy *in God* – this would, moreover, be impossible – but one can and must love one's enemy because God ordains as much, for himself, because of the Cause he is. The enemy is thus *inimicus*, not *hostis*. One can imagine what Schmitt would have done with this passage, how he would have articulated it on to Christian politics and on to the properly political texts of Saint Augustine. Augustine says this at the heart of the *Confessions*: 'Blessed are those who love you, and love their friends in you and their enemies for your sake.'[18]

Was this a digression? We shall go no further for the moment. This is perhaps enough to de-configure, if not disfigure, the exemplary paradigms, the classifications, and the customary periodizations. The fact that Saint Augustine and Montaigne (among others) continue to develop, deploy and make explicit Aristotelian and Ciceronian motifs, to claim authority for themselves in the letter of these texts while undoubtedly submitting them to a sort of infinite transplantation, to an uprooting and a transplantation *of the infinite*, is enough to cause us to suspect something untimely, some non-identity with self, in each of the presumed models: Greek, Roman, Christian. Later, and again on the subject of fraternity between brothers, we shall speak of other revolutions without revolution – the French Revolution, for example – and its relation to Saint Augustine among others.]

When Diogenes Laertius reads off Aristotle's bequest, the issue is more than one of friendship. The lead is hardly hidden from view; it only disappears, to appear again a little further on. Instead of citing a sentence written by Aristotle, Diogenes is content with reporting the *Memoirs* of Favorinos, which themselves report sayings which are supposedly Aristotle's. Some series of apophthegms seem to line up aphorisms. The deductive law seems non-apparent. Under their surface discontinuity, a secret logic is controlling the reported sayings and the indirect propositions. Immediately following this domestic quip, if you like, on the way in which the soul of friends inhabits more than one body, and on the arithmetical oddity that then transforms the habitat into a haunting fear (how might a single soul inhabit more than one body without haunting them?), here are two aphorisms on the brevity of life, on the economy of survival and on the blindness of the gaze: among men, there are the savers: they believe they are immortal; they economize, rein themselves in, abstain, dispense with expenditure as if they have to live for ever (*ōs aei zēsoménous*); then there are those who spend and dispense without calculation because life is too short, as if they are about to die the next minute (*ōs autíka tethnēxomēnous*). As for the question of knowing why so much time is spent on the handsome, Aristotle would have rejected it as a blind question (*tuphlou, éphē, to erōtēma*). Why? Because one must be blind not to know the answer in advance: beauty itself? Or because only a blind person is interested in beauty, in the visibility of bodies?

More or less under the safekeeping of writings to which reference is sometimes made, Aristotle's sayings thus consigned are most often inspired, like all wisdom, by an ethical or political concern: equality, reciprocity (we might say a mutualism, a Friendly Society of *antiphileîn* which we shall later distinguish, as rigorously as possible, however difficult it sometimes remains, from egalitarianism and social security), distributive or proportional justice, a certain concept of the rights of men or of the human person. All these themes come to conspire in the murmur of an ambiguous sigh: ω φίλοι, οὐδείσ φίλοσ, a cryptic phrase whose grammar, written form, and initial accentuation still remain to be determined. Let us repeat: for the moment we are writing it without accents. In particular without an accent on the ω, without an underscored iota and without a spirit. This letter will have sketched, so as to give it space and form, a sort of crypt. Replete with twin ghosts. Around the crypt, mourning and ritual, in the course of centuries, ceremonies repeat themselves, and incantatory formulas inherited across generations of priests, and philological haunting, for love of a phrase: the history of a canonical sentence − a history, then, of exegesis, the work of the copyist: transcription, translation, tradition. All the transfers imaginable. But around a so-discreet diacritical mark, the underscored mark of a single letter which appears and disappears, around another pronunciation − in other words, around a way of *saying* otherwise. It would all come down to a difference in the way of accentuating, chanting, therefore of addressing the other. Would such a history really have depended on a single letter, the ω, the omega opening its mouth and tossing a sentence to the other? Hardly anything at all? Less than a letter?

Yes, it will have been necessary to decide on an aspiration, on the softness or hardness of a 'spirit' coming to expire or aspire a capital O, an ω: is it the sign of a vocative interjection, ω, or that of a pronominal dative, ω with a *hoi*, and hence an attribution − the friends, φίλοι, remain motionless, indifferent to what is happening to them in either case, the vocative or the nominative?

ω φίλοι, οὐδείσ φίλοσ.

What does that change? Everything, perhaps. And perhaps so little. We shall have to approach prudently, in any case, the difference created by this trembling of an accent, this inversion of spirit, the memory or the omission of an iota (the same iota synonymous in our culture for 'almost nothing'). We shall have to approach these differences wherever they count: in the modality of the uttering, the meaning of the sentence, the choice of philosophemes – in the very politics conforming to, or exploiting them [*qui s'y plient ou emploient*].

Notes

1. 'For it is love, the thing that gives us our word for friendship . . .'; 'from this a flame bursts forth, whether of love or of friendship', *Laelius de Amicitia*, VIII, 26; XXVII, 100.

2. *Slaves by Choice*, [trans. Malcolm Smith, Egham: Runnymede Books, 1988], p. 48.

3. Chapter 2 and *passim*.

4. We are quoting – as we often do, but here without modifications – M.L. Steinhauser's translation of Schmitt's preface [hitherto untranslated in English], in *La notion du politique*, *Théorie du partisan*, Flammarion, 'Champs', p. 41. It is not without interest that Schmitt cites, in the original German (1542), the chronicle (*Cillierchronik*) of a noble Slovene family. Schmitt quotes from a book by Otto Brunner published in 1939: '*Aristoteles spricht, das etlich weis sprechen und mainen, und spricht es mitsambt in, das freundtschaft und krieg ursach sindt der stiftung und störung.*'

5. '*Mía psukhē dúo sómasin enoikousa.*' In the *Eudemian Ethics* (VII, 1240b 2–15) there are formulas whose letter is the closest to this reported statement. But here, already, Aristotle reports something said, not without manifesting a certain reserve: 'Further, we say about friendship such things as that friendship is equality (*os isótes philótēs*), and true friends have but a single soul (*mían psukhen*). All such phrases point back to the single individual; for a man wishes good to himself in this fashion. . . . And wishing the existence above all of the friend, living with him, sharing his joy and his grief, unity of soul with the friend, the impossibility of even living without one another, and the dying together are characteristic of a single individual. (For such is the condition of the individual and he perhaps takes pleasure in his own company (*ísōs omilei autyos autó.*) . . . And for this reason it seems possible for *a man to be at enmity with himself;* but so far as he is single and indivisible, he is an object of desire to himself. Such is the good man, the man whose friendship is based on excellence, for the wicked man is not one but many . . .' (emphasis added.)

6. From the beginning of the essay 'On Friendship', Montaigne evokes the authority of the 'Ancient schools' to justify not only the inadequation of the marriage model to the model of perfect friendship but the incapacity of the female sex even to approach it. And it is certainly not insignificant for what is of import to us at this exact point, that the justification is couched in the logic of the gift, the market or commerce. Marriage is a free market ('a market to which only the entrance is free' – which is counted as a liability – free, that is, contractual and reversible by definition), and a

market above all, not having its signification, its end and its form in itself. It is a market without immanence, without autonomy and without the disinterestedness that fit friendship: while the 'market' of marriage is normally made 'for other purposes', 'in friendship there is no traffic or commerce except with itself'. In this, friendship is freer than the 'market' whose 'entrance is free' ('Our "willing freedom" produces nothing more properly its own than affection and loving friendship': p. 208). Furthermore, the fault lies less with marriage than in woman, in her sex:

> In addition, women are in truth not normally capable of responding to such familiarity and mutual confidence as sustain that holy bond [*saincte couture*]* of friendship, nor do their souls seem firm enough to withstand the clasp of a knot so lasting and so tightly drawn. And indeed if it were not for that, if it were possible to fashion such a relationship, willing and free, in which not only the soul had this full enjoyment but in which the bodies too shared in the union – where the whole human being was involved – it is certain that the loving-friendship would be more full and more abundant. But there is no example yet of woman attaining to it, and by the common agreement of the Ancient schools of philosophy she is excluded from it. (p. 210)

When he sends La Boétie's sonnets to Madame de Grammont, Montaigne is intent on warning her about certain verses, those that 'were written in favour of his future wife in that time when he was preparing his marriage, and which already smack of God knows what marital coldness'.

7. p. 208. Here again the Ciceronian theme, always working through presence and proximity (*propinquitas*). The law is that which is close. Although Cicero maintains that social bonds grow stronger to the extent that men are close to one another (*ut quisque proxime accedere*), that men *naturally* prefer their fellow citizens to foreigners (*peregrini*), their relatives to others (*propinqui quam alieni*), if he is intent on recalling that it is 'nature' itself that 'brings about' a friendship between relatives, Cicero specifies that this familial friendship can come to lack a sufficiently firm and stable base (*firmitatis*). Friendship is not always sufficiently durable and steadfast – '*bébaios*', as it would have been expressed in the Greek tradition. Hence the advantage of friendship over a *propinquitas* (the proximity of the close and familial alliance), which may sometimes lose this good feeling, this favourable disposition (*benevolentia*), this wanting-the-good which is never absent from friendship. This *benevolentia* associated by Cicero with *caritas* is the best gift of the gods but, in general, unites 'no more than a handful of individuals' (V, 19, 20). We are slowly approaching that arithmetic concealed in the enigma of 'O my friends . . .'.

The conclusion of *De Amicitia* firmly ties the bond of friendship to virtue as that which correctly assures the firm basis of the bond. That which in friendship is '*bébaios*', following this Greek lead, is what binds it to virtue. And it is recalled precisely through

---

* Further on, Montaigne will speak again of 'the seam [*couture*] that joins [souls] together', on the page preceding the exposition on perfect friendship, namely friendship among men: 'brotherly harmony' is a 'solder binding brothers together'; the vocabulary of the artifice, *seam* and *solder*, are as important as – if not more important than – fraternity itself. Montaigne insists on this point: friendship is not and must not be a *natural* fraternity, but a fraternity of alliance, adoption, election, oath. Why, then, this 'natural' figure? Why this adherence or this reference again to a natural bond, if one has set out to de-naturalize? Why does the natural schema remain? This is our question.

an address to friends: '*Virtus, virtus inquam*, I tell you – you, Gaius Fannius and you, Quintus Mucius: it is virtue, yes, virtue, that initiates and preserves friendship. For virtue assures harmony (*convenentia rerum*), stability, earnestness.' The whole passage is dominated by a metaphorics of glint, light, and fire. The glint of virtue is reflected from one to the other, and the reflection creates participation. The light becomes fire, and 'from this [reflection] a flame breaks forth, whether of love or of friendship (*ex quo exardescit sive amor sive amicitia*). Both terms, after all, are derived from the verb "to love" (*Utrumque enim ductum est ab amando*).' After this Cicero distinguishes love from friendship: if to love, the act of loving, in both friendship and love, is always disinterested, advantage in fact does grow out of friendship, even if it is not sought (XXVII, 100).

8. This is yet another Ciceronian topos, a quasi-quotation from *Laelius de Amicitia* ('I have been bereaved of a friend such as the world will never see again – at least, so it seems to me. One thing I am sure of is there was never such a one before. . . . How beloved he was of his fellow citizens was made clear by the mourning at his funeral. . . . For I cannot agree with those who in the last few years have begun to . . . say that the soul dies with the body and that death is the end of all things. I am more inclined to accept the point of view expressed by men of earlier days – by our own ancestors, for example, who so scrupulously observed the honours due to the dead'; and after a eulogy of Greater Greece and its institutions, after recalling shared political and personal cares, the hope that 'for all time to come men will remember my friendship with Scipio': 'in all the course of history men can name scarcely three or four pairs of friends (*paria amicorum*)' (11–15). To the couple Laelius and Scipio must be added the other masculine couples cited here or elsewhere by Cicero: Orestes and Pylades, Theseus and Pirithoüs, Damon and Phthias.

9. Cited in the entry 'Fraternity' in the *Dictionnaire critique de la Revolution française* by François Furet and M. Ozouf, Paris: Flammarion 1988, ch. IV. Reissued in the collection 'Champs' 1992, p. 210.

10. p. 207. Jean-Claude Fraisse provides an excellent clarification of this point of Aristotelian discourse. On the subject of 'ideas of reciprocity and equality' guiding justice, Fraisse points out, in effect: 'This is all identical to what friendship realizes. Yet the paths are not the same: while bringing about friendship among citizens seems to be the lawgiver's ideal,★ the existence of friendship makes the existence of justice and legislation useless.† While justice proceeds by constraint . . . friendship . . . is linked to virtue alone. . . . Thus do we see Aristotle being careful to avoid the slightest corruption of friendship by law.'

11. Emphasis added. In the wily reasoning of this page, which we are unable to follow here as meticulously as we should, the parenthesis seems to imply that if Montaigne gives his approval to unconditional obedience in certain cases, it must remain informed by reason and by virtue, without which there is no perfect friendship. Virtue and reason are not empirical conditions but appertain to the structure of sovereign and unconditional friendship. In the same move, the unconditionality cannot be *blind*. Faithful obedience is trusting, and trust is enlightened a priori by reason as well

---

★ *Nicomachean Ethics*, VIII, 1, 1115a 22–6; *Politics*, II, 4, 1262b 7–9.

† *Nicomachean Ethics*, VIII, 1, 1155a 26–7: 'when men are friends they have no need of justice, while when they are just they need friendship as well', p. 1825 [revised Oxford translation].

as by virtue which, in each of the two friends, were, from the beginning, indissociable from what binds their two wills together in the same 'harness'. As a consequence, the position taken by Montaigne appears less opposed to Cicero's than it would at first seem. Concerning the same example – Montaigne has then borrowed it from him once again – Cicero manifests an unequivocal hostility towards Caius Blosius:

> Wrongdoing, then, is not excused if it is committed for the sake of a friend; after all, the thing that brings friends together is their conviction of each other's virtue; it is hard to keep up a friendship if one has deserted virtue's camp. . . . Let us, then, lay down this law for friendship: we must not ask wrongful things, nor do them, if we are asked to. For if a man should declare that he has done a thing of this kind for a friend's sake, the excuse does him no honour and is absolutely unacceptable even in ordinary affairs, and especially so if the act was treasonable (*contra rem publicam*) (*Laelius de Amicitia*, XI, XII).

12. Ibid., V, 18.

13. Ibid., VIII, 26.

14. *The Confessions* [trans. P.S. Pine-Coffin, Penguin Books, 1961], pp. 77, 78–80.

15. *Retractations*, II, VI, 2 [as quoted by the editors of the French edition of the *Confessions* – my translation – Trans.]

16. *Confessions*, IV IX, 14, p. 79. [Pine-Coffin's translation is too telegraphic at this point: '. . . if we do not return love for love' gives short shrift to Augustine's Latin, which Derrida has respected more closely: 'if he does not love his beloved, redoubled in love (*si non amaverit redamentem*) or if he is not redoubled in love for his beloved (*aut si amantem non redamaverit*)' – Trans.]

17. *Confessions*, IV, X, 15, p. 80.

18. '*Beatus qui amat te et amicum in te et inimicum propter te*': ibid., IV, IX, 14, p. 79.

8

Recoils

In truth, those who have subscribed in complete confidence to the vocative reading that we have been pretending to follow from the outset ('O my friends, there is no friend') have not even been properly haunted by the possibility of such a secret. They have gone so fast as to be unaware of its existence. Unless the haunting begins where the extravagance of the sentence thus accentuated is troubling enough to become unforgettable to the point of obsession, thereby allowing the unsuspectable to become unconsciously suspect. And those who have allowed it, those who have preferred the interjection to the dative, the eloquence of the interpellation to the attributive assertion, are by no means few in number. To my knowledge, those who have cited, celebrated, even published the vocative sentence under examination in henceforth canonical discourses have all, without exception, read the *ōméga* as an interjection, a vocative O, which is anything but certain – which would in fact be rather dubious, as we shall show. Montaigne, Florian, Kant, Nietzsche, Blanchot and Deguy, for example, rely on this reading. And the same goes for the French, German, and Spanish translations of Diogenes Laertius that we have been able to check.[1] This, then, is the most widespread reading, the only one to have become legendary, the one to which 'On Friendship' subscribes, where Montaigne distinguishes great friendship, 'sovereign master friendship', not only from 'those other common friendships' but, indeed, from 'the most perfect of their kind'. The bond uniting me to the soul of the friend is not only the knot of an attachment between two, between two equals, two subjects, or two symmetrical wills. This bond places me under the law of the other. It disjoins and disproportions me, inspiring a confidence, a faith, a 'fidence' [*fiance*] *greater in the other than in myself*, and this disymmetry itself, alone, marks the rupture between knowing and loving, reason and affect; between knowledge and the heart – or the body and the 'entrails'. Here, 'ardent affection'; there, coldness. The knowledge we have of each other may be symmetrical and reflective, equally shared in the glass of a mirror; it is nevertheless autonomous on both sides. As for trust, it could never be measured in this way; in truth it cannot be measured, it hails from the 'depths' ['*le fin fond*'], it is not aligned on knowledge – even if, in its own sublime way, it also has such knowledge: I must trust the other more than myself, and this sliver of mirror is indeed the sign that my friendship reaches towards, and is sustained in, the other. It depends more on the other than on myself. Passion and heteronomy:

> Our souls were yoked together in such unity, and contemplated each other with so ardent an affection, and with the same affection revealed each to each other right down to the very entrails, that not only did I know his mind as well as I knew my own but I would have entrusted myself to him with greater assurance than to myself. ('On Friendship', p. 213)

This 'fidence' does not bear upon this thing or that: I do not trust the other more than myself relative to this or that object, this or that decision for which I would thus depend on his counsel, his wisdom, knowledge, or experience. No, it is on the subject of my very self, 'deep down' in myself; it is regarding myself, in the inner recess of my 'regarding myself', that I entrust myself, without measure, to the other. I entrust myself to him more than to myself, he is in me before me and more than me. 'Because it was him; because it was me': another Aristotelian topos[2], another Ciceronian topos (*'Est enim is* [*verus amicus*]*, qui est tamquam alter idem*'[3]). Heteronomic trust exceeds the reflexive forms of knowledge and consciousness of a subject, all the certitudes of an *ego cogito*. No *cogito* can measure up to such a friendship. I think from out of it, it thinks me before I even know how to think. It needs only to become evil to start looking like the Evil Genius.

Providing, however, that this friendship is not confused with the others, that the homonymy does not lead us astray. This is the moment when Montaigne quotes Aristotle, and trusts that he is quoting an interjection. He is seeking to limit its range to 'common and customary' friendships, those that can also turn into hatred (Montaigne, then, would not have been at all surprised at the Nietzschean reversal; he would have limited it to 'common' friendships and enmities):

> Let nobody place those other common friendships in the same rank as this. I know about them – the most perfect of their kind – ... you would deceive yourself. In those other friendships you must proceed with wisdom and caution, keeping the reins in your hand: the bond is not so well tied that there is no reason to doubt it. 'Love a friend', said Chilo, 'as though some day you must hate him: hate him, as though you must love him.' That precept which is so

detestable in that sovereign master friendship is salutary in the practice of
friendships which are common and customary, in relation to which you must
employ that saying which Aristotle often repeated: 'O my friends, there is no
friend!' (pp. 213–14)

Is Montaigne therefore following Diogenes Laertius? Does he not, once
again, distort the Aristotelian thematic, while developing and deploying its
letter? Does not the heteronomic disproportion of sovereign friendship,
once translated into the political realm, endanger the principle of equality,
mutuality, and autarky which, it would seem, inspires Aristotle? But our
question at every moment concerns *political translation*. It is indeed a
question of knowing the rules of translation, but first of all of making sure
that translation is possible and that everything can be translated into politics.
Is the political a universal translating machine?

We continue, then, to wonder what it might well mean for lawgivers to
'have shown more concern for friendship than for justice', as Montaigne
likes to say Aristotle liked to say. Concerning, for example, proportional
justice or a measurable equality of rights, *qua* human rights, Diogenes is
intent on saying on two occasions, and in two slightly different forms, what
Aristotle never failed to say on the subject – that his concern was for the
human qua human, the human before the individual, the human prior to all
moral difference differentiating the human and the individual. If a man
gives (for example, to someone unworthy – a conman, for instance – he
gives to the human, to the humanity of the human in him, not to his
character, to his manner of life [*tropos*], or to his morality): 'He was accused
of taking pity on a knave. He answered that he was thinking of the man,
not of his morals.'[4] He thereby invokes the form or essence of the human.
This humanity of the human destroys the finite proportionality that would
ordain the calculation of worth, to give following only this rule. A *principle
of infinity* has already entered the proportionality. In proportioning everything on the scale of the human, in measuring everything against the
standard of my friendship for the humanity of the human being, I no longer
hold to the *finite* proportion of empirical determinations or of law (the
conman is worth less than the gentleman, etc.). This excess of one
proportion over another heralds, in certain respects, the excess found in
Montaigne that is of interest to us. But here it remains measured by a
generality (the human in each human being – in every man and woman)
and not by the singularity of an attachment, by the 'affection' or sovereign
friendship of a couple the likes of which is seen once in every three
centuries. The problem of inegalitarian heteronomy remains intact. Unless

equality, a certain equality, could be saved in respect of disymmetrical and heteronomic singularities. This equality would be at once calculable and incalculable; it would count on the incalculable.

The same logic is at work on the subject of freedom, when Diogenes reports another of Aristotle's sayings. This one speaks of freedom, as well as of servitude, in a language closer to that of *On Willing Slavery* than to the one sometimes attributed to it by the *doxa* which greatly reduces its complexity. Once again, it is approximately the same question as before: 'He was accused of giving alms to a knave: He answered (for the fact is related in this manner): "I have given alms not to the individual, but to the man."'[5] He gave it not to a man, to a particular man, but to the human, to the humanity of the human race. This sentence can be compared to the *Nicomachean Ethics* (1161b). Aristotle recalls the friendship due to the slave, but the slave *qua* human, not *qua* slave. What makes the difference, here, what finally justifies friendship, is the soul or the life (*psukhé*) of the slave. More precisely, *psukhé* in so far as it will not be reduced to the technical, to the machine, to the automat or to the tool (*órganon*). The soul is what makes the slave a man. One could not be friends with an *órganon* as such. The slave is an animate tool (*émpsukhon órganon*), the tool is an inanimate slave (*ápsukhos doulos*). In so far as he remains a tool, the slave will never inspire friendship. But the animate tool is also a man, and there is general agreement that there is something *just* (*dikaion*), that there is a relation of justice between all men – that is, between beings capable of entering into a community of sharing or participation (*koinónēsai*) according to law (*nómos*) or convention (*sunthékē*), the suitability of convention. To say that one can be friends with a slave *qua* man (*kai philía dí, kath óson ánthrōpos*) is to imply, in the same systemic cohesion, a series of indissociable concepts: friendship (*philía*), man (*ánthrōpos*), soul (*psukhé*), the just (*díkaion*), law (*nómos*), and the contract (*sunthékē*). A few lines above, Aristotle had underscored the bond between justice, friendship, and communal sharing (*koinōnía*).[6] Two consequences for friendship can immediately be drawn:

1. Friendship is irreducible and heterogeneous to the tool (*órganon*), to instrumentalization or – if one can widen or modernize things in this way – to all technical dimensions.

2. This same axiomatic dooms friendship in advance to democracy *qua* its destiny. There is here not a fact but a tendential law, a relation of proportion: since there are more shared things where citizens are equal, since communal sharing implies more law, more contract and convention, democracy is, then, more favourable to friendship than tyranny (1161b 5–10). For the paternal relation is a royal or monarchical one; the relation

between a man and his spouse is aristocratic. But the relation of *brothers* is properly 'political' (often translated: 'democratic' [Salomon translates it: 'that of a commonwealth']). The *politeía* is the brothers' affair (*tôn adelphôn*: *Eudemian Ethics*, 1241b 30). Tyranny, oligarchy and democracy (Aristotle says simply *dêmos* here) are derived from these three forms. Between the political as such, fraternity, and democracy, their co-implication or mutual appurtenance would be quasi-tautological.

This concept of democracy is confirmed in the *Eudemian Ethics* (1236 ab): it is a politics of friendship founded on an anthropocentric – one could say humanist – concept. To man alone, in so far as he is neither animal nor god, is appointed the primary and highest friendship, that from which all the others receive their name, as it were, even if they are not simply its homonyms or synonyms, even if they are not its species, and even if they do not relate to this primary sense in a simply equivocal or univocal way. This friendship *in the primary sense* (*ê prôtê philía*), which is also the highest, if not the universal, sense, is that of friendship founded upon virtue (*di'aretên*). It is reserved to man, since it implies this faculty of decision, of deliberation or reflective choice (*proaíresis, boúleusis*) which appertains to neither animals nor to God. A system link will be easily recognized here between this properly human faculty (neither animal nor divine) of deliberation or calculation, on the one hand, and on the other, the concepts of law (*nómos*), convention (*sunthêkê*), or community (*koinônía*) which, as we noted above, are implied in friendship as well as in democracy, and which, furthermore, bind together, in their very essence, friendship and democracy. There is no friendship, at least *in this primary sense*, with animals or with gods. There is no friendship, either, between animals or gods. No more so than democracy, fraternity, law, community, or politics.

But are things this simple? Is one entitled to speak *only* of friendship in the primary sense, of friendship founded on virtue, without slipping into aporias and contradictions? These aporias and contradictions are perhaps of another order than those Aristotle announces as such, while promising to undo them. Having multiplied the aporias (*aporeitai de polla peri tês philías*), beginning with those of all values that seem worthy of friendship (likeness, unlikeness, the contrary or the useful), the *Eudemian Ethics* had, as it were, set down the task: beyond these opinions (*dóxai*), to find a definition, prior, precisely, to a *lógos* of friendship allowing both for an account of different opinions on this subject 'and to put an end to aporias and contradictions'.[7]

We would like to approach here, perhaps, other aporias and other contradictions, knots of thought which *perhaps* promise something else (and this 'perhaps' to which we hold is perhaps no longer a mere working hypothesis). In any case, these knots would no longer promise such an analytical outcome. They would no longer submit to being understood by such a programme, by the tasks and bonds of such a *lógos* of friendship. Consequently, they would no longer submit to being named, adequately, 'aporia' or 'contradiction' – at least in this sense, in the *lógos* of this *lógos*. They would exceed it – not towards the space or the hope of satisfactory solutions, in a new architectonic, analytical, or dialectical order, but in the direction of a sort of hyper-aporetic. It would be the arche-preliminary condition of another experience or another interpretation of friendship, and, by this very fact, the condition, at least negative, of another political thought – that is, another thought of decision and responsibility as well.

Politics of friendship: our theme thus invites us to privilege – indeed, to isolate – the place of the political in the general logic of this hyper-aporetic, in the hierarchy or architectonic proposed by Aristotle. On the one hand, as we have seen, the work of the political, the properly political act or operation, comes down to creating (producing, making, etc.) the most possible friendship (1234b 22–3). This tendential law – one might say this *telos* – seems, in the same move – to bind friendship to politics – in their origin as well as their end. If the political carries out its work in the very progress of friendship, then the two motifs, as well as the two movements, seem contemporaneous, co-originary and coextensive. In each and every aspect, friendship would be political. Is this not confirmed in Book III of Aristotle's *Politics*? Does it not stress that everything that comes to pass in the *polis* is 'the work of friendship (*philías érgon*)'? That the deliberate choice (*proaíresis*) of a living-together (*tou suzēn*) is friendship itself (1280 b 13)? Be it a matter of living together, cohabiting in the same place (*tópos*), contracting marriages or participating in the life of the phratry, offering sacrifices, etc. – all this, in effect, defines the *pólis*. Let us note in passing that the emphasis here is on the familial bond *qua* 'phratry'. The phratry is certainly not dominated by the position of the brother (*adelphós*), but it could never, in its very derivation, be totally alien to the brother's position. The *télos* of the State (*pólis*) is the 'good life (*to eu zēn*)', and the good life corresponds to the positivity of a living together (*suzēn*). This is nothing other than friendship in general. The *pólis* not only cannot not set itself up in dispersion or separation, but it cannot even be gathered *into one place* to answer in reaction to injustice or to be content with ensuring commerce. The *final* project of a community (*koinōnía*) of the good life, for families, houses, filiations, is required. And this is in view of a perfect and autarkic life (*zōēs teleías khárin kai autárkous*: 1242a, 11–12). The force and movement of this social bond *qua* political bond, the *télos* assuming its origin no less than its end, is indeed *philía*. *Philía* seems, therefore, to be thoroughly political. Its binding or attractive force binds the state (the city, the *pólis*) to the phratry (family, generations, fraternity in general) as much as to place.

This is indeed a difficult conclusion to accept in the light of a reading of other analyses. Even if *all* friendship is in some respect political, strictly or properly political friendship is only one kind of friendship. Above all, it is not the primary or the highest of its forms. One wonders how this disjoining in the very concept of the political, where it articulates itself on to the political, is to be interpreted. Why does its range seem to exceed itself or to annex a shadow which sometimes follows, sometimes precedes it? Why does the political seem to begin before the political?

Lower in the hierarchy, under 'primary' friendship, under the friendship of virtue, two other kinds of friendship share at least the same name. The third and last is grounded in pleasure (*día to ēdú*): it is unstable and most often found among young people. But concerning what is of the utmost importance to us here, the second type of friendship has something troubling about it for the very order of this conceptuality as a whole. In question is a friendship grounded neither in virtue nor in pleasure, but in usefulness (*día to khrésimon*). Unlike friendship between parents (*suggenikē*) or friendship among comrades (*etairikē*), so-called political friendship is grounded in association or community in view of the useful. The political community (*koinōnía*) is therefore neither the family nor comradeship. But given that the point of our question has for some time now directed us towards the political question of the family and, within it, to fraternity, we are obliged to take a closer look.

The family is a friendship; Aristotle says so explicitly (*oikía d'estí tis philía* – *Eudemian Ethics*, 1242a 28). *Oikía* is the family, but also the *house* in the broad sense of the term: race as well as domesticity. Now this *economic* friendship, this parental or domestic friendship, also constitutes a community (*koinōnía*), and thus features a kind of justice (*díkaion ti*). Even in the absence of *pólis*, there would be a kind of justice, notes Aristotle (ibid.). In other words, the family, in this broad sense, features the two traits of the political (community and justice – but it would be better to say 'law') where the political as such has not yet appeared, nor appeared indispensable. Familial friendship is therefore *already* political, where it is *not yet* political. But the question of the brother returns in this equivocation or in this contradiction of already-not-yet (which could be found up to and including the Hegelian concepts of family, bourgeois society and the State)[8].

Familial or *syngenic* friendship in effect comprises several species, several forms or figures (*éidē*). The excursus found in the *Eudemian Ethics* contains

only two of them: friendship between brothers and between father and
son. Neither woman, daughter nor sister is named at this point. Although
they are not excluded, they appear at least derivative or exterior to this
syngenealogical cell. But more precision is needed around this crucial point.
If the feminine figure seems exterior to the determining centre of familial
friendship (father/son/brothers), this does not mean for Aristotle that all
friendship is excluded, in general, between man and woman, husband and
wife. It means only – and here is the exclusion – that such a friendship
belongs neither to properly familial or syngenic friendship nor to friendship
in the highest sense, primary or virtuous friendship. This friendship is based
on the calculation of the useful, a friendship of partnership (*koinōnía*), hence
one of a political kind (*gunaikos de kai andros philía ōs khrḗ simon kai
koinōnía*, 1242a 32). Community between man and woman relates to useful
goods; it is a community of services, and hence political. In this sense, it is
true that it is more just if, as Aristotle notes above, the most just (*díkaion*) is
found in friendship grounded on usefulness, for such is political justice (*to
politikon díkaion*: 1242a 11–12).

Let us be still more precise and, if possible, more just. We have been
following the *Eudemian Ethics* as closely as possible. In the *Nicomachean
Ethics*, in which numerous developments intersect with the former work,
Aristotle not only proclaims once again that friendship between husband
and wife is in conformity to nature (*kata phúsin*). He adds that the inclination
to form couples and to procreate is even *more natural* than the inclination to
form a political community. The family is anterior to the city, and more
necessary. But the thing is that, unlike animals, the human family goes
beyond creation. Couples form not only for the sake of reproduction;
because of the division of work, they spread out into life as a whole. Man
and woman bring to the couple their 'own' capacities. This is a community
for usefulness, and sometimes – this must never be excluded, and Aristotle
never does exclude it – for pleasure. The two secondary friendships (of
pleasure and of usefulness) are capable, therefore, of uniting husband and wife
in a familial couple. Now among the secondary friendships, there is indeed
politics. Up to this point, we have nothing but what is set out in the
Eudemian Ethics. The clarification brought to bear by the *Nicomachean Ethics*
on our previous subject, seemingly in contradiction with it, is that *philía*
between spouses may also, sometimes, be grounded in virtue: this would
make conjugal *philía* a friendship *par excellence*, primary friendship. For this
to be the case, each party must have its own virtue so that both, reciprocally,
may profit from and delight in (*khaírein*) the virtue of the other. The enjoyment of this mutual delight, the joy of this mutual *khaírein* that delights in

and profits from the other's virtue, and even his or her *jouissance*, is friendship *par excellence*, the virtuous friendship of spouses. Very well. But this does not last. If it does, it is owing to the children, who are the indispensable link of the bond (*súndesmos*). Without children, spouses part, their bonds unravel (*dialúontai*). The children are the common good, and only that which is common can maintain conjugal union. In other words, in short, conjugal friendship cannot be grounded in virtue, and thus be grounded durably (for duration is an essential trait of virtue) unless there are children. The child is the virtue of the parents. This virtue is deposited, bequeathed, delegated to the child. The difference from animal procreation is the testament.

Now we have seen, and will verify once again, that the bond with children, the friendship between parents and children, is ordained to the father–son relation. The daughter is not named. Aristotle had just recalled, precisely in the *Nicomachean Ethics*, that if the affection between parents can take on several forms or figures, if it is '*polueidês*', all of these species seem to depend on paternal love (*pasa ek tês patrikês*: 1161b 15–20).

Without following up at this stage the taxonomic refinements that abound in the Aristotelian casuistic, let us retain at least its most determining criteria, at the points of greatest import to us – that is, in following out our guiding thread.

1. In the androcentric family unit, the father–son relation is distinguished from the fraternal relation according to the type of equality involved: propositional or analogical equality in the first case (*kat'analogían*), numerical equality (*kat'arithmón*) in the second. This is why, Aristotle states, there is proximity between fraternity and comradeship (1242a 5). This proximity constitutes a major stake from the moment interest is taken in equality in the city, and an account is needed for the figurability of the brother: the possibility of calling a true comrade brother – legitimate brother, not bastard brother. For let us not forget that it is not the fraternity we call natural (always hypothetical and reconstructed, always phantasmatic) that we are questioning and analysing in its range and with its political risks (nationalism, ethnocentrism, androcentrism, phallocentrism, etc.), it is the brother figure in its renaturalizing rhetoric, its symbolics, its certified conjuration – in other words, the process of *fraternization*. There is no – there could never be a – political fraternization between 'natural' brothers. But here Aristotle stresses the resemblance or proximity between fraternity (which he supposes to be natural) and comradeship. And exactly in so far as it concerns equality, in all places where it can be a political model. Having remarked that friendship between brothers is eminently the friendship of

comrades, friendship grounded in equality (*ē de tôn adelphôn pros allélous etairikē málista ē kat'isótēta*), Aristotle quotes Sophocles:

> for I was not declared a bastard brother to him;
> but the same Zeus, my kind, was called
> the father of us both. (1242a 35–9)

The symbolic paternity of Zeus founds the equality of allied brothers, and therefore genealogical legitimacy: confraternity without bastardization.

2. There are, then, three kinds of friendship, respectively founded, as we recall, on (1) *virtue* (this is *primary friendship*); (2) *usefulness* (for example, political friendship); and (3) pleasure. Now each species divides up into two: according to equality or according to difference (Aristotle says: according to superiority). In this move, justice too will divide into two, following numerical or proportional equality. Communities will organize the sharing out sometimes in terms of equality, sometimes in terms of the other. When numerically equal sums of money are contributed, they are shared according to their number; if the sums contributed are unequal, the money is shared out proportionally. When the inferior inverts the proportion and links up the terms crosswise (*kata diámetron*), the superior comes off the worse in the exchange: friendship or community remains that of service rendered, the liturgy (*leitourgía*) of public service; the proportion must therefore be restored and the profit, the benefit, the gain (*kérdos*) compensated. This is the distinguished role of honour (*timé*), of esteem or entitlement to consideration. This entitlement to honour belongs by nature (*phúsei*) to the archon, to the ruler or to the god. The evaluation of honour is that of a priceless price. Priceless, honour would be what saves friendship from calculation and raises it above the bargaining of rendered services. Above a certain recognition (the thanks of commerce, the market of patronage), hence the recognition of gratitude, but in the name of another recognition: the recognition of entitlement to honour.

Honour thus removes *philía* from the market. But providing that *philía* is strictly proportioned to a *hierarchy*! – and to a hierarchy which naturally (*phúsei*) attributes it to the rule, to the beginning and to command, to the archon and to the god in their relation to the ruled.[9] Honour still commands from the site of the incalculable, but the incalculable is naturally in hierarchical form – and naturally so from the standpoint of *arkhé*. This hierarchization is nothing other than the sacralization of the beginning, *qua* command. And as it is on the side of god, it is on the side of the father. Of him of whom the brothers ('natural' or by alliance, but always by alliance, is it not; always by election or convention) say they are the legitimate sons, pure of all bastardization. Honour is on this side, it withdraws itself from the market only by reason of this proper filiation. This leads us to another important distinction.

If political friendship essentially depends on usefulness, it may nevertheless be subdivided into *legal* political friendship – nomic (*nomikē*) friendship – and *ethical* (*ēthikē*) political friendship. Cities (*póleis*) may be friends with one another, and citizens (*polítai*) as well. If there is no longer what is called usefulness – which also supposes mediation, the means/ends relation, etc. – but, rather, an immediate, 'from hand to hand' relationship, States and citizens no longer know themselves as such. Everything passing 'from hand to hand' is neither of the useful nor of the political order. As for the ruler/ ruled relation (*árkhon/arkhómenon*), it is neither natural (*phusikon*) nor of the order of the kingdom (*basilikón*). It supposes the alternation of turns, 'by turns'. This 'by turns' is destined not to do good or to do well, as God would, but to distribute received goods and the liturgy of rendered services fairly. For political friendship, *qua* absolute principle and general truth, *desires equality*; it has as its decided and declared (*boúletai*) project to ground itself in equality. This is the moment when the distinction between the *legal* and the *ethical* intervenes. Political friendship is attentive to equality as well as to the thing (the affair, *prágma*), to the former as much as the latter, to one inasmuch as it also relates to the other. This is what political friendship 'looks to (*blépei*)' and what concerns it. As in a market, in commerce between sellers and buyers. Equality and the thing, the equality of things, therefore the third party and the common measure: an account and a fixed wage [*gage*] are necessary: a salary, a fee, a counter-value (*misthos*). Aristotle quotes Hesiod: 'A fixed wage for a friend (*misthros andri phílo*)', which has sometimes been translated: 'short reckonings make long friends'. When it is grounded on consent, consensus, convention (*omología*), this friendship is at once political and legal (*nomikē*). It is, then, a matter of a homology of reciprocity, as in the case of a contract, an agreement between two subscribing parties. When, on the other hand, the parties leave the matter to each other's discretion, in a sort of trust without contract, credit becoming an act of faith, then friendship 'wants to be' moral, ethical (*ēthikē*) and of the order of comradeship (*etairikē*). Why is it that in this latter case recriminations and grievances abound? Because this ethical friendship is against nature (*para phúsin*). Indeed, those who associate themselves in this way wish to have both friendships at once, one in the service of interest (based on usefulness) *and* one appealing to virtue (the reliability of the other), friendship of the second type *and* primary friendship. Here we have an equivocal calculation, a barely honest accumulation – in sum, a way of backing these two horses of friendship. Through the sober aridity of his discourse, Aristotle thus describes a tragedy as much as a comedy, major and minor calculations: this irrepressible desire to overinvest in a friendship or a love, to count on a profit in renouncing profit, to expect a recompense, if only a narcissistic or symbolic one, from the most disinterested virtue or generosity. With the help of a distinction which should not be judged a summary one, Aristotle never gives up analysing the ruses that enable one friendship to be smuggled into another, the law of the useful into that of pleasure, one or the other into virtue's mask. Those who prefer 'ethical' friendship believe it is possible to dispense with the legal, nomic form of political friendship; they disregard the contract or mutual agreement, thus opening themselves up to disappointment. Moreover, it is in 'useful' friendship, and within it, then, political friendship, that the greatest number of grievances and recriminations are encountered. Friendship based on virtue is, by definition, impeccable. As for friendship based on pleasure, friends part and bonds unravel once the enjoyment has run its course: the friends have had their delight, they have given, received, offered; they have had, and do not request anything more. Of course, all the forms of 'aporia' then spring up – aporia is Aristotle's word (*Eudemian Ethics*, 1243a 14–35) – as to the criteria of the just, and when we must determine what is just (*dei krínein to dikaíon*) from the vantage point of quantity or quality: the vantage point of the enjoyment of what is given or of the rendered service. On this count, how are we to get the person giving and the person receiving to agree? Who gives and who receives? It goes without saying that if political friendship considers the 'homology' (the contractual agreement) and the thing, it is less just, its justice is less 'friendly (*dikaoiosúne philikê*)' than ethical friendship, which counts on intention, will, and choice (*proaíresis*). The fundamental conflict lies in the opposition of the beautiful and the useful: ethical friendship is certainly 'more beautiful', but useful friendship is more necessary.

The criterion is painfully lacking if we are to judge the just where friendship 'based on usefulness' and friendship 'based on pleasure' end up intersecting in a couple that may very well be called, then, a couple of friends or a couple of lovers. What is lacking at this point is the straight line, the straight and narrow path (*euthuôría*). When the straight and narrow path does not appear, it becomes difficult to measure the just. This happens with lovers, with 'erotics (*epi tôn erôtikôn*)' when one of them seeks pleasure and the other usefulness. And undoubtedly when the sharing out of these quests becomes equivocal. Everything can function as long as love is there. When love ceases, the two lovers strive to calculate their respective share, and they wage war, like Python and Pammenes. But in this confusion of friendships, the conflict is not limited to the beloved. It arises everywhere when the straight and narrow path recoils, along with the common measure: between the master and his disciple, the doctor and his patient, the musician and the king. One then indeed wonders when such a measure would ever be accessible, capable of regulating any social exchange. And how do you calculate the just salary, or an equality of proportion, be it a case of instruction, medicine, technique or art?

In each case of this 'aporia', each time it becomes impossible to 'judge the just' in friendship, each time a grievance consequently arises, not between enemies but between friends who, as it were, have been misled, and have misled each other because they have first mistaken friendships, confusing in one case friendship based on virtue with friendship based on usefulness, in another, legal and ethical friendship, etc. – each time that the common measure and the straight and narrow path are in default for these friends who are indeed friends, but have not managed to concur on friendship, one wanting one of its forms, the other yet another, a third wanting more than one in the same, etc. – each time in the grievance one can address to the other, calling him 'friend' but telling him that in their case there is no friendship: here where I am talking to you, my friend, there is no friend. This is indeed a question of accounts, once again, and of equality, of calculation between calculabilities, or calculation between the calculable and the incalculable. Friend, there is no measure of equality, I cannot count on you, don't count on me any longer, etc.

Is this what, according to Diogenes Laertius, Aristotle meant? Probably not at the moment when he is said to have uttered O *phíloi, oudeis phílos* (but in what manner, according to which spirit?) – not directly, in any case, not in a straight line, not in this form. But then – what did he mean?

Let us return to Diogenes by another detour. If the three friendships (based on virtue, usefulness, pleasure) require equality, we have seen that a certain friendship can also entail superiority. Aristotle says this is another species of friendship, that of the divinity for man, of the governor for the governed, of the father for the son and the husband for the wife. Moreover, these friendships differ between themselves and imply no absolute reciprocity. In the development devoted to this inequality Aristotle evokes friendship with the dead, a friendship which knows without being known (*Eudemian*

Ethics, 1239ab; see above, Chapter 1). The requirement of reciprocity is one of the most obscure themes of the doctrine. In certain cases, when superiority is excessive or 'hyperbolic', Aristotle judges the expectation of reciprocity incongruous, as for example in the case of God. Hence one must not ask to be loved in return (*antiphileîsthai*) or to be loved in like measure to one's own love. On the other hand, the reciprocity of *antiphileîn* does not mean equality. If friends are friends in equality, a certain reciprocity without equality can also bring together beings who love each other but would not, for all that, be friends (1239a 20). Now, it is in a concatenation of sentences informed by this question of reciprocity and mutual justice that the exclamation attributed to Aristotle is reported by Diogenes Laertius:

'To the question how we should behave to friends, he answered, "As we should wish them to behave to us." He defined justice (*dikaisosúnē*) as a virtue of the soul (*aretēn psukhēs*) which distributes according to merit. Education he declared to be the best provision for old age. Favorinus in the second book of his *Memorabilia* mentions as one of his habitual sayings that "He who has friends can have no true friend". Further, this is found in the seventh book of the *Ethics*.' One part of the enigma concerns the little word 'true' ('no true friend') which the French and English translations judge necessary or charitable to add to the text, without further ado – in the French translation the word 'true' is between parentheses, no doubt to stress the value of insistence often connoted by *oudeis* (no one or nothing, truly, no one or nothing worth its weight, absolutely no one, no (friend) deserving consideration, truly deserving the name of friend). The other part of the enigma lies in the syntactic instability – indeed, the apparent grammatical undecidability – of the sentence of which we have already spoken at such length.

The time has perhaps come to decide the issue. It would be fitting in this case to give one's reasons for deciding, for deciding to opt for one side rather than the other, even if – let us reassure ourselves – a tiny philological *coup de théâtre* cannot prevail in the venerable tradition which, from Montaigne to Nietzsche and beyond, from Kant to Blanchot and beyond, will have bestowed so many guarantees to the decision of a copyist or a rushed reader in staking a bet on a tempting, so very tempting, reading, but an erroneous one, and probably a mistaken one. Luckily for us, no orthographic restoration or archival orthodoxy will ever damage this other, henceforth sedimented archive, this treasure trove of enticed and enticing texts which will always give us more food for thought than the guard-rails with which we would protect them. No philological fundamentalism will ever efface the incredible fortune of this brilliant invention. For there is here, without doubt, a staggering artifact, the casualness of an exegetical move as hazardous as it is generous – indeed, abyssal – in its very generativity. Of how many great texts would we have been deprived had someone (but who, in fact?) not one day taken, and perhaps, like a great card player, deliberately feigned to take, one omega for another? Not even one accent for another, barely one letter for another, only a soft spirit for a hard one – and the omission of the subscript iota.

And yet. We shall not say here what is true or false. But why should we not honour another passage? The passage from a neat but less probable, less convincing reading to one that is more discreet, more steadfast, more patient in the experience of the text? This passage could resemble a substitution, undoubtedly, even the correction of an error. But what should in truth be in question is something else – a less normalizing procedure, we hope. More respectful of the great ancestors. Without a trial around probity but in a concern for philological probability. In order not to go against a sort of statistical realism. There is in effect an *improbable* version, the one we know, the one we have been ceaselessly citing: the odds are less in its favour, as we shall attempt to show, and nothing convincing can come to its defence. However improbable it may be, this version will retain its titles – there can be no doubt about that – its coats of arms, a rich and henceforth archived tradition, a *canonical* authority protected by great names. It will have lined the library shelves of this tradition with illustrious variants, and remains available like a priceless stock. Better, like a capital with bottomless surplus-value. Another, more probable version, can henceforth make – or, rather, find – its way again. Without any value of orthodoxy, without a call to order, without discrediting the canonical version, this one might well engage, on other paths, sometimes at the intersection of the original one, with new adventures of thought. This other wager will certainly be less risky, since it corresponds to the greatest probability. It will call into play another ante, another bias, certainly, but without absolute assurance. There will be a pledge and a wager, as in all readings, there will be speculation on possible interest, where it is not only a question of spelling, grammar, and accentuation.

Several questions arise. They urge us on, but we must distinguish them, even if we are unable to give a complete answer to each one:

1. Where is the grammatical uncertainty in the 'construction' of Diogenes Laertius' text?
2. Who translated it differently? How was it done?
3. Are there grounds for the other translation? Why?

4. Does this other reading change anything in the original analysis? What?

1. According to the way the ω (*ōméga*) is written in *O phíloi, oudeis phílos*, we are confronted with either a vocative interjection (*ōméga* with smooth breathing and a circumflex accent) – this is the reading that has traditionally prevailed: 'O my friends, no friends' – or the dative of a pronoun (*ōméga* with rough breathing, circumflex accent and iota subscript, *hoi*). This reading has not been retained by the tradition: 'he for whom there are friends (a plurality or multitude of friends) has no friend'; or again: 'too many friends means no friend'. Paraphrased: he who has too many has none. This would be, in sum, a thesis on the number of friends, on their suitable number, and not on the question of the existence of the friend in general.

2. This second translation is not unheard-of, even though it never comes to the foreground of discussion. It is true that this translation is flaccid and apparently lacklustre. We shall call it the recoil, the recoil version, the labour and the manoeuvre of recoiling: it is in effect more modest, laborious, craft-like and painstaking, it restrains the provocation, it adds or suppresses a coil, it counts the coils, attempting to flatten out the phrase, and above all, with this additional or withdrawn coil, it reopens the question of multiplicity, the question of the one and that of the 'more than one' (of the one *qua* woman and the 'more than one', of the feminine one and the 'more than one' feminine one as well, of the feminine one and the 'more than one' feminine one, etc.). It thus explicates the grave question of arithmetical form which has been our obsession from the beginning: how many friends – men and women friends?

So far as I know,[10] there is an English edition of the text, giving for the Greek ω φίλοι, οὐδείσ φίλοσ: '*He who has friends can have no true friend.*'[11]. This could also be translated: 'cannot have any true friend'.

Then there is an Italian translation: '*Chi ha amici, non ha nessun amico*', 'He who has friends, has no friend.'[12]

Then another German translation: '*Viele Freunde, kein Freund.*'[13]

But first of all, the translation closest to the source, in the best economy of its literal form, in Latin: *Cui amici, amicus nemo.*[14]

3. So it all comes down to less than a letter, to the difference of breathing. The third question (what grounds would there be for such a translation, and hence, for preferring such a written form?) requires a broader answer, in a more probabilistic style. Supposing that up against an

original manuscript, or a first reliable (*bébaios!*) transcription, we had the means to choose between the two versions, such a possibility of literal deciphering, however interesting and determining it may be, seems to me, here, of secondary importance. It comes after and alongside other criteria: the internal coherence of Diogenes Laertius' text, the systemic consequence ruling the Aristotelian text to which it refers. For one too often forgets to take into account – as one should, however – the following sentence: '*alla kai en tô epdómo tôn Ethikôn esti*': 'Further, this is found in the seventh book of the *Ethics*', as the English translation gives it. '*Alla*' can take on the value of 'what is more', 'at least', 'but also', 'moreover' (*Further, anche, auch, tambien*, are the translations we have quoted). The point is to recall that the saying reported by rote is found (*esti*) *also, moreover, 'into the bargain*', in the seventh book of the *Ethics*. Diogenes would, in sum, be suggesting: for those who would rely only on the written word, without taking me at my word or without trusting the *Memorabilia* of Favorinos, they can refer to proof and seek confirmation or support for the reading in the text of the master. The same thought is also found elsewhere, consigned and archived in a book by Aristotle.

One then begins to have doubts. Reading a reference as precise, as attentive, as cautious as this one, one begins to have doubts about the canonical version. For the contents of the interjection, the theme of the great apostrophe, the equivalent of the major tradition, *cannot be found* in Aristotle, it would seem – in any case, nowhere in the seventh book of the *Ethics*. On the other hand, the recoil version has more than one reference to account for it, to justify the dative, and hence to make Diogenes' clarification in the ensuing sentence intelligible. More than one reference, hence more than one confirmation, more than one support: in both *Ethics* and – this clue should close the discussion – in the seventh book of the *Eudemian Ethics*.

4. This leads us to the final question. We shall set out to split it into two. This will not, when the time comes, prevent us from combining them: *content* and *form*.

A. *Content*. In the seventh book of the *Eudemian Ethics* (1244b) Aristotle undertakes an analysis of the relations between friendship and self-sufficiency. It is indeed a matter of a problem, even an *aporia* – Aristotle's usual word returns here – the aporia of autarky (*autarkeia*). As Jean-Claude Fraisse rightly notes[15], this aporia also belongs to the *Lysis* tradition. A virtuous man, a good man, a man sufficient unto himself, in the way God is – would such a man need a friend? Would there be a friend for him? And if a friend were sought out of insufficiency, would the *good* man be the most autarkic, the most self-sufficient, depending only on himself in his initiatives and in mastery over himself? If the virtuous man is a happy man, why would he need a friend? In autarky, one needs neither useful nor pleasant people, not even company. 'So that the happiest man will least need a friend, and only as far as it is impossible for him to be independent.' This question of measure, then, opens up a space in which, it seems to me, one can then identify the declaration that might indeed be the sentence or one of the sentences attributed to Aristotle by Diogenes. Immediately following is Aristotle's declaration: 'Therefore the man who lives the best life must have fewest friends, and they must always be becoming fewer, and he must show no eagerness for men to become his friends, but despise not merely the useful but even men desirable for society' (1244b 10). The chain seems clear and tightly linked: if virtue can unite with happiness only in autarky, the virtuous man should tend to dispense with friends; he must do everything in his power not to need them. In any case, a multiplicity of friends must be avoided, rarity must be sought after, thereby tending towards absolute scarcity – extreme scarcity, as it were – at the risk of having no friend: *cui amici, amicus nemo*.

If this reconstitution were not sufficient, if one were not content with this reference to the Seventh Book of the *Eudemian Ethics*, the one explicitly evoked by Diogenes Laertius, then one could go to the *Nicomachean Ethics*. In the Ninth Book (9–10, 1170b 20–1171a 20), the same theme is handled with such elegance and so extensively that there would no longer be room for doubt. The arithmetical or met'arithmetical motif of *extreme scarcity* serves as its prop for an intertwining of themes which come to wind themselves around it, in a natural, elegant, supple, economic movement. Whether it be a matter of hospitality or politics, useful or virtuous friendships, poets or lovers, scarcity is worth more, and sometimes *to the extreme*. Scarcity sets the price, and gives the measure to true friendship. A scarcity which gives the measure, but one which one does not quite know how to measure. Is it not incommensurable? The word *hyperbole* crops up twice [the English translation gives: *excessive*]. Instead of following up this development in detail, let us be satisfied with moving to the outermost point of these two hyperboles.

·*First hyperbole.* In the first place, far from seeking to make the greatest possible number of friends, it would be better, as Hesiod says, to be neither the host of many guests (*polúxeinos*) nor inhospitable (*áxeinos*), neither xenophilic nor xenophobic, hence neither 'friendless (*áphilos*)' nor polyphilic, hospitable to *too many* friends, amenable to friendship to the point of excess (*kat'uperbolén*). No hyperbole; just a happy medium, a measured measure. But where does it stop? Next, a small number of friends should suffice, whether they be sought for the sake of usefulness or for that of pleasure, just as a small amount of seasoning in food is enough. As for friends based on virtue, must one, on the other hand, have the greatest possible number? Or is there a measure, as in the population of the *polis*? Ten men is not enough, one hundred thousand is too many, says Aristotle. In the *Politics*, he distinguishes between *pólis* and *éthnos* in referring to what would today be called a demographic 'threshold of tolerance'. Over a given number of people, as we would translate in modern terms, this is no longer the State but the nation, with all the problems created for the democratic model by demography. Since we are dealing here, as regards number, with an analogy between friendship and the *polis*, between friendship and what constitutes the political *as such*, it should be noted that Aristotle does not recommend a determined number but, rather, a number falling between given limits (*to metaxu tinôn orisménôn*). Happy medium, moderation, proper measure. For one cannot parcel oneself out among too many friends. Furthermore, and for this very reason, these friends must be friends of one another. This limits their number even more – who has never come across this limit in his or her experience?

Second hyperbole. The example of love, of sensuous love, as it is translated. Eros is a 'hyperbole' of *philía*. A hyperbolic scarcity. Eros addresses only one at a time (*pros ena*). But this is also the case with great friends, those whose friendship the poets praise. These hymns to friendship always concern couples. Never more than two friends.

Although the end of Aristotle's development seems to issue in a concession or an exception (to have too many friends is to be complacent, it is to be the friend of no one, *except* in the case of properly political friendship for fellow citizens) rarity still remains the law of all friendship grounded in virtue. Rarity is the virtue of friendship. He who has friends – too many friends – has no friend. The recoil version thus recommends a recoil. Friendship is what it must be – virtuous – only under the condition of a recoil or a retreat: several friends, one, two, three (but how many, exactly?), who are like brothers. . . .[16]

B. *Form*. What difference is there, from the vantage point of the structure of the utterance, between the *canonical* version and the *recoil* version?

(a) The first speaks *to* friends, the second *of* friends. Opening with the vocative O, the famous interpellation harbours what some would call a 'performative contradiction' (how can you claim to address friends when you tell them there are no friends? A serious philosopher should not play such a game which, moreover, damages the transparency and necessary univocity in the communicational space of democracy, etc.[17]). With all the reversals, all the revolutions it engenders *ad infinitum*, the above 'performative contradiction', as we have amply seen, has the advantage of quickening – indeed, of dramatizing – a desire for friendship which, never renouncing what it says should be renounced, at least opens thought up to another friendship. As for the recoil version, it appears to remain merely reportive [*constatif*]. It is not an appeal or an address, but a declaration without an exclamation mark, a description or a definition. In a neutral tone, calmly, without a gaping-mouthed clamour, it claims to speak to what is. It no doubt still defines the truth of a contradiction (he who has many friends in truth has none), but this contradiction is pointed out from the position of a third party; it is not a self-contradiction which would come to torment the very act of enunciation.

(b) To define the relation between the two versions, one cannot be satisfied with a simple opposition, however evident, between an apostrophe and a reportive utterance. Such an opposition would be of limited interest, especially for what we are calling here, so as to appeal to them, politics of friendship. What is precisely of interest to us is the chiasmus that the call structure introduces between the two versions. If the interjection of the canonical version launches a call which cannot be reduced to a report, the articulated phrase as a whole comprises, includes, clasps, a reportive-type declaration ('O my friends, *there is no friend*'). This report is common to both versions. But in the apostrophe, the reportive determination forms the substantial content of a non-reportive utterance, a call in whose impulse this content is, as it were, carried up, swept off, overrun: I am speaking to you, calling you my friends, to tell you this: there are no friends. If there were a performative contradiction, it would then arise between this reportive moment and the form or performative force which included it and carries it along. This performative form *already itself* entails, in effect, prior to this other report – that there is no friend – an enveloped reportive assertion (if I say 'O friends', I am supposing they are friends and that you are a friend). This enveloped report or observation [*constatation*], already at work in the vocative interjection (O friends), collides with the explicit, included, second observation: there is no friend.

Conversely – and here is the chiasmus – reportive as it claims to be, the recoil version must indeed entail in turn a performative address. To whom is it said that he who has friends has none? Whether it receives an answer or not, the question is ineluctable. Everything is indeed prepared to sensitize to what will always remain inevitable in it, as if someone wished the addressee, the addressee of this sentence of uncertain origin (the auditor, the reader, them or her, you, all of us), to begin or end up wondering: to whom is this discourse addressed? And in what mode?

It has often been noted that there is no cut-and-dried reportive utterance. Some 'primary' performative value is always presupposed in it: an 'I am speaking to you', 'I am telling you that', 'I assure you or promise you that – I want to say something and I will get to the end of my sentence', 'listen to me', 'believe me', 'I am telling the truth', etc. Even if, in the recoil version, you stick to the mere assertion of a report (for he who has friends, several friends, too many friends, more than one friend, for him there are no friends), it was indeed necessary that the assertion be *addressed* and that the address contain some performative force. We do not know to whom Aristotle is said to have said this or that, but it is not only the reader or auditor who is 'entailed' by the structure of the utterance. A minimum of friendship or consent must be supposed of them; there must be an appeal to such a minimal consensus if anything at all is to be said. Whether this appeal corresponds, *in fact*, to a comprehension or an agreement, if only on the meaning of what is said, appears to us secondary with regard to the appeal itself. The appeal is coextensive to the most reportive moment of the report. In short, there is indeed some form of silent interjection, some 'O friends', in the recoil version. It rings in the performative space of a call, prior to its very first word. And this is the irrefutable truth of the canonical version. As if, through and despite its philological precipitation, it were calling back to its truth the recoiling of the most convincing and most probable version. What the latter wanted to say is the call, is that which *will have been* 'O my friends, there is no friend'. And this also holds for its Nietzschean quasi-reversal: the same chiasmus is at work. All the versions therefore inscribe the thetic kernel of a neutral declaration (no friend), one which *witnesses or registers* [*prend acte*], within and under the condition of an agitated scene, in the restless act of an inter-rogation and an apostophe which *appeals*.

Where are we heading? Our intention is not to suggest an exercise in reading or to play off the two great competing mythical phrases against a '*speech act*' theory, albeit reduced, as here, to its rudiments. We wish only to recall, in order to appeal to them, the two great *destinies* of the sentence, destinies in which necessity and destination, the law and the other, strike up an alliance. The first destiny: however it is read, in the canonical or recoil version, and whoever its author, such a sentence is addressed to someone. The fact that this is absolutely necessary does not prevent – on the contrary, it commands – that the task of determination or identification of this addressee remain unfulfilled and always exposed to some undecidability. This is analytically inscribed in its event as well as in its structure. But when we say 'someone', we seem to be presupposing (1) that his gender is indifferent (neuter, that is to say, following the tradition, preferably masculine); (2) that this someone could, in a limited case, be one person, and that this 'only one' would be enough to meet the conditions of possibility of the utterance. Now it is not possible (in any case, not for a human being – and shortly we shall show the anthropocentric implications of the utterance in question) to be neuter in gender. And secondly – another destiny or 'destinerrancy' – it is impossible to address only one person, only one man, only one woman. To put it bluntly and without pathos, such an address would have to be *each time one single time*, and all iterability[18] would have to be excluded from the structure of the trace. Now, for only one person to receive a single mark once, the mark must be, however minimally, identifiable, hence iterable, hence interiorly multiple and divided in its occurrence – in any case in its eventness [*événementialité*]. The third party is there. And the one *qua* 'more than one' which simultaneously allows and limits calculability. This drama or this chance of a singular multiplicity is witnessed in both versions, if only in the divide, within each of them, of singular and plural. Whatever way they are read, through all the possible modalities of reading (and we are a long way from their exhaustive examination; we would need a dozen sessions at least), both say that there is not *a* friend, a sole friend, some friend, no friend; both say *a* friend is not (*oudeis phílos*). And both declare as much against a backdrop of multiplicity ('O friends', or for him who has 'friends'). *Independently of all determinable contexts*, they could want to say, and both in unison, and they say so at any rate, with or without our consent: *there is never a sole friend*. Not that there would be none, but that there never is one. And one is already more than one, with or without my consent. And I want this and do not want it. I do not want it because the desire for a unique friendship, an indivisible bond, an 'I love you' one time, one single eternal time, one time for all time(s), will never cease. But I do not want it. Montaigne said as much of the indivisible love bonding him to his friend's soul, to the soul of the other 'man'. For he never stopped pining after the desire for multiplication lodged within the very interior of indivisibility, which proliferates for the very reason of singular indivisibility: from the moment when, in 'indivisible' friendship, 'each gives himself so entirely to his friend', he cannot fail to be 'grieved that he is not twofold, threefold or fourfold, and that he does not have several souls, several wills, so that he could confer them all to this subject'. Whatever this 'subject' may be, and whatever 'to confer' means, indivisibility harbours the finite and the infinite in itself simultaneously. Hence the possibility *and* impossibility of the calculation. Whether it is given or promised, indivisibility is immediately infinite in its finiteness. It appears as such only in the desire for repetition and multiplication, in the promise and the memory that divide the indivisible in order to maintain it. Furthermore it is here, preeminently, that the enemy is within, in the place of the friend. Friend and enemy take up their places in taking the place of the other, one becoming, prior to the slightest opposition, the ambiguous guardian, both the jailer and saviour, of the other. *Canonical* or *recoil*, both versions speak to the infinite in the 'none', the becoming 'not one' of someone of either gender. This multiplicity makes the taking into account of the political inevitable, from out of the innermost recesses of the most secret of secrets. It cuts across what is called the question of the subject, its identity or its presumed identity with self, a supposed indivisibility which ushers in the accounting structure for which it appears to be designed. Indivisible in its calculable identity, it loses, by the same token, the indivisibility of its incalculable singularity, and one divides the other.

We said: *independently of all determinable contexts*. Does one have the right to read like this? No, certainly not, if one wishes to imagine a sentence or a mark in general without any context, and readable as such. This never occurs, and the law remains unbreachable. But for the same reason, a context is never absolutely closed, constraining, determined, completely filled. A structural opening allows it to transform itself or to give way to another context. This is why every mark has a force of detachment which not only can free it from such and such a determined context, but ensures even its principle of intelligibility and its mark structure – that is, its *iterability* (repetition *and* alteration). A mark that could not in any way detach itself from its singular context – however slightly and, if only through repetition, reducing, dividing and multiplying it by identifying it – would no longer be a mark. Now this is exactly what occurs in the history of our sentence. Its entire history, from the beginning, will have consisted in abandoning of a unique context and an indivisible addressee. This will have been possible only because its original addressee (friend or enemy, but absolutely not neuter) will have first been multiple, potentially detached from the context of the first occurrence. In a way – willingly or reluctantly, consciously or not – every presumed signatory of the sentence under scrutiny also re-marks this, says it, says the 'more than one' of the addressee, the friend-enemy, 'more than one [*plus d'un*]' or the 'more than a [*plus qu'un*]': for example, a feminine 'one', a feminine other. This sentence cannot be signed or incorporated, it cannot be shifted elsewhere, anywhere, without re-marking this 'destinerrancy' due to the *'more than (a) one [plus d'un ou plus qu'un]'* of destination. And this is friendship, and this is war! And however the 'more than a' is understood, is it not the abyss of 'more than one'? An other, masculine or feminine, but ultimate solitude as well? (Later, Hölderlin: 'But where are the friends'; and 'More than one of them / Is reluctant to return to the source'; and 'Here it happens that I am alone'.)

'Aristotle' – let us call him by that name – had indeed to address (himself) [*devait bien s'addresser*, also: 'had to address (himself) well']. Let us not even mention the circle of his living disciples, the presumed addressees of all his philosophemes and theorems. The most theoretical of each of his remarks – indeed, of the most theoretistic [*théorétistes*] among them – could never be neuter. Each of his judgements, and his judgements on judgement, had to let itself be orientated towards a reader or a listener. They had to set out to convince, to demonstrate, to produce an effect. A particular addressee whose place is marked in the very structure of the utterance might not belong to the circle of immediate presence – he or she was even capable of not belonging – but also had to find himself called by an allocution, by a speech gesture which was not limited to the theoretical, reportive, 'judicative' context. Hence no neutrality was possible around the two poles of this speech gesture, whatever the theoretical thesis posed at the time (there is or there is not a friend, an enemy; there are friends or there are not many, a few, just one, etc.). This speech gesture will never allow itself be neutralized, and its saying cannot be reduced to the said; we know a priori that he *was addressing*, as a friend or an enemy, a friend or an enemy. Or both: we know that he was addressing both, in turn or simultaneously. This move beyond the theoretico-reportive sphere could not fail to be a project: a project of friendship or of enmity, as one will say, or both at the same time; and a project of the corresponding political community, one of singularity or multiplicity (this is of little importance here). But such a project is irrepressible, and as old as the sentence.

Will it be said – this would indeed be tempting – that beyond all the dialectics whose ineluctable experiences we multiply, beyond the fatal syntheses or reconciliations of opposites, the dream of an unusable friendship survives, a friendship beyond friendship, and invincible before these dialectics? And that it first of all stems from this evidence that 'Aristotle' – let us call him by that name – at least asked the other to hear him, understand him, to be enough of a friend to do so, and therefore to consider him – Aristotle – as a friend, *qua* the friend of a promise of friendship? And even at the very moment of saying 'no friend'? This request for friendship, this offer of friendship, this call to coming together in friendship, at least to hear, the time it takes to hear, at least to finally *agree*, the time it takes to agree on the meaning of the sentence, even if it were still saying, in the saying of its said, the worst in dialectics, is this, this saying of the said, not, then, the 'I love you, listen' of the 'I love you; do you hear me?'. Is it not, then, this 'perhaps you can hear me in the night . . .', an inflexible hyperbole of *philía* – inflexible not in the sense of some indestructible, rigid and resistant solidity, but because its featherweight vulnerability would offer no foothold for a reversal of any kind, for any dialectical opposition? And if politics were at last grounded in this friendship, this one and no other, the politics of *this* hyperbole, would this not be to break with the entire history of the political, this old, tiring and tired, exhausted history?

Temptation indeed. It is that of the book you are reading – there can be no doubt about it – but it is also the temptation this same book owes itself to resist, owes itself a time of resistance. Not to resist so as to deny, exclude or oppose, but precisely to keep the temptation in sight of its chance: not to be taken for an assurance or a programme. Again the question of the *perhaps*, the paradoxical conditions for an event or a decision. For not only could it never be a matter of *grounding* anything, above all of grounding a politics, on the virtue of a 'perhaps'. But above all else, doomed as it may be to hyperbole, the logic of agreement or hyperbolic consent presupposes a little too quickly that the person addressing the other wishes to be heard, read, understood, wishes first of all to address some*one* – and that this desire, this will, this drive, are *simple*, simply identical to their supposed essence. If we believe and are saying that this is in no respect true, it is not to make a case for the demoniac by allowing it to appear, by staging it or leaving the stakes of the question in its favour. But we cannot, and we *must* not, exclude the fact that when someone is speaking, in private or in public, when someone teaches, publishes, preaches, orders, promises, prophesies, informs or communicates, some force in him or her is also striving *not to* be understood, approved, accepted in consensus – not immediately, not fully, and therefore not in the immediacy and plenitude of tomorrow, etc. For this hypothesis there is no need – this may appear extravagant to some people – to revert to a diabolical figure of the death instinct or a drive to destruction. It is enough that the paradoxical structure of the condition of possibility be taken into account: for the accord of hyperbolic lovence to be possible and, in the example we have just examined, for me to hope to be understood beyond all dialectics of misunderstanding, etc., the possibility of failure must, in addition, not be simply an accidental edge of the condition, but its haunting. And the haunting must leave an imprint right on the body it seems to threaten, to the point of merging indissociably with it, as inseparable from it as its essence or essential attributes. And it is impossible not to aspire to this haunting failing which no 'good' decision would ever accede to responsibility, failing which nothing, no event, could ever happen. Undecidability (and hence all the inversions of signs between friendship and its opposite) is not a sentence that a decision can leave behind. The crucial experience of the *perhaps* imposed by the undecidable – that is to say, the condition of decision – is not a moment to be exceeded, forgotten, or suppressed. It continues to constitute the decision as such; it can never again be separated from it; it produces it *qua* decision *in and through* the undecidable; there is no other decision than this one: decision in the matter and form of the undecidable. An undecidable that persists and repeats itself through the decision *made* so as to safeguard its decisional essence or virtue as such. This same necessity can be translated differently – we have done so elsewhere: the instant of decision must remain heterogeneous to all knowledge as such, to all theoretical or reportive determination, even if it may and must be preceded by all possible science and conscience. The latter are unable to determine the leap of decision without transforming it into the irresponsible application of a programme, hence without depriving it of what makes it a sovereign and free decision – in a word, of what makes it a decision, if there is one. At this point, practical performativity is irreducible to any theorem; this is why we have stressed the performative force which had to prevail in both versions of a sentence which in any case, in addressing another, could not count on any assurance, any purely theoretical criterion of intelligibility or accord; it *could not* count on such assurance, but above all *it had to* and *desired not to want* to count on such an assurance, which would destroy in advance the possibility of addressing the other as such. To express this in the case of a telegram: 'I love you' cannot and must not hope to prove anything at all. Testimony or act of faith, such a declaration can decide only providing it wants to remain theoretically undecidable, improbable, given over in darkness to the exception of a singularity without rule and without concept. Theoretically, it can always flip into its opposite. Without the possibility of radical evil, of perjury, and of absolute crime, there is no responsibility, no freedom, no decision. And this possibility, as such, if there is one, must be neither living nor dead.

How this madness can then negotiate with what it is not, how it can be protected and translated in the good sense of 'things', in proofs, guarantees, concepts, symbols – in a *politics*, *this* politics and not another – this is the whole of history, of what is called history. But every time it will be singular, singularly iterable, as will the negotiation and contamination of singularity and concept, exception and rule. Furthermore – another side of the same law – the request or offer, the promise or the prayer of an 'I love you', must remain unilateral and dissymmetrical. Whether or not the other answers, in one way or another, no mutuality, no harmony, no agreement can or must reduce the infinite disproportion. This disproportion is indeed the condition of sharing, in love as well as in friendship. In hatred as well as in detestation. Consequently, the desire of this disproportion which *gives* without return and without recognition must be able not to count on 'proper agreement', not to calculate assured, immediate or full comprehension. It must indeed desire that which goes to make the essence of desire: this non-assurance and this risk of misunderstanding. And in not knowing *who*, in not knowing the substantial identity of *who* is, prior to the declaration of love, at the origin of who gives and who receives, *who* is in possession or not of what happens to be offered or requested. Here, perhaps, only here, could a principle of difference be found – indeed an incompatibility between love and friendship, at least according to the most conventional meaning of these words in 'our' culture, and supposing such a difference could ever manifest itself in its rigorous purity. If such an essential incompatibility or heterogeneity in their provenance were to be granted, despite everything claimed on the subject by those (we have referred to several of them) who derive love and friendship from the same passion, this would not mean that love and friendship cannot associate, or cohabit, or alternate, or naturally enrich themselves among those who love each other. It would mean only that friendship supposes a force of the improbable: the *phenomenon* of an appeased symmetry, equality, reciprocity between two infinite disproportions as well as between two absolute singularities; in the case of love, it would raise or rend the veil of this phenomenon (some would be tempted to say that it would reveal its hidden, forgotten, repressed truth) to uncover the disproportion and dissymmetry as such. The absolute dis-pair [*dés-espoir*] of an absolute act of faith and renunciation. But since we have evinced doubts on the possibility of these two essences ever manifesting themselves in their purity, *as such*, we are here dealing only with hyperbolic limits.

Our objective was not to start down this path, but only to draw attention to a clue: in the *canonical* version as well as in the *recoil* version, Aristotle's sentence named *phílos*, the friend, not the lover or the beloved (of either gender). The question of knowing if it was a loved or a loving friend was no more clearly articulated than, in its Nietzschean obverse, the question of knowing whether the person who names the enemy is the enemy of enemies (and everything would indeed lead us to suppose that he or she could very well be the friend of enemies). In other words, when one names the friend or the enemy, a reciprocity is supposed, even if it does not efface the infinite distance and dissymmetry. As soon as one speaks of love, the situation is no longer the same. If one wished to translate in terms of love what Aristotle's sentence says of the friend, of friends, and – as we believe it does – to friends, such a task would no doubt be fascinating (it would take another book) but altogether more dangerous ('love, no love', 'loves, no love'; 'my love, there is no love (happy? virtuous? reciprocal?)'; 'my loves, there is no love', 'my loves, there is no lover nor beloved (of either gender)' – these are just a few of the translations which would be neither analogous nor homologous, above all because they would fail to name and to determine the 'who' (lover, loved one) which, for Aristotle's sentence, was the friend, the friends. And let us not even mention the parentheses: their violence as much as their untranslatability.

Here, we shall once again have to acknowledge the necessity of this 'zigzag' which we would like to show, marks the history-without-history of what the French call *amitié*. This history does not consist in a linear succession or in a continuous accumulation of paradigms, but in a series of ruptures which intersect their own trajectories before turning back along a different one: all the mutations, all the new configurations, repeat, on the very day after they open, the same archaic motif of the day before yesterday without which they could not even come to speak their language. For another of these 'zigzags' that we have already multiplied, we must once again return to Aristotle, where, precisely, the motif of autarky ruled the arithmetic of scarcity. As we remember, the ideal of the virtuous sage prescribes that he be independent and self-sufficient, hence able to do without others, as much as possible: few friends, the fewest possible.

In an extremely simplified schema, we might say that the interpretation of this law appeals to *two great logics*. It is still a matter of true friendship (primary friendship, *prótē philía*, in the *Eudemian Ethics*; perfect or accomplished friendship, *teleía philía*, in the *Nicomachean Ethics*). One of these logics can make of friendship *par excellence* (Montaigne's sovereign friendship) an *arkhé* or a *télos*, precisely, towards which one must tend even if it is never reached. No more than the absolute scarcity of friends can or must be reached, in the case of a man. In this case, this inaccessibility would be only a distancing in the immensity of a homogeneous space: a road to be travelled. But the inaccessibility can be interpreted *otherwise*. *Otherwise*

– that is to say, in terms of a thought of alterity which makes true or perfect friendship not only inaccessible as a conceivable *telos*, but inaccessible *because it is inconceivable* in its very essence, and hence in its *telos*.

On the one hand, one would thus have a conceivable and determinable *telos* which *in fact* cannot be reached: one cannot reach it and it cannot happen, it cannot happen to us. This is a new way of interpreting, outside all context, the 'no friend'. There is no friend, purely and simply because perfection is too difficult, and that's that. We had not yet alluded to this difficulty.

On the other hand, the *telos* remains inaccessible because it is inconceivable, and inconceivable because it is self-*contradictory*. Inaccessibility would then have an altogether different sense, that of an interdictive bar in the *very concept* of friendship. As Aubenque rightly puts it: '*perfect friendship destroys itself*.'[19] It is contradictory in its very essence. On the one hand, in effect, *one must* want the greatest good for the friend – hence one wants him to become a god. But *one cannot* want that, one cannot want what would then be wanted, for at least *three reasons*.

1. Friendship with God is no longer possible because of his remoteness or separation (*Nicomachean Ethics*, VIII, 7, 1159a 5). Presence or proximity are the condition of friendship, whose energy is lost in absence or in remoteness. Men are called 'good' or 'virtuous' from the vantage point of aptitude, possibility, *habitus* (*kath'éxin*), or in act (*kat'enérgeian*). It is the same for friendship: friends who sleep or live in separate places are not friends in act (*ouk energousi*). *The energy of friendship draws its force from presence* or from *proximity*. If absence and remoteness do not destroy friendship, they attenuate or exhaust it, they enervate it. The proverb on this subject quoted by Aristotle indeed makes the point that for him, absence or remoteness is synonymous with silence: friends are separated when they cannot speak to one another (this is *aprosēgoría*, non-allocution, non-address, a rare word appearing in this proverb of unknown provenance: '*aprosēgoría has undone many a friendship*'). It is, then, not only a matter of distance between places, although Aristotle mentions this too, but of what, for him, will go hand in hand with topological separation: the impossibility of allocution or colloquium. (Question: how would this discourse have handled telecommunication in general? And how would it deal today with the telephone and all the new dis-locations which dissociate the allocution of co-presence in the same place? People can speak to each other from afar – this was already possible, but Aristotle took no account of it.) Again an aporia:

but when one party is removed to a great distance, as God is, the possibility of friendship ceases. This is in fact the origin of the difficult question [the aporia] (*aporeitai*) whether friends in the final analysis really wish for their friends the greatest goods, as for example for them to be gods, for in this case they would no longer be their friends, since friends are goods. (VIII, 9, 1159a 5–11)

No friendship with God is possible because this absence and this separation also signify the absence of common measure for a proportional equality between God and me. Then one cannot speak with *this* God: it is a case of absolute *aprosēgoría*. God cannot even be addressed to tell him there is no friend. *One cannot, therefore, want God for a friend.*

2. The other reason is that friendship orders me to love the other as he is while wishing that he remain as he is and do so following his human nature, 'only so long as he remains a man' (ibid.). In its origin and its end, in its primary sense or its culmination, friendship is still the *distinctive feature of man*. One cannot, therefore, want to deify the friend while wishing that he remain what he is, that he remain a man.

3. And yet – the third and undoubtedly the most radical of the reasons – the man of friendship, *qua* man of virtue, *should nevertheless resemble God*. Now God has no need of a friend; he thinks himself, not some other thing. The *nóēsis nóēseōs*, the thought of thought characteristic of the Prime Mover as well as, in the same tradition, absolute knowledge in Hegel's sense, could not care less about friendship because it could not care less about the other. Perfect or true friendship, that of the just and virtuous man who would resemble God, thus tends towards this divine *autárkeia* which can very easily dispense with the other and hence has no relation to friendship with the other, no more so than to its death. Precisely in a development devoted to autarky, Aristotle underscores this sort of aporia:

> For because a god is not such as to need a friend, we claim the same of a man who resembles a god. But by this reasoning the virtuous [*spoudaîos*] man will not even think, for the perfection of a god is not in this, but in being superior to thinking of anything beside himself. *The reason is that with us welfare involves a something beyond us, but the deity is his own well-being.*[20]

In sum, it is of God (or man in so far as he should or would want to resemble Him) that one must think in saying 'there is no friend'. But one then thinks of someone who cannot think or who thinks nothing other than self, who does not think to the extent that he thinks nothing but self.

Now if man has friends, if he desires friends, it is because man thinks and thinks the other.

Friendship *par excellence* can only be human but above all, and by the same token, there is thought for man only to the extent that it is thought *of the other* — and thought of the other *qua thought of the mortal*. Following the same logic, there is thought, there is thinking being — if, at least, thought must be the thought of the other — only in friendship. Thought, in so far as it is to be *for man*, cannot take place without *philía*.

Translated into the language of a human and finite *cogito*, this gives the formula: I think, therefore I am the other; I think, therefore I need the other (in order to think); I think, therefore the possibility of friendship is lodged in the movement of my thought in so far as it demands, calls for, desires the other, the necessity of the other, the cause of the other at the heart of the *cogito*. Translated into the logic of a divine *cogito*, of the *cogito* of *this* god: I think, therefore I think myself and am sufficient unto myself, there is no (need of a) friend, etc. O friends (you other men), for me there is no friend. This is how such a god would speak, if he were to come down to speak. Divine might be the word that still holds us back. Divine remains a particular truth of Aristotle's saying, as soon as friends can be addressed, as we have just verified, only providing they are men. In any case, it suffices that the concept of perfect friendship be contradictory for someone to raise his voice and say 'O my friends, there is no friend'.

Under the condition of the *cogito*. But all thought does not necessarily translate into the logic of the *cogito*, and we may meet up again, on another path, with this affinity of *phileîn*, of thought, with mortality.

Notes

1. Thus there is, to my knowledge, unanimity among the 'canonical' citations, the most famous or the most popular among them, even if the situation is more complex for the existing translations in use. Clues will have to suffice for our argument, since one translation has prevailed, not the other. This certainly does not justify the failings of the investigation. I have not checked all the existing translations in the world. The version I am calling the canonical one also justifies itself through recourse to existing translations. Here are a few:

In French: '*O mes amis, il n'y a pas d'ami (véritable)*'. Diogène Laërce, *Vie, Doctrines et Sentences des philosophes illustres*, traductions, notice et notes par R. Genaille, Garnier–Flammarion, 1965, t. 1, p. 236.

In German: '*O Freunde, nirgends ein Freund!*' *Des Diogenes Laertius Philosophische Geschichte Oder Von dem Leben, den Meinungen und merkwürdigen Reden der Berühmtesten*

Philosophen Griechenlands aus dem Griechischen das erstemal ins Deutsche übersetzt, Leipzig, im Schwickertschen Verlage, 1806.

In Spanish: '*Oh amigos! no hay ningún amigo*', Diogenes Learcio, *Vidas de los más ilustres filósofos griegos*, Orbis, Barcelone, 1985, Traducción del griego, prólogo y notas, José Ortiz y Sainz, vol. 1, p. 189.

Unlike the translations we will soon be quoting, which construct the sentence differently, these three translations share the fact that they do not give the Greek text on the facing page. One therefore cannot know how, in the view of the translator, the *ōmēga* is to be accentuated.

2. *Eudemian Ethics*, 1240b 5–10.

3. *Laelius de Amicitia*, XXI, 80 ('for the true friend is, so to speak, a second self'). We shall meet this topos again between Michelet and Quinet.

4. '*Ou ton trópon, eípein, alla ton ánthropon ēléēsa*', V, 17, 4–5.

5. *Lives of the Eminent Philosophers*, V, 21, 3–4: '*ou tố anthrópō, phēsín, édōka, alla tố anthrōpíno*'.

6. *Nicomachean Ethics*, 1159b 25–30.

7. 1235b 12: '*Kai tas aporías lúsei kai tas enantiíseis*'.

8. I take the liberty of referring the reader to *Glas*, pp. 133–4 and *passim*.

9. *Tố árkhonti phúsei kai theố pros to arkhómenon*', 1242b 20.

10. Here again I must remind the reader that this is not an exhaustive investigation. These *factual* limits will never be justifiable, but my aim has been in the first place to set up the bearings for the possibility and stakes of an alternative reading – this is what I am doing here; I am not dealing with the worldwide philological state of the question. Here I should thank the men and women friends who have helped me along these international paths, through the several languages, libraries or bibliographies to which I refer, be they Latin, Italian, Spanish, English, or German: Giorgio Agamben, Maurizio Ferraris, Cristina de Peretti, Aileen Philips, Elisabeth Weber.

11. Diogenes Laertius, *Lives of Eminent Philosophers*, with an English translation by R.D. Hicks, vol. 1. The Loeb Classical Library, Harvard University Press, Cambridge, MA and London 1925–91, pp. 464–5.

12. Diogene Laerzio, *Vite dei filosofi*, c. di Marcello Gigante, ed. Laterza, Roma–Bari 1962, p. 204.

13. Diogenes Laertius, *Leben und Meinungen . . .*, t. 2, Von Otto Apelt, *unter Mitarbeit* von H.G. Zekl, Hamburg 1967 (second edition).

14. Diogenis Laerti, *De clarorum philosophorum vitis, dogmatibus et apophtegmatibus. Libri decem ex italicis codicibus nunc primus excussis recensuit*, C. Gabr. Cobet . . . Parisis, Ed. Ambrosia Firmin Didot . . . MDCCCV.

15. Fraisse, *Philiá*, p. 238.

16. Without jumping the gun, without neglecting a leap which resembles an infinite leap, let us nevertheless take note of the numerous analogies which regularly align Christian friendship or fraternity with the Aristotelian, even Ciceronian, tradition. The rule of religious orders in retreat, starting from a certain date, includes a recommendation of scarcity for monks: 'Those wishing to live as monks in a hermitage are allowed to be as many as three, four maximum', we read in the *Opuscules* of Saint Francis of Assisi (cited in *La Règle des frères mineurs*, Éditions françiscaines, Paris 1961, p. 58).

17. On particular present-day aspects around this 'performative contradiction', I must refer the reader to *Mémoires – pour Paul de Man*, ch. III.

18. On this point we must refer the reader to 'Signature Event Context' in *Margins of Philosophy* [trans. Alan Bass, University of Chicago Press 1982] and to *Limited Inc.* [trans. Samuel Weber, 2nd edn, Evanston, Il: Northwestern University Press 1990].

19. 'Aristotle on Friendship', the appendix to *La Prudence chez Aristotle*, PUF, 1963, p. 180. This five-page essay forcefully establishes a series of conflicts or contradictions that concern not only 'friendships that are imperfect, or grounded in some misunderstanding' but 'the very essence of friendship' (ibid., Aubenque's emphasis).

20. '*Aítion d'óti ēmin men to eu kath'éteron, ekeíno de autos autou to eu estín.*' *Eudemian Ethics*, VII, 12, 1245b 14–19, quoted and translated by Aubenque, p. 183.

9

'In human language, fraternity . . .'

I am meditating a work, not one line of which yet exists. It would consist in establishing the relation between the Christian dogma and the political and social forms of the modern world. . . . Why then do they always advise us to wait for the realization of Christianity in the tomb? Are they afraid of disinheriting the dead? . . . The Church has ceased to perform miracles; but *humanity, and France particularly, have done them for her.* . . . Saint Augustine, representing the old Roman mind, comes and closes the free discussion of ideas.

> E. Quinet, 'Why the dogma of *human brotherhood* was inscribed so late in civil and political law', in *Christianity, in Its Various Aspects, from the Birth of Christ to the French Revolution*[1]

And in this great tradition there is not only a connected series of events but there is also progress. France has continued the Roman and Christian work that Christianity had promised, and France has delivered. *Brotherly equality* had been postponed to the next life, but she taught it as the law on earth to the whole world.

This nation has two very powerful qualities that *I do not find in any other.* She has both the principle and the legend: the idea made more comprehensive and more humane, and the tradition more connected and coherent.

This principle, this idea, which was buried in the Middle Ages under the dogma of grace, is called *brotherhood in the language of man.* . . .

This nation, considered thus as the asylum of the world, is much more than a nation. It is a living brotherhood.

> Michelet, *The People*[2]

This book is more than a book, it is myself. That is why it belongs to you. It is myself and it is you, my friend, I dare say.... The entire variety of our work together began in the same living roots: The sentiment of France and the idea of the father-country.

Accept it, then, this book of the People, *because it is yourself, because it is myself.* By your military origins, by my industrial ones, we ourselves represent, much as others perhaps, the two modern aspects of the People, and its recent occurrence.

Michelet to Edgar Quinet[3]

The sacred word of the new age, *Fraternity* – the woman can spell it, but does not yet know how to read it.

Michelet, *L'Amour*[4]

Who could ever answer for a discourse *on* friendship without *taking a stand?* The urgency of this question is no way lessened by the fact that this discourse on friendship, this *de amicitia,* claims to be theoretical or philosophical. Who will answer for a treatise *perí philías* without taking a stand, hence without assuming the *responsibility* of this stand – friend or enemy, one *or* the other; indeed, one *and* the other? Can one speak of love without declaring one's love, without declaring war, beyond all possible neutrality? Without avowing, if only the unavowable?

Now what have we been doing up to now? We said at the beginning that citing the citation of a citation was perhaps to assume, in one's own name, the responsibility of no enunciation. Perhaps this may not even be addressing you, truly you, right here. An example of this *aprosēgoría,* this *keeping silent,* silence kept, this speech kept at a distance at which Aristotle said a friendship would not survive for long. Or a language at an incalculable distance?

Once again it must be said (but to whom?): these matters are not so simple. Am I totally irresponsible for what I *said* from the moment I am irresponsible for *what* I said? Am I irresponsible for *the fact that* I spoke (the fact of having spoken) from the moment I do not hold myself responsible for what I have said, for the contents of my speech, for that which in fact I have contented myself with reporting? Defined by what are commonly called conventions, a certain number of artificial signs come here to attest the following: even if I have yet to say something determined *in my name* when, to start off with, I pronounced, without any other protocol, 'O my friends, there is no friend', one has the *right* (but what is this right?) to suppose that *I* am nevertheless *speaking in my own name.*

It is then a matter of the name *borne*, the *bearing* or the *basis* [*le port ou le support*] of the name – and the *relation* to the name. The *range* of the name – this is the question that has been bringing all its weight to bear here. It is in effect in the power of the name to be able to survive the bearer of the name, and thus to open up, from the very first nomination, this space of the epitaph in which we have recognized the very space of the *great* discourses on friendship.

(We have not privileged the great discourses on friendship so as to submit to their authority or to confirm a hierarchy but, on the contrary, as it were, to question the process and the logic of a canonization which has established these discourses in a position of exemplary authority. The history of friendship cannot be reduced to these discourses, still less to these *great* discourses of a *philosophical* genre. But precisely to begin the analysis of the forces and procedures that have placed the *majority* of these *major* discourses in the *major* position they have acquired, all the while covering over, reducing, or marginalizing the others, one must begin by paying attention to what they say and what they do. This is what we wish to do and say.)

You hold me responsible, *personally responsible*, by the mere fact that I am speaking. Responsible, for example, for the decision to begin by quoting Montaigne, rather than saying something else, before saying anything at all. Holding me *responsible*, personally responsible, you imply, with the utmost rigour, some kind of knowledge relative to what *person* and *responsibility* mean.

What is happening at this very moment? This could issue in a 'pragmatic' type of description. Suppose I am invited to speak to you (but exactly how and by whom, finally? And who invites you to read a book, that is, to invite the word of another into your home, and to put you in charge of it, at this very moment? And how many of you are there, exactly?). A hypothesis, then: invited to speak to you, while you would be alone or assembled to listen to me, then to examine me – in short, to *answer me* – I have already answered an invitation and am therefore addressing you who are beginning to answer me. Your rejoinder is still *virtual* as regards the content of the answer, but you already effect it *in act* through this first response consisting in the attention paid (with more or less *energy*, as Aristotle would say) or at least the attention promised to a discourse, whether the promise be kept or not, to whatever degree it be kept or not (infinite problems).

With this distinction between potentiality and act, we are already virtually installed in the *dominant* code, in the very constitution of one of philosophy's great canonical discourses on friendship, the discourse of the very philosopher quoted by Montaigne – Aristotle – whose major features we are questioning, the axiomatic and hierarchy-creating power diffused by its renown. This irradiation began before Aristotle (with Plato, etc.) and continues well beyond him, to be sure, well beyond Epicureanism and Stoicism, beyond Cicero, certain Church Fathers, and several others. But we thought it necessary to begin, precisely, by questioning the most canonical of the canonical, in this place in which is concentrated, for us in the West, the potential of maximum signification of the dominant power in its most assured authority. Will it be possible to (re)turn or to go elsewhere, beyond or below this potential of irradiation?

But even to pose this question, and precisely to suspend it on a 'perhaps', we risk reaccrediting, with all its conceptual machinery, the potentiality/ act distinction, the one between *dúnamis* and *enérgeia*. It is never far away, in the *Nicomachean Ethics*, when it is a matter of distinguishing between the 'good' who, always few in number, are friends in the rigorous sense of the term, in the proper sense, simply friends, absolutely friends (*aplôs phíloi*), and the others who are friends only by accident or by analogy with the first (VIII, 6, 1157b 1–5); the same distinction is never far away when the issue is that of distinguishing between, on the one hand, friendship *par excellence*, the friendship of virtue (the *prótè philía* of the *Eudemian Ethics* or the *teleía philía* of the *Nicomachean Ethics*) and, on the other, derived friendships, those grounded in usefulness or pleasure. Neither is the distinction ever far away when, having defined three forms of government or constitution (*politeía*), the *Nicomachean Ethics* sets out three corresponding types of friendship, each of them proportional to relations of justice (VIII, 10, 1160a 31 and 13; 1161a 10), in such a way that if man is a 'political' being made to live in society (IX, 9, 1169b 28), and if, then, he is in need of friends, properly political friendship is nevertheless only a species of friendship, a derived one, the useful friendship demanded for concord, accord, consensus (*homónoia*). All these divides suppose the potentiality/act distinction, the accident/essence distinction, etc. And such distinctions would be called up *here*, and therefore necessarily implied or implemented – claims Aristotle in sum – by the correct use and understanding of the Greek word *philía*, by its very semantic constitution. By everything named *friendship*, by every- thing whose 'true name is *friendship*', as Nietzsche said in *The Gay Science* (para. 14).

Let us then suppose, *concesso non dato*, that one can today *translate* by *'friendship'*, by *Freundschaft*, by *amitié*, etc., these Greek words *philía*, *homónoia*, and all those which, one following upon the next, are inseparable from them. That would amount, here, to considering the possibility of this translation ensured, and the possibility of thinking thought, *qua* the thought of the same or the thought of the other, in the pathbreaking [*frayage*] of this transfer, train or tramway named *philía, Freundschaft, friendship, amitié.*

Aristotle knew that this translation poses a critical problem, already from within the Greek language. His own language had to revert, in effect, to the same word, *philía,* for different and derived senses, inadequate to *philía prótè* and *teleía philía.* The entire discourse of the two *Ethics* on *philía* can be read as a discourse on language, on the word *philía:* its uses, its contexts, its measured equivocation, its legitimate or improper translations.

Now, even supposing, *concesso non dato,* that these words can be translated with no remainder, the questions of responsibility remain here among us (but then how many of us are there?). How is this responsibility to be exercised in the best possible way? How will we know if there is *philía* or *homónoia* between us, if we are getting on well, at what moment and to what degree? How are we to distinguish between ourselves, between each of us who compose this as yet so undetermined 'we'?

Let us therefore suppose that you hold me responsible for what I say by the mere fact that I am speaking, even if I am not yet assuming responsibility for the sentences I am quoting.

Then, perhaps, you will grant me this: that as the first result of a practical demonstration, the one that has just taken place – even before the question of responsibility was posed, the question of 'speaking in one's own name', countersigning such and such an affirmation, etc. – we are caught up, one and another, in a sort of heteronomic and dissymmetrical curving of social space – more precisely, a curving of the relation to the other: prior to all organized *socius,* all *políteia,* all determined 'government', *before* all 'law'. Prior to and before all law, in Kafka's sense of being 'before the law'.[5]

Let's get this right: prior to all *determined* law, *qua* natural law or positive law, but not prior to law *in general.* For the heteronomic and dissymmetrical curving of a law of originary sociability is also a law, perhaps the very essence of law. What is unfolding itself at this instant – and we are finding it a somewhat disturbing experience – is perhaps only the silent deployment of that strange violence that has always insinuated itself into the origin of the most innocent experiences of friendship or justice. We have begun to respond. We are already caught up, we are caught out, in a certain responsibility, and the most ineluctable responsibility – as if it were possible to think a responsibility without freedom. We are invested with an undeniable responsibility at the moment we begin to signify something. But where does this begin? Does it ever begin? This responsibility that assigns freedom to us *without leaving it with us*, as it were – we see it coming from the other. It is assigned to us by the other, from the place of the other, well before any hope of reappropriation allows us the assumption of this responsibility – allowing us, as we say, to assume responsibility, *in the name, in one's own name*, in the space of *autonomy*, where the law one gives oneself and the name one receives conspire. In the course of this experience, the other appears *as such* – that is to say, the other appears as a being whose appearance appears without appearing,[6] without being submitted to the phenomenological law of the originary and intuitive given that governs all other appearances, all other phenomenality *as such*. The altogether other, and *every other (one) is every (bit) other*,[7] comes here to upset the order of phenomenology. And good *sense*. That which comes before autonomy must also *exceed* it – that is, succeed it, survive and indefinitely overwhelm it.

In general, when one is dealing with law (*nómos*), the same good sense opposes autonomy, even autarcky, to heteronomy. Here we have the epitome of good sense, the unimpeachable in its uncontestable authority. Yet this oppositional logic *must* perhaps *be* distorted, in order to prepare, from afar, the 'political' translation of what thus '*must be*'. It is in fact a question of a 'what must be', and the relations between autonomy and heteronomy from the place of this *what must be*.

In a word – and since it is good, for the sake of clarity, to multiply the anticipations and announce the heading – the point here is that of a 'political' translation of which the risks and difficulties – indeed, the aporias – could never be exaggerated. Having made a *problematic* scansion appear in a sort of history of friendship, a scansion which would have introduced dissymmetry, separation and infinite distance in a Greek *philía* which did not tolerate them *but nevertheless called for them*, it would now be a matter of suggesting that a democracy to come – still not given, not thought; indeed, put down or repressed – not only would not contradict this dissymmetrical curving and this infinite heterogeneity, but would in truth be demanded by them.

Such a dissymmetry and infinite alterity would have no relation to what Aristotle would have called inequality or superiority. They would indeed be incompatible with all sociopolitical hierarchy *as such*. *It would therefore be a matter of thinking an alterity without hierarchical difference at the root of democracy.* We shall see later that, beyond a certain determination of law and calculation (measurement, 'metrics'), but not of law or or justice in general, this democracy would free a certain interpretation of *equality* by removing it from the phallogocentric schema of *fraternity*. The former would have been determining in *our* traditional, canonical, dominant concept of friendship, and simultaneously – despite the differences and discontinuities that we should never ignore or neglect – in the apparent '*finitism*' of Greek and Roman philosophical culture and in '*infinitist*' testamentary culture, particularly in its Christian form. And in the preceding chapter, we were intent on showing how the philosophical horizon of *philía* (with everything it supposes, of course) carries in its determination, in the very form of its finity *qua* horizon, the potential but inexorable injunction of its infinitization, and hence also that of its Christianization. The privilege we are bestowing here on the latter, in what is, all in all, a history of fraternization, a history *qua* fraternization, in particular in its revolutionary ecstasies, would be justified – provisionally – only by the role it played, in the place of the theologico-political graft between the Greek and Christian worlds, in the construction of models and the political discourse of modern Europe.

Questions, then: in what sense may one still speak of equality – indeed, of symmetry – in the dissymmetry and boundlessness of infinite alterity? What right does one have to speak still of the political, of law, and of democracy? Must these words totally change their meaning? Let themselves be translated? And what, then, will be the rule of translation?

A moment ago we were evoking an excessive assignation of responsibility. What does responsibility have to do with *what is called friendship*? We are indeed saying 'what is called friendship', and we stress this precaution. That again looks like a quotation, as if we had to strive unceasingly to recall that before knowing what friendship is and what we mean by this word, here and now, we must first deal with a certain use of the word 'friendship'. Referring first to the Anglo-Saxon distinction between 'using' and 'mentioning', between the gesture consisting in making use of a word and that of referring to a word between parentheses (by citing it, naming it, by provisionally suspending its use), let us say that we should first of all mention the uses of the word 'friendship', as well as the interpretations and experiences (for experiences are also interpretations) to which this 'friendship' gives rise.

For we should not forget that we are first speaking in the tradition of a certain concept of friendship, within a given culture – let us say our own, or at least the one from which a 'we' is staking its chance. Now if this tradition harbours within it dominant structures, discourses which silence others, by covering over or destroying the archive, a tradition is certainly not homogeneous, nor, within it, is the determination of friendship. Our main concern will indeed be to recognize the major marks of a tension, perhaps ruptures and in any case scansions, within this history of friendship, the canonical figure of friendship.

To make ourselves once again more sensitive to this heterogeneity and its internal potentialities, to make it and them a springboard for a leap further out, let us return to the 'canonical' version. Let us listen one final time, let us listen once again to Montaigne listening to Diogenes listening to Aristotle, but translating him too, interpreting him, *authorizing* him: 'O my friends, there is no friend'. The painful and plaintive irony of the address also speaks the certainty of a strange affirmation. The sentence – we have heard it – is launched like a sort of apostrophe. Someone in effect turns towards his friends: 'O my friends . . .' – but the apostrophe turns on itself, it bears in itself a predicative proposition, it envelops an indicative declaration. Claiming to state a fact, it also utters a general truth in the form of a judgement: 'there is no friend'. We have already pointed out that the general truth of the *fact* refers to the friend ('no friend', *oudeis phílos*, indefinite singular, the negativity of just anyone) and seems to contradict in act the very possibility of the apostrophe, its possibility of being *serious* and eluding fiction, when it claims to be addressing friends, particular determined friends, not just any friends, and friends in the plural: friends are indeed necessary, I must posit or suppose their existence if I am thus to address certain of their number, if only to tell them that 'there are no friends'. To be sure, there is also a contradiction in the reportive utterance or in the aforementioned *recoil* verson. And it remains. How will you affirm non-contradictorily that having *some* friends is to have *no* friend? But this contradiction is shown, denounced, objectified, stated, perhaps played out, between two meanings of the word friend or two quantities (the plural and the singular); it in no way affects the act of uttering, as would a 'performative contradiction'.

However vivacious and present it remains, this 'performative contradiction' could still be handled as a mere piece of nonsense, a logical absurdity – indeed, in the best of cases, and if this does not distract us from the gravity of the political affair, as the playful exercise of a paradox, a pleasant fiction, a fabulous pedagogy. Yes, but provided that it really is a question of a simple performative contradiction – that is, *as long as and provided that* the two enunciative structures are sufficiently symmetrical to be mutually opposed and contradictory. Provided, therefore, that they make up a sentence and belong to a *presently homogeneous* ensemble.

Now this is not necessarily the case.

While its performative force sweeps up the entire sentence, while its form overwhelms and comprises within itself the alleged report, the apostrophe resembles at one and the same time a *recall* and a *call* [*appel*, also 'appeal'].

First of all, a call, for it points towards a future. Thus one addresses friends by calling them friends. They are addressed presently in and of the future: O my friends, be my friends, I love you, love me, I will love you, let us exchange this promise, we will exchange it, will we not ... (Let us recall: Friendship, as Aristotle also said, 'seems to consist in loving rather than in being loved',[8] a proposition whose power of dislocation, infinitization and dissymmetricalization we have not finished meditating); listen to me, be alert to my call, to my complaint, to my expectation, understand and be sympathetic, I request of you sympathy and consensus, become these friends to whom I aspire. Yield to what is at one and the same time a desire, a request, and a promise – one can also say a prayer. And let us not forget what Aristotle says of prayer (*eukhé*): it is a discourse (*lógos*) but one which, in some ways like a performative, is neither true nor false.[9] We know that there are no friends, but I pray you, my friends, act so that henceforth there are. You, my friends, be my friends. You already are, since that is what I am calling you. Moreover, how could I be your friend, how could I declare my friendship (and it consists in loving rather than in being loved), if friendship were not still to come, to be desired, to be promised? How could I give you my friendship there where friendship would not be in default, if there already were such a thing? More precisely, if the friend were not in default? If I give you friendship, it is because there is friendship (perhaps); it does not exist, *presently*. In any case, it is not at my disposal.

(Let us note in passing that the logic of this call – 'You-my-friends-be-my-friends-and-although-you-are-not-yet-my-friends-you-are-already,-since-that-is-what-I-am-calling-you' – comes under the structure and the temporality of what we have been calling on several occasions a messianic teleiopoesis.)

For neither the 'recoil' version nor the 'canonical' apostrophe says: 'there is no friendship', but 'there is no friend'. Perhaps because we have an idea of friendship and what it should be, in the ideality of its essence or the culminated perfection of its *telos* (*teleía philía*), an idea of invincible friendship in the face of all scepticisms, perhaps it is *in the name of friendship* that we must indeed acknowledge (*constater*) that if there is friendship, if there is indeed a promised friendship, alas, 'there is no friend'. Is that not what Montaigne means in the context determined by his most thematic intention, a context which prevails in this passage up to a certain point? Is is not in reference to the 'common friendships', 'ordinary and common-place' ones, that one must sigh in complaint? These common friendships are not this 'sovereign master friendship', and this is why 'there is no friend', no friend worthy of the name, in those friendships.

But if *presently* there is no friend, let us act so that henceforth there will be friends of this 'sovereign master friendship'. This is what I call you to; answer my call, this is our responsibility. Friendship is never a present given, it belongs to the experience of expectation, promise, or engagement. Its discourse is that of prayer, it inaugurates, but reports (*constate*) nothing, it is not satisfied with what is, it moves out to this place where a responsibility opens up a future.

The fraternal figure of friendship will often bestow its features, allegorical or not, Greek or Christian, on what all revolutionary oaths involve with respect to responsibility to a future. Witness the turbulent history of the word and concept of *fraternity* during and after the French Revolution, in and around the Republican motto, the 'holy motto of our forebears' as Pierre Leroux said[10] – a motto which, nevertheless, does not appear in the Declaration of Human Rights, the Constitution of 1793, or the Charter of 1830, but only in an addendum to the Constitution of 1791, then in the 1848 Constitution which at last seals the establishment of the new Trinity.

But the apostrophe 'O my friends' also turns towards the past. It recalls, it points to that which must indeed be supposed in order to be heard, if only in the non-apophantic form of prayer: you have already marked this minimal friendship, this preliminary consent without which you would not hear me. Otherwise you would not listen to my call, you would not be sensitive to the element of hope in my complaint. Without this absolute past, I would not have been able, for my part, to address you thus. We would not be together in a sort of minimal community – but also incommensurable to all others – speaking the same language or praying for translation against the horizon of a same language, if only to manifest disagreement, if a *sort of friendship* had not already been sealed, before all contracts; if it had not been avowed as the impossible that resists even the avowal, but avowed still, avowed as the unavowable of the 'unavowable community': a friendship prior to friendships, an ineffaceable friendship, fundamental and groundless, one that breathes in a shared language (past or to come) and in the being-together that all allocution supposes, up to and including the declaration of war.

Is this incommensurable friendship, this friendship of the incommensur-able, indeed the one we are here attempting to separate from its fraternal adherence, from its inclination to take on the economic, genealogical, ethnocentric, androcentric features of fraternity? Or is it still a fraternity, but a fraternity divided in its concept, a fraternity ranging infinitely beyond all literal figures of the brother, a fraternity that would no longer exclude anyone?

Here we are in the vicinity of the gravest of problems. It will have been understood that it is not our intention to denounce fraternity or fraternization. Of course, no one will contest the fact that all movements (Christian or revolutionary ones, for example) celebrating fraternity or fraternal friendship have universal range and theoretically challenge the limits of natural, literal, genetic, sexually determined (etc.) fraternity. Michelet's gesture would be a good example: the assumption and overcoming of Christian fraternity in favour of the universal and revolutionary fraternity in the Enlightenment style, etc. The passages quoted as this chapter's epigraphs are telling in this context. So many others could confirm the force of this movement. In Michelet there is even, to be sure, this hyperbolization of the fraternity concept which extends it not only beyond all boundaries but indeed beyond all juridical, legislative, and political determinations of the law. How can one oppose the generosity of so many analogous formulas to the one cited above: 'Fraternity is the law beyond the law'?

Whence, then, our reticence?

In keeping this word to designate a fraternity beyond fraternity, a fraternity without fraternity (literal, strict, genealogical, masculine, etc.), one never renounces that which one claims to renounce – and which returns in myriad ways, through symptoms and disavowals whose rhetoric we must learn to decipher and whose strategy to outwit. Is it by chance, is it in the name of a 'law beyond law,' that Michelet couches this discourse on sublime fraternity in considerations (on the nation, the homeland, France, or womankind) of which the least that can be said is that their literalness, their literalism, does not readily brook transformation? According to what a Michelet, for example, says of the homeland, of the nation, of France, the alleged universalism of the discourse can be agreed upon only by way of the exemplarist logic in which we have recognized the profound strategy of all nationalisms, patriotisms, or ethnocentrisms.

To give examples of the exemplarism we are putting into question, enunciations such as the following could be multiplied indefinitely: 'She [France] found she was herself, and even as she was proclaiming the future common right of the world, she distinguished herself from the rest of the world more than she had ever done before.' Or again: 'The homeland is the necessary initiation to the homeland of all mankind.' Or yet again: 'France is a religion.' 'France has been the pontiff of the Age of Enlightenment.' And above all, then: 'This nation, considered thus as the asylum of the world, is much more than a nation. It is a living brotherhood.'[11]

Let us not forget that this fraternity is another name for friendship. The last words of the book, whose author believes it will 'remain the profound basis of democracy',[12] recall this: 'All I have in this world – my friendships – I offer them up to her, and give to my country the beautiful name handed down by ancient France. I lay them all at the altar of the *Great Friendship*.'[13] National singularity gives the example of universal friendship or fraternity, the living example, the ideal example in the sense Cicero gives to the word *exemplar* in *De Amicitia*. And this is said universally in the French language, in which what is called, 'in human language, fraternity', is uttered. To be exemplary, infinitely universal, French fraternity has as much need of being literal, singular, incarnate, living, idiomatic, *irreplaceable*, as fraternity *tout court* does, in order to become exemplary of universal fraternity, of being literally fraternal: that is to say, where a woman cannot replace a man, nor a sister a brother. The woman is not yet fraternal enough, not friend enough; she does not yet know what 'fraternity' means; above all she does not know what it will and should mean, she does not understand – *not yet* – the fraternal promise. She knows the word well enough, but she does not possess the concept; she reads it as one reads in nursery school, she reads it without reading it. She reads it literally but does not yet have access to what it thinks in spirit – and so it is the sacred that she misses, and history and the future, no less: 'She can spell the sacred word of the new age, *Brotherhood*, but cannot yet read it.' Not yet.

This is so well expressed. And *L'Amour* is so replete with the love of women that one feels mean indeed in showing the slightest irony in the face of such vibrant eloquence, sometimes moving, always generous. And precisely so authentically democratic. Finally, so democratically well-intentioned, and so disarming. Actually more disarming than disarmed. For in the final analysis. . . . The book claims to be 'the profound base of democracy', and one indeed sees that it is unprepared, for the moment, to open universal democratic fraternity to those – in truth, to *those women* – who would precisely, in its view, not yet be ready for it – *not yet*. This logic of the 'not yet' slightly complicates matters and allows women to hope – or, at least, universal fraternity to hope – but this interests us all the more since, in the next chapter, we will again come across universal fraternity at work, in an analogous context (*mutatis mutandis*) in a distant relative of Michelet, but so far removed that no cousinly affinity between them would be imaginable: Nietzsche. Is not the thing all the more telling? The thing? The woman, the sister.

Let us strive to be more equitable. If the thing does not allow itself to be thus classified, if it remains more ambiguous, ironic (again the woman, 'eternal irony of the community', as Hegel said); if the thing still leaves room for other reversals, it is not only because Michelet's *L'Amour* exudes the goodness of the man, the husband, the father. It is not because his phallogocentrism or his andro-gallo-fraternocentrism is also an exemplary universalism, and hence boundlessly generous. Why then? In his unbounded desire to give and take away at the same time, unreservedly to demonstrate his love of woman, to whom he denies any maturity in the historical experience of promised friendship, Michelet does not fail to bestow on woman more than he takes away. For here he is suddenly ready to concede to her, in the contortion of a gesture which will immediately contradict itself, the very thing he had placed in the extreme hyperbole of fraternity – that is: being a 'law beyond the law'. Well, then, it would be *almost* the same for woman – if it were not the opposite, and if it did not immediately annul itself in its antithesis. Woman is *like* absolute fraternity, she resembles it, like law beyond the law, justice beyond justice. She is 'more than just'. Except for the fact that she destroys, with justice, what she thus is, what she could be, what she is without being it: pure friendship. Let us read. Having remarked: 'She can spell the sacred word of the new age, *Brotherhood*, but cannot yet read it', the author of *L'Amour* continues:

'She sometimes seems to be above the virtues of the new age. She is *more just than just* – she is chivalrous, and extremely generous. *But justice transcended destroys justice itself.*'[14]

Fraternization is always caught up, like friendship itself, in a vertiginous process of hyperbolization. There is always someone, something, more fraternal than the brother, more friendly than the friend, more equitable than justice or the law – and the measure is given by the immensity and incommensurability of this 'more'. Thus it is refused while simultaneously given. As incalculable as that indivisible subject of which we were speaking above: the condition of possibility and impossibility of calculation, the condition of a decision which nevertheless becomes immediately impossible and of secondary importance once a subject is what it is: indivisible and identical to itself, subject to everything *except* to something ever really happening to it, actually affecting it. The *mechanism* of hyperbolization (for there is something of the mechanical and the technical in this regularity) works away at this semantics in the strict and proper sense of the term. The paradox is in this: that the strict, literal, restrained sense is not, as one might believe, what a literal sense promises, announces or defers in the figure of the figure, in the figurative sense. The strict sense conceals the literal sense, which would be on the same pole as the figurative sense, on the opposite pole of the strict sense: thus true fraternity, fraternity in the literal sense, would be universal, spiritual, symbolic, infinite fraternity, the fraternity of the oath, etc., not fraternity in the strict sense, that of the 'natural' brother (as if such a thing ever existed), the virile brother, by opposition to the sister, the determined brother, in this family, this nation, this particular language. And what we are picking up here around fraternity, *qua* the dominant schema of friendship, transports its upsetting hyperbole into friendship, as into all its associated semantic values.

What, then, is friendship *in the literal sense*? Does this question still make sense, precisely? In a rather Aristotelian gesture, will one say of friendship that, if it is caught up in the bonds of fraternity *in the strict sense*, it possesses only an *accidental, analogical* or *equivocal* relation to friendship, hence to fraternity *in the literal sense*?

The question then becomes, it returns and becomes again: 'What is friendship *in the literal sense*?' Is it ever present? What is presence for this *philía próte* or this *teleía philía* of which we have glimpsed the aporia? 'What is the essence of friendship?', 'What is a friend?', 'What is a feminine friend?'

If we are not even *close* to an answer, it is not only owing to the great number of *philosophical* difficulties still awaiting us. It is not only because we have discerned the presence of this value of *presence* at the very heart of that which was to be defined, which the *entire* tradition that we have acknowledged hitherto pre-defined or pre-understood precisely as the virtue of presence, the truth of *proximity*: the friend is the near one and friendship grows with presence, with allocution in the same place. This is its truth, its essence, its mode of existence, etc. If we are not even *close* to an answer, nor perhaps to a grasp of the question as one of proximity, this is – in a principled, preliminary, both simple and abyssal way – because the question 'what is (*tí estin*)', the question of the essence or the truth, has *already* deployed itself, as the question *of* philosophy, *from out of* a certain *experience* of *phileín* and *philía*.

The question 'What is friendship?', but also 'Who is the friend (both or either sex)?' is nothing but the question 'What is philosophy?'.

Was ist das – die Philosophie?[15] In the conference bearing this title,

Heidegger pinpoints the moment when the *philefn* of Heraclitus' *philefn to sophón*, having been determined as the 'originary accord' or 'harmony' (*ein ursprünglicher Einklang, harmonía*), would have become tension towards a search – a *question*, precisely – a jealous, nostalgic, and tense (*strebende Suchen*) inquisition, an investigation 'determined by Eros': the desire and tension of *órexis*.[16] Thought (*Das Denken*) would have become philosophy only in the wake of this eroticization of questioning around being ('*Was ist das Seiende, insofern es ist?*'). 'Heraclitus and Parmenides were not yet "philosophers".' The 'step' to philosophy would have been prepared by sophistry, then accomplished by Socrates and Plato. Guided by a vigilant reading of this interpretation, we could attempt to follow the discreet lead of an unceasing meditation on friendship in Heidegger's path of thinking.[17] In the course of this meditation we encounter, in particular, a strange and isolated allusion to the hearing of the 'voice of the friend (*Stimme des Freundes*] which every *Dasein* carries with it'.[18] The existential analytic of *Dasein*, which 'carries' (*trägt*) this voice within it, is – let us not forget – neither an anthropology nor a sociology, nor an analytic of the subject, the person, consciousness, the *psukhé* or the self; neither an ethics or a politics. For all these disciplines presuppose it. This bestows on the voice of the friend – and therefore on friendship itself – an especial ontological signification, in a chapter on *Dasein und Rede, Die Sprache*, and not even in the analytic of *Mitsein*. This strange voice, at once both interior and coming from without, is perhaps not unrelated to the 'voice' of consciousness (*Gewissen*) of which Heidegger also proposes an existential analytic (*Sein und Zeit*, paras 57 ff.). The provenance of the call, its *Woher*, is an *Unheimlichkeit* (para. 58) which would be sufficient to uproot all mere domesticity if it did not play a more ambiguous but spectral and always decisive role in Heidegger's discourse. The voice of the call is always felt to be a *foreign* voice, a non-intimate one ('*unvertraut* – *so etwas wie eine* fremde *Stimme*) by the 'One' of the everyday (para. 57). The gender of this 'friend' is not determined; we would thus be tempted to graft on to this reading a question posed elsewhere on the subject of the word *Geschlecht* and the question of sexual difference in Heidegger.[19]

The sophistic moment would signify a scission in the thought of harmony. To heal this wound, to calm this discord or this false note in the harmony of the *Einklang*, to reconstitute the originary *philefn* thus inter-rupted, the worried and nostalgic philosopher asks 'what is . . .?'. It thereby becomes what it is, philosophy, as if, beneath the question 'what is? (*ti estin*)', or 'what is being?', 'the beingness of being (*ti to on*)?', philosophy was implicitly asking: what has happened? What has occurred? – in other words: What has happened to *phileîn* or to originary *Einklang*? Why has the harmony been interrupted? Why the discord and the false note? Why has *lógos* been affected thus, this logos which means the gathering of the One?

These same questions should lead, through the thinker's *Gespräch* with the poet, a speech between two which always supposes some friendship, towards two types of texts: on the one hand those that address Hölderlin ('*Wo aber sind die Freunde?*, in *Andenken*[20]), and on the other hand, those addressed to Trakl, to the figures of 'the friend who follows the stranger', to those of the brother and sister, precisely around this motif of *Geschlecht*.[21] But the question 'What is philosophy?', philosophy *qua philía tou sophóu*, is repeated and interpreted by Heidegger, often in the ringing out of *phileîn* as it rings in the Heraclitean sentence ('*Der Spruch Heraklits: phúsis krúptesthai phileî*'). Heidegger translates *philía* as accorded favour (*Gunst*), benevolent protection, good grace.[22] 'In *phúsis* reigns the benevolence of what accords or is accorded, as the favourable of the favour.'[23] Or again: 'We understand *phileîn* as favour or solicitude.'[24] *Philía* would name here the essential, reciprocal or alternative (*wechselweise*) relation between rising, opening or opening up (*Aufgehen*) and the decline or the covering-over (*Untergehen* [*Sichverbergen*]) of *phúsis*.

What does to accord mean? In what language is it accorded to be able to hear it?

Qua philía, phúsis accords. It is the accord, the accord in itself of harmony and given accord, but its solicitude for revelation is also accorded to the dissimulation of self: accord in itself of what is accorded in rising and what is accorded in decline, the *Aufgehen* as well as the *Untergehen*. And, as always for Heidegger, under the law of a *lógos* that assembles and gathers up. The gathering (*Versammlung*) always prevails, even if it accords the tensions of a false note. *Phúsis* and *philía*, *phúsis qua philía*: one, like the other, guards this at once generous and jealous relation to itself, as it were, it loves (in) hiding: [*elle aime à se cacher*], *kruptesthai phileîn*. It loves to hide and only loves in hiding, it loves providing it is hidden. The withdrawal of the sense of decency [*pudeur*] here bestows movement itself, it bestows originarily, and not in the twilight of some sin; it bestows the gift of what thus couples, in order to accord them, *phúsis* and *philía*, and *phúein* to *phileîn*, with one another.

And on the path of this *phúein* (to be born, to grow, to sprout up, to grow up, to mature), on the path of this generation *qua phileîn*, one might be tempted here to retrace the genealogy of this genealogy, that of this genealogism which we have so insistently recognized in the political figures of *philía*, in particular in autochthonism and its fratrocentrism. Would it be so difficult to find the trace of Greek autochthonism in Heideggerian thought? No one has the slightest doubt, so evident seems the trace.

Up to a certain point, we must, to be sure, account for Heidegger's concern with avoiding anachronism in this hearing of *philía* and *phileîn*. Now the most serious deafness would consist, according to him, in anthropologizing, psychologizing, subjectifying *phileîn*. Heidegger would appear to incriminate modern metaphysics for this deafness, in any case the post-Christian philosophy of subjectivity. It sometimes seems difficult to follow him along this epochal scansion, especially when he excludes Aristotle from this anthropologization of *philía* or *phileîn*. The subject/object opposition is no doubt anachronistic. But how can he claim that the anthropological – indeed, psychological – vantage point remains foreign to Aristotle? It is also true that Heidegger does not then speak of a discourse on *anthropos* or on *psukhé in general*, but of what is called in *modern times* anthropology or psychology. These are the so-called disciplines that would depend on a metaphysics of subjectivity, on an interpretation of the human *qua* subject. This allows us to read, in the same passage, that Christianity constitutes the preparatory stage of an education of the passions, and even a psychology. The first consequence, if Heidegger is to be followed here, would be that *all* the discourses of friendship that we have evoked hitherto, all the post-Aristotelian treatises *de amicitia*, whether Roman, neo-Roman or not, come under a 'Christian metaphysics of subjectivity'. And the same consequence would hold for all the 'politics' that we have been trying to decipher. They would remain politics of psychological subjectivity, exactly as would the concept of the political from which they claim to stem. Treatises, confessions, poems, fictions, would have begun, without exception, by subjectifying, anthropologizing, psychologizing – indeed, Christianizing – *philía*.

Now, for the Greeks there would be no psychology. No anthropological 'subject'. Aristotle's treatise *Perí psukhés* would have nothing to do with a 'psychology'. In its very accomplishment, metaphysics would become 'psychology'. Psychology and anthropology would be 'the last word' of metaphysics. Psychology and technics go 'hand in hand'.[25] Whatever the status of this epochal distribution and the problems it creates, the conclusion would be clear: when Heidegger evokes the friend or friendship, he does so in a space which is not – or no longer, or not yet – the space of the person or the subject, nor that of *ánthrōpos*, the object of anthropology, nor that of the *psúkhé* of psychologists. Nor, therefore, that of an attendant politics.

When, in a rather late text, Heidegger attempts to return to an experience of speech or of language (*Sprache*) sufficiently originary to precede, as it were, questioning itself (*das Fragen*); when he recalls that this questioning – the very moment of research, knowledge, philosophy – presupposes a certain acquiescence (*Zusage*), an accord given to *Sprache*, engaged in it, he finds again, perhaps, that agency of *phileĩn* which has not yet become *philosophía*: a questioning tension, an eroticization of a *Streben*, a jealous, nostalgic, mournful or curious contraction of Eros; then, against this backdrop, metaphysical subjectivization, psychologization, politicization.

(We have attempted elsewhere, more than once, to recognize and draw the consequences of such an arche-originary pledge preceding all questioning. When we propose here to think a certain experience of the *perhaps* 'prior to' the possibility of such a pledge which must be found suspended therein, we can only raise the stakes in a Heideggerian warning against the 'subjective', 'psychological', 'metaphysical' interpretation of *philía* and its 'politics'. But our aim is to propel this movement in another direction, and here towards a thought of friendship which could never thrive in that 'gathering' (*Versammlung*) which prevails over everything and originarily accords *philía* to *phúsis* and *lógos*.)

It is perhaps in a region thus withdrawn from metaphysical subjectivity that for Heidegger 'the voice of the friend' rings out. The issue is perhaps what we were calling above a minimal 'community' – but also incommensurable to all others, speaking the same language or praying, or weeping, for translation against the horizon of a sole language, if only to manifest a disagreement: friendship prior to friendships. One would have to add: 'prior to' enmity.

This promise before friendships would be linked to the 'yes, yes', this promise of memory that we have attempted to analyse elsewhere. The double affirmation must remain essentially risky, threatened, open. Above all, it cannot allow itself to be defined or posited, it cannot be reduced to a determined position. As such, it eludes opposition. It is therefore not yet 'political' – at least, not in the strictly coded sense of the tradition Schmitt claims to have defined. We could, then, *resituate* the 'concept of the political'.

Without going back over the affinities of this 'concept' with a certain politics, in a context dominated by national socialism, at this precise point the attempt can in fact be made at least to discern topical differences: between Heidegger's subject and Schmitt's on the one hand, between these two poles and what we have been attempting to articulate, here or elsewhere.

Against the backdrop of a sort of historical community or an affinity of co-appurtenance whose features would have to be reconstituted, Schmitt seems first of all to share with Heidegger a firm conviction: one must get behind the subjectal or anthropological determination of the *Freund/Feind* couple. Likewise, one would have to remove all corresponding or dependent determinations: psychological, anthropological, moral, aesthetic, economic. To shed light on the affinity and difference between Heidegger and Schmitt, we must return again to some of the latter's analyses, in order to reread them differently, especially with respect to Schmitt's logic or ontology of 'real possibility':

> The specific political distinction to which political actions and motives can be reduced is that between friend and enemy. . . . The distinction of friend and enemy denotes the utmost degree of intensity of a union or separation, of an association or dissociation. It can exist theoretically and practically, without having simultaneously to draw upon all those moral, aesthetic, economic, or other distinctions [to wit: the distinctions mentioned above: good–evil, beautiful–ugly].[26]

> The friend and enemy concepts are to be understood in their concrete and existential sense, not as metaphors or symbols, not mixed and weakened by economic, moral, and other conceptions, least of all in a private-individualistic sense as a psychological expression of private emotions and tendencies. They are neither normative nor pure spiritual [*rein geistigen*] antitheses.[27]

> War is still today the most extreme possibility. One can say that the exceptional case has an especially decisive meaning which exposes the core of the matter. For only in real combat is revealed the most extreme consequence of the political grouping of friend and enemy. From this most extreme possibility human life derives its specifically *political* tension.
>
> A world in which the possibility of war is utterly eliminated, a completely pacified globe, would be a world without the distinction of friend and enemy and hence a world without politics. It is conceivable that such a world might contain many very interesting antitheses and contrasts, competitions and intrigues of every kind, but there would not be a *meaningful antithesis* whereby men could be required to sacrifice life, authorized to shed blood, and kill other human beings. For the definition of the political, it is here even irrelevant whether such a world without politics is desirable as an ideal situation. The phenomenon of the political can be understood only in the context of the ever present possibility

of the friend-and-enemy grouping, *regardless of the aspects which this possibility implies for morality, aesthetics, and economics.*

War as the most extreme political means discloses the possibility which underlies every political idea, namely, the distinction of friend and enemy. This makes sense only as long as this distinction in mankind is actually present (*real vorhanden*) or at least potentially possible (*real möglich*). On the other hand, *it would be senseless (sinnwidrig) to wage war for 'purely' religious, 'purely' moral, 'purely' juristic, or 'purely' economic motives. The friend and enemy grouping and therefore also war cannot be derived from these specific antitheses of human endeavor.* A war need be neither something religious nor something morally good nor something lucrative.[28]

All in all, Schmitt proposes a deduction of the political as such from a place in which there was as yet no such thing as the political. Between the originary and the derived, the opposition must be rigorous and clear-cut (and *this* oppositional logic, *on this point*, is common to Heidegger and Schmitt). To deduce the political, the enemy as such must be thought – that is, the possibility of a properly political war:

> If there really are enemies in the ontological sense as meant here, then it is logical (*sinnvoll*), but of an exclusively political logic (*aber nur politisch sinnvoll*), to repel and fight them physically. . . . For as long as a people exists in the political sphere, this people must, even if only in the most extreme case – and whether this point has been reached has to be decided by it – determine by itself the distinction of friend and enemy. Therein resides the essence of its political existence. . . . The justification of war does not reside in its being fought for ideals or norms of justice, but in its being fought against a real enemy. All confusions of this category of friend and enemy can be explained as results of blendings of some sort of abstractions or norms.[29]

If Schmitt determines the political in terms of the enemy rather than those of the friend, this is doubtless no merely inconsequential dissymmetry. As we recalled above, Schmitt relies on a necessity he calls a dialectical one. If a politics of friendship rather than war were to be derived, there would have to be agreement on the meaning of 'friend'. But the signification of 'friend' can be determined only from within the friend/enemy opposition. In his deduction of the political, Schmitt in fact reverts to this oppositional logic, to the friend/enemy opposition, to the possibility of war rather than to the dissymmetrical fact of enmity. Here, we are heading towards a question which would perhaps concern the possibility of an experience of friendship outside or on the near side of this oppositional or 'polemological' logic, and hence, also, of the *purity* that the latter seems to require.

Now, although Heidegger shares Schmitt's concern with oppositional purity, it would no doubt be vain to seek in his work such a *determining* deduction of the political. Is this a lack, an absence suffered or desired? Is it because, moving back under this determination, towards a more originary zone, Heidegger no longer possessed the means of a determining derivation? Is it the modernity of such a determination which is in default? But where, and whose? Heidegger's or modernity's itself? And what if Heidegger, in Schmitt's very logic, had understood this properly modern depoliticization of a world in which the enemy concept loses its limits? And what if Heidegger had thought this depoliticization (nihilist, in sum, he would have said) is but the truth of politics, of the metaphysical concept of politics carried out to its culmination? Schmitt would then in this case become the last great metaphysician of politics, the last great spokesperson of European political metaphysics. Questionable or not (the issue will not be discussed here), such a hypothesis would lack, it seems to us, neither interest nor verisimilitude – nor, precisely, promise for political thought, for politics as such. For what is not in the least paradoxical and the least interesting in the Schmittian attempt is precisely this reactive stubbornness in conserving, restoring, reconstituting, saving or refining the classic oppositional distinctions at the very moment when, bringing his attention to bear on a certain modernity (that of 'technics', of war indissociable from technics, partisan war or the Cold War, wars in progress or wars to come), he is forced to register the effacement of fundamental distinctions, *qua* metaphysical, theologico-political – let us say, rather, onto-theological – distinctions.

How can Schmitt be surprised? How can he bemoan the problems encountered through a reflection whose object is the friend/enemy distinction, when he himself admits that 'our age . . . simultaneously produces engines of nuclear extermination and effaces the distinction between war and peace'? Does he not dream of improving the instrument of a classical theory (which moreover, according to him, would never have been of great use) to adjust it to a modernity, to a modern theory of the political and a modern polemology which can perfectly well dispense with such an instrument? Schmitt can thus write:

> The era of systems is over. The beginning of the great epoch of the European republic (*Epoche des europäischen Staatlichkeit*), three hundered years ago, saw the birth of magnificent systems of thought. It is no longer possible, in our age, to construct the like. The only thing possible today is a historical retrospective gathering up the image of that great epoch of *jus publicum Europaeum*, with its

concepts of the State, of war, and of the just enemy, in the consciousness of its systematics.[30]

Further on, he notes that the Cold War provokes

the rupture of these axes of coupled concepts which up to now have sustained the traditional system of limits and forms imposed on war. The Cold War totally ignores the classic distinctions between war, peace, and neutrality, between the political and the economic, military and civilian, soldier and civilian, with the exception of the friend/enemy distinction, whose logic presides at the birth of war and determines its nature.

Nothing surprising, then, if the old English word foe★ has left the four-hundred-year-old lethargy of its archaism to return to common usage, over the past two decades, next to the word enemy. In an age which simultaneously produces devices of nuclear extermination and effaces the distinction between war and peace, how is one, consequently, to prevent the pursuit of a reflection whose object is the friend/enemy distinction?[31]

Here again, through deviations which one must refrain from reducing and which would demand patient work, Heidegger shares Schmitt's disquiet; he subscribes to his diagnosis and prognosis: the distinction between war and peace is disappearing in the technological deployment of modern wars *qua* 'world wars'. A world war is no longer a war, nor is it, obviously, peace. Now Heidegger:

The 'world wars' and their character of 'totality' *und ihre 'Totalität'*) are already a consequence of the abandonment of Being (*Seinsverlassenheit*). They press toward a guarantee of the stability of a constant form of using things up (*Vernutzung*). Man, who no longer conceals his character of being the most important raw material, is also drawn into this process. Man is the 'most important raw material' because he remains the subject of all consumption. He does this in such a way that he lets his will be unconditionally equated with this process, and thus at the same time become the 'object' of the abandonment of being. The world wars are the antecedent (*Vorform*) form of the removal (*Beseitigung*) of the difference between war and peace. This removal is necessary since the 'world' has become an unworld (*Unwelt*) as a consequence of the abandonment of beings by Being's truth. . . . Changed into their deformation of essence (*zu ihrem Unwesen abgeändert*), 'war' and 'peace' are taken up into erring (*Irrnis*), and disappear into the mere course of the escalating manufacture of what can be manufactured

★ Foe: (*Shorter Oxford Dictionary*): 1. in early use, an adversary in deadly feud or mortal combat; now one who hates and seeks to injure another (Old English) 2. One belonging to a hostile army or nation, an enemy in battle or war (Middle English).

(*Machen von Machbarkeiten*), because they have become unrecognizable with regard to any distinction. The question of when there will be peace cannot be answered not because the duration of war is unfathomable, but rather because the question already asks about something which no longer exists, since war is no longer anything which could terminate in peace.[32]

That which Schmitt and Heidegger have in common, it would seem, is the credit given to *opposition*: not only oppositional logic (dialectical or not, the one the Nietzsche of the 'dangerous perhaps' smiles at), not only pure distinctions, pure opposition between the originary and the derived, but oppositionality itself, ontological adversity, that which holds adversaries together, assembling them in *lógos qua* ontological *pólemos*.[33] Despite these affinities, one could wager that Heidegger would have considered the Schmittian discourse as a tribute paid once again, on the part of a lucid theoretician, to a post-Christian metaphysics of subjectivity incapable of posing authentic ontological questions and carrying all his concepts to their level. Notably around these values of 'possibility', of 'actual' or 'present' 'possibility' which play an organizing role in *The Concept of the Political*. And even more so around the friend/enemy couple, a couple of subjects, a couple that finally leaves unquestioned the very question of *what* in the last instance a subject (individual or collective) is, and *what* friendship or its opposite is.

The very possibility of the question, in the form 'what is ...?', thus seems, from the beginning, to suppose this friendship prior to friendships, this *anterior* affirmation of being-together in allocution. Such an affirmation does not allow itself to be simply incorporated and, above all, to be *presented* as a present-being (substance, subject, essence or existence) in the space of an ontology, *precisely because it opens this space up*. The 'I-who' to which Nietzsche's statement refers in *Human All Too Human* ('*Ruf ich, der lebende Tor*') would not necessarily suppose, in its grammatical appearance, the presence of such a subject, of a present-being *qua* subject. Therefore, of a calculability of this *one* indivisible and identical to itself, this *one* to which, all in all, nothing can happen which would affect it in its being, divide it or spoil it; no decision, above all, whereby this identity to self would be called into play; nothing, then, that would not float on the surface of a substantial and unmoving autonomy.

Behind the logical play of the contradiction or the paradox, perhaps the 'O my friends, there is no friend' means initially and finally this overrunning of the present by the undeniable future anterior which would be the very movement and time of friendship. Does not the sentence avow an undeniable future anterior, the absolute of an *unpresentable* past as well as future – that is, traces that can be disavowed only in convoking them into the daylight of phenomenal presence?

A temporal torsion would thus knot the predicative proposition ('there is no friend') to the inside of the apostrophe ('O my friends'). The torsion of the dissymmetry would envelop the theoretical observation or knowledge in the performativity of a prayer that it could never exhaust.

This dissymmetry brings us back to the *question of the response.*

How is the *question of the response* to be linked to the question of responsibility? And why make friendship a privileged locus for this reflection? A brief grammar of the response – or rather, of 'responding' – will afford a preliminary insight into our reasons. We are sketching such a grammar in terms of a language, the French language, but – *at least in this case* – the concepts do not seem altogether limited by this language. This is not to say that they hold *in general* beyond all languages (syntax and lexis) but that, in this context, they appear translatable within a group of European languages which authorize us here to question something like *our* culture and our concept of responsibility. Suffice it to say that this grammar, however schematic, will be a little more than a grammar.

One says 'to answer for', 'to respond to', 'to answer before'. These three modalities are not juxtaposable; they are enveloped and implied in one another. One *answers for*, for self or for something (for someone, for an action, a thought, a discourse), *before* – before an other, a community of others, an institution, a court, a law. And always one *answers for* (for self or for its intention, its action or discourse), *before*, by first responding *to*: this last modality thus appearing more originary, more fundamental and hence unconditional.

1. One *answers for self*, for what one is, says, or does, and this holds beyond the simple present. The 'self' or the 'I' thus supposes unity – in other words, memory that answers. This is often called the unity of the subject, but such a synthesis of memory can be conceived without necessarily reverting to the concept of *subject*, in any case without a subject *qua* living being (this predicate is difficult to reduce as long as the word 'subject' still means something not arbitrarily or conventionally ascribed to the semantic history of the word). This unity is never assured in itself *qua* empirical synthesis; the so-called *proper* name becomes the agency to which the recognition of this identity is confided. 'I' am assumed to be responsible for 'myself' – that is, for everything imputable to that which bears my name. This imputability presupposes freedom, to be sure – a non-present

freedom; but also that what bears my name remains the 'same', not only from one moment to the next, from one state of that which bears my name to another, but even beyond life or presence in general – for example, beyond the self-presence of what bears the name. The agency called here 'the proper name' cannot necessarily be reduced to the registered name, patronymic or social reference, although these phenomena are most often its determining manifestation.

The question of the proper name is obviously at the heart of the friendship problematic. Pre-socratic *philía* was perhaps capable of doing without the proper name, at least without what we are calling the proper name, if it is true, as Heidegger claims, that *philía* is older than subjectivity. But supposing that the proper name rigorously presupposes a concept of subjectivity (nothing seems less assured), we have a real problem thinking friendship without the proper name, whether it corresponds to a registered patronymic or not. The friendship for La Boétie, as Montaigne says, was first friendship for a name. The name preceded their encounter. More precisely, this encounter or '*accointance*' took place long before 'I met him and first made me acquainted with his name, thus preparing for that loving friendship . . .':

> Meditating this union there was, beyond all my reasoning, beyond all that I can say specifically about it, some inexplicable force of destiny. We were seeking each other before we set eyes on each other – both because of the reports we each had heard, which made a more violent assault on our emotions than was reasonable from what they had said, and I believe, because of some decree of Heaven: we embraced each other by our names.[34]

2. One first responds to the other: to the question, the request, the prayer, the apostrophe, the call, the greeting or the sign, the adieu of the other. This dimension of *answering qua* responding *to* – appears more originary than the others for two reasons. On the one hand one does not answer for oneself in one's own name, one is responsible only before the question, the request, the interpellation, the 'insistence' of the other. On the other hand, the proper name structuring the 'answering for oneself' is in itself *for the other* – either because the other has chosen it (for example, the name given to me at birth, one I never chose, which ushers me into the space of law) or because, in any case, it implies the other in the very act of naming, in its origin, finality and use. The *answering* always supposes the other in a relation to self, it keeps the sense of this dissymmetrical 'anteriority' down to the apparently most interior and most solitary autonomy of the 'as regards self',

of interior consciousness and moral consciousness jealous of its independence – another word for freedom. This dissymmetrical anteriority also marks temporalization as the structure of responsibility.

3. Answering *before*: this expression seems first to modalize the 'responding to'. One anwers *before* the other because, first of all, one responds *to* the other. But this modalization is more than and different from an exemplary specification. And it plays a decisive role whose effects we should register. The expression 'before' marks in general, right on the idiom, the passage to an institutional agency of alterity. It is no longer singular but universal in its principle. One responds *to* the other, who can always be singular, and must in one respect remain so, but one answers *before the law*, a court, a jury, an agency authorized to represent the other legitimately, in the institutional form of a moral, juridical, political community. We have here two forms or two dimensions of the *respect* entailed in all *responsibility*.

Considering the rigour, the force and the originality that Kant confers on this concept, will we say that respect introduces a new configuration into this philosophical history of friendship whose canon we have been questioning? Let us first note in passing that these two words, *respect* and *responsibility*, which come together and provoke each other relentlessly, seem to refer, in the case of the former, to languages of the Latin family, to distance, to space, to the gaze; and in the case of the latter, to time, to the voice and to listening. There is no respect, as its name connnotes, without the vision and distance of a *spacing*. No responsibility without response, without what speaking and hearing *invisibly* say to the ear, and which takes *time*. The co-implication of responsibility and respect can be felt at the heart of friendship, one of the enigmas of which would stem from this distance, this concern in what concerns the other: a respectful separation seems to distinguish friendship from love.

Kant is undoubtedly the first, the first with such critical and thematic rigour, to have set out to locate what is proper to this friendly respect. There is no friendship without 'the respect of the other'. The respect of friendship is certainly inseparable from a 'morally good will' (the tradition of *virtue* in the *próté philía*, from Aristotle to Cicero and Montaigne). However, it cannot, for all that, be simply conflated with *purely moral* respect, the one due only to its 'cause', the moral law, which finds in the person only an example. To respect the friend is not exactly to respect the law. One can have friendship for a person: an example of respect for the moral law. One has no friendship for law, the cause of moral respect.

The fundamental passage that the *Doctrine of Virtue* devotes to friendship is formidably complex.[35] Kant quotes in turn, in a slightly different form, Aristotle's saying, and as if by chance, having hailed the great couples of friends, always men, only men. And in this short treatise on friendship – entitled, however, 'On the Most Intimate Union of Love with Respect in Friendship' – there is not the slightest allusion to woman, nor even to sexual difference. As for the great couples of great men, they furnish this analysis with its only historical example, in truth a mythological and Greek one, and cue the only proper names present in it. Kant, it is true, does not fail to note that he places himself, here, in the historical and canonical space of citation. He is then held by the law of a genre, an almost literary genre, a kind of novel:

> Friendship thought as attainable in in its purity or completeness (between Orestes and Pylades, Theseus and Pirithoüs) is the hobby horse of writers of romances. On the other hand Aristotle says: My dear friends, there is no such thing as a friend! The following remarks may draw attention to the difficulties in perfect friendship. (p. 148)

What difficulties? And what are the schemata which, here again, impose themselves if we are to think these difficulties, to establish them in their concepts and to propose solutions for them? As always, Kant inscribes the most original and the most necessary critical signature in the lineage of a tradition. Following the Aristotelian distinction to which Montaigne also remained faithful, Kant begins by saying that he will speak of friendship in so far as it is 'considered in its perfection'. But he confers on this perfection the perfectly rigorous status of what is called an idea in the Kantian sense. In its perfection, therefore – that is, *qua* an unattainable but practically necessary idea – friendship supposes both *love* and *respect*. It must be equal and reciprocal: reciprocal love, equal respect. One has the duty to tend towards and to nurture this ideal of 'sympathy' and 'communication' (*Mitteilung*). For though friendship does not produce happiness, the two feelings composing it envelop a dignity; they render mankind *worthy* of being happy. First difficulty: if it is a duty to thus tend towards a *maximum* of good intentions, if 'perfect friendship' is a 'simple idea', how will 'equality' in the 'relation to one's neighbour' be ensured in the process? For example, the equality in each of the constituent parts of a like duty (thus 'reciprocal benevolence'). For reciprocity is not equality, and the criteria which would *ensure* that sentiments are equally reciprocal, equally intense or ardent in reciprocity are lacking. The intensity or force, the 'ardour', of love (which is united with respect in friendship) can break the equality while maintaining the reciprocity. Even more seriously, Kant asks, cannot this ardour of love, this 'excessive ardour in love', this very excess, provoke the loss 'of the respect of the other'? For we come now to the major difficulty in the very idea of friendship, inherent in the *contradictory* character and hence the unstable balance of these two feelings which are opposed *qua* fusional 'attraction' (*love*) and 'repulsion' which keeps at a distance (*respect*).

We should register here a first limit, in our view an extremely significant one. In order to describe or present this contradiction (which formally recalls the contradiction in the Aristotelian concept of friendship as we set it out above), Kant affords himself no other resource than the natural law put at his disposal by the science or metaphysics of nature: the law of universal attraction (and repulsion). It will be said that this is a manner of speaking, a rhetoric of presentation. Perhaps, but for Kant *there is no other*, and he devotes no critical attention to it. Even when, from this situation described in natural terms, he claims to be able to draw up a rule or maxim. He writes:

> For love can be regarded as attraction and respect as repulsion, and if the principle of love bids friends to draw closer, the principle of respect requires them to stay at a proper distance from each other. This limitation on intimacy, which is expressed in the rule that even the best of friends should not *make themselves too familiar with each other*, contains a maxim that holds not only for the superior in relation to the inferior but also in reverse. (p. 261; emphasis added)

The maxim of this rule concerns, as is often the case in this analysis, the necessity of *testimony*, of the testimony of respect that cannot, for all that, be reduced to the 'outward manifestations' of respect. When the superior finds his pride wounded, he may consent to not receiving testimony of the respect due him, but then this consent must last only a *moment*. The maxim commands that it last only a moment, failing which the unmarked respect is irremediably lost, even though it may be mimicked in the 'outward manifestations' of a ceremonial. Hence an (exterior) testimony of respect is needed which must be the exterior of an interior, an *expression* and not a simple exteriority. And it must be capable of steadfastly resisting the ordeal of time, it must be steady and reliable, or – let us say it once more in Greek – 'bébaios'.

Yet with this imperative of a distance (albeit 'proper', as he says) Kant introduces into the continuum of a tradition, which is none the less confirmed by him, a principle of *rupture* or *interruption* that can no longer be easily reconciled with the values of proximity, presence, gathering together, and communal familiarity which dominate the traditional culture of friendship. Or at least, Kant grants the necessity of this distance, even if it never totally escaped the attention of his predecessors, a more rigorous philosophical status, and the dignity of a law with its rule and maxim. And what Kant here calls perfect friendship *qua* 'moral' friendship (which he distinguishes from aesthetic friendship) is no longer in any sense of the term what Aristotle called 'ethical' friendship (itself distinguished from 'nomic' or legal friendship[36]). If this respectful distance from the other was not countered by love and attraction, it ought to become infinite. Furthermore, a double objection to this distance can be levelled at Kant: (1) in the name of what *moral right* is the infinity of this respect owed the other to be limited? (2) Why and how should a law presented as natural (the 'force of attraction' coming to be opposed to the 'force of repulsion') intervene here to limit the respectful distance? And why would this distance be presented *as* repulsion? The double objection would concern not only the concept of friendship but that of love as well. Why would love be only the ardent force of an attraction tending towards fusion, union, and identification? Why would the infinite distance which opens respect up, and which Kant wished to limit by love, not open love up as well? And even more so, perhaps, in the love experience or in lovence in general, as if it were necessary to say the converse: the infinite distance in love, a certain kind of coming together in friendship? And why would the moral principle be on the side of friendship, not on that of love? Would this bear no relation to the masculine model of friendship, of the virility of virtue, which, as we shall prove, is for Kant, too, the ultimate authorizing agency?

This, then, is our hypothesis, and we are going to attempt to support it. It requires that we pay attention to what Kant calls 'the friend of man'.

Let us not forget that we are speaking here of virtue, of purely moral friendship, not of 'aesthetic' friendship, which does not suppose the respect of the other. Kant is neither very gentle nor very tender with friendship. He doesn't think friendship should be tender. The friendship of Kant is not gentle, and if it were to become so, Kant would put us on our guard against it. He is quick to recall the suffering and the sacrifice, as well as the cost, involved in such friendship. Kant needs this negativity, even if 'it is a heavy burden to feel chained to another's fate and encumbered with his needs'. Friendship must therefore not be a social security, a mutual benefit insurance, and the assistance on which the other must be able to count could never be the end, the 'determining ground', of friendship. Help and assistance are nevertheless necessary, but once again, under the heading of 'outward manifestations' of heartfelt benevolence. For this inner benevolence is never directly accessible, originarily and 'in person', as a phenomenologist would say, but only in 'appresentation' with the help of an outward sign: with the help of testimony. In other words, one must help the friend – not to help him, not because he needs assistance, or because that would be the principle or the end of friendship, but in order to give him the signs of friendship.

Why, in sum, is Kant so suspicious of tenderness and gentleness, of *teneritas amicitiae*? This paradoxical movement must be correctly understood, for it sheds indirect light on the Kantian concept of love and, above all, introduces a *catastrophic* complication into the *natural* law of attraction/repulsion which none the less organizes this friendly 'doctrine of virtue'. Let us first of all say it succinctly: an excess of tenderness tends towards reciprocal possession and fusion (excessive attraction) and – following this, or as a consequence! – this measureless gentleness inevitably leads to interruption – indeed, to rupture. This, then, is a case (the tenderness of reciprocal possession) where *attraction leads to rupture*, where attraction becomes the quasi-synonym of repulsion. Too much love separates, interrupts, threatens the social bond. Following this logic, the most paradoxical consequences are unleashed or, on the contrary, never fail to become rigorously bound, to the point of strangulation, in a *double bind*: the natural law of attraction/repulsion is perverted into a principle of absolute disorder. Here we have, in fact, a situation in which the principle of repulsion would have to be compensated not by attraction, which would lead to a worse repulsion, an interruption or a rupture, but by repulsion itself (repulsion against repulsion: painful respect). This, too, is a situation in which the principle of attraction would have to be compensated not by repulsion, which would lead to rupture, but by attraction itself (attraction against attraction: a slightly but not too tender friendship). The enemy – the enemy of morality, in any case – is love. Not because love is the enemy, but because, in the excessive attraction unleashed by love, enmity and war are allowed to take place. Love harbours hate within itself. Reciprocal possession and fusion towards which the tender one risks tending is nothing else but a principle of (non-natural) perversion at the heart of the natural law of attraction and repulsion. It could be compared to a death instinct or a demonic principle. It would end up haunting virtue. If this is indeed the case, friendship would then be at one and the same time the sign, the symptom, the representative of this possible perversion, yet also what protects us from such perversion. The evil and the remedy for the evil.

Under these conditions, how could the concept of moral perfection not be contradictory? This, in any case, is the reading of these lines we are proposing: although they are couched in a rather conventional mode of moderating wisdom, as in the midst of *cultivated* people in a select club, they nevertheless carry a terrible message, a message of terror, news of death: love is the evil, love can be evil's vehicle and evil can always come out of love, the radical evil of the greatest love. Abandon is the evil: abandon unto oneself or unto the other. And this begins very simply on the threshold, with 'feeling' — with the appearance of feeling or *affect* in general. Against *abandon*, a sole response: 'rules', and 'strict' rules at that:

> Although it is sweet to feel in such possession of each other as approaches fusion into one person, friendship is something so delicate (*teneritas amicitiae*) that it is never for a moment safe from interruptions if it is allowed to rest on feelings, and if this mutual sympathy and self-surrender are not subjected to principles or rules preventing excessive familiarity and limiting mutual love by requirements of respect. Such *interruptions* are common among uncultivated people, although they do not always result in a *split* (for the rabble fight and make up). Such people cannot part with each other, and yet they cannot be at one with each other since they need quarrels in order to savour the sweetness of being united in reconciliation. But in any case the love in friendship cannot be an *affect*; for emotion is blind in its choice, and after a while it goes up in smoke. (p. 262; original emphasis)

The black painting of a black-tinged passion. If one now compares this bedevilment of love (it's simply a question of turning the page) to the appearance of a certain *black swan*, then another landscape of Kantism offers up an unconscious to be read. And it is certainly not the unconscious of only that philosopher named Immanuel Kant.

What is the secret of this black swan? Secrecy [*Le secret*].

A reflection on the Kantian ethics and politics of friendship should in fact organize itself around the concept of secrecy. The concept seems to (secretly) dominate this *Conclusion of the Elements of Ethics*, and to mark problematically the ideal of friendship *qua* communication (*Mitteilung*) or egalitarian sharing. In contradistinction to aesthetic friendship,[37] moral friendship demands absolute confidence, a confidence such that 'two people' must share not only their impressions, but even their secret judgements. The political stakes are obvious: Kant concludes that true friends ought to be able to say anything to each other on questions of government, religion, etc. This is quite dangerous, and *rare* indeed are *reliable* friends, those, then, who are able to renounce all public profit, all political or institutional consequence, to the possession or circulation of this secret. They are few and far between, and this cautions prudence. The existence and necessity of secrecy are hence correlative to the *scarcity* of which we have spoken at such length. It is owing to secrecy that it should be said: he who has many friends has none. What is rare, in fact, is not only men worthy of friendship, worthy of the secret we wish to entrust them with, but friends in couples. It should come as no surprise here if, once again, precisely on the subject of secrecy, we come across the topos of Cicero and Montaigne: a great friendship comes along once every three or four centuries (yet another implied difference with love, no?). But no friendship without the possibility of absolute secrecy. A friend worthy of such secrecy is as improbable, and perhaps as impossible to find, as a *black swan*.

A black swan: the poetic figure of this 'rare bird' is taken from a satire by Juvenal.

> Every man has his secrets and dare not confide blindly in others, partly because of a base cast of mind in most men to use them to one's disadvantage and partly because many people are indiscreet or incapable of judging and distinguishing what may or may not be repeated. The necessary combinations of qualities is seldom found in one person (*rara avis in terris, nigroque simillima cygno**), especially since the closest friendship requires that a judicious and trusted friend be also bound not to share the secrets entrusted to him with anyone else, no matter how reliable he thinks him, without explicit permission to do so.
>
> This (merely moral friendship) is not just an ideal but (like black swans) actually exists here and there in its perfection.

The black swan is found in Book VI, not Book II. And Kant (but did he ever read Juvenal?) should know that Juvenal was speaking not of a friend but of a woman 'more chaste than the Sabines who, with their scattered hair, threw themselves between the combatants'. 'She has everything going for her: who could take her on as spouse? (*quis feret uxorem cui constant omnia?*)'.

Let us not dwell longer than is necessary on the experiences of the betrayed secret of which Kant murmurs a confession here. Let us consider

---

* Juvenal, Sat. II, 6, 165 ('a bird that is rare on earth, exactly like a black swan').

only the following *three* surprising subjects that do not surprise Kant to any great extent. *Three oddities* will in fact have been noticed in passing:

1. No one knows exactly what a secret is, and Kant doesn't know either: only an infinite intelligence (one excluded here from the ranks of mankind) could give lessons to those whose 'lack of intelligence' prevents them from appreciating what must remain secret. For there are no secrets in nature – no one has ever encountered one there: the secret is that which one *thinks* [*croit savoir*] *must* remain secret because an *engagement* has been entered upon and a *promise* made in certain non-natural conditions. Now to the extent that, as Kant remarks, this also depends on 'intelligence', no one knows absolutely in all certainty where discretion begins and ends – no one, no finite subject, by definition, ever has the required theoretical intelligence to know for sure. Kant, therefore, is speaking of a secret which he must know no one ever knows enough about, of which, therefore, one never knows anything of absolute value. The secret is not, fundamentally, an object of knowledge. It is as if Kant did not know what he is talking about.

2. If there is a problem with secrecy, on the other hand, it is in so far as there are two friends *plus one* ('another friend, believed equally reliable', notes Kant), and to the extent that this discourse on secrecy supposes the couple's rupture. It supposes in any case that the third party, *qua* friend, as reliable and as equal as the other two, is already around. More than one, then, and consequently, yet another 'more than one' (for the third party can also have a reliable friend, to whom he or she could say 'swear that you will not repeat what I swore not to repeat', etc.). Hence N + 1 – this is the beginning of friendship, where a secret is both possible and impossible. Always the same arithmetic, always the same calculation: impossible and necessary.

3. Despite or because of this third party, the originary irruption of this *more than one*, and despite the disorder this third party creates from the outset, this other friend as the condition of a different friend, the black swan is the *only occurrence* (random and improbable, but not excluded) of an *event of friendship* which bestows an effective chance, *in history*, to the idea of moral friendship. When Kant writes: 'This (merely moral friendship) is not just an ideal but (like black swans) actually exists here and there in its perfection', he wants to say, I suppose, that this purely moral friendship is not *only* an ideal (what it first of all is) but can also, sometimes, in history (*perhaps!*), take form in the black swan.

This black swan is a brother. For Kant, it is a brother.

Why? We have just spoken of purely moral friendship. It can, then, happen that this friendship 'actually exists' 'here and there' and 'from time to time': 'the black swan!'. And it is the bond between two men, with the minor but inevitable complication of the third man, and the supplementary friend of whom we have just caught a glimpse. But there is also what Kant calls *pragmatic* friendship: this one, out of love, burdens itself with the ends of other men, this time of an indeterminate number. 'Pragmatic' friendship could never achieve the purity or perfection desired, that is, 'requisite for a precisely determinant maxim'. It remains, therefore, the 'ideal of a wish'. In the concept of reason it is infinite, in experience it is finite. In both cases, there is the rare but real uprising of the 'black swan', a limited but effective experience of pragmatic friendship, the taking place of the phenomenon of friendship. In history, in space and in time: yes, friendship does happen. Hence sensibility is a part of the game. And this cannot happen except against a backdrop of what unites mankind, this effective and sensible sharing out [*partage*] whose *aesthetic* dimension is thus required. What happens must be able to happen. And the condition of possibility must be universal. All this supposes, then, a general or generic possibility, the possibility of what Kant calls here the *friend of man*.

The *friend of man* loves the whole human race. Whatever happens, he shares in what happens to other men, through sensibility – '*aesthetically*', says Kant. He rejoices with them when something good happens (the 'black swan', pragmatic and humanitarian solidarity, however insufficient it may be), and will never disturb this joy without profound regret. This very regret is the sign that he is the friend of the whole human race. But if the 'friend of man' concept entails sensibility and aesthetic community, it also corresponds to an infinite rational rigour – that is, an Idea. This is what distinguishes the friend of man from the 'philanthropist' who is content with merely loving mankind, without being guided by this Idea.

Now what is this Idea? Having stressed that 'the expression "*a friend* of man" is somewhat narrower in its meaning than "one who merely loves man (*als der des Philanthropen, die Menschen bloß liebenden Menschen*)', Kant establishes this Idea: it is not only an intellectual representation, a representation of *equality* among men, but *consideration* for this representation of equality, a '*just consideration*' for such a representation. Equality *is necessary*. There is no equality, but there must be. For it is *obligation* that the soundness or justice of this *consideration* adds to the representation: 'the Idea that in putting others under obligation by his beneficence he is himself under obligation'. Consequently, equality is not only a representation, an intellectual concept, a calculable measure, a statistical objectivity; it bears within itself a feeling of obligation, hence the sensibility of duty, debt, gratitude. This is inscribed in sensibility, but only in sensibility's relation to the purely rational Idea of equality. This is the condition for the existence of something called 'the friend of man', 'the friend of the whole race'. It goes without saying that cosmopolitanism, universal democracy, perpetual peace, would not have the slightest chance of being announced and promised, if not realized, without the presupposition of such a friend.

And it is a brother. The black swan is a brother, for he can appear, however infrequently, from time to time, only providing he is already the friend of man. He must belong to this race to which the friend of man belongs, who is the friend of the whole race. He must be the brother of these brothers. For just when Kant has defined in this way, in the 'strictest' sense of the term, the friend of man, he tells us how the phenomenon of this idea of obliging equality is to be *represented*: as a father and brothers. Submissive and equal brothers. The men are brothers, and the father is not a man: 'all men are represented here as if they were brothers under one father who wills the happiness of all'.

This structure corresponds − with the curtness of a philosophical rigour that would have to be reconstituted in Michelet, Quinet, or others − to the secularization, in the style of the Enlightenment, of Christian friendship the promise of which the friends of the French Revolution (and Kant must be counted a member) said that it was the implementation, achieved in history − projected as such, in any case. This friendship is quite fraternal. It binds brothers together between themselves but not with the father, who wills the happiness of all and to whom the sons submit. There is no friendship for the father, one is not the friend of the one who makes friendship possible. One can be grateful to him, since one is obliged to him. There is even reciprocal love with the father, but this reciprocal love (non-equal) is not friendship. In friendship a respect that is not only reciprocal but thoroughly equal is required. This is impossible with the father; it is possible only with brothers, with what is represented as brothers. Friendship for the one who makes friendship possible would be a temptation of pride. And the father, who is not a brother, is not a man. Kant continues, and concludes:

> *All men are here represented as brothers under one universal father who wills the happiness of all.* For the relation of a protector, as a benefactor, to the one he protects, who owes him gratitude, is indeed a *relation of mutual love, but not of friendship, since the respect owed by each is not equal.* The duty of being benevolent as a friend of man (a necessary humbling of oneself) and the just consideration of this duty serve to guard against the pride that usually comes over those fortunate enough to have the means for beneficence.[38]

Let us recall that this discourse concludes the *Elements of Ethics* and belongs to a *Doctrine of Virtue*. The determination of friendship *qua fraternity* therefore tells us something essential about ethics. It also tells us something irreducible about the essence of virtue. It tells us its universal political horizon, the cosmopolitical idea of all virtue worthy of the name. This would be reason enough to place fundamental value on this 'doctrine'. But this text, this *presentation* of the doctrine, is of import to us also because it locates, with remarkable topical precision, the place of the brother, the brother *qua* place. Especially *qua* topical place. Indeed, Kant says: 'All men are here represented as brothers under one universal father'.

It could be said that this is merely a representation, a presentation, a manner of speaking, an image or a schema of the imagination *in view of* the idea of equality and *in view of* responding to the obligation attached to it, responding to it and answering for it responsibly. To be sure. Or it will be said: no more than those who, throughout history, have linked friendship to fraternity (everyone, let us agree, all those who have spoken of friendship, the brothers, the fathers and the sons who are brothers – all those, at least, whose speech we remember because it managed to make itself heard) – no more than them, therefore, does Kant confuse this fraternity with the fraternity called 'natural', strict, literal, sensible, genetic, etc. To be sure. But, on the one hand, the schema of this presentation has become indispensable. One cannot and must not dispense with it. One should no longer be able to. On the other hand, *qua* sensible or imaginal schema, in its very necessity, it remains linked to sensible or imaginal fraternity, to the *virility* of the *congeneric*. And this adherence has become indivisible, it is *posited* as such, it sees itself as necessary, it does not wish to be conventional, or arbitrary, or imaginary. Failing which, Kant could have proposed another figure to speak of human community or of the universal equality of finite beings. He could have diversified the examples to name the link of kinship. Why did he not say, for example, the cousin, the uncle, the brother-in-law, the mother-in-law, the aunt or the mother? Let us see fair play here: why did he not speak of the sister?

The *anthropological* schema of the family is doing all the work here. It is the desire for *one* family. Not even for the family in general, that thing too obscure for us to claim to be able to speak abstractly about, but for one family which can speak to us of the family, invent it and afford itself the favour of a representation. A family renders this service, it renders itself indispensable and renders indispensable the rendered service. At the centre of *this* familial schema, at the centre of what can again be called *oikeiótēs*, the brother occupies the unique place, the place of the irreplaceable. In this place of the irreplaceable, a 'pure practical reason' is welded indivisibly to an anthropology, and even, as we shall soon see, to a *pragmatic anthropology*.

We must know that the place of the irreplaceable is quite a singular place indeed. If it is irreplaceable, as the place, as the *khóra*, it is so as to receive substitutable inscriptions. It is the place of possible substitution. It can never be confused with that which occupies it, with all the figures which come to be inscribed therein and pass themselves off as the copies of a paradigm, the examples of an irreplaceable exemplar.

Is it not from the place of this very place that we gaze over the *horizon*, awaiting the black swan that does not come every day of the week? A place can never be situated anywhere but under a *horizon*, from out of this limit which opens up and closes off at one and the same time. Is it not from off this bank and under this horizon that a political phallogocentrism has, *up to this point*, determined *its* cosmopolitical democracy, *a* democracy, *qua* cosmo-phratrocentrism?

Up to this point, at least *up until now*, through countless tremors. Some of them, in the past, have been so violent that, at least *up to this point*, they have not even been interpreted. Their traces have still to be gathered up, registered, archived by those in charge of the management of their memory, the archons of the same family. These tremors have only just begun, for the history we have been speaking of is only several thousand years old: the time of a twinkling of an eye.

But what are we doing when we say 'up to this point'?

To what 'perhaps' can this pledge be given?

(*France, enfranchisement, fraternity*. We have just been speaking of pledges. They are here inscribed in a plural heritage: more than one culture, more than one philosophy, more than one religion, more than one language, more than one literature. And more than one nation. Among all these given pledges, an *ineffaceable* lock maintains this book close to France.

I would not attempt to deny it.

Perhaps [*Peut-être*] is itself, as we observed at the appropriate time, a French word. No translation could do it justice. This book is not written only in French, for this would be to claim for French the exemplary privilege of translation of all other idioms, and that of remaining the only point of passage for all conversations, as if a French interpreter were claiming the exorbitant role of third-party universal translator while insisting on the rights of a sublime monolingualism. No, there is still more. It must indeed be said of this book, in the chapter now coming to a close and in the next one, that it sets itself up to *work and be worked relentlessly* [*s'acharne lui-même*]. I understand this French term '*acharner*' in the hunter's sense of the term, where it comes down to setting up *a decoy of flesh*. This book set itself up to *work and be worked relentlessly*, close to the thing called France. And close to the singular alliance linking nothing less than the history of fraternization to this thing, France – to the State, the nation, the politics, the culture, literature and language which answer for the name 'France' and, when they are called by this name, answer to it. From before the time of the French Revolution (Montaigne was only an example), then during the Revolution and in its aftermath (Michelet and Quinet were only examples in their turn, and we have and will hear other voices, sometimes breaking with tradition within the tradition – those, for example, of Bataille, Blanchot, Lévinas, Nancy or Deguy). But of course at the perceptible hinge between these two chapters, and in order to let the literary or poetic legend, the *moment of language*, ring out again from one century into the next, we must listen to the colossal figure of Victor Hugo. He must be watched giving in to the vertigo of French exemplarity, to what is most fraternally universal and revolutionary in it. Indeed, the most perceptive and most blind declarations of this visionary of Europe, of Humanity, of Technics, in the twentieth century were dedicated to the brother. But above all Hugo wrote eloquent, generous but, alas, also symptomatic pages on the subject of what every brother owes to France. To 'sublimated France', to be sure, as he put it so well. But *fraternity* is universal only in first being *French*. Hugo declaims this French universality with the generous frankness that Francis Ponge associated with the 'Frenchness' in which Hugo had already praised the values of 'enfranchisement'. Essentially and as example, to be a brother is to be French. Above all, and *naturally*, if you are the eldest brother. For everything we are saying about fraternity must be said about the 'natural law' concept which will always fundamentally have been, like 'generosity' itself, inseparable from it. The brother concept is indispensable to anyone – Victor Hugo, for example – who would set out to think *Humanity* as a *Nation*. From the very moment of its 'embryo-genesis'.

Let us listen (I must 'select' or 'underscore'; I regretfully excise the spirit from these sentences that I encourage you to read in full and in one sitting, again and again, for their own sake). It begins as follows, with France (and it is a text which begins, like Ponge's poem, with 'It seems that France begins'):

In the twentieth century, there will be an *extraordinary nation*. It will be a great nation, but its grandeur will not limit its freedom. It will be famous, wealthy, thinking, poetic, cordial to the rest of humanity. *It will have the sweet gravity of an older sibling. . . . The legislation of this nation will be a facsimile of natural law, as similar to it as possible.* Under the influence of this motive nation, the incommensurable fallow lands of America, Asia, Africa and Australia will give themselves up to civilizing emigration . . . The *central nation* whence this movement will radiate over all continents will be to other societies what the model farm is among tenant farms. It will be more than a nation, it will be a civilization; better than a civilization, it will be a *family.* Unity of language, currency, measure, meridian, code; fiduciary circulation to the utmost degree, money bills making anyone with twenty francs in his purse a person of independent means; an *incalculable surplus-value resulting from the abolition of parasitical mechanisms* . . . The illiterate person will be as rare as the person blind from birth; the *jus contra legem* [will be] understood. . . . The capital of this nation will be Paris, and will not be named France; it will be called Europe. Europe in the twentieth century, and in those following, even more transfigured, will be called Humanity. *Humanity, definitive nation. . . .* What a majestic vision! There is in the *embryo-genesis* of peoples, as in that of beings, a sublime hour of transparency. . . . Europe, one with itself, is germinating there. *A people, which will be France sublimated, is in the process of hatching. The profound ovary* of progress, once fertilized, carries the future, in this presently distinct form. This nation to come is palpitating in present-day Europe, like the winged being in the reptile larva. In the next century, it will spread both its wings: one the wing of freedom, the other of will.

The fraternal continent is the future. May everyone enrol now, for this immense happiness is inevitable. Before having its people, Europe has its city. The *capital* of this people that does not yet exist exists already. This seems a prodigy; it is a law. The foetus of nations behaves like a human foetus, and the mysterious construction of the embryo, at once vegetation and life, always begins *with the head.*[39]

Let no one accuse me of unjustly incriminating the figure of fraternity – already so greatly, generously, brilliantly infused by Hugo himself with genetic rhetoric and sublimated organicism – with the supplementary accusation of phallocentrism or androcentrism. The brother is neither the universal class hospitable to women or sisters, nor a spiritual figure replaceable in its clear-cut *determination* – one would even say in its sexual resolution. The *virility of the brother* is an ineffaceable letter *in* Victor Hugo's text. Here is the proof:

What has befallen Paris? Revolution.

Paris is the pivotal city around which, on a given day, history has turned. . . .

The Commune is rightful; the Convention is right. This is superb. On one side the Populace, but sublimated; on the other, the People, but transfigured.

And these two animosities have a love, the human race, and these two collisions result in Fraternity. This is the magnificence of our revolution.

It is certain that the French Revolution is a beginning. *Nescio quid majus nascitur Iliade.*

Take note of this word: *Birth.* It corresponds to the word Deliverance. To say the mother has delivered is to say the child is born. To say France is free is to say the human soul has reached adulthood.

True birth is virility.

On the fourteenth of July 1789, the hour of the *virile* age struck.

Who accomplished the fourteenth of July?

Paris.

. . .

The word *Fraternity* was not thrown in vain into the depths, first from the heights of Calvary, then from those of 1789. What the Revolution wants, God wants.

. . . Jerusalem releases the True. It is where the supreme martyrdom pronounced the supreme words:

Freedom, Equality, Fraternity. Athens releases the Beautiful. Rome for the Great. . . . Paris, the place of revolutionary revelation, is the human Jerusalem.[40]

Like Marx, Hugo wishes at one and the same time to swear and to abjure; he is seen at once welcoming and chasing, convoking and conjuring the spectre away. In his *Peace Declaration* (signed at Hauteville House in May 1867, during the International Exhibition), the man who had just written: 'Great poetry is the solar spectre of human reason'[41] is appealing here to fraternization to put an end, once and for all, 'to ghosts', 'to phantoms', to the 'spectre', to death itself. And against Christ, the spectre of spectres: like Marx he borrows one of Christ's sayings to say, in sum, 'let the dead bury the dead'. The speech of a brother. Hugo had begun by recalling that this Paris of fraternity was also the Paris of 'literary revolution' ('Paris after 89, after the political revolution, accomplished 1830, the literary revolution' . . . 'this Louvre out of which would emerge equality, this *Champ-de-Mars* out of which would emerge *fraternity*. Elsewhere armies are forged; Paris is a forge of ideas'); he had also described with extraordinary lucidity the future of 'telegraphy', the technology 'which sends your own writing in a few minutes to a place two thousand leagues away', 'the trans-atlantic cable', the 'propeller in the ocean while we await the propeller in the atmosphere'; he had also praised Voltaire, 'the representative, not of French genius, but of universal spirit'; and here come the brothers to put an end to the phantom (in Greek one would say: to put an end to the *phantasm*):

Unity is forming; hence union. *Man One is Man Brother*, Man Equal, Man Free. . . . The immense winds of the future stir with peace. What can be done in the face of this *storm of fraternity* and joy? Alliance, alliance! cries out the infinite. . . . Why do you want to make us believe in *ghosts*? Do you imagine we do not know that war is dead? It died the day Jesus said: *Love one another!* and the only life left in war was henceforth that of a spectre. Yet following Jesus' departure, the night lasted for almost another two thousand years – the night air is amenable to phantoms – and war was able to continue prowling in this darkness. But the eighteenth century arrived, with Voltaire the morning star, and the Revolution its dawn, and now it is the full light of day. . . . Are you the ones attacking, Germans? Is it us? Who is to be incriminated? Germans, *All men* [in English in the text], you are All-the-Men. We love you. We are your fellow citizens in the city of Philosophy, and you are our countrymen in the land of Freedom. . . . *France means enfranchisement. Germany means Fraternity.* Can you imagine the first word of the democratic formula waging war on the last? . . . Let the spectre be gone! . . . From out of those very bodies lying cold and bloody on the battlefield springs forth, in the form of remorse for kings, reproach for peoples, the *principle of fraternity*. . . . What are all these peoples . . . doing in Paris? They are here to be France. . . . They know there exists a people of reconciliation, a house of democracy, an open nation, welcoming *anyone who is brotherly or wishes to be so*. . . . What a magnificent phenomenon, a cordial and marvellous one, this extinguishing of a people *evaporating into fraternity*. O France, adieu! You are too great to be only a country. One separates from one's mother, who becomes a goddess . . . and you, France, become the world.[42])

Notes

1. [Trans. C. Cocks, London: Longman, Brown, Green & Longmans, 1846], pp. 45–52; emphasis added.

2. Trans. John P. McKay, Urbana, Chicago, London: University of Illinois Press 1973, p. 191; emphasis added.

3. Michelet, *Le Peuple*, introduction and notes P. Viallaneix, Paris: Flammarion 1984, p. 57. Emphasis added. As a footnote points out: 'the friendship between the two men . . . never lapsed'. Initiated by Victor Cousin into the philosophy of history, one translating Vico and the other Herder, simultaneously, together at the Collège de France in 1842, united in the struggle against the priest-party, they mutually dedicate the two works I have just cited. And do not hesitate, if one is to judge by the choice of words, to talk to one another like a Montaigne and a La Boétie, who would have grown old together at the Collège de France.

4. 1856, Book V, Chapter 6, 'Does unity obtain?', Vienna: Manz, p. 305.

5. Here I allow a reference to 'Before the law' [trans. Avital Ronell, enlarged trans. Christine Roulston, in Derek Attridge (ed.) *Acts of Literature*, London: Routledge 1992 (1985)].

6. See 'Violence and Metaphysics', in *Writing and Difference* [trans. Alan Bass, London and Chicago: University of Chicago Press/Routledge & Kegan Paul 1978].

7. ['*tout autre est tout autre*': I have followed here David Wills's translation, in Derrida, *The Gift of Death*, University of Chicago Press 1995, ch. 4, pp. 82–8. – Trans.]

8. *Nicomachean Ethics*, VIII, 9, 1159a 25–30.

9. See '*all' outē alethēs outē pseudes*'. On certain stakes of this proposition which are crucial today, see 'How to Avoid Speaking: Denials' [trans. Ken Frieden, in Sandford Budick and Wolfgang Iser, eds., *Languages of the Unsayable: The Play of Negativity in Literature and Literary Theory*, New York: Columbia University Press 1989], pp. 3–70.

10. Quoted by François Furet and Mona Ozouf in the fine article devoted to this theme in their *Dictionnaire critique de la Révolution française*, pp. 199ff. We learn, among so many other things in this work, that Leroux 'prefers to place fraternity in the middle of the motto, as the affective term linking freedom and equality' (p. 212). For Louis Blanc and Buchez, on the other hand, fraternity should appear first, at the origin or principle, as its divine origin dictates.

The Christian roots of the motif explain at once the attraction and the repulsion of a 'fraternity', its to-and-fro movements throughout revolutionary and post-revolutionary history:

> For where else can we find a better justification for the 'consanguinity established by nature among the inhabitants of the earth'; where else, then, a justification of fraternity, than in the Christian religion? . . . This consciousness of a link between the Christian message and the Revolution was to find its full use in federative ceremonies, in dramaturgies of the abolition of differences: the priests celebrating them recall that, to create a perfect society, all particular interests must be snuffed out, as in the example of this invention of Christ, 'gentle fraternity'. . . . The Gospel itself intended – Fauchet's federative oath stresses the point – 'to spread over all the earth the sacred fire of universal fraternity' . . . the link between Christianity and Revolution . . . explains the appearance, at the sides of freedom and equality, of fraternity, to achieve what was felt as another Trinity. (pp. 202–3)

Analysing the phenomena of fraternization, recalling the 'obsession of the [fraternal] oath', the habit of greeting, from 1791, as 'brothers and friends', of signing 'salvation and fraternity', the same article rightly stresses the 'infinite enlargement' (p. 204) of fraternization, this potential of infinitization which is so important to us here and in which, above, we could identify a Christian logic only after acknowledging *also*, in the same move, with all its subsequent consequences, the deployment of a Greek memory. When have these two memories been more efficiently coupled, and come face to face, than in the ideal instant of what is called the French Revolution?

11. *Le Peuple*, pp. 178, 181, 190, 190, 191.

12. Preface to the 1866 edition, p. 247.

13. Ibid., p. 210.

14. Ibid., p. 305. Emphasis added. The following 'scene' should be read, really read: in a bed, between spouses who love each other. Nothing is missing: they are talking about a political 'secret', an 'enemy of public welfare', a wanted criminal, an enemy of law and justice. The husband hesitates to 'betray law, justice', to give 'a victory to injustice'. The wife: 'But you are saving your enemy. . . . Be great. . . . And be good to me. Make this beautiful sacrifice for me. It will make me feel young again.'

Yes. What was stated above is now confirmed: 'Woman is always higher or lower than justice. Love, holiness, chivalry, magnanimity, honour; all of that she feels marvellously, but law she feels more slowly' (p. 304).

15. Günther Neske, Pfullingen 1956. *What is Philosophy* was a lecture given in Cérisy-la-Salle, Normandy, in August 1955. [Trans. Jean T. Wilde and William Kluback, Albany, New York, NCUP.]

16. 'The *phileîn to sophón*, that already mentioned harmony with *sophón*, *harmonía*, thus became *órexis* [yearning], a *striving* for *sophón*. *Sophón* – the being in Being – is now especially sought. Because the loving is no longer an original harmony with *sophón* but is a particular striving towards *sophón*, the loving of *sophón* becomes "*philosophía*". The striving is determined by Eros' [English trans. p. 51].

17. We have broached this task in a still preliminary way in 'Heidegger's Ear, Philopolemology, *Geschlecht IV'* [trans. John P. Leavey, Jr, in J. Sallis (ed.) *Reading Heidegger*, Indiana University Press 1991].

18. *Being and Time*, para 34 [trans. John Macquarrie and Edward Robinson, New York: Harper 1962], p. 163.

19. '*Geschlecht*: Sexual Difference, Ontological Difference.' *Research in Phenomenology*, XIII, 1983, 64–85. Also 'Heidegger's Hand (*Geschlecht II*)' [trans. John P. Leavey Jr in *Deconstruction and Philosophy: The Texts of Jacques Derrida*, Chicago University Press 1987].

20. See also Heidegger's text under the same title in *Erläuterungen zu Hölderlins Dichtung*, Klostermann, Frankfurt-am-Main 1951. Jean Launay translated it into French under the title 'Souvenir', in *Approche de Hölderlin*, Paris: Gallimard 1973. Having noted that 'the unison of the same thoughts and hence coappurtenance are revealed as the substance and constancy of friendship', Heidegger quotes the verse 'But where are the friends? Bellarmin/with his comrades?'. Heidegger dwells at length on the unicity of this 'true question' (there is no other in the poem) which might well be addressed *to* friends – the only ones who speak, who speak to each other and are in agreement – rather than posed *on the subject of* friends (p. 163). One would have to follow up more thoroughly than is possible here the Heideggerian meditation on the singular One, the 'More than one' ('More than one/Is reluctant to go to the source') and the 'Now it is that I am alone', from the standpoint of which the poetic meaning of the question 'But where are the friends?' is announced: 'We know them not. The other has already arrived home. He has begun now, *at home*, what can properly be called the way to the source' (pp. 175–6).

21. I shall take up this question in a forthcoming essay (*Geschlecht III*), and refer the reader to the remarkable works of David Farrell Krell, especially *Intimations of Mortality*, Pennsylvania State University Press, University Park and London 1986, pp. 163ff; and to 'Passage à la soeur, Heidegger et Geschlecht', in *Le Passage des frontières*, Galilée 1994, p. 459.

22. See the 1943–44 course on Heraclitus, *Gesamtausgabe*, ed. Manfred S. Frings, 1979, Bnd 55, pp. 127ff.

23. *Gönnen, Gewähren*. '*In der phúsis waltet die Gunst*', p. 132. We have stressed these heavily charged words '*walten*' (reign, dominate, prevail) and '*Gewalt*' (force, violence, power, etc.) in 'Heidegger's Ear' and in 'Force of Law'.

24. '*Wir verstehen das* phileîn *als die Gunst und das Gönnen*' (p. 136).

25. 'In the Greek world, there is no psychology. Aristotle's treatise *Perí Psukhés* has

nothing to do with a "psychology". In the accomplishment of metaphysics, metaphysics becomes "psychology" – that is, psychology and anthropology are the last word of metaphysics: psychology and technics go hand in hand.' Ibid., p. 130.

26. Schmitt, CP, p. 26.

27. Ibid., pp. 27–8.

28. Ibid., pp. 35–6; emphasis added.

29. Ibid., pp. 49–50.

30. Preface to CP, p. 17 of the German edition. This preface recalls the retrospective proposed in Nomos der Erde, 1950.

31. Ibid., p. 18 of the German edition.

32. 'Überwindung der Metaphysik', in Vorträge und Aufsätze, Neske 1954, pp. 88–9. The quoted section, later published in the Darmstadt Cahier Barlach, is from fragment XXVI of notebooks from 1936 to 1946. [The English translation, 'Overcoming Metaphysics', is by Joan Stambaugh in Heidegger, The End of Philosophy, London: Souvenir Press 1975, pp. 103–4.]

33. We hope we have demonstrated this in 'Heidegger's Ear'.

34. 'On Friendship', p. 212 [translation slightly modified].

35. It constitutes precisely the Conclusion of the Elements of Ethics in the Doctrine of Virtue, Metaphysics of Morals, second part, paras 46–7, [trans. Mary Gregor, Cambridge University Press 1991].

36. See above, Chapter 8 , pp. 204–5.

37. On this point the reader can consult the extraordinary Appendix on 'virtues of society (virtutes homileticae)', and read what is said about humanitas aesthetica, which adds grace to virtue. Grace is not virtue; it belongs to these exterior works, these ornaments, these parerga of virtue, to be sure, but to add grace to virtue is a duty of virtue! Even if this be a matter of 'small change', like 'sweetness of language', 'politeness', 'hospitality', the 'ease with which one lets oneself be approached', etc., – in a word, neither friendship nor friendliness, but amiability. We shall meet this 'small change' in a moment, in Anthropology from a Pragmatic Point of View.

38. Kant, p. 264. Emphasis added [translation modified].

39. Victor Hugo, 'L'avenir', in Paris (Introduction to the Paris Guide), Paris 1867, pp. 5, 9, 11–15.

40. 'Suprématie de Paris', in ibid., pp. 54, 60, 62, 63, 67, 72, 74.

41. 'Fonction de Paris', in ibid., p. 83. The meaning of spectre is different here, but up to what point? The relation is not that of simple homonymy. ('The hearth of reason is necessarily the hearth of art. Paris enlightens in both respects; on one side real life, on the other ideal life. . . . Truth bestows pristine light; by cutting through this strange milieu called the past, it remains light and becomes volume. One of the powers of genius is that it is a prism. It remains reality and becomes imagination. Great poetry is the solar spectre of human reason.') The first poem of the youthful period of the author of 'Phantoms' was a classic 'Ode to Friendship'. This poem, the first to be chosen for Hugo's Cahiers de vers français, sings of Castor and Pollux, Orestes and Pylades, the name and the virtues.

42. 'Peace Declaration', in Paris pp. 104–6, 110, 114, 118–24.

10

'For the First Time in the History of Humanity'[1]

> We were friends and have become estranged. But this was right. . . . That we have to become estranged is the law *above* us; by the same token we should also become more venerable for each other – and the memory of our former friendship more sacred. There is probably a tremendous but invisible stellar orbit in which our very different ways and goals may be included (*einbegriffen*) as small parts of this path; let us rise up (*erheben wir uns*) to this thought. But our life is too short and our power of vision too small for us to be more than friends in the sense of this sublime possibility (*erhabenen Möglichkeit*)! – Let us then believe in our star friendship even if we should be compelled to be earth enemies (*Erden/Feinde*).
>
> Nietzsche, 'Star Friendship', in *The Gay Science*[2]

Up until now: up until now, in sum, and still just a second ago, we were speaking of life's brevity. How short will life have been, too short in advance, '*Aber unser Leben ist zu kurz*', says the friend of *Sternen-Freundschaft*.

Up until now we have been speaking of the infinite precipitation into which an eschatological sentiment of the future throws us. Imminence, a world is drawing to a close, fatally, at a moment when, as we were saying a moment ago, things have only just begun: only a few brief millennia, and it was only yesterday that 'we were friends' already.

This is the way fraternal friendship goes. We have just had a hint that fraternal friendship is not without affinity with the history of an ascension. Not a progress but an elevation, a sublimation, no doubt in affinity with what Kant defines also as the stellar sublimity of the moral law ('the starry heavens above me, the moral law within me'). The profound height, the altitude of the moral law of which fraternal friendship would be *exemplary* – 'schematic' or 'symbolic', to use Kant's technical language, according to whether the figure, the presentation or the hypotyposis of the brother would be related to the understanding or to reason.

This narrative can be told as the history of humanity. Let us be more precise: of a *humanization* of man that would have been reflected into *fraternization*.

(As you will have noticed, we have deliberately refrained from recourse to 'illustrations' to 'actualize' our analyses or in an attempt to demonstrate their necessity *today*, by delving into the most spectacular 'news' on political scenes: local, national, European or worldwide. We have done so through a concern with sobriety: first, we do not want to exploit that which, as it were, *screens out* reflection by projecting itself with the pathetic and 'sensational' violence of images on to a too easily mediatizable scene. Then again, these examples are in the mind, heart and imagination of anyone who would be interested in the problems we are dealing with here; such people, let us hope, will have found the path of these mediations by themselves. Lastly, the overabundance of such 'illustrations' would have swamped the least of our sentences. Be it a matter of new forms of warfare, of what is confusedly called the 'return' of the 'religious', of nationalism, of ethnocentrism (sometimes dubbed 'tribal' so as not to put off the other person living with us, at home); upheavals of 'number', of demographic calculation in itself and in its relations to democracy, or to a democratic 'model' which will never have been inscribed in the culture or religion of an *immensely ever-growing majority* of the world's population; unprecedented statistics on what can no longer even be tranquilly called 'immigration' and all forms of population transfer; the restoration or calling into question of citizenship in terms of territory or blood; unheard-of forms of theologico-political intervention on a worldwide, inter- or trans-state scale; the refoundation of state structures and international law (in progress or to come, etc.) – the list would be endless: *all* the themes broached here are, to all intents and purposes, situated at the articulation between these 'present-day examples' and the history of problematics that we are striving to reconstruct or deconstruct. But they demand, above all, implicitly or explicitly, a new topic of these articulations. A single example, one that serves as the pretext for this parenthetical paragraph: a rigorous, critical, non-dogmatic definition of what is called today the *humanitarian* – with its ever more specific organizations, the accelerated multiplication of its interventions, its both continental and international scope, its complex relations with governmental and non-governmental institutions, its medical, economic, technical, militaro-policing dimensions, the new rights that this 'humanitarianism' seeks between the usual 'United Nations' type of intervention and a right to interfere, to invent, etc. – all of this demands a conceptual and practical reformulation. But this cannot be done without a systematic, and *deconstructive*, coming to terms with the tradition of which we are speaking here. For example, what would the definition of 'humanitarian' be in its unheard-of forms with respect to what Kant calls – let us recall – 'the friend of man', a concept Kant intends to keep separate from that of the 'philanthropist'? In what respect does the humanitarian participate in this process of fraternizing humanization that we are questioning here? Another question: what would be today, in a new system of law, a crime against humanity? Its recent definition is no longer sufficient. It will be said that the question is very old, and this is true, but it is also as new, still intact, pregnant, replete, heavy with a future whose monstrosity, by definition, is nameless.[3])

Hence, the categorical imperative: not to betray humanity. 'High treason against humanity' is the supreme perjury, the crime of crimes, the fault against the originary oath. To betray humanity would be to betray, quite simply, to fall short of virtue – that is, short of the virtue of fraternity. In that humanity, one should never betray one's brother. Curse or speak ill of him. Another way of saying: only the brother can be betrayed. Fratricide is the general form of temptation, the possibility of radical evil, the evil of evil.

Kant reports elsewhere, *another time*, Aristotle's saying. In the canonical version, of course, with the vocative and the exclamation mark: '*Meine lieben Freunde: es giebt keinen Freund!*' And he will tell us a story, to get us to give credence to a sort of crime against humanity.

As we were suggesting a moment ago, it is indeed a matter of anthropology, and of *Anthropology from a Pragmatic Point of View*. Its 'didactic' speaks to us of appearance, of this appearance authorized and even recommended by morality. Deceptive appearance is not as bad as all that, is not always inadvisable, Kant concedes. Nature was wise enough to implant in mankind a felicitous aptitude for being deceived. Certainly illusion does not save virtue, but in saving appearance, illusion renders virtue attractive. Proper exterior appearance commands consideration: 'an appearance which is not demeaning to associate with', *sich nicht gemein zu machen*, Kant writes, thinking again of women, of course, and adding immediately afterwards, as a first example: 'Womankind is not at all satisfied when the male sex does not appear to admire her charms.'[4] To which – strict as he always is, careful to select the Latin designation which will speak the law of the concept – he adds a reserve, the reserve of reserve – modesty, *pudicitia*: 'Modesty

[*Sittsamkeit*] (*pudicitia*), however, is self-constraint which conceals passion; nevertheless, as an illusion it is beneficial (*als Illusion sehr heilsam*), for it creates the necessary distance between the sexes so that we do not degrade the one as a mere instrument of pleasure (*zum blossen Werkzeuge des Genusses*) of the other.'

Modesty has the virtue of saving the other, man or woman, from its instrumentalization, from its degradation to the rank of means in view of an end – here, enjoyment. Keeping us away from the technical, from the becoming-technical of desire, modesty is therefore eminently moral and fundamentally egalitarian. Owing to modesty, the two sexes are equal before the law. But let us not forget that this modesty is classed under illusions, salutary appearances, in a sub-chapter devoted to comedy, to roles played in society, to deceit and to mirages. Like 'propriety', *decorum*, 'beautiful appearance', 'politeness' – all related themes – modesty might well be a moral subterfuge. It would equalize the sexes by moralizing them, getting the woman to participate in universal fraternity: in a word, in humanity. The modest woman is a brother for man.

Let us not conclude from this that she becomes less desirable for all that. Precisely the contrary! Modesty would then belong to a *history* [*une histoire*], a history of fraternization, a history *qua* fraternization, which begins in a non-truth and *should end up making non-truth true*. Is this not what Kant says immediately afterwards? He has just named modesty, propriety and the beautiful appearance. Here is the moment when he recalls Aristotle:

> Politeness (*politesse* [in French in the text]) is an appearance of affability which instils affection. *Bowing and scraping* (compliments) and all courtly gallantry, together with the warmest verbal assurance of friendship, are not always completely truthful. 'My dear friends,' says Aristotle, 'there is no friend.' But these demonstrations of politeness do not deceive because everyone knows how they should be taken, especially because signs of well-wishing and respect, though originally empty, gradually lead to genuine dispositions of the soul (*zu wirklichen Gesinnungen dieser Art hinleiten*).

It is indeed a matter of a history of truth. A matter, more precisely, of a trial of *verification*, *qua* the history of a becoming-true of illusion. A history which is *made qua* the story *one tells to oneself and others*: history is made while the story is being told; it is made in being related.

(This Kantian history of truth *qua* the history of an error could be converted by a good philosophical computer into Hegelian software, then into Nietzschean – it's already happening, isn't it?)

Such a history of *verification* is inseparable from the history of *humanization qua fraternization*. As a consequence, the crime against humanity – what Kant will call 'high treason against humanity' – consists in not taking into account a history, precisely, of this history that makes that which was only appearance, illusion, 'small change' (*Scheidemünze*: we have already noted this Kantian obsession: currency *qua* devalued currency, even counterfeit money[5]) become true and serious. The crime against humanity would be to disdain currency, however devalued, illusory or false it may be; it would be to take counterfeit money for counterfeit, for what it is, and to let it come into its truth as counterfeit money. The crime would be not to do everything in one's power to change it into gold – that is, into virtue, morality, true friendship. To do this, as we shall see, one must leave childhood, and this is always the sign whereby Kant recognizes Enlightenment. It will always be asked, of course, on which side lies the greatest deception: on the side of the person who, in the name of truth, mocks the difference between real and counterfeit money; or – and this is Kant – the person who would entrust virtue with the obligation of changing small change into gold – on pain of betraying mankind, of being indicted for 'high treason against humanity':

> Every human virtue in circulation is small change; only a child takes it for real gold. Nevertheless, it is better to circulate pocket pieces than nothing at all. In the end, they can be converted into genuine gold coin, though at a *considerable loss* (*mit ansehnlichem Verlust*). To pass them off as nothing but counters which have no value, to say with the sarcastic Swift that 'Honesty [is] a pair of Shoes worn out in the Dirt', and so forth, or to slander even a Socrates (as the preacher Hofstede did in his attack on Marmontel's *Bélisaire*), for the sake of preventing anyone from believing in virtue, all this is high treason perpetrated upon humanity (*ein an der Menschheit verüber Hochverrath*). Even the appearance of the good in others must have value for us, because in the long run something serious can come from such a play with pretences (*Verstellungen*) which gain respect even if they do not deserve to.

The emphasis is mine. Kant says nothing of the price to be paid, of this 'considerable loss' that can accompany the becoming-gold of currency, the becoming-truth of the simulacrum, its *verification* or its *authentication*. Who comes off worst? What exactly would be lost?

We had recalled two dimensions in the relation to the other: *respect* and *responsibility*, stressing that which, from the vantage point of what might be called aesthetic in the Kantian sense, the former owes to the spatial figure of distance and gaze, the latter to the time of speech. These two dimensions intersect in the ethics or the virtue of friendship: responsible friendship *before* reason, when reason makes the Idea of equality an obligation. The absolute respect and responsibility of brothers before one another but in so far as they must be respectful and responsible before the father, this time *reciprocally but not equally in either case, in a love and not in a friendship, in a reciprocal but not symmetrical love.*

In principle this double dimension maintains the absolute singularity of the other and that of 'my' relation to the other, as a relation of the other to the other I am myself, as its other for itself. But the relation to the singularity of the other also passes through the universality of law. This discourse on universality can determine itself in the regions of morality, of law or of politics, but it always appeals to a third instance, beyond the face-to-face of singularities. This is why we have been so attentive, in Kant's text, to the uprising of the third friend, and to the question of secrecy that it opens up and forever keeps from closing.

The third party always witnesses a law that comes to interrupt the vertigo of singularity, this double singularity or dual in which one might see the features of a narcissism, in the most conventional sense of the term. Would we have here more than one model of friendship, more than one example as regards what Cicero called the example, the *exemplar*, the friend *qua* model and portrait – self-portrait in which I project my ideal image? If this were hypothetically the case, one of these models could find its motto in one of the Aristotelian definitions of the friend as 'another oneself'[6] or in the legendary response of Montaigne ('If you press me to say why I loved him, I feel that it can only be expressed by replying: "Because it was him: because it was me."'[7]).

The other model (if it be other, and if it does not deploy the traps that the first sets the other) would rather inspire particular sentences of Zarathustra, who so often addresses the friend as a brother, beginning with the address on virtue ('My brother, if you have a virtue and it is your own virtue, you have it in common with no one'[8]). Another model, at least as regards its form. The form of desire: to interrupt the jealous narcissism of the dual relation, which always remains imprisoned between 'me' and 'me', 'I' and 'me'; to do everything possible to keep it from sliding into the abyss of specular jealousy. Is there a worse jealousy than jealousy of self? In truth, is there any other? Is one ever jealous of another? Jealous of someone besides one's very own brother? Who is the *more-than-one*, the supplement of the *one-in-excess*?:

'One is always one too many around me' – thus speaks the hermit. 'Always once one – in the long run that makes two!'

I and Me are always too earnestly in conversation with one another: how could it be endured, if there were not a friend? For the hermit the friend is always the third person: the third person is the cork that prevents the conversation of the other two from sinking to the depths.[9]

We were saying that this was another model of friendship. But is there more than one model here? And is it a matter of alternatives? Are there really two different, even antagonistic or incompatible, structures? Perhaps they imply one another – a supplementary ruse – at the very moment when they seem to exclude one other. Does not my relation to the singularity of the other *qua* other, in effect, involve the law? Having come as a third party but always from the singularity of the other, does not the law command me to recognize the transcendent alterity of the other who can never be anything but heterogeneous and singular, hence resistant to the very generality of the law?

Far from dissolving the antagonism and forcing the aporia, this co-implication, it is true, only aggravates them – at the very heart of friendship.

The singularity/universality divide has always divided the experience, the concept and the interpretation of friendship. It has determined other oppositions within friendship. Schematically: on the one hand, the secret-private-invisible-illegible-apolitical, ultimately without concept; on the other, the manifest-public-testamonial-political, homogeneous to the concept.

Between the two terms of the opposition, the *schema* or the *familial symbol* (we will henceforth understand the terms 'symbol' and 'schema' in the Kantian sense: between the sensible singularity of intuition and the generality of the concept or Idea). On the one hand, fraternal friendship appears essentially alien or rebel to the *res publica*; it could never found a politics. But on the other, as we have proved, from Plato to Montaigne, Aristotle to Kant, Cicero to Hegel, *the great philosophical and canonical discourses on friendship* will have explicitly tied the friend-brother to virtue and justice, to moral reason and political reason.

The principal question would rightly concern the hegemony of a philosophical canon in this domain: how has it prevailed? Whence derives its force? How has it been able to exclude the feminine or heterosexuality, friendship between women or friendship between men and women? Why can an essential inventory not be made of feminine or heterosexual experiences of friendship? Why this heterogeneity between *érōs* and *philía*?

Why cannot such a history of the canon be reduced to a history of philosophical concepts or texts, nor even to a history of 'political' structures as such – that is, structures determined by a concept of the political, by this concept of the political? Why is it a matter of a history of the world itself, one which would be neither a continuous evolution nor a simple succession of discontinuous figures? From this vantage point, the question of friendship might well be at least an example or a lead in the two major questions of 'deconstruction': the question of the history of concepts and (trivially) so-called 'textual' hegemony, history *tout court*; and the question of phallogo-centrism.[10] Here *qua* phratrocentrism.

These philosophical canons will have posed the moral and political conditions of an authentic friendship – and vice versa. These discourses also differ among themselves – no one would claim the contrary – and, well beyond what we have just delineated, they call for long and careful analyses. Such analyses should in particular not decide too quickly, in the name of the law, to identify morality and politics: it is sometimes in the name of morality that one has removed friendship from the separations and criteria of politics.

Hence the endless raising of the stakes whose law we have attempted to formalize. This law confounds Aristotle, for example, when he attempts to place friendship above the law and politics. ('When men are friends they have no need of justice, while when they are just they need friendship as well, and the truest form of justice is thought to be a friendly quality.'[11]) But if friendship is above justice – juridical, political, or moral – it is therefore also immediately the most just. Justice beyond justice. Fraternity *qua* 'law beyond law' (Michelet). In all forms of government or consititu-tion (royalty, aristocracy, timocracy, republic or *politeía* – and democracy as the least evil of constitutions: 'for in its case the form of constitution is but a slight deviation'[12]), one sees a form of friendship coterminous with relations of justice appear. And if, in tyranny, friendship and justice play only an insignificant role, the opposite is the case in democracy where, as we have seen, the brother relation prevails.[13] It should also be recalled that justice has two dimensions, one non-written, the other codified by law; therefore, likewise, friendship grounded in usefulness – the case in political friendship – may be moral or legal.[14] The oppositions we are thus recalling seem to dominate the interpretation and experience of friendship in our culture. An unstable domination undermined from within, but all the more imperious for that.

What relation does this domination maintain with the *double exclusion* we see at work in all the great ethico-politico-philosophical discourses on friendship: on the one hand, the exclusion of friendship between women; on the other, the exclusion of friendship between a man and a woman? This double exclusion of the feminine in this philosophical paradigm would then confer on friendship the essential and essentially sublime figure of virile homosexuality. If, in the schema or the familial symbol, this exclusion privileges the figure *of the* brother, the name of the brother or the name *of* 'brother'[15], rather than the name (of the) father, it would be all the more necessary to relate this political model, especially that of democracy, to the tradition of the Decalogue, notably in its Christianization (which would not be terribly original, let us admit), as well as to the rereading of the Freudian hypothesis on the alliance between brothers – *after* but already *before* the parricide, *in view* of a murder all the more useless, all the more interfered with in its act by the simulacrum or the phantasm (which does not limit the effectiveness of its effects) since it bestows even more power on the dead father, and must indeed *presuppose* moral (egalitarian and universalist) law to explain the shame and remorse which, according to Freud, would have ensued in the wake of the crime, and then – and *only then*, have grounded egalitarian law *qua* the interdict of killing.

(Having stressed the problems and paradoxes of the Freudian hypothesis elsewhere,[16] I prefer not to return here, despite its importance, to the reference in *Totem and Taboo* or *The Man Moses*. . . . To sound the keynote of a development to come, and notably concerning the Christianization of the fraternal community, let us be content here with situating a comic, vertiginous, and highly significant episode in the history of psychoanalysis itself. In question is the politico-strategic strategy of the relations between Freud and his momentary Christian ally, Jung. One letter from Ferenczi says more, by itself, than any glosses, which we will not bother with here. We shall quote several passsages, following the selective principle of several themes: the psychoanalytic challenge to a 'mutualist' logic of all democratic communities, hence to *philía par excellence*; the dissymmetry of the analysand/analyst relation; the heterogeneity between transference (*qua* 'love', as Freud said) and all possible friendship; the irreversible transcendence of the archontic or founding agency with regard to the founded institution; the irreversible transcendence of the paternal position with regard to a fraternal community, singularly in its *Christian* form; the structural resistance of Christianity to psychoanalysis; the theory of the sovereign exception *qua* the power of the father (of psychoanalysis) of self-analysis for a unique and therefore 'first time in the history of humanity', etc. – the whole lot assumed with the utmost seriousness by one of the first disciples, without the slightest irony, in an address to the father that we shall also take seriously, despite the outburst of laughter – terminable interminable – which will rock us to the end. To the end – that is, as long as we will be saying, in reading such a letter (for example), that really, if something has not happened to psychoanalysis *up until now*, this is indeed typical of psychoanalysis; and that undoubtedly nothing will never happen to it, especially not in the chain of generations of its founding fathers, unless psychoanalysis itself would already have happened in this non-event, the event of this non-event, and this would be what, perhaps, we must strive to think, to live, and finally to admit. Here, then, are a few excerpts, but the whole volume should be read from the first page to the last:

> Dear Professor, I thank you for your detailed letter. Jung's behavior is uncommonly impudent. He forgets that it was *he* who demanded students from the 'analytic community' and that they be treated like patients. But as soon as it has to do with him, he doesn't want this rule to be valid anymore. *Mutual analysis* is nonsense, also an impossibility. Everyone must be able to tolerate an authority over himself from whom he accepts analytic correction. You are probably the only one who can permit himself to do without an analyst; but that is actually no *advantage* to you, i.e., for your analysis, but a necessity: you have no peer or even superior analyst at your disposal because you have been doing analysis fifteen years longer than *all* others and have accumulated experiences which we others still lack. – Despite all the deficiencies of self-analysis (which is certainly lengthier and more difficult than being analyzed), we have to expect of you the ability to keep your symptoms in check. If you had the strength to overcome in yourself, without a leader *(for the first time in the history of humanity)* [Ferenczi's emphasis], the resistances which all humanity brings to bear on the results of analysis, then we must expect of you the strength to dispense with your lesser symptoms. . . .
>
> . . . I, too, went through a period of rebellion against your 'treatment'.
>
> . . . Jung is the typical instigator and founder of religion. The *father* plays almost no role in his new work; the *Christian community of brothers* [Ferenczi's emphasis] takes up all the more room in it. – His book [*Metamorphoses and Symbols of the Libido*, published in the *Jahrbuch* in 1911–12] has a frightfully repellent effect on me; I loathe its content and its form; its superfluous slyness, superficiality, and cloyingly poeticizing tone make me hate it. Imagine – I still haven't finished reading it.

Much further on in the same letter, Ferenczi tells two of his dreams, with accompanying drawings. Two more excerpts:

I. . . . [(Indistinct) A woman stands on a table and protects herself from the snake by tightly pressing on her dress.] *You* and your sister-in-law play a role in this dream . . .

II. . . . My younger brother, Karl, has just cut off his penis to perform coitus (!). I think something like: that is not necessary, a condom would have been sufficient! . . .[17]

The *double exclusion* of the feminine would not be unrelated to the movement that has always 'politicized' the friendship model at the very moment when one strives to rescue it from thoroughgoing politicization. The tension is here on the inside of the political itself. It is at work in all the discourses that reserve politics and public space to man, domestic and private space to woman. This is also, for Hegel, the opposition of day and night – and therefore a great number of other oppositions.[18]

What is Nietzsche's place in this 'history'? And why do we thus unceasingly return to him? Does he confirm in depth this old tradition which refuses woman the sense of friendship, *for the moment* ('not yet', as Michelet also said)?

Many indications seem in fact to confirm this. Beginning with Zarathustra's sentences in 'Of the Friend'. *Three times over* it is said that 'woman is not yet capable of friendship' ('*Deshalb ist das Weib noch nicht der Freundschaft fähig: . . . Noch ist das Weib nicht der Freundschat fähig:*' . . . '*Noch ist das Weib nicht der Freundschaft fähig*').

These three times must be respected. They concatenate immediately, but what a leap from one to the next! The song 'Of the Friend' began with the speech of the Hermit, as one recalls (always more than one, always one too many, always one time one, that makes two, and three will be necessary to counter the specular jealousy between *I* and *me*, etc.). But the hermit is too attracted to the depths or the abyss, he is nostalgic for elevation; he is dreaming of a friend to gain altitude. This is all a matter of belief. What does the friend's nostalgia reveal? That we wish to *believe* in the other because we want, in vain, to believe in ourselves. This nostalgia has some affinity with the one Heidegger believes he is able to pick up at the origin of philosophical *philía*. It therefore fires the envy towards the other as well as towards self. We envy each other. Love would be but the attempt to leap beyond this envy. And the aggression whereby *we make an enemy*, whereby we make ourselves our own enemy, is only a reaction. It hides and reveals, at one and the same time, our vulnerability. The true fear, the true respect, then pronounces: 'At least be my enemy! (*Sei wenigstens mein Feind!*)'. Zarathustra takes on the tone of a Blake ('*Do be my enemy for*

Friendships sake!') to address an enemy, to speak to him in the name of friendship. There is more friendship, and more nostalgia, in speaking *to* one's enemy – more precisely, in begging the other to become one's enemy – than in speaking *of the* friend without addressing him. There would thus be more declared friendship, more avowed community, in the *canonical* version of the Aristotelian sentence 'O my friends . . .', than in the reportive version of the *recoil*, which states and registers the bottom line *on the* friend and *on* friends. Even more friendly, more declared and avowed in its friendship, would be the inverted apostrophe 'O enemies! . . .'. If there is more respect or fear here, it is because this demand for enmity comes from someone who dare not entreat the other to give him friendship: 'At least be my enemy!' he then says. Conclusion: if you want a friend, you must wage war on him, and in order to wage war, you must be capable of it, capable of having a 'best enemy'.

A eulogy of friendship will now follow, drawing the ineluctable consequence of this axiom. To be capable of this friendship, to be able to honour in the friend the enemy he can become, is a sign of freedom. Freedom itself. Now this is a freedom that neither tyrants nor slaves know. Therefore, it is a political translation of the axiom. The slave and the tyrant have neither friend nor enemy. They are not free and 'equal' enough for that. With this political conclusion, Zarathustra brings up the case of woman. She is at once tyrant and slave, and that is why she (still) remains incapable of friendship, she knows only love. This thesis concerns not only woman, but the hierarchy between love and friendship. Love is *below* friendship because it is an above/below relation, one of inferiority and superiority, slavery and tyranny. It is implied, then, that friendship is freedom plus equality. The only thing missing is fraternity, and we are coming to that. Thus is the first of the three sentences engendered: 'In woman, a slave and a tyrant have all too long been concealed. For that reason, woman is not yet capable of friendship: she knows only love.' Feminine love causes only 'injustice' and 'blindness' to be seen in all that is not loved. In other words, woman remains incapable of respecting the enemy, of honouring what she does not love. Incapable of such a respect, incapable of the freedom entailed by that respect, she could never have either friends or enemies *as such*. Only a free and respectful consciousness could ever attain to this *as such*, this phenomenal essence of the friend or enemy, as well as of the couple they form.

Such a judgement on the subject of woman has political value. It is a political judgement confirmed by the second sentence, the one immediately following, inscribing this political condemnation in its most traditional system. Incapable of friendship, enmity, justice, war, respect for the other, whether friend or enemy, woman is not man; she is not even part of humanity. Still addressing his friend as a brother, especially in speaking in truth to him of ends and virtues ('*Wahrlich, mein Bruder*...', he regularly says), Zarathustra declares here that woman is the outlaw of humanity – in any case as regards the question of loving, if not that of childbirth and suckling; the nurturing mother is perhaps human (like a 'cow') but not the lover that woman can be – woman, to whom friendship still remains inaccessible: 'Woman is not yet capable of friendship: women are still cats and birds. Or, at best, cows.'

Now here we see a sort of apostrophical reversal: the third sentence. Confirming what has just been pronounced on women, Zarathustra suddenly *turns towards* men – he apostrophizes them, accusing them, in sum, of being in the same predicament. Woman was not man, a man free and capable of friendship, and not only of love. Well now, neither is man a man. Not yet. And why not? Because he is not yet generous enough, because he does not know how to give enough to the other. To attain to this infinite gift, failing which there is no friendship, one must know how to give to the enemy. And of this, neither woman nor man (up until now) is capable. Under the category of 'not yet' (*noch . . . nicht*), hence this 'up until now' that we were questioning above, man and woman are equal in this respect. Up until now, they are equally late, although woman is lagging behind man. They are equal in avarice (*Geiz*), equally unable to give and love in friendship. Neither one (not yet, up until now) is one of these true brothers, these friends or enemies, these friends *qua* possible enemies, those whom Zarathustra nevertheless already, starting now, addresses and appeals to (teleiopoetically). This is the third sentence: 'Woman is not yet capable of friendship. But tell me, you men, which of you is yet capable of friendship?/Oh your poverty, you men, and your avarice of soul! (*und euren Geiz der Seele!*) As much as you give to your friend I will give even to my enemy, and will not have grown poorer in doing so.'

One must be patient in the face of this 'not yet', and meditate in all due time the 'up until now' positioned on the threshold of this dissymmetrical gift. For it extends also to man (*Mann*), but first and foremost, again, to Zarathustra's brother. He bears the future of a question, of a call or a promise, a complaint or a prayer. In the performative mode of the apostrophe. There is no friendship as yet, it has not yet begun to be thought. But, in a sort of mourned anticipation, we can already name the friendship that we have not yet met. A threshold naming: we are saying here, on the threshold, that we *already* think that we do not yet have access to friendship. May we have it one day! Such is the exclamation mark, the singular clamour, of this wish. This is Zarathustra's 'O my friends, there is neither friend nor enemy'.

The end of the song rings out in a still more singular way. For is not what has just been repeated, doubled, parodied, perverted and assumed also the Gospel message? Is it not, more precisely, that which commands us to love our enemies as universal brothers, beyond our own family and even our own biological (foster, uterine, or consanguine) brothers? Yes and no – we shall have to return to this. Here now, after the raising of the stakes on the Christian heritage, is the reimplementation of the Aristotelian heritage, around the opposition we have already encountered between the friend and the companion. Fundamentally, that of which man will have been capable up until now – at least up until now – is certainly not perfect friendship (*teleía* or *próte philía*), only comradeship. Now comradeship must be surpassed. But given that it can be surpassed only in giving infinitely to the enemy, which Aristotle never said, the Gospels must be played against Aristotelian virtue and against Greek friendship *par excellence*. This is enough to discourage anyone wishing to establish a reassuring historical scansion – that is, a decidable and clear-cut one – to make this strategy coherent. It would be better to give up the idea immediately and think up different ways of doing history or the historian's profession. For that which thus defies the tranquillity of the historian is a strategy of friendship, a war for friendship. Friendship is now the stake of these endless strategies. And must not one think, or at least approach, this other history, hence this other friendship, to leave comradeship? Comrades, try again! Zarathustra is speaking of friendship also to historians and theologians – and this is the end of his song: 'There is comradeship: may there be friendship! (*Es gibt Kameradschaft: möge es Freundschaft geben!*).' Since this '*es gibt*' and this '*geben*' immediately follow a definition of friendship by the gift, for the friend as well as for the enemy ('*Wie viel ihr dem Freunde gebt, das will ich noch meinem Feinde geben*'), it can be supposed that the 'there is' ('*es gibt*') or the 'may there be' ('*möge es geben*') give themselves only to the extent of the gift. The gift is that which gives friendship; it is needed for there to be friendship, beyond all comradeship.

But as woman has not yet attained to friendship because she remains – and this is love – 'slave' or 'tyrant', friendship to come continues to mean, for Zarathustra: freedom, equality, fraternity. The fragile, unstable and recent motto, as we have seen, of a republic. Unless it appeals to a friendship capable of *simultaneously* overwhelming philosophical history (Aristotelian, as we have just seen) and Enlightenment fraternity *qua* the sublation [*relève*] (we have seen enough signs of this) of Christian fraternity: three friendships in one, the same, in sum, with which one must break.

Another song leads us on to this path, one that begins shortly after 'Of the Friend'. 'Of Love of One's Neighbour' (*Von der Nächstenliebe*) seems to oppose friend to neighbour, and blatantly to the neighbour of the Gospels. In truth, it does not *oppose* friend to neighbour, it wishes to raise it *above* the neighbour – and this in the name of the far-off and of the future. The neighbour is believed, like his name, to be close and present. Friendship is a thing of distance, a thing of the future; hence 'Do I exhort you to love of your neighbour? I exhort you rather to flight from your neighbour and to love of the most distant (*Fernsten-Liebe*)'. Zarathustra thus addresses brothers not yet born, his brothers to come but supposed *already* to be prepared to hear him where they are as yet still incapable of doing so. And this is why they must be spoken to. Ready to hear, they will be ready when they have heard. This teleiopoetic word accomplishes the Gospel word in perverting it, it sets it awry and de-natures it, but in order to keep its promise. If this Gospel word promises spiritual fraternity, beyond milk and blood (but owing to other blood, to another eucharistic body – this is the whole question, and Zarathustra does not fail to take it up); if the word of Christ thus promises the true filiation of brothers of the 'father who is in heaven', is this not in terms of a love of neighbour which prescribes, *as does Zarathustra*, the love of one's enemies? One becomes a brother, in Christianity, one is worthy of the eternal father, only by loving one's enemy as one's neighbour or as oneself. Here we have the profit of a sublime economy, an economy beyond economy, a salary that is transformed into the gold of non-salary. Let us cite here only Matthew, aware nevertheless that we are on the brink of a work of infinite reading:

> You have heard the commandment, 'You shall love your countryman but hate your enemy.' My command to you is: love your enemies, pray for your persecutors. This will prove that you are sons of your heavenly Father, for his sun rises on the bad and the good, he rains on the just and the unjust. If you love those who love you, what merit is there in that? Do not tax collectors do as much? And if you greet your brothers only, what is so praiseworthy about that? Do not pagans do as much? In a word, you must be made perfect as your heavenly Father is perfect.[19]

Does not Zarathustra also entreat the friend to come around to an absolute gift that breaks with the ruse of this sublime economy? Is not the friendship for his brother *qua* neighbour and son of God still in search of the pure gold of an infinite wage? Does it not still seek – to pick up once again the Kantian motif that we evoked above – the best exchange rate for virtue? In any case, it is in the name of the friend who 'bestows' that Zarathustra advises against the love of one's neighbour, but a wageless, unrequited bestowal.

The gift he then names must also belong to the finite world. One would thus have to think the dissymmetry of a gift without exchange, therefore an infinite one – infinitely disproportionate, in any case, however modest it may be, from the vantage point of terrestial finitude. From under its horizon without horizon. For we have just suspected infinitization itself of being an economic ruse. A certain 'gild' is denounced in the same song, and it would be like a Christian seduction, the love of one's neighbour as the manoeuvring hypocrisy of a perverse seduction, a stratagem to mislead the other towards oneself:

> You cannot endure to be alone with yourselves and do not love yourselves enough: now you want to mislead your neighbour into love and gild yourselves with his mistake (*und euch mit seinem Irrtum vergolden*).

Such a finitism would then revert from Christian to Greek, if we could still rely on this distinction, which we are doing less and less often:

> I do not teach you the neighbour but the friend. May the friend be to you a festival of the earth and a foretaste of the Superman.
> I teach you the friend and his overflowing heart. But you must understand how to be a sponge if you want to be loved by overflowing hearts.
> I teach you the friend in whom the world stands complete, a vessel of the good – the creative friend, who always has a completed world to bestow.
> And as the world once dispersed for him, so it comes back to him again, as the evolution of good through evil, as the evolution of design from chance.
> May the future and the most distant be the principle of your today: in your friend you should love the Superman as your principle.
> My brothers, I do not exhort you to love of your neighbour: I exhort you to love of the most distant.
> Thus spoke Zarathustra.[20]

Three remarks before interrupting – as we must – these songs. They concern the *gift*, the *superman*, and the *spectre*.

1. *The gift*. This friend of the most distant belongs to the finite earth, to be sure, not to the world of Christian hinterworlds. But far from limiting

the gift that he perhaps then gives, his finitude infinitizes it. Zarathustra's friend, this friend to come, this friend of the far removed, does not give this or that, in just any economy (in which the virtuous would still want to be paid[21]), he gives a world, he gives all, he gives that in which all gifts may appear; and like all gifts, this gift of the world must nevertheless be determined: it is *this* world, a completed world. A friend who does not give you *the* world, and a world which, because it exists, has form and limit, being this world and not another, gives you nothing. To think this friendship, which would be neither Greek nor Christian, this gift would have to be thought as the gift of the world, and above all (*but* above all) as gift of a finite world.

2. *The Superman*. To be sure, he is awaited, announced, called, to come, but – contradictory as it may seem – it is because he is the origin and the cause of man. He is the originary (*Ursache*) cause of man. Man is called – and called into question – by his cause. His cause is naturally beyond him. With regard to this friend promised, announced, hoped for (always following the same thrust of the messianico-teleiopoetic *perhaps*) the friendship against which these men and women were judged up until now, and judged incapable, *owing to a lack of humanity*, precisely, and of liberty – well, this very friendship, this friendship to come, would still be too human. At the very least it deserves its name 'friendship', and properly human friendship, only providing it lets itself be transfixed by the expectation of the superman to come. But to come as cause or origin, – that is, as immemorially past. This is the only possible experience of a 'most distant' that remains approachable only in being unapproachable. Fundamentally, all the concepts of a friendship of presence and proximity whose anthropological, anthropocentric or humanist character we have been emphasizing hitherto would be situated and delimited here. Even if this anthropocentrism were also, sometimes, anthropo-theological or onto-theological, the profound structure of the concept would not be modified. Its centre of gravity would remain as close as possible to proximity, in the present of the closest.

3. *The spectre*. In a passage that we were reading above,[22] and precisely in *Human All Too Human*, Nietzsche, as it were, had resurrected 'phantom friends', those who have not changed while we have been transformed. These friends returned as the phantom of our past – in sum, our memory, the silhouette of the ghost who not only *appears* to us (*phantasmata*, phenomena, phantoms, things of sight, things of respect, the respect which returns and comes down to the spectre), but an *invisible* past, hence a past that can speak, and speak to us in an icy voice, 'as if we were hearing

ourselves'. Here, this should be exactly the opposite, since it is a question of the friend, of the superman whose present friendship urges the arrival. Not the past friend, but the friend to come. Now what is coming is still spectral, and it must be loved as such. As if there were never anything but spectres, on both sides of all opposition, on both sides of the present, in the past and in the future. All phenomena of friendship, all things and all beings to be loved, belong to spectrality. 'It is necessary to love' means: the spectres, they are to be loved; the spectre must be respected (we know that Mary Shelley brought our attention to the anagram that makes the spectre in respect become visible again). And here we have the sentence addressed by Zarathustra to his brother. Here is what the song 'Of Love of One's Neighbour' promises him: the friend to come, the *arrivant* who comes from afar, the one who must be loved in remoteness and from afar, the superman – and it is a spectre:

> Higher than love of one's neighbour stands love of the most distant man and of the man of the future; higher still than love of man I account love of causes and of phantoms (*die Liebe zu Sachen und Gespenstern*).
>
> This phantom that runs along behind you, my brother, is fairer than you; why do you not give it your flesh and bones? But you are afraid and you run to your neighbour. (p. 87)

A spectral distance would thus assign its condition to memory as well as to the future *as such*. The *as such* itself is affected with spectrality; hence is it no longer or not yet exactly what it is. The disjunction of spectral distance would, by this very fact, mark both the past and the future with a non-reappropriable alterity.[23]

Thus, at least, spoke Zarathustra. We have refrained from substituting Nietzsche's name for his, as if, from one ghost to another, it never came down to the same one. Things are already unattackable and inappropriable enough as they are for each ghost. Neither should one rush to consider a single one of Zarathustra's sentences as Gospel. Having commanded them to be capable of facing the enemy, of respecting, fearing, honouring him; having recalled that a humanity in default of an end also defaults itself – is itself lacking in humanity – Zarathustra demands of his disciples that they leave him: repudiate me, be ashamed of the one who 'perhaps has deceived you'. 'For the man of knowledge must not only love his friends: he must also be able to hate his enemies!' This is the immense song 'Of the Bestowing Virtue', in whose end, in a neo-evangelical scene, Zarathustra addresses his brothers to promise his return. Then, after the separation, after the repudiation, another love – friendship itself – will be possible. Zarathustra swears, invites, bids, demands the oath:

> Now I bid you (*Nun heisse ich euch*) lose me and find yourselves, and only when you have all denied me will I return to you.
>
> Truly, with other eyes, my brothers, I shall **then seek** my lost ones; with another love I shall then love you.
>
> And once more you shall have become my friends and children of one hope: and then I will be with you a third time, that I may celebrate the great noontide with you. . . .
>
> '*All gods are dead: now we want the Superman to live*' – let this be our last will, one day, at the great noontide!

This is only the end of Part One. To relaunch it, it will become the epigraph of Part Two. The entire path of this abyssal altercation with Christian fraternity had begun, as we will recall, with the evocation of the hermit. As Zarathustra is also addressing another brother to come, but one who is already listening to him, there would be – among all the tasks that thus assign themselves to us but which, alas, we have to give up pursuing – an ancient and new history to relate and to make, from this point of view, of Christian fraternity: not only its theme, its concept and its figures but its orders, *fraternities* as institutions (an analogous and equally urgent investigation would deal with the figure of the brother in Arabo-Islamic culture – and with the 'Muslim brothers'). Faced with this task, our shortcoming has no avowable justification here. Let it nevertheless be clear that we believe in the gravity of the obligation which the limits of this work oblige us to shirk. We have insisted sufficiently on the indefinite recoils of the discourse and strategy of Zarathustra in order not to be convinced in advance that the history of the brother in the Bible and in the Koran, as is the case in the history of orders called 'fraternities', contains in itself, here or there, in one fold or recoil or another, reason enough for finding ourselves beside Zarathustra or his disciples rather than in a posture of confrontation.

Let us hold at least to this evidence: these songs of Zarathustra are also songs of mourning. He is taking leave, he asks to be repudiated, he will return, and the returning ghost who promises his brothers that they will then be his brothers or friends is indeed a testament, a 'this is my body' offered again to them.

As if there were no interminable mourning other than the mourning of the brother, and as if the friendship we have been speaking about would dry up after this impossible mourning: only by deferring it can this friendship begin to mourn. There is no possible introjection or incorporation; this is the canon of friendship. Successful, a death without remainder, or an ideal death, the mourning of the brother would run too great a risk of allowing the father to return. This is what, at any price, the brothers' conjuration desires – anything but the return of the father! – what we have hitherto been calling friendship, the one conjured away by Zarathustra *as well as* the one in the name of which he bids his brothers to come – one friendship against the other, but one along with the other. As if friendship were playing against the love of the father. And as if the scene could be framed thus: without a woman.

Let us backtrack for a moment. If the great canonical meditations on friendship (Cicero's *De Amicitia*, Montaigne's 'On Friendship', Blanchot's *L'amitié*, for example) belong to the experience of mourning, to the moment of loss – that of the friend or of friendship – if through the irreplaceable element of the named they always advance in testimonial order to confide and refuse the death of the unique to a universalizable discourse ('. . . my friends, there is no friend': Aristotle–Montaigne; 'But what has become of my friends?': Villon; *'Wo aber sind die Freunde?'*: Hölderlin), if by this token they simultaneously *found* and *destabilize*, if they restore, because they threaten them, a great number of oppositions (singular/universal, private/public, familial/political, secret/phenomenal, etc.), and perhaps *all* oppositions, can it be said that the relative invariance of this model is *itself* fractured and fractures *itself* [se *fracture* elle-même], and opens on to its own abyss? Going back over all the motifs that we have just touched upon (the ethics and politics of friendship, death, the name, fraternity, etc.), reconsidering all these oppositions, could we not discern two major ruptures in what, for sheer convenience, would be called *the history of friendship*, whereas a certain friendship might very well (we have seen so many indications of this) shake up the most traditional concept of historicity? And how are they to be related to the *double exclusion* of the feminine, the exclusion of friendship between a man and a woman and the exclusion of friendship *between* women? The categories of 'not yet' and of 'up until now' make this assurance tenuous. It might well urge us to stop speaking simply of exclusion. We have attempted to show that the Graeco-Roman model, which seems to be governed by the value of *reciprocity*, by homological, immanentist, finitist – and rather politist – concord, bears within itself, nevertheless, potentially, the power to become infinite and dissymmetrical. Montaigne (whom we are reading here as an example of a canonical paradigm) undoubtedly inherits most of these features. But when he breaks with the reciprocity and discreetly introduces – it seems to me – heterology, transcendence, dissymmetry and infinity, hence a Christian type of logic ('. . . he infinitely surpassed me'; 'I would have entrusted myself to him with greater assurance than to myself'; '. . . For the very writings which Antiquity have left us on this subject seem weak to me compared to what I feel'), he also accomplishes the so-called Greek model of friendship. That which ensures the mediation or the solder – in any case, a certain continuity between the two times – that which also relates to the exclusion of woman, if only in the form or the pretext of 'not yet', is the brother, and, more precisely, the name, the name 'brother' and the brother's name. We have quoted, without bringing them into comparison, two of Montaigne's declarations. One praised the name 'brother', the other the brother's name. Let us recall them. One spoke the name 'brother' in its genericity: 'The name *of* brother is truly a fair one and full of love: that is why La Boétie and I made a brotherhood of our alliance.'[24] The other spoke the brother's name, in its singularity. Montaigne, speaking precisely of the testamentary piece that forms the starting point of 'On Friendship', enunciates in two steps the incredible time of the name. The name ensures the 'fraternal solder' in that it precedes, as it were, the encounter with the friend and bestows on friendship a 'force' and an 'effort' which imparts existence to it prior to its existence, as it will also allow it, by the same dismembering of the surviving stance [*survivance*], to exist after it has existed. Owing to the name, friendship begins prior to friendship; owing to the name, friendship survives friendship; friendship always begins by surviving. One might just as well say friendship is never there; it's as simple as that. Nor the friend of which, from this point of view, there are none. As we were saying, Montaigne enunciates this in two steps.

1. First as the heir or legatee of the friend, 'with death on his lips':

This is all I have been able to recover of his literary remains, I the heir to whom, with death on his lips, he so lovingly willed his books and his papers – apart from the slim volume of his works which I have had published already.

Yet I am particularly indebted to that treatise, because it first brought us together: it was shown to me long before I met him and first made me acquainted with his name; thus preparing for that loving-friendship between us which as long as it pleased God we fostered so perfect and so entire that it is certain that few such can even be read about, and no trace at all of it can be found among men of today.[25]

2. Next, when he does have to admit (but who, in the urge to quote a saying which seems to carry an ineffable singularity beyond the name, will have noticed it?) that the 'Because it was him; because it was me' goes 'beyond all my reasoning' only by virtue of the name, owing to the name. The name is the cause of everything in this friendship. The time of the name is what bestows this force of approach, this power of proximity or of 'union' which defies discourse: the name against the discourse, before and after it; the name *qua* force, affection, mediation, these nameless concepts (without common names) which speak the effect of the proper name. As in the passage quoted just a moment ago, God is named in the place where this name is so mysteriously active. Only the name of God and 'some decree of Heaven' can account for this reason of the name, for these effects of the name. Of the proper name, of course, and of a famous name, which comes more easily to men than to women, to brothers than to sisters, to sons than to daughters:

> . . . the seam which joins them together. . . . If you press me to say why I loved him, I feel that it can only be expressed by replying: 'Because it was him; because it was me.' Mediating this union there was, beyond all my reasoning, beyond all that I can say specifically about it, some inexplicable force of destiny. We were seeking each other before we set eyes on each other – both because of the reports we each had heard, which made a more violent assault on our emotions than was reasonable from what they had said, and, I believe, because of some decree of Heaven: we embraced each other by repute, and at our first meeting, which chanced to be at a great crowded town-festival, we discovered ourselves to be so seized by each other, so known to each other and so bound together that from then on none was so close as each was to the other. (p. 212)

Concerning what is of import to us here, the two features of the name must undoubtedly be held together. On the one hand, the name constitutes the very structure of the testamentary survival stance, hence of a certain spectrality: the name survives a priori, if this can be said, its bearer and the person to be called, before and afterwards, beyond presence. But this general and structural feature is also enframed [*arraisonné*], in a *certain* history, as the chance of filiation, of the *inherited* name, as well as of *renown* (and Montaigne speaks as often of the proper name as of the renown which brings this legendary name to the cognizance of the friend to come, thereby giving birth to friendship). Under the two forms of this enframing (inheritance of the name and social renown) *this* history leaves less chance to the woman, to the daughter, to the sister. We are not saying *no* chance, but *less* chance. When one speaks of hegemony – that is, the relation of forces – the laws of structure are tendential; they are determined not (do not determine) in terms of *yes or no*, hence in terms of simple exclusion, but in those of differential force, *more or less*. It is fitting here to emphasize the impossibility of a *sheer* exclusion in order to account for effects of repression, hence for returns of that which should not return: symptoms and disavowals that this very law can produce and reproduce, never failing in fact to do so.

Hence one can no longer speak here of a *simple* fracture and say that it is Judaeo-Christian. Nor that it depoliticizes the Greek model nor that it shifts the nature of the political.

Is another event then produced when, with Nietzsche or Blanchot, we come to call the friend by a name which is no longer that of the near one or the neighbour, and undoubtedly no longer the name of man? The words rupture or interruption – as we have just confirmed – are not sufficient for the determination of what occurs with Nietzsche, especially given the authority with which the brother still dominates all the reversals. Consequently, as we suggested at the beginning, we cannot and should not elude this other question: of all that which, in our time, responds to the event of which Nietzsche was at one and the same time the signatory and the witness, the cause and the effect, might we say, following certain signs that would lead us to believe it, that in some places of thought, for some – few in number, it is true – an unprecedented rupture will have taken place? Or rather, an unprecedented thought of rupture or of interruption as the place of friendship? We are obviously thinking – as we also indicated at the beginning – of Blanchot, Bataille and everything radiating around their work without their wanting, for all that, to become its centre or source, which in fact they are not. We would wish neither, *on the one hand*, to efface the singularity of their name, of their names, of their thought(s), their work(s), above all their friendship (another person would say: of the friendship of this legendary pair of friends of this century to which, Kant would add, a third reliable friend came to join them, already in fact being there from the very beginning – Lévinas – and the fact that these three knew each other to different extents is of little importance) nor, *on the other hand*, would we want to capitalize around them all the original thoughts linked to them or to which they themselves have referred, expressly or not.

The remaining question – about which it can be asked what is left once these questions have finished ringing out – is one whose novelty we will keep in the very form which Plato gave it in *Lysis*, at the moment of his leavetaking following his failure: not 'what is friendship?' but who is the friend? Who is it? Who is he? Who is she? *Who*, from the moment when, as we shall see, all the categories and all the axioms which have constituted the concept of friendship in its history have let themselves be threatened with ruin: the subject, the person, the ego, presence, the family and familiarity, affinity, suitability (*oikeiōtēs*) or proximity, hence a certain truth and a certain memory, the parent, the citizen and politics (*polítēs* and *politeía*), man himself – and, of course, the brother who capitalizes everything?

The stake of this question is, of course, *also* political. The political belongs to this series, even if it is sometimes placed in the position of the series' *transcendental*. Is it possible, without setting off loud protests on the part of militants of an edifying or dogmatic humanism, to think and to live the gentle rigour of friendship, the law of friendship *qua* the experience of a certain ahumanity, in absolute separation, beyond or below the commerce of gods and men? And what politics could still be founded on this friendship which exceeds the measure of man, without becoming a theologem? Would it still be a politics?

What happens politically when the 'Who' of friendship then distances itself from all these determinations? In its 'infinite imminence' – let us listen to Blanchot – the 'who' exceeds even the interest in knowledge, all forms of knowledge, truth, proximity, and even as far as life itself, and the memory of life. It is not yet an identifiable, public or private 'I'. Above all, as we are going to hear, it is some 'one' to whom one speaks (if only to tell him or her that there is no friend), but of whom one does not speak. This, no doubt, is why Blanchot must prefer the vocative and canonical version to the recoil version:

> We have to renounce knowing those to whom we are bound by something essential; I want to say, we should welcome them in the relation to the unknown in which they welcome us, us too, in our remoteness. Friendship, this relation without dependence, without episode, into which, however, the utter simplicity of life enters, implies the recognition of a common strangeness which *does not allow us to speak of our friends, but only to speak to them*, not to make of them a theme of conversations (or articles), but the movement of understanding in which, speaking to us, they reserve, even in the greatest familiarity, an infinite distance, this fundamental separation from out of which that which separates becomes relation. Here, discretion is not in the simple refusal to report confidences (how gross that would be, even to think of), but it is the interval, the pure interval which, from me to this other who is a friend, measures everything there is between us, the interruption of being which never authorizes me to have him at my disposition, nor my knowledge of him (if only to praise

him) and which, far from curtailing all communication, relates us one to the other in the difference and sometimes in the silence of speech.[26]

Consequently, if the testament or the epitaph remains the place of a *De Amicitia* for our time, all the signs of orison find themselves – if not negated or inversed, then at least suspended in a non-negative neutrality. Such a neutrality calls into question not only our memory of the friend, our thought of fidelity, but our memory of what 'friendship' has always meant. And yet we do sense that this discreet violence accomplishes an injunction which was already working away at the legacy of this tradition, and was being demanded from within our very memory. On the death of the friend, the 'measurelessness of the movement of dying', the 'event' of death reveals and effaces at the same time this 'truth' of friendship, if only the truth of the far-off places of which Zarathustra spoke. Oblivion is necessary:

> ... not the deepening of the separation, but its effacement, not an enlarging of the caesura, but its levelling, and the dissipation of this void between us where once developed the frankness of a relation without history. In such a way that at the present time that which was close to us has not only ceased its approach, but has lost even the truth of extreme remoteness. We are able, in a word, to remember. But thought knows that one does not remember: without memory, without thought, it already struggles in the invisible where all falls back into oblivion. This is the place of profound pain. It must accompany friendship into oblivion. (p. 329)

Oblivion must [*Faut l'oubli*]. Friendship without memory itself, by fidelity, by the gentleness and rigour of fidelity, bondless friendship, out of friendship, out of friendship for the solitary one on the part of the solitary. Nietzsche already demanded this 'community without community', this bondless bond. And death is the supreme ordeal of this unbinding without which no friendship has ever seen the light of day. The book has as its epigraph these words of Georges Bataille:

> ... friends to the point of this state of profound friendship in which a forsaken man, forsaken by all his friends, meets in life he who will accompany him beyond life, himself lifeless, capable of free friendship, detached from all bonds.

The moment when the hyperbole seems to engage with the greatest risk, with respect to the inherited concept of friendship and all the politics that have ever spun out of it (Graeco-democratic or Christiano-revolutionary) is when the 'without sharing' and the 'without reciprocity' come to sign friendship, the response or the responsibility of friendship. Without sharing and without reciprocity, could one still speak of equality and fraternity? We are again quite close to Nietzsche, although we are already invited to think a proximity of the distant to which Zarathustra called us (he must have had to suppose it too, teleiopoetically) and always under the neutral and non-dialectizable law of the *'pas'* ['step' or 'not'] and the 'X without X'.

> And yet, to the proximity of the most distant, to the pressure of the most weightless, to the contact of what does not reach us – it is in *friendship* that I can respond, a friendship unshared, without reciprocity, friendship of that which has passed leaving no trace. This is passivity's response to the un-presence of the unknown.[27]

How could such a 'response' ever translate into ethical or political responsibility, the one which, in the philosophical and Christian West, has always been associated with friendship? The preceding pages respond (admirably and from within the same 'logic') to this question of responsibility. As in the passage we have just quoted, they are written to and inspired by the figure of Lévinas, the other great friend, the other unique friend, in a friendship of thought which is not exclusively one of thought. If this language seems 'impossible' or untenable with regard to the common sense of friendship, where it has commanded all the canonical discourses we have mentioned thus far, it is also because it is written in terms of *a writing of the disaster*. The disaster is less friendship's (for friendship) than one without which there is no friendship, the disaster at the heart of friendship, the disaster of friendship or disaster *qua* friendship. Star friendship (*Sternen-Freundschaft*).

Without being able to do justice here to these immense books, in particular *L'Amitié* or *The Writing of the Disaster*, let us fall back, under the sign of friendship, admiration and unmitigated gratitude, to several passages in which what is most enigmatic, if not most problematic, in friendship receives the keenest attention:

Let us do so in three steps, taking up three questions: (1) the question of the *community*; (2) the *'Greek* question'; (3) the question of *fraternity*.

1. *The question of the community.* It will be asked what 'common' can still mean as soon as friendship goes beyond all *living* community? What is being *in common* when it comes to friends only in dying? And what is it that renders this very value of the common valueless, valueless for thinking

friendship, if not, fundamentally, this testamentary structure that we have constantly seen at work in all the great discourses on friendship? In order to think this 'call to dying in common through separation', Blanchot decides he must undo or suspend the gift, the very generosity of the promise which, according to Nietzsche, remained the essential feature of the friend to come. Here, we are no longer in affinity with Nietzsche – with one Nietzsche, in any case (for there is always more than one):

> Friendship is not a gift, or a promise; it is not generic generosity. Rather, this incommensurable relation of one to the other is the outside drawing near in its separateness and inaccessibility. Desire, pure impure desire, is the call to bridge the distance, to die in common through separation. (p. 50)

Whatever can be thought of the gift or the promise from which such a friendship would free itself, from which it should indeed abstain, whatever can be thought of this duty or this possibility, it is true that in translating gift and promise by 'generic generosity', in associating them so closely – nothing could be less self-evident[28] – risks are avoided, notably the political risks which, as we have pointed out, return incessantly: naturalization, the genericity of genre, race, *gens*, the family or the nation; and return, more precisely, with the features of fraternity. But once the necessity of all these neutralizations has been honoured ('the outside drawing near in its separateness', 'pure impure desire'), once it has been clearly pointed out that the common is not the common of a given community but the pole or the end of a *call* ('the *call* to bridge the distance, to die in common through separation'), the whole question remains: what is being called the *call*, and what is being called 'common'? Why these words again, when they no longer mean what they were always thought to mean? When they still mean what they were believed not to mean – a meaning to which a memory, another memory, another friendship, ought to awaken them again? The question is not only the one which brings on semantic vertigo, but the one which asks 'what is to be done?': What is to be done today, politically, with this vertigo and its necessity? What is to be done with the 'what is to be done?'? And what other politics – which would nevertheless still be a politics, supposing the word could still resist this very vertigo – can this other communality of the 'common' dictate to us?

This type of question envelops another. If, through 'the call to die in common through separation', *this* friendship is borne beyond being-in-common, beyond being-common or sharing, beyond all common appur-tenance (familial, neighbourhood, national, political, linguistic and finally generic appurtenance), beyond the social bond itself – if that is possible – then why elect, if only passively, this other with whom I have no relation of this type rather than some other with whom I have none of the sort either? Why would I call this foreigner my friend (for we are speaking of this absolute foreigner, if only the neighbourhood foreigner, the foreigner within my family) and not the other? Why am I not the friend of just anyone? Am I not, moreover, just that, in subscribing to such a strong and at the same time disarming and disarmed proposition? There could never be any appeasing response to this question, of course. But the hypothesis can come up that, if this is the way things are, it is because the friendship announced in this language, the one promised or promising without promising anything, is perhaps of the order neither of the common nor of its opposite, neither appurtenance nor non-appurtenance, sharing or non-sharing, proximity or distance, the outside or the inside, etc. Nor therefore, in a word, that of the community. Not because it would be a community without community, 'unavowable' or 'inoperative', etc., but simply because it would have nothing to do, with regard to what is essential in that which is called friendship, with the slightest reference to community, whether positive, negative, or neutral. This would (perhaps) mean that the aporia requiring the unceasing neutralization of one predicate by another (relation without relation, community without community, sharing without sharing, etc.) calls on significations altogether different from those of the part shared or held in common, regardless of the sign – positive, negative or neutral – assigned to them. This desire ('pure, impure desire') which, in lovence – friendship or love – engages me with a particular him or her rather than with *anybody* or with all hims and all hers, which engages me with these men and these women (and not with all of either and not with just anyone), which engages me with a singular 'who', be it a certain number of them, a number that is always small, whichever it is, with regard to 'all the others', this desire of the call to bridge the distance (necessarily unbridgeable) is (perhaps) no longer of the order of the common or the community, the share taken up or given, participation or sharing. Whatever the sentence constructed with these words (affirmative, negative, neutral or suspensive), it would never be related to what we persist in naming with these well-worn words: lovence, friendship, love, desire. Consequently, if there were a politics of this lovence, it would no longer imply the motifs of community, appurtenance or sharing, whatever the sign assigned to them. Affirmed, negated or neutralized, these 'communitarian' or 'communal' values always risk bringing a brother back. Perhaps this risk must be assumed in order to keep the question of the 'who' from being politically enframed by the schema of being-common or being-in-common, even when it is neutralized, in a question of identity (individual, subjective, ethnic, national, state, etc.). The law of number and of the 'more than one' which goes all through this book would not be any less crucial and ineluctable but it would, then, call for an altogether other language.

2. *The Greek question.* Despite the infinite distance separating his thought of friendship from what we have called, all the way to its hyperbolic paradoxes, the Greek 'model' of friendship, and no doubt from the very idea of a 'model', why does Blanchot see fit, at one moment, to praise Greek *philía*, the 'exalted virtue' it demands and which is found only in 'a few of us'? Why is it precisely when he too is speaking of *philía* as a 'model' (Blanchot's term) that he quotes in turn Aristotle's sentence in its canonical version ('O my friends, there is no friend')? But this time, having taken account of everything we have just heard, the 'there is no friend' can and must become laden with the newest and most rebellious of significations: there is no longer a friend in the sense of what the entire tradition has taught us.

And yet. And yet, a certain heritage is still affirmed, reaffirmed, providing it is 'still capable of being enriched'. We shall first read this passage, but its sheer existence indeed attests to – rather, confirms – the fact that no actual rupture is possible, determinable, even advisable, even from the greatest distancing, and that the history we are referring to is not articulated in this way.

In question again is a sort of epigraph. Here are the last pages of *Michel Foucault as I Imagine Him*,[29] a text first written for a journal, 'the day following Foucault's death':

. . . asked about his projects, he [Foucault] suddenly exclaimed: 'Oh! First I'm going to concern myself with myself!' His comment is not easy to elucidate, even if one considers a bit hastily that, like Nietzsche, he was inclined to seek in the Greeks less a civic morality than an individual ethic permitting him to make of his life – what remained of it for him to live – a work of art. And it was thus he would be tempted to call on the ancients for a revalorization of the practices of friendship, which, although never lost, have not again recaptured, except for a few of us, their exalted virtue. *Philía*, which, for the Greeks and even Romans, remains the model of what is excellent in human relations (with the enigmatic character it receives from opposite imperatives, at once pure reciprocity and unrequited generosity), can be received as a heritage always capable of being enriched. Friendship was perhaps promised to Foucault as a posthumous gift, beyond passions, beyond problems of thought, beyond the dangers of life that he experienced more for others than for himself. In bearing witness to a work demanding study (unprejudiced reading) rather than praise, I believe I am remaining faithful, however awkwardly, to the intellectual friendship that his death, so painful for me, today allows me to declare to him, as I recall the words attributed by Diogenes Laertes to Aristotle: '*Oh my friends, there is no friend.*'

Instead of giving in to the indecency of the cold reading of the rhetoritician which would uncover the sublime calculations imposed on this extraordinary declaration of friendship in mourning, instead of analysing the writing of a 'so painful' fervour which still submits to the obligation of weighing each word on the scene (the concession, the parentheses, the 'perhaps', the strict qualification of an essentially 'intellectual' friendship, etc.), let us limit ourselves to two points.

1. First of all, the *theme* is indeed that of the Greek 'model'. As it seems hardly compatible with the thought of friendship which Blanchot, in *L'Amitié* and elsewhere (especially in *The Writing of the Disaster*), had carried to the extremity of an uncompromising and, at the same time, gentle rigour, the entire effort – not to say the painful torsion – of this epigraph will consist in emphasizing above all: (1) the aporias which make this Greek model scarcely readable, enigmatic if not objectionable; and (2) the necessity, by way of consequence, *of not receiving* this heritage, in any case not without transforming it or enriching it (no doubt to the point of contradicting it at the heart of its contradiction). As this unconditional allusion to an 'exalted virtue' which he, in sum, promotes – this 'exalted virtue' that 'a few of us' have 'recaptured' – is, in Blanchot's work, undoubtedly a hapax, the eulogy of 'the model of what is excellent in human relations' can only be immediately blurred, complicated, neutralized ('with the enigmatic character it receives from opposite imperatives, at once pure reciprocity and unrequited generosity'). Since everything Blanchot has thought and written *elsewhere* on friendship should lead him to wish not to inherit from this model, the allusion to a heritage which is nevertheless necessary or indisputable must take place under the condition that the heritage be 'enriched', 'always capable of being enriched', and, since the heritage has 'opposite imperatives', let us understand enriched by the very thing it is not or which it excludes from within itself. For what else could ever enrich one, if not what one is not, what one does not have, what one can neither have or have been? The Greek model of *philía* could never be 'enriched' otherwise than with that which it has violently and essentially attempted to exclude.

2. Does the *formal* structure – this time formal more than thematic – does the composition, not to say the rhetoric, of these two pages not confirm this profound indecision, as if one could neither inherit nor not inherit what is left for us to inherit, the heritage of a culture, the heritage of a friend? Of course, it was necessary to speak of the Greek affair, notably because Foucault, for whose memory this text pre-eminently wants itself to be and describes itself as intended, was working on it before his death (and although *philía* remains strangely marginalized, not to say left in silence, in his last works, at least those published to date). But what is literally retained, in a declaration which means to bear witness to a work rather than to a person ('in bearing witness to a work'), for a work for which the question is not partisan praise (for it 'demands study (unprejudiced reading) rather than praise'[30]), that which is kept in what finally is such a problematic heritage – this cumbersome model of Greek *philía* – is a reported sentence, and one which says what? – that there is no friend. The testimony of friendship (of 'intellectual friendship') is declared in the form of a sentence recalling that there is no friend, which neutralizes the declaration of friendship, pluralizes the address (O friends) and leaves the Greek model to put itself, by itself, into question. All by itself – this is what the model does best. Blanchot keeps the address. He does not speak of *the* friend or of friends, he speaks to Foucault, but to a dead Foucault to whom he thus declares, presently ('posthumous gift' of a 'friendship' 'perhaps promised'), and in the plural: 'O my friends, there is no friend.' What is thus declared presently to Foucault ('today allows me to declare to him'), that is, the 'intellectual friendship' to which Blanchot 'believes he is remaining faithful', is thus accompanied (without accompanying itself), following a colon, by a time of remembrance ('I recall'). But a time of remembrance which recalls, no doubt out of modesty and reserve, less the friend than the saying attributed to Aristotle which says there is no friend. The incredible audacity of this 'as' [*tandis que*], following a colon, opens a solitary subordinate clause; it suspends the entire declaration in an *epokhē* of this intemporal time which is suited to mourning but also annuls in advance everything that could indeed be said in this saying and declared in this declaration. A colon: will an act of punctuation ever have unfurled a veil of mourning in this way, suspending even the logical sequence, letting only contiguity appear, the contemporaneousness of two temporal orders simply juxtaposed, without an inner relation between them? Will one ever have punctuated with more rigour, economy, reserve, even leaving open the hypothesis (but let us not dwell on this here) that there, perhaps, no one is around for anyone any longer, and that this is indeed death, this dying

of which Blanchot has complained, so often, so profoundly, not that it is fatal but that it remains impossible? Like friendship, perhaps: 'I believe I am remaining faithful, however awkwardly, to the intellectual friendship that his death, so painful for me, today allows me to declare to him, as I recall the words attributed by Diogenes Laertes to Aristotle: "Oh my friends, there is no friend."' This is shown (performatively), by the fact, attested here, that this friendship could not have been declared during the lifetime of the friend. It is death that 'today allows me' to 'declare' this 'intellectual friendship', 'as . . .'. May thanks be given to death. It is *thanks* to death that friendship can be declared. Never before, never otherwise. And never if not in recalling (while thanks to death, the friend recalls that there are no friends). And when friendship is declared during the lifetime of friends, it avows, fundamentally, the same thing: it avows the death thanks to which the chance to declare itself comes at last, never failing to come.

Without seeking to conceal it, it will have been undersood that I wish to speak here of those men and women to whom a bond of friendship unites me – that is, I also want to speak *to them*. If only through the rare friendship I am naming, which always occasions in me a surge of admiration and gratitude. To my knowledge, among the aforementioned, those who cite Aristotle's quasi-citation, always in the canonical version, there is, besides Maurice Blanchot, Michel Deguy. In a more Roman tradition (a Latin quotation) whose path he has not indicated to me, Deguy concentrates on the Aristotelian reminder, against Plato, of the singularity of *this*, of *this* friend. Let us cease speaking of friendship, of the *eídos* of friendship; let us speak of friends. This is the enormous vein, the inexhaustible *tópos* of the quarrel Aristotle believed it was necessary to pick with Plato's ghost. Now here we have what is happening to us today with the ruin which affects us and which we have adopted as our theme: this collapse of the friendship concept will perhaps be a chance, but, along with Friendship, the collapse carries off the Friend too, and there is nothing fortuitous in the fact that the sudden burst of this chance at the heart of the ruin is still linked, in what in our time is most untimely, to literature, to the 'literary community', of which *The Unavowable Community* also speaks. (Is not literature today, in the saturation of a geopolitical process of a becoming-worldwide [*mondialité*], the very thing which remains intolerable to the intolerance of the theological-political systems for which, the idea of democracy having no unconditional virtue, no speech can elude the space of theological-political authority? Absolute theologization *qua* absolute politicization?) For it is above all a question of poetry and literature in the pages Deguy devotes to '*O amici mei*', and the word 'literature' is the only word, along with 'friendship', or with the singularity of 'this one', that he wishes to underscore:

O amici mei

> If a certain Latin tradition is to be believed on this subject – *O Amici mei, sicut Aristoteles dicere solitus est, nullus est amicus!* – it is under the heading of *friendship* that Aristotle undertook to ruin the capital letters of Platonism, and called to the witness stand the *ousia prôtê: this* man. O my friends, there is no Friend.[31]

Under the sign of the capital letter in ruins, where Friendship should give way to friends who henceforth no longer answer the call to the witness stand, a narrative could follow (for it would be a question of narrative, signed by someone who presents himself, with all due irony, as a reader for 'a major publisher', the same one, as a matter of fact, which houses the great work of Bataille and Blanchot). The narrative would be prepared only 'to tell stories of the monuments and ruins of friendship'. Such a hypothesis is handled, poetically and philosophically, through a number of themes which have appeared to us, up until now, to embody the enigma: sexual difference, misogyny and the monastic order of 'brothers' ('What is thought of love can be said in favour of friendship, the alibi allows one to speak of the amiable. There are two conditions conducive to the firing of the spirit: that of the "Muse", prosopeia of eros, and now "libido", and sexual difference forces poetry to cry out its adieu: "A single being is absent and everything comes alive . . .". The second is the womanless condition, outside of difference, and this is the monastic flame-up of the spirit, "philosophy", which sometimes takes flight from out of a little misogyny (which can be misandry in the community of women)'), the 'free and dissymmetrical relationship' of the 'most generous', again from out of a 'dying in common' ('. . . singing over dying together'), and lastly, above all, the war of friendship between family and literature:

> Most men will have existed only through and for their families; when men live and die in being loved, commented on, at times a little deplored. Among the despairing attempts to exist beyond the family: writing, or . . . loving; which carries off, alters, adulters. Of the other, an other, truly other, ravishes: it is a god. And see how, as soon as they are torn away from the family by love, they found a family. Unless they die in loving, loving to die, Tristan and Juliet, this is the choice left them by *literature*.

(Remember, says the conjugal quarrel, that we are not of the same family. And this is why we have never really spoken of the same thing.)

3. Lastly, *fraternity*. What can the name 'brother' or the call to fraternity still mean when one or the other arises in the speech of friendship which, like that of Blanchot – at least in his *L'Amitié* or *The Writing of the Disaster* – has so radically delivered itself from the hold of all determined communities, all filiation or affiliation, all alliances – families or peoples – and even all given generality, if only by a 'gift, a promise, a generic generosity'? We have already noted that allusions to fraternity are rare in Blanchot. But for this very reason, for this reason as well, these allusions are worth dwelling upon. Besides the brief, obviously affirmative, connotations we have already examined in *The Unavowable Community*,[32] a particular generous declaration of friendship addressed to the Jews and to Judaism requires us to question what it says or does not say of the friendship of which *L'Amitié* speaks:

> It is obviously the Nazi persecution (which was in operation from the beginning, unlike what certain professors of philosophy would wish to convince us of – to have us believe that in 1933, when Heidegger joined, national-socialism was still a proper, suitable doctrine, not deserving of condemnation) which made us feel that *the Jews were our brothers* and that Judaism was more than a culture and even more than a religion, but, rather, the foundation of our relationships with the other [*autrui*].[33]

I shall not hazard an interpretation of this definition of Judaism, although I sense both its highly problematic character and its imposing necessity (which is of course unquestionable, from the moment one decides to call Judaism the very thing one thus defines: a question of a circle with which we cannot here engage again). Putting aside, then, what is most difficult in this definition, but supposing, precisely, that Judaism is 'the foundation of our relationships with others', then – and this will be my only question – what does 'brothers' mean in this context? Why would *autrui* be in the first place a brother? And especially, why '*our* brothers'? Whose brothers? Who, then, are *we*? Who is this 'we'?

(Reading this sentence, and always in view of the admiring and grateful friendship which binds me to the author, I was wondering, among other questions (more than one): why could I never have written that, nor subscribed to it, whereas, relying on other criteria, this declaration would be easier for me to subscribe to than several others? In the same vein, I was wondering why the word 'community' (avowable or unavowable, inoperative or not) – why I have never been able to write it, on my own initiative and in my name, as it were. Why? Whence my reticence? And is it not fundamentally the essential part of the disquiet which inspires this book? Is this reserve, with respect to the above definition of Judaism, insufficiently Jewish, or, on the contrary, hyperbolically Jewish, more than Jewish? What, then, once again, does 'Judaism' mean? I add that the language of fraternity seems to me just as problematic when, reciprocally, Lévinas uses it to extend humanity to the Christian, in this case to Abbot Pierre: 'the fraternal humanity of the stalag's confidential agent who, by each of his movements, restored in us the consciousness of our dignity. The man was called Abbot Pierre, I never learned his family name.'[34])

It is rather late in the day now to issue a warning. Despite the appearances that this book has multiplied, nothing in it says anything *against* the brother or against fraternity. No protest, no contestation. Maligning and cursing, as we have seen often enough, still appertain to the inside of the history of brothers (friends or enemies, be they false or true). This history will not be thought, it will not be recalled, by taking up *this* side. In my own special way, like everyone else, I believe, I no doubt love, yes, in my own way, my brother, my only brother. And my brothers, dead or alive, where the letter no longer counts and never has, in my 'family' and in my 'families' – I have more than one, and more than one 'brother' of more than one sex, and I love having more than one, each time unique, of whom and to whom, in more than one language, across quite a few boundaries, I am bound by a conjuration and so many unuttered oaths.

Where, then, is the question? Here it is: I have never stopped asking myself, I request that it be asked, what is meant when one says 'brother', when someone is called 'brother'. And when the humanity of man, as much as the alterity of the other, is thus resumed and subsumed. And the infinite price of friendship. I have wondered, and I ask, what one wants to say whereas one *does not want* to say, one knows that one should not say, because one knows, through so much obscurity, whence it comes and where this profoundly obscure language has led in the past. *Up until now.* I am wondering, that's all, and request that it be asked, what the implicit politics of this language is. For always, and today more than ever. What is the political impact and range of this chosen word, among other possible words, even – and especially – if the choice is not deliberate?

Just a question, but one which supposes an affirmation. If my hypothesis must remain a hypothesis, it cannot be undone with a pledge. The pledge of a testimony irreducible to proof or certitude, as well as to all theoretical determination. If one wishes to retranslate this pledge into a hypothesis or a question, it would, then, perhaps – by way of a temporary conclusion – take the following form: is it possible to think and to implement democracy, that which would keep the old name 'democracy', while uprooting from it all these figures of friendship (philosophical and religious) which prescribe fraternity: the family and the androcentric ethnic group? Is it possible, in assuming a certain faithful memory of democratic reason and reason *tout court* – I would even say, the Enlightenment of a certain *Aufklärung* (thus leaving open the abyss which is again opening today under these words) – not to found, where it is not longer a matter of *founding*, but to open out to the future, or rather, to the 'come', of a certain democracy?

For democracy remains to come; this is its essence in so far as it remains: not only will it remain indefinitely perfectible, hence always insufficient and future, but, belonging to the time of the promise, it will always remain, in each of its future times, to come: even when there is democracy, it never exists, it is never present, it remains the theme of a non-presentable concept. Is it possible to open up to the 'come' of a certain democracy which is no longer an insult to the friendship we have striven to think beyond the homo-fraternal and phallogocentric schema?

When will we be ready for an experience of freedom and equality that is capable of respectfully experiencing that friendship, which would at last be just, just beyond the law, and measured up against its measurelessness?

O my democratic friends . . .

Notes

1. From one of Ferenczi's letters to Freud; see below, p. 280
2. Book Four, para. 279, trans. W. Kaufmann, New York, Vintage 1974, pp. 225–226.
3. [See the epigraph to Derrida's *Of Grammatology*: the future is 'that which breaks absolutely with constituted normality and can only be proclaimed, *presented*, as a sort of monstrosity': trans. Gayatri Spivak, Johns Hopkins University Press 1976, p. 5. – Trans.]
4. *Anthropology from a Pragmatic Point of View*, [trans. Victor Lyle Dowdell, Carbondale and Edwardsville, Southern Illinois University Press 1978], p. 38.
5. See above, ch. 9, pp. 257–8.
6. '*ésti gar o phílos állos autos*', *Nicomachean Ethics*, IX, 4, 1166a 32. Aristotle posits here that man, with his friend, is in a relation similar to the one he has to himself. He then defers the question of whether there can be friendship between a man and himself, only to return to it further on, answering in the affirmative. It is in terms of this

friendship for self that friendship can extend to other men. The best I can wish for my best friend is what I wish for myself in the highest degree (1168b 5).

7. Montaigne, *Essays*, p. 212.

8. '*Mein Bruder, wenn du eine Tugend hast, und es deine Tugend ist, so hast du sie mit niemandem gemeinsam*' [trans. R. Hollingdale, Penguin Classics 1961].

9. "*Einer ist immer zu viel um mich*" – *also denkt der Einsiedler.* "*Immer einmal eins* – *das gibt auf die Dauer zwei!*"

Ich und Mich sind immer su eifrig im Gespräche: wie wäre es auzuhalten, wenn es nicht einen Freund gäbe?

"*Immer ist für den Einsiedler der Freund der Dritte: der Dritte ist der Kork, der verhindert, daß das Gespräch der Zweie in die Tiefe sinkt*"', *Vom Freunde*, in *Also sprach Zarathustra* [trans. R. Hollingdale, Harmondsworth, Penguin 1961], p. 82.

10. And even of sacrificial 'carno-phallogocentrism'. See *Points de suspension*, Galilée 1992, p. 294 [*Points . . .: Interviews 1974–1994*, ed. Elisabeth Weber, trans. Peggy Kamuf and others, Stanford University Press 1995], pp. 280–81.

11. *Nicomachean Ethics*, VIII, 2, 1155a 25.

12. Ibid., 10, 1160b 18–20.

13. *Eudemian Ethics*, VII, 9, 1241b 30.

14. *Nicomachean Ethics*, VIII, 15, 1162b 20; *Eudemian Ethics*, VII, 10, 1242b 30.

15. The brother*'s* name or the name *of* brother: Montaigne again, on his friendship with La Boétie: 'The name of brother is truly a fair one and full of love: that is why La Boétie and I made a brotherhood of our alliance' p. 208).

16. *Before the Law*.

17. Budapest, 26 December 1912, in *The Correspondence of Sigmund Freud and Sándor Ferenczi*, vol. 1, 1908–14 [trans. Peter T. Hoffer, The Belknap Press of Harvard University Press, Cambridge, MA and London 1993], pp. 449–51.

18. On all these problems, and again on the ethico-political question of the woman/wife, the sister, and the brother in Hegel, I refer the reader to *Glas*, Galilée 1974 [trans. John P. Leavey Jr and Richard Rand, Lincoln and London: University of Nebraska Press 1986].

19. *The Gospel According to Matthew*, V, 43–8 [trans. Members of the Catholic Biblical Association of America, from *The New American Bible*, World Publishing 1972]. This is evidently the passage to which Schmitt refers (see above, ch. 4, pp. 88–9).

20. *Thus Spoke Zarathustra*, pp. 87–8.

21. 'You want to be paid as well, you the virtuous! Do you want reward for virtue and heaven for earth and eternity for your today?', ibid. 'Of the Virtuous', p. 117. The reference is undoubtedly, among many other possibilities, to the Gospel according to Matthew, cited above. But the logic of wages is everywhere in the Gospels.

22. Chapter 4.

23. In a recent and beautiful essay, Alexander Garciá Düttmann says of this passage and of 'Star Friendships' that it is a question of an 'originary alter-ation' *qua* a non-dialectizable, non-*relevable*, un-sublatable distancing. See 'What is called Love in all the Languages and Silences of the World: Nietzsche, Genealogy, Contingency', in *Imago*, Fall 1993, p. 314.

24. Montaigne, 'On Friendship, p. 220.

25. Ibid., pp. 206–7.

26. *L'Amitié*, Gallimard 1971, pp. 328–9. Emphasis added.

27. Maurice Blanchot, *The Writing of the Disaster* [trans. Ann Smock, Bison Book Edition, University of Nebraska Press 1995], p. 27.

28. Elsewhere I have suggested the opposite: that the gift ought to exclude the too natural value of generosity. See *Donner le temps*, Galilée 1991, p. 205 [trans. Peggy Kamuf, *Given Time, 1. Counterfeit Money*, University of Chicago Press 1992], p. 162.

29. Fata Morgana 1986, pp. 63–4 [trans. Jeffrey Mehlman, Zone Books 1987], pp. 108–9.

30. The work of the lost friend should not be 'praised' – it is the same word as the one used in the text on Bataille, so many years before, which we cited above: 'if only to praise him'.

31. *Le Comité. Confessions d'un lecteur de grande maison*, Champ Vallon 1988, pp. 88–9.

32. '. . . the heart of fraternity: the heart of the law', p. 47.

'The problem of being committees of action without action, or circles of friends which would disown their former friendships in the name of an appeal to friendship (comradeship without preconditions) which would carry the exigency of being there, not as a person or subject, but as the demonstration of a brotherly, anonymous, and impersonal movement.

The presence of the "people" in its limitless power which, so as not to limit itself, accepts *to do nothing*'. (p. 55)

33. A letter to Salomon Malka, *L'Arche*, no. 373, May 1988. Emphasis added, obviously.

34. *Emmanuel Lévinas, 'Qui êtes-vous?'*, Interview with F. Poirié, La Manufacture, 1987, pp. 84–5, cited in M.A. Lescourret, *Emmanuel Lévinas*, Flammarion 1994, p. 121.